Inequality and Economic Integration

Globalization and economic integration have impacted on the quality of life and individual well-being across the world. Attempts to evaluate the impact on income dispersion from this process have been extremely controversial. *Inequality and Economic Integration* provides the first real attempt to build up a theoretical framework and indices examining the relationships between the recent acceleration in economic integration and inequality among persons and countries. The aim is to enable social and political institutions to monitor increasing disparities in well-being and social exclusion.

The contributions in this volume cover different subfields of economics and examine both the negative and positive spillover effects of economic integration on individuals, social groups and nations. Since the impact of globalization on the most deprived people is multidimensional in nature, the theoretical framework is extended to inequality in a multivariate context where several individual characteristics are simultaneously considered.

Francesco Farina is Professor of Economics at Siena University, Italy.

Ernesto Savaglio is Associate Professor of Economics at University 'G. D'Annunzio' of Chieti-Pescara, Italy.

Routledge Siena Studies in Political Economy

The Siena Summer School hosts lectures by distinguished scholars on topics characterized by a lively research activity. The lectures collected in this series offer a clear account of the alternative research paths that characterize a certain field. Different publishers printed former workshops of the school. They include:

Macroeconomics: A Survey of Research Strategies
Edited by Alessandro Vercelli and Nicola Dimitri
Oxford University Press, 1992

International Problems of Economics Interdependence
Edited by Massimo Di Matteo, Mario Baldassarri and Robert Mundell
Macmillan, 1994

Ethics, Rationality and Economic Behaviour
Edited by Francesco Farina, Frank Hahn and Stefano Vannucci
Clarendon Press

Available from Routledge:

The Politics of Economics and Power
Edited by Samuel Bowles, Maurizio Franzini and Ugo Pagano

The Evolution of Economic Diversity
Edited by Antonio Nicita and Ugo Pagano

Cycles, Growth and Structural Change
Edited by Lionello Punzo

General Equilibrium
Edited by Fabio Petri and Frank Hahn

Cognitive Processes and Economic Behaviour
Edited by Nicola Dimitri, Marcello Basili and Itzhak Gilboa

Environment, Inequality and Collective Action
Edited by Marcello Basili, Maurizio Franzini and Alessandro Vercelli

Inequality and Economic Integration
Edited by Francesco Farina and Ernesto Savaglio

Inequality and Economic Integration

Edited by
Francesco Farina and
Ernesto Savaglio

Routledge
Taylor & Francis Group
LONDON AND NEW YORK

First published 2006
by Routledge
2 Park Square, Milton Park, Abingdon, Oxon OX14 4RN

Simultaneously published in the USA and Canada
by Routledge
270 Madison Ave, New York, NY 10016

Routledge is an imprint of the Taylor & Francis Group

Typeset in Times New Roman by
Newgen Imaging Systems (P) Ltd, Chennai, India
Printed and bound in Great Britain by
Antony Rowe Ltd, Chippenham, Wiltshire

British Library Cataloguing in Publication Data
A catalogue record for this book is available
from the British Library

Library of Congress Cataloging in Publication Data
A catalog record for this book has been requested

ISBN10: 0–415–34211–2
ISBN13: 9–78–0–415–34211–7

Contents

Figures

Tables

Contributors

Elisabetta Croci Angelini, Professor of Economics, University of Macerata, Dipartimento di Studi sullo Sviluppo Economico, Piazza Oberdan, 3-62100 – Macerata (Italy).

Anthony B. Atkinson, Professor of Economics, Nuffield College, University of Oxford, New Road, Oxford OX1 1NF (Great Britain).

Simone Borghesi, Assistant Professor, University of Pescara, Dipartimento di Metodi Quantitativi e Teoria Economica, viale Pindaro, 42, 65127 Pescara (Italy).

Andrea Brandolini, Economic Research Department, Banca d'Italia, via Nazionale, 91 00184 Rome (Italy).

Daniele Checchi, Professor of Economics, Department of Economics, Business and Statistics, University of Milan, via Conservatorio, 7, 20122 Milano (Italy).

Valentino Dardanoni, Professor of Economics, Department of Economics, Business and Finance, University of Palermo, Viale delle Scienze (Parco D'Orleans) 90128 – Palermo (Italy).

Francesco Farina, Professor of Economics, University of Siena, Dipartimento di Economia Politica, Piazza San Francesco, 7, 53100 Siena (Italy).

Marc Fleurbaey, Professor of Economics, CATT, Faculté de Droit Economie Gestion, Université de Pau, Av. du Doyen Poplawski, BP 1633, 64016 PAU CEDEX (France).

Jean-Luc Gaffard, Professor of Economics, Faculty of Law and Economics, University of Nice-Sophia Anthipolis, IDEFI, Institut de Droit et d'Economie de la Firme et de l'Industrie 250, rue Albert Einstein 06560 Valbonne (France).

Ugo Pagano, Professor of Economics, University of Siena, Dipartimento di Economia Politica, Piazza San Francesco, 7, 53100 Siena (Italy).

Frederick van der Ploeg, Professor of Economics, Department of Economics, European University Institute, Villa San Paolo, via della Piazzuola, 43, 50133 Florence (Italy).

Lionello F. Punzo, Professor of Economics, University of Siena, Dipartimento di Economia Politica, Piazza San Francesco, 7, 53100 Siena (Italy).

Ernesto Savaglio, Associate Professor, University of Pescara, Dipartimento di Metodi Quantitativi e Teoria Economica, viale Pindaro, 42, 65127 Pescara (Italy).

Alain Trannoy, Professor of Economics, Université de Marseille, EHESS, GREQAM-IDEP, Vieille Charité, 2 rue de la Charité – 13002 Marseille (France).

Alessandro Vercelli, Professor of Economics, University of Siena, Dipartimento di Economia Politica, Piazza San Francesco, 7, 53100 Siena (Italy).

John A. Weymark. Professor of Economics, Vanderbilt University, Department of Economics, VU Station B #351819, 2301 Vanderbilt Place, Nashville, TN 37235-1819 (USA).

Jeffrey G. Williamson, Laird Bell Professor of Economics, Department of Economics, Harvard University, Littauer Center, Room, 216, Cambridge, MA 02138 (USA).

Introduction

Francesco Farina and Ernesto Savaglio

In the last two decades, the acceleration in economic integration has affected the quality of life and the standard of living. The elimination of barriers to trade in goods and services, the liberalization of capital markets, the transnational mobility of workers, the worldwide diffusion of information and communication technologies boosting Foreign Direct Investment (FDI) and the outsourcing of production processes in newly developing areas constitute an unprecedented clustering of technological and institutional innovations. More generally, a variety of structural changes in international politics have hugely narrowed the distance among nations as well as among individuals. In most advanced countries, economic integration has also been fostered by the expanding role of the market after privatization programmes, pro-market legislation and the rolling-back of redistribution and stabilization policies.

The evaluation of the impact on income dispersion stemming from these globalization processes is a controversial issue. For the same period, Bourguignon and Morrison(2002) show that the interpersonal world income disparity is broadly constant according to the Gini inequality index. However, the *between-country* income inequality appears to be decreasing, mainly as an effect of the Southeast Asia and China high growth rates (Sala-i-Martin, 2002). Based on this evidence, the Washington consensus praises globalization as a Pareto-improvement in the worldwide social welfare that will sooner or later be beneficial to all individuals. Yet, the Gini index of interpersonal world income inequality is widening, in the population-weighted computation by Milanovic (2002) aimed to take into account the income polarization between urban and rural populations in India and China. Therefore, inequality criteria allow for different implications, while apparently globalization is not a homogenizing process smoothing out disparities in the individual standard of living.

The aim of this volume is to expound and possibly clarify the relationship between globalization and inequality. The included contributions cover different sub-fields of economics and witness how strongly the scientific community is committed to the refinement of categories and empirical tools. After a Historical overview, chapters are organized in three categories: Income inequality, Globalization and well-being and Multidimensional inequality.

In his historical introduction J.G. Williamson (Globalization, income distribution, and history) observes that the deceleration following a period of faster economic integration may have a varying impact on economic growth and inequality. After the discovery of the New World, several constraints hampered the expansion of world trade. In the aftermath of the Second World War, the strengthening in economic relations brought about high growth rates. In most advanced countries, national and local policies aimed at compensating the *losers* from economic integration impeded that the rise of *between-country* income inequality could be followed by the rise of the *within-country* income inequality. Williamson concludes that conflicts of interest are much easier to compromise when economic growth is sustained and led by sound economic forces.

Part I and Part II of the volume focus on how and to what extent acceleration in economic integration affects inequality in income and well-being. Wage inequality represents the main indicator of income disparities across individuals. A plurality of economic and institutional factors affect labour earnings. In the advanced countries, trade openness has reduced the wage level of low-skilled worker, as an effect of higher imports of the low-skilled intensive products and a lower labour demand for the low-skilled workers. Furthermore, technical change paves the way to the rise in wages and salaries of the high-skilled workers belonging to top deciles of the earnings distribution. Labour market institutions also influence wage dispersion. The fall in the wages of the low-skilled workers is restrained by the bargaining power of the unions and welfare benefits preserve their quality of life. Since legislation enforcing job protection or minimum wage negatively impact on the employment and participation rates, labour market deregulation is expected to induce a higher employment rate.

Atkinson and Brandolini (Earnings dispersion to income inequality in European and US labour market) describe a variety of interactions between earnings inequality, the labour market and redistributive institutions. Wage dispersion depends on the share of unskilled workers, the skill premium and the unemployment rate. The tax and benefits system reduces the rise in inequality caused by globalization and technical progress. However, the more the employment rate is depressed, the more the question of the welfare state sustainability negatively impinges on the degree of coverage, in terms of both the number of the individuals insured and the generosity of the benefits. The authors remark how different employment rates and redistribution systems entail a diverging downward movement for the United States and the European Union of the earnings distribution Lorenz curves.

Croci Angelini and Farina (The size of redistribution in OECD countries: does it influence wage inequality?) show that the redistributive institutions, in their interaction with the labour market and the technological opportunities of the firms, affect wage dispersion. The decision on the degree of redistribution is motivated by the society's preference for 'risk insurance'. According to heterogeneous preferences for redistribution determined by the median voter's income with respect to the average level, they distinguish four systems of social protection in the OECD countries. The impact of redistribution in reducing the market income dispersion is much wider in the Scandinavian and the Continental countries compared to the Mediterranean and the Anglo-Saxon countries. The authors provide econometric evidence for the claim that the redistribution makes the implementation of both skill-biased technical change and labour market deregulation not only socially sustainable but also employment-enabling.

An ethically acceptable degree of inequality can be better evaluated in a dynamic perspective. If income positions are interchangeable passing from one generation to the next, market economy could promote equality of opportunities. The analysis of the temporal evolution of one resource distribution within a given population is the aim of the work of Checchi and Dardanoni (Social mobility). They discuss social mobility as the intra-/inter-generational transmission of inequality in the long run. The authors show how to have more mobility means to allow for a reduction in equality of opportunities. A society is certainly less unequal if everybody, independently of his/her ancestors, has access to all available social positions. Moreover, a mobile society is not only even, but also efficient, since the more talented people excel regardless their social origins. Finally, Checchi and Dardanoni argue that to define and then measure social mobility is a difficult task, because of the multidisciplinary nature of the mobility concept. Nevertheless, there is no doubt that a greater degree of mobility opportunities ensures that the social inequality is not perpetuated over time.

The well-being of individuals depend on a variety of personal characteristics. Borghesi and Vercelli (Global health) draw our attention to the circumstance that health conditions are at the crossroad of many issues linking the determinants of well-being. Economists are more and more conscious that the influence of growth and income inequality on health conditions interacts with the double-way correlations among health on one side, and the environment and population dynamics on the other side. Globalization, while boosting per capita income growth, endangers the conditions for sustainability. The economic 'short-termism' triggered by globalization may depress educational attainments and exacerbate environmental degradation, thus worsening the quality of life. The authors show that individuals in the lowest deciles of the income distribution suffer from relative deprivation in health. They are likely to be excluded from both the workforce and the social networks, and as a consequence their life expectancy is even reduced.

Economic integration has exposed individuals to the risk of contingencies negatively affecting their well-being, but also heterogeneity across growth rates counts much in shaping standard-of-living profiles. Gaffard and Punzo (Economic integration and cross-country convergence: exercises in growth theory and empirics) investigate the interplay between economic integration and the evolutionary path of per capita income among countries. Technical progress differently impacts on the economic structures in different areas. The diversity of patterns of growth in Europe, United States and Japan have been deeply shaped by country-specific fluctuations around potential of both actual employment and output. As it is also witnessed by the experience of transition countries in Eastern Europe and Latin America, globalization by no means makes different growth paths to collapse in a unique steady state. Since the interpersonal income dispersion greatly depends on the specific growth characteristics, in order to set up the most appropriate re-equilibrating policies, a deeper understanding of the different institutional underpinnings of growth regimes is needed.

Van der Ploeg (Are the welfare state and redistribution really so bad for the economy? effects of reciprocal altruism, consumer rivalry and second best) discusses whether public institutions should take into account the increase in individual risk to which we are exposed after globalization. He claims that the rationale for promoting redistributive policies in an increasingly individualistic environment relies on beliefs held by people about the efficiency and the ethical foundations of a public insurance system. So doing, the acceptance of high tax and high welfare benefits can be traced back to the importance of reciprocity in fostering cooperative behaviour across individuals. The fact that individuals care about relative income and mutually monitor the level of their respective effort in promoting the social welfare is at the origin of the economic success of countries with large welfare institutions. In a second best world, the most sensible policy to cope with inequality consists in institutions devoted to the protection of both market incentives and 'disadvantaged' individuals.

The problems faced by nations undertaking an economic integration are magnified by the heterogeneity of welfare institutions. Pagano (Cultural diversity, European integration and welfare state) tackles the problem of conciliating the need for public and merit goods provision with high preference heterogeneity across the integrating European countries. Differently from the United States, whose cultural standardization makes social insurance difficult to be accepted, cultural diversity within the EU at the same time requires and obstacles a comprehensive system of social protection. A limited cultural standardization, as a substitute for social protection, could be promoted only at a cost of penalising social groups unable to substitute cultural standardization for social insurance. Granted that a free choice among different systems of social insurance and redistributions is ruled out, the solution suggested by Pagano consists in a system of mutual insurance among the different welfare systems, making economic integration compatible with social protection.

Chapters in Part I and Part II indicate that globalization tends to concentrate a majority of human resources (human capital, intellectual property rights, institutions for lower and upper education) in the hands of the top social groups making inequality increase. The comprehension of the multifaceted interconnections between inequality and globalization is far to be easy. The previous analyses suggest that new tools are required in order to capture the multidimensional worsening of individual living conditions due to globalization. In this perspective, Part IV of the volume is theoretical in nature and represents a complete survey of the complex problem of extending the ranking principles from the univariate to the multivariate inequality case. Classical literature on economic inequality measurement depicts disparity of an attribute (typically income) in a given population. Since people differ in many aspects besides income, this seems an unsatisfactory approach. Many scholars have then attempted to extend the unidimensional inequality criteria to a multivariate context where several individual characteristics are simultaneously considered.

Theoretical arguments have been provided which justify the use of standard stochastic dominance and Lorenz dominance for making comparisons of individual welfare in terms of inequality. Trannoy (Multidimensional egalitarianism and the dominance approach: a lost paradise?) focuses on a generalization of the Lorenz criterion to the multidimensional case and on the dominance approach with symmetric and asymmetric treatment of the personal characteristics. In fact, Trannoy first discusses the advantages to compare two multivariate distributions by using the notion of price majorization and then reviews the stochastic dominance approach to multidimensional disparity. He thinks over inequality in a unidimensional context as a quiet world, where the fundamental result of Hardy, Littlewood and Pölya (1934) allows us to live in a sort of theoretical paradise where everything works. On the contrary, there exists no similar gem for multidimensional inequality, but few approaches that do not provide a unified field.

Economists draw positive and normative conclusions from results provided by several *a priori* selected inequality indices. Weymark (The normative approach to the measurement of multidimensional inequality) provides a comprehensive review of the literature on normatively based dominance criteria in a multidimensional inequality setting. Following the approach to the univariate inequality measurement, a multidimensional inequality index is axiomatically constructed according to a two-step aggregation procedure. At the first stage, an evaluation (utility) function measures the well-being of each individual endowed with an allocation of attributes and a unidimensional (utility) distribution is obtained by aggregation. In the second stage, the individual utilities are collected by a univariate inequality index and an overall social evaluation is then supplied. The required crucial assumption is the decomposability property of the evaluation function used to rank multivariate distributions according to their social desirability. Weymark discusses the set of axioms used for generalizing to multivariate distributions the most widely applied inequality indices, namely the class of inequality indices of Atkinson-Sen-Kolm, the class of generalized entropy (inequality) indices and finally the class of Gini multidimensional indices.

A critical examination of the main contributions to the new field of multidimensional inequality is provided by Savaglio's work (Three approaches to the analysis of multidimensional inequality). According to the different methodology applied, he divides the existing literature, extending the one-dimensional inequality criteria to a multidimensional context, in three main approaches. The first one relies on Social Evaluation Functions (SEF) which are additive separable. The assumption of separability is quite an unrealistic hypothesis, as the correlation between individual attributes is a rather pervasive phenomenon. The second approach consists in the multidimensional extension of some (well known classes of) univariate inequality indices. The main criticism to this research approach is the loss of information we suffer when the comparison of multivariate distributions is limited to comparing scalars. The third approach evaluates multidimensional inequality using tools of convex analysis. Savaglio argues that the results of this latter approach are analytically sophisticated and difficult to implement when one turns to the *empirical* evaluation of disparity.

A more policy oriented appraisal of multidimensional inequality is presented by Fleurbaey (Social welfare, priority to worst-off and dimensions of individual well-being). He examines an axiomatic extension of some one-dimensional measurement criteria of individual well-being to essentially multidimensional measures of 'primary goods' and/or 'capabilities'. In such a setting, individual preferences over different dimensions are to be taken into account. Starting with the Pigou–Dalton principle of transfers and its specifications, inequality aversion is introduced in (personal and then) social preferences. In so doing, the author proposes a method to construct a SEF that avoids interpersonal comparisons and relies on ordinal preferences. According to such multidimensional inequality approach, a SEF of *maxmin* type singles out as the only tool satisfying a set of mild-looking conditions on preferences for equity. Finally, Fleurbaey applies his methodology to labour market, where people differ for the quantity of labour they offer and net income they earn and to the measurement of economic globalization.

We have considered economic integration as influencing many inequality dimensions, stressing that economic research urges new tools for analysing multidimensional disparity. While much work remains to be done, some policy proposals stemming from the presented contributions are worth to be evaluated.

References

Bourguignon, F. and Morrison, C. (2002) 'Inequality among World Citizens: 1820–1992', *American Economic Review*, 92: 722–744.

Hardy, G., Littlewood, H. and Polya, G. (1934) *Inequalities*, Cambridge: Cambridge University Press.

Milanovic, B. (2002) 'True World Income Distribution, 1988 and 1993: First Calculation Based on Household Surveys Alone', *Economic Journal*, 112: 51–92.

Sala-i-Martin, X. (2002) *The World Distribution for Income (Estimated from Individual Country Distribution)*, NBER Working Paper no. 8933.

Part I

Inequality in an historical perspective

1 Globalization, income distribution and history

Jeffrey G. Williamson

1.1 Globalization and world inequality

Globalization in world commodity and factor markets has evolved in fits and starts since Columbus and de Gama sailed from Europe more than 500 years ago. This chapter begins with a survey of this history in order to place contemporary events in better perspective. It then asks whether globalization raised world inequality. This question can be split into two more: What happened to income gaps between nations? What happened to income gaps within nations? This chapter stresses on the second two questions, the reason being that answers to these have more relevance for policy and for the ability of a globally integrated world to survive. Indeed, at various points in the chapter, I ask whether global backlash in the past was driven by complaints of the losers. Finally, this chapter also stresses the contribution of world migration to poverty eradication.

Recent scholarship has documented a dramatic divergence in incomes around the globe over the past two centuries. Furthermore, all of this work shows that the divergence was driven overwhelmingly by the rise of between-nation inequality, not by the rise of inequality within nations (Bourguignon and Morrisson, 2002; Dowrick and DeLong, 2003; Pritchett, 1997). Figure 1.1 uses the work of François Bourguignon and Christian Morrisson to summarize these trends, and it confirms that changing income gaps between countries explains changing world inequality. However, the fact that the rise of inequality within nations hasn't driven the secular rise in global inequality hardly implies that it has been irrelevant, and for two reasons: first, policy is formed at the country level, and it is changing income distribution within borders that usually triggers policy responses; and second, it is the political voice of the losers that matters, and they can be at the top, the bottom, or the middle of that distribution.

I start by decomposing the centuries since 1492 into four distinct globalization epochs. Two of these were pro-global, and two were anti-global. I then explore whether the two pro-global epochs made the world more unequal, and whether it produced backlash.

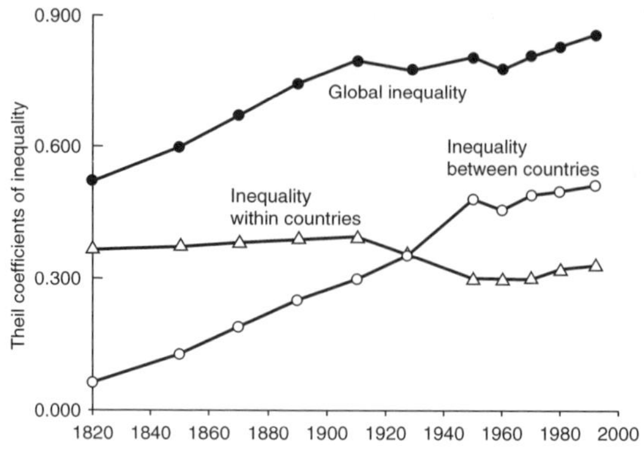

Figure 1.1 Global inequality of individual incomes, 1820–1992.

Source: Bourguignon and Morrisson (2001). The "countries" here consist of 15 single countries with abundant data and large populations plus 18 other country groups. The 18 groups were aggregates of geographical neighbors having similar levels of GDP per capita, as estimated by Maddison (1995).

1.2 Making a world economy

1.2.1 Epoch I: anti-global mercantilist restriction 1492–1820

The Voyages of Discovery induced a transfer of technology, plants, animals, and diseases on an enormous scale, never seen before and maybe since. But the impact of Columbus and da Gama on trade, factor migration, and globalization was a different matter entirely. For globalization to have an impact on relative factor prices, absolute living standards and Gross Domestic Product (GDP) per capita, domestic relative commodity prices, and/or relative endowments must be altered. True, there was a world trade boom after 1492, and the share of trade in world GDP increased markedly (O'Rourke and Williamson, 2002). But was that trade boom explained by declining trade barriers and global integration? A pro-global decline in trade barriers should have left a trail marked by falling commodity price gaps between exporting and importing trading centers, but there is absolutely no such evidence. Thus, "discoveries" and transport productivity improvements must have been offset by trading monopoly markups, tariffs, non-tariff restrictions, wars, and pirates, all of which served to choke off trade.

Since there is so much confusion in the globalization debate about its measurement, it might pay to elaborate on this point. Figure 1.2 presents a stylized view of post-Colombian trade between Europe and the rest of the world (the latter denoted by an asterisk). MM is the European import demand function (i.e. domestic demand minus domestic supply), with import demand declining as the home market price (p) increases. SS is the foreign export supply function (foreign supply minus foreign demand), with export supply rising as the price abroad (p^*) increases. In the absence of transport costs, monopolies, wars, pirates, and other trade barriers, international commodity markets would be perfectly integrated: prices would be

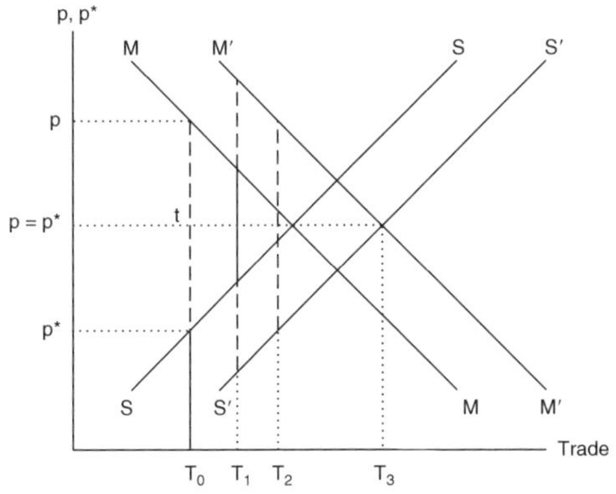

Figure 1.2 The European overseas trade boom 1500–1800.

the same at home and abroad, determined by the intersection of the two schedules. Transport costs, protection, war, pirates, and monopoly drive a wedge (t) between export and import prices: higher tariffs, transport costs, war embargoes, and monopoly rents increase the wedge while lower barriers reduce it. Global commodity market integration is represented in Figure 1.2 by a decline in the wedge: falling transport costs, falling trading monopoly rents, falling tariffs, the suppression of pirates, or a return to peace all lead to falling import prices in both places, rising export prices in both places, an erosion of price gaps between them, and an increase in trade volumes connecting them.

The fact that trade should rise as trade barriers fall is, of course, the rationale behind using trade volumes or the share of trade in GDP as a proxy for international commodity market integration. Indeed, several authors have used Angus Maddison's (1995) data to trace out long-run trends in "commodity market integration" since the early nineteenth century, or even earlier (e.g. Findlay and O'Rourke, 2003). However, Figure 1.2 makes it clear that global commodity market integration is not the only reason why the volume of trade, or trade's share in GDP, might increase over time. Just because we see a trade boom doesn't necessarily mean that more liberal trade policies or transport revolutions are at work. After all, outward shifts in either import demand or export supply could also lead to trade expansion. Thus, Figure 1.2 argues that the *only* irrefutable evidence that global commodity market integration is taking place is commodity price convergence. However, we cannot find it.

If it wasn't declining trade barriers that explains the world trade boom after Columbus, what was it? Just like world experience from the 1950s to the 1980s (Baier and Bergstrand, 2001), it appears that European income growth – or growth of incomes of the landed rich – might have explained as much as two-thirds of the trade boom over the three centuries as a whole (O'Rourke and Williamson, 2002).[1] The world trade boom after Columbus would have been a lot bigger without those anti-global interventions.

1.2.2 Epoch II: the first global century 1820–1913

The 1820s were a watershed in the evolution of the world economy. International commodity price convergence did not start until then. Powerful and epochal shifts towards liberal policy (e.g. dismantling mercantilism) were manifested during that decade. In addition, the 1820s coincide with the peacetime recovery from the Napoleonic wars on the continent, launching a century of global *pax Britannica*. In short, the 1820s mark the start of a world regime of globalization.

Transport costs dropped very fast in the century prior to the First World War (O'Rourke and Williamson, 1999). These globalization forces were powerful in the Atlantic economy, but they were partially offset by a rising tide of protection. Declining transport costs accounted for two-thirds of the integration of world commodity markets over the century following 1820, and for *all* of world commodity market integration in the four decades after 1870, when globalization backlash offset some of it (Lindert and Williamson, 2003). The political backlash of the late nineteenth century and interwar period was absent in Asia and Africa – partly because these regions contained colonies of free trading European countries, partly because of the power of gunboat diplomacy, and partly because of the political influence wielded by natives who controlled the natural resources that were the base of their exports. Thus, the globally induced domestic relative price shocks were even bigger and more ubiquitous in Asia and Africa than those in the Atlantic economy (Williamson, 2002). To put it another way, commodity price convergence between Europe and the periphery was even more dramatic than it was within the Atlantic economy.

In short, the liberal dismantling of mercantilism and the worldwide transport revolution worked together to produce truly global commodity markets across the nineteenth century. The persistent decline in transport costs worldwide allowed competitive winds to blow hard where they had never blown before. True, there was an anti-global policy reaction after 1870 in the European center but it was nowhere near big enough to cause a return to the pre-1820 levels of economic isolation. On the other hand, these globalization events were met with rising levels of protection in Latin America, the United States, and the European periphery, and to very high levels. However, I postpone until the end of this chapter the question as to whether it was globalization backlash that triggered protection in the periphery or whether it was something else.

Factor markets also became more integrated worldwide. As European investors came to believe in strong growth prospects overseas, global capital markets became steadily more integrated, reaching levels in 1913 that may not have been regained even today (Clemens and Williamson, 2004b; Obstfeld and Taylor, 2003). International migration soared in response to unrestrictive immigration policies and falling steerage costs (Chiswick and Hatton, 2003; Hatton and Williamson, 1998), but not without some backlash: New World immigrant subsidies began to evaporate toward the end of the century, political debate over immigrant restriction became very intense, and, finally, the quotas were imposed. In this case, it is clear that the retreat from open immigration policies to quotas was driven by complaints from the losers at the bottom of the income pyramid, the unskilled native born (Chiswick and Hatton, 2003).

1.2.3 Epoch III: beating an anti-global retreat 1913–1950

The globalized world started to fall apart after 1913, and it was completely dismantled between the wars. New policy barriers were imposed restricting the ability of poor populations to flee miserable conditions for something better, barriers that still exist today, a century later. Thus, the foreign-born share in the US population fell from a pre-1913 figure of 14.6 percent to an interwar figure of 6.9 percent. Higher tariffs and other non-tariff barriers choked off the gains from trade. Thus, barrier-ridden price gaps between Atlantic economy trading partners doubled, returning those gaps to 1870 levels (Findlay and O'Rourke, 2003; Lindert and Williamson, 2003: Table 1). The appearance of new disincentives reduced investment in the diffusion of new technologies around the world, and the share of foreign capital flows in GDP dropped from 3.3 to 1.2 percent (Obstfeld and Taylor, 1998: 359). In short, the interwar retreat from globalization was carried entirely by anti-global economic policies.

1.2.4 Epoch IV: the second global century after 1950

Globalization by any definition resumed after the Second World War. It has differed from pre-1914 globalization in several ways. Most important by far, factor migrations are less impressive: the foreign-born are a much smaller share in labor-scarce economies than they were in 1913, and capital exports are a smaller percentage of GDP in the post-Second World War United States than they were in pre-Second World War Britain (Obstfeld and Taylor, 1998: Table 11.1). On the other hand, trade barriers are probably lower today than they were in 1913. These differences are tied to policy changes in one dominant nation, the United States, which has switched from a protectionist welcoming immigrants to a free trader restricting their entrance.

Hecksher and Ohlin theory teaches us that trade can be a substitute for factor migration. While modern theory is more ambiguous on this point, history is not: in the first global century, before quotas and restrictions, factor mobility had a *much* bigger impact on factor prices, inequality, and poverty than did trade (Taylor and Williamson, 1997). Perhaps this explains why the second global century has been much more enthusiastic about commodity trade than about migration.

1.3 Did the second global century make the world more unequal?

1.3.1 International income gaps: a postwar epochal turning point?

The Bourguignon and Morrisson evidence in Figure 1.1 documents what looks like a mid-twentieth century turning point in their between-country inequality index, since its rise slows down after 1950. However, the Bourguinon and Morrisson long-period data base contains only 15 countries. Using postwar purchasing-power-parity data for a much bigger sample of 115, Arne Melchior *et al.* (2000) actually document a *decline* in their between-country inequality index in the second half of the twentieth century, and Xavier Sala-i-Matin (2002) shows the same when focusing on poverty. The first three authors document stability in between-country inequality up to the late 1970s, followed by convergence. Other studies find the same fall in between-country inequality after the early 1960s, but perhaps the most useful in identifying an epochal regime switch is that of Andrea Boltho and Gianni Toniolo (1999), who show a rise in between-country inequality in the 1940s, rough stability over the next three decades, and a significant fall after 1980, significant enough to make their between-country inequality index drop well below its 1950 level. Did the postwar switch from autarky to global integration contribute to this epochal change in the evolution of international gaps in average incomes?

1.3.2 Trade policy and international income gaps: late twentieth-century conventional wisdom

Conventional (static) theory argues that trade liberalization should have benefited Third World countries more than it benefitted leading industrial countries. After all, trade liberalization should have a bigger effect on the terms of trade of countries joining the larger integrated world economy than on countries already members.[2] And the bigger the terms of trade gain, the bigger the GDP per capita gain.

So much for theory. Reality suggests the contrary. After all, the postwar trade that was liberalized the most was in fact intra-OECD trade, not trade between the OECD and the rest. Anti-global policies in the Third World served to lower its GDP below what might have been, but that policy was consistent with the anti-global ideology prevailing in previously colonial Asia and Africa, in Latin America where the great depression hit so hard, and in eastern Europe dominated as it was by state-directed USSR. Thus the succeeding rounds of liberalization over the first two decades or so of General Agreements on Tariffs and Trade (GATT) brought freer trade and gains from trade mainly to OECD members. However, these facts do *not* suggest that late twentieth-century globalization favored rich countries. Rather, they suggest that globalization favored all countries who liberalized and penalized those (poor preindustrial) who did not.

There is, of course, an abundant empirical literature showing that liberalizing Third World countries gained from freer trade after the OECD leaders set the liberal tone, after the 1960s.

First, a large National Bureau of Economic Research (NBER) project assessed trade and exchange-control regimes in the 1960s and 1970s by making calculations of deadweight losses (Bhagwati and Krueger, 1973–1976). However, these studies used models which did not allow protection a chance to lower long-run cost curves as would be true of the traditional infant-industry case, or to foster industrialization and thus growth, as would be true of those modern growth models where industry is the carrier of technological change and capital deepening. Second, analysts have contrasted the growth performance of relatively open with relatively closed

Table 1.1 Trade-policy orientation and growth rates in the Third World, 1963–1992

Trade policy orientation	*Average annual rates growth of GDP per capita (in %)*		
	1963–1973	*1973–1985*	*1980–1992*
Strongly open to trade	6.9	5.9	6.4
Moderately open	4.9	1.6	2.3
Moderately anti-trade	4.0	1.7	−0.2
Strongly anti-trade	1.6	−0.1	−0.4

Source: Lindert and Williamson (2003).

Note
Table 3 based on the World Bank data.

economies, as illustrated in Table 1.1. Yet, countries that liberalized their trade also liberalized their domestic factor markets, liberalized their domestic commodity markets, and set up better property-rights enforcement. The appearance of these domestic policies may deserve more of the credit for raising income. Third, there are country event studies which show that when Third World trade policy regimes changed dramatically, their growth performance improved (Dollar and Kraay, 2000a). Fourth, macroeconometric analysis has been used in an attempt to resolve the doubts left by simpler historical correlations. The most famous of these is by Jeffrey Sachs and Andrew Warner (1995), but many others have also confirmed the openness-fosters-growth hypothesis for the late twentieth century.

1.3.3 When the twentieth-century leader went open: the United States

The recent American surge in wage and income inequality generated an intense search for its sources. First, there were the globalization sources. These included the rise in unskilled worker immigration rates, due to rising foreign immigrant supplies and to a liberalization of US immigration policy. Increasing competition from imports that used unskilled labor intensively was added to the globalization impact, a rising competition due to foreign supply improvements (aided by US outsourcing), international transportation improvements, and trade-liberalizing policies. Second, there were sources apparently unrelated to globalization, like a slowdown in the growth of per worker skill supply and biased technological change that cut the demand for unskilled relative to skilled workers.

The debate evolved into a "trade versus technology" contest, although it might have learned far more by greater attention to immigration and skills (or schooling) supply, and by attention to the century *before* the 1970s. Some agree with Adrian Wood (1998) that trade was to blame for much of the wage widening. Others reject this conclusion, arguing that most or all of the widening was due to a shift in technology that has been strongly biased in favor of skills. Robert Feenstra and Gordon Hanson (1999) guess that perhaps 15–33 percent of the rising inequality was due to trade competition. In any case, everyone seems to agree that going open in late twentieth century was hardly egalitarian for America.

1.3.4 Globalization, inequality, and the OECD

The United States wasn't the only OECD country to undergo a recent rise in inequality. The trend toward wider wage gaps has also been unmistakable in Britain. Although there wasn't much widening in *full-time labor earnings* for France or Japan, and none at all for Germany or Italy, income measures that take work hours and unemployment into account reveal some widening even in those last four cases. A recent study surveyed the inequality of disposable household income in the OECD since the mid-1970s (Burniaux *et al.*, 1998). Up to the mid-1980s, the Americans and British were alone in having a clear rise in inequality. From the mid-1980s to the mid-1990s, however, 20 out of 21 OECD countries had a noticeable rise in inequality. Furthermore, the main source of rising income inequality after the mid-1980s was the widening of labor earnings. The fact that labor earnings became more unequal in most OECD countries, when *full-time* labor earnings did not, suggests that many countries took their inequality in the form of more unemployment and hours reduction, rather than in wage rates.

1.3.5 Globalization, inequality, and the Third World

The sparse literature on the wage-inequality and trade liberalization connection in developing countries is mixed in its findings and narrow in its focus. Until recently, it had concentrated on six Latins and three East Asians, and the assessment diverged sharply between regions and epochs. Wage gaps seemed to fall when the three Asian tigers liberalized in the 1960s and early 1970s. Yet wage gaps generally widened when the six Latin American countries liberalized after the late 1970s (Hanson and Harrison, 1999; Robbins, 1997). Why the difference?

As Adrian Wood has rightly pointed out, historical context was important, since other things were not equal during these liberalizations. The clearest example where a Latin wage widening appears to refute the egalitarian Stolper-Samuelson prediction was the Mexican liberalization under Salinas in 1985–1990. Yet this pro-global move coincided with the major entry of China and other Asian exporters into world markets, forcing Mexico to face new competition in all export markets. Historical context could also explain why trade liberalization coincided with wage widening in other Latin countries, and why it coincided with wage narrowing in East Asia in the 1960s and early 1970s. Competition from other low-wage countries was far less intense when the Asian tigers pulled down their barriers in the 1960s and early 1970s compared with the late 1970s and early 1980s when the Latin Americans opened up.

But even if these findings were not mixed, they could not have had a very big impact on global inequalities. After all, the literature has focused on nine countries that together had less than 200 million people in 1980, while China by itself had 980 million, India 687 million, Indonesia 148 million, and Russia 139 million. All 4 of these giants recorded widening income gaps after their economies went global. The widening did not start in China until after 1984, because the initial reforms were rural and agricultural and therefore had an egalitarian effect. When the reforms reached the urban industrial sector, China's income gaps began to widen. India's inequality has risen since liberalization started in the early 1990s. Indonesian incomes became increasingly concentrated in the top decile from the 1970s to the 1990s, though this probably owed more to the Suharto regime's ownership of the new oil wealth than to any conventional trade-liberalization effect. Russian inequalities soared after the collapse of the Soviet regime in 1991, and this owed much to the handing over of state assets to a few oligarchs.

1.3.6 Border effects, limited access, and the Third World

Income widening in these four giants dominates global trends in within-country inequality, but how much was due to pro-global policy? Probably very little. Indeed, much of the inequality surge during their liberalization experiments seems linked to the fact that the opening was incomplete and selective. That is, the rise in inequality appears to have been based on the exclusion of much of the population from the benefits of globalization. China, where the gains since 1984 have been so heavily concentrated in the coastal cities and provinces, offers a good example. Those that were able to participate in the new, globally linked economy prospered faster than ever before, while the rest in the hinterland were left behind, or at least enjoyed less economic success. China's inequality had risen to American levels by 1995, but the pronounced surge in inequality was dominated by the rise in urban–rural and coastal–hinterland gaps, not by widening gaps within any given locale. This pattern suggests that China's inequality – like that of Russia, Indonesia, and other giants – has been raised by differential access to the benefits of the new economy, not by widening gaps among those who participate in it.

Consider another example. In the aftermath of GATT-related liberalization in 1986 and of North American Foreign Trade Agreement (NAFTA)-related liberalization in 1994, Mexico has undergone rising inequality, not falling inequality as most observers predicted. However, Gordon Hanson (2002) has shown that much of this result can be traced to an uneven regional stimulus and, in particular, to the boom along the US border. Is it only a matter of waiting for these "border effects" to spread? Apparently, since Raymond Robertson (2001) has shown that the Stolper-Samuelson predictions work just fine for Mexico after 1994, if one allows for a reasonable three to five year lag.

1.4 Did the first global century make the world more unequal?

1.4.1 Global divergence without globalization

Figure 1.1 documents the rise of income gaps between nations since 1820. While the evidence may not be as precise, we also know that global income divergence started long before 1820. Indeed, international income gaps almost certainly widened after 1600 or even earlier. Real wages, living standards, health, and (especially) output per capita indicators all point to an early modern "great divergence" which took place between European nations, within European nations, and between Europe and Asia. Real wages in England and Holland pulled away from the rest of the world in the late seventeenth century. Furthermore, between the sixteenth and the eighteenth centuries the landed and merchant classes in England, Holland, and France pulled far ahead of everyone – their compatriots, the rest of Europe, and probably any other region on earth. This divergence was even greater in real than in nominal terms, because luxuries became much cheaper relative to necessities (Hoffman *et al.*, 2002). Thus, global inequality rose long before the First Industrial Revolution. Industrial revolutions were never a necessary condition for widening world income gaps.

Despite the popular rhetoric about an early modern world system, there was no true globalization move after the 1490s and the voyages of de Gama and Columbus. Intercontinental trade was monopolized, and huge price markups between exporting and importing ports were maintained even in the face of improving transport technology and European discovery. Furthermore, most of the traded commodities were non-competing: that is, they were not produced at home and thus did not displace some competing domestic industry. In addition, these traded consumption goods were luxuries out of reach of the vast majority of each trading country's population. In short, pre-1820 trade had only a trivial impact on the living standards of anyone but the very rich. Finally, the migration of people and capital was only a trickle before the 1820s. True globalization began only after the 1820s.

Thus, while global income divergence has been with us for more than four centuries, globalization has been with us for less than two. Globalization has never been a necessary condition for widening world income gaps. It happened with and without globalization.

1.4.2 When the nineteenth-century leader went open: Britain

Britain's nineteenth-century free-trade leadership, especially its famous Corn Law repeal in 1846, offers a good illustration of how the effects of global liberalization depend on the leader, and how the effects of going open can be egalitarian for both the world and for the liberalizing leader. The big gainers from British trade liberalization were British labor – especially unskilled labor – and the rest of Europe and its New World offshoots, while the clear losers were British landlords, the world's richest individuals (Williamson, 1990). How much the rest of the world gained (and whether British capitalists gained at all) depended on foreign-trade elasticities and induced terms of trade effects. But since these terms of trade effects were probably quite significant for what was then called "the workshop of the world," Britain must have distributed considerable gains to the rest of the world as well as to her own workers. Workers – especially unskilled workers – gained because Britain was a food-importing country and because labor was used much less intensively in import-competing agriculture than was land. Whether and how much the periphery gained also must have depended on deindustrialization there, a long-run force I explore further later.

History offers two enormously important historical cases where the world leader going open had completely different effects: pro-global liberalization in nineteenth-century Britain was unambiguously egalitarian at the national and world level; American liberalization in the late twentieth century was not.

1.4.3 European followers and the New World

What about the globalization and inequality connection for the rest of Europe and its New World offshoots? Two kinds of (admittedly imperfect) evidence document distributional trends within countries participating in the global economy. One relies on trends in the ratio of unskilled wages to farm rents per acre, a relative factor price whose movements launched inequality changes in a world where the agricultural sector was big and where land was a critical component of total wealth. It tells us how the typical unskilled (landless) worker near the bottom of the income pyramid did relative to the typical landlord at the top (w/r). The other piece of inequality evidence relies on trends in the ratio of the unskilled wage to GDP per worker (w/y). These trends tell us whether the typical unskilled worker near the bottom was catching up with or falling behind the income recipient in the middle.

When w/r and w/y trends are plotted for the Atlantic economy against initial labor scarcity between 1870 and First World War (Williamson, 1997), they conform to the conventional globalization prediction. Inequality fell and equality rose in land-scarce and labor-abundant Europe either due to trade boom, or to mass emigration, or to both, as incomes of the abundant factor (unskilled labor) rose relative to the scarce factor (land). In addition, those European countries which faced the onslaught of cheap foreign grain after 1870, but chose not to impose high tariffs on grain imports, recorded the biggest loss for landlords and the biggest gain for workers. Those who protected their landlords and farmers against cheap foreign grain (like France, Germany, and Spain) generally recorded a smaller decline in land rents relative to unskilled wages. To the extent that globalization was the dominant force, inequality should have fallen in labor-abundant and land-scarce Europe. And fall it did. However, these egalitarian effects were far more modest for the European industrial leaders who, after all, had smaller agricultural sectors and for whom land (owned by those at the top) was a smaller component of total wealth.

Symmetrically, globalization had a powerful inegalitarian effect in the land-abundant and labor-scarce New World. Not surprisingly, Latin America, the United States, Australia, Canada, and Russia all raised tariffs to defend themselves against an invasion of European manufactures and the deindustrialization it would have caused (Coatsworth and Williamson, 2004). Indeed, the levels of protection in the United States, Canada, Australia, Latin America, and the European periphery were *huge* compared to Continental Europe: in the 1880s the United States and Latin America had tariffs *five to six times* higher than Western Europe, and the European periphery had levels *three times* higher!

1.4.4 Terms of trade gains in the periphery before 1913

Terms of trade movements might signal who gains the most from trade, and a literature at least two centuries old has offered opinions about whose terms of trade should improve most and why (Diakosavvas and Scandizzo, 1991; Hadass and Williamson, 2003). Classical economists thought the relative price of primary products should rise given an inelastic supply of land and natural resources. This conventional wisdom took a revisionist U-turn in the 1950s when Hans Singer and Raoul Prebisch argued that since 1870 the terms of trade had deteriorated for poor countries exporting primary products, while they had improved for rich countries exporting industrial products.

The terms of trade can be influenced by changes in transport costs and changes in policy. It can also be influenced by other events, such as world productivity growth differentials across sectors, demand elasticities, and factor supply responses. But since transport costs declined so dramatically in the first global century, this is one likely source that served to raise *everybody's* terms of trade. Furthermore, and as we have seen, rich countries like Britain took a terms-of-trade hit when they switched to free trade by mid-century, an event that must have raised the terms of trade in the poor, nonindustrial periphery even more. But in some parts of the periphery, especially before the 1870s, other factors were at work that mattered even more, and they *greatly* reinforced these pro-global forces.

Probably the most powerful nineteenth-century globalization shock did not involve transport revolutions at all. It happened in Asia, and it happened in mid century. Under the persuasion of American gun ships, Japan switched from virtual autarky to free trade in 1858. In the 15 years following, Japan's foreign trade rose from virtually nil to 7 percent of national income (Huber, 1971). In home markets, the prices of exportables soared and prices of importables slumped. As a consequence, Japan's terms of trade rose by a factor of 4.9 over those 15 years. Thus, declining transport costs and a dramatic switch from autarky to free trade unleashed a powerful terms of trade gain for Japan. Other Asian nations followed this liberal path, most forced to do so by European muscle. Thus, China signed a treaty in 1842 opening her ports to trade and adopting a 5 percent *ad valorem* tariff limit. Siam adopted a 3 percent tariff limit in 1855. Korea emerged from its autarkic Hermit Kingdom with the Treaty of Kangwha in 1876, undergoing market integration with Japan long before colonial status became formalized in 1910. India went the way of British free trade in 1846, and Indonesia mimicked Dutch liberalism. In short, and whether they liked it or not, Asia underwent tremendous improvements in their terms of trade by this policy switch, and it was reinforced by declining transport costs worldwide.

For the years after 1870, there is better evidence documenting terms of trade movements the world around, country by country (Coatsworth and Williamson, 2004; Hadass and Williamson, 2003; Williamson, 2002). Contrary to the assertions which Prebisch and Singer made a half-century ago, not only did the terms of trade improve for a good share of the non-Latin American poor periphery up to the 1890s, but they improved a lot more than they did in Europe.Why am I able to report such different historical findings than did Prebisch and Singer, or than did Arthur Lewis a little later? One reason is that Prebisch and his followers were motivated by deteriorating terms of trade in Latin America after the 1890s, while I am casting a wider net. Another is that I have only reported the terms of trade performance during the first global century, not during the anti-global interlude that followed.

A third reason is that the peripheral terms of trade reported here are those which prevailed in each home market, not the inverse of those prevailing in London or New York. In a world where transport costs plunged steeply, everybody could have found their terms of trade improving, but some primary producers in the periphery actually enjoyed the biggest pre-war improvements. If other members of the periphery did not enjoy the same big gains, it was not the fault of globalization induced by transport revolutions and liberal policy.

This pre-1913 terms of trade experience seems to imply that globalization favored some parts of the poor periphery even more than it did the rich center, and to that extent it must have been a force for more equal world incomes. That inference is probably false. Over the short run, positive and quasi-permanent terms of trade shocks of foreign origin will always raise a nation's purchasing power, and the issue is only how much. Over the long run a positive terms-of-trade shock in primary-product-producing countries should reinforce comparative advantage, pull resources into the export sector, thus causing deindustrialization. To the extent that industrialization is the prime carrier of capital-deepening and technological change, then economists like Singer were right to caution that positive external price shocks for primary producers might actually *lower* growth rates in the long run. Of course, small-scale, rural cottage industry isn't the same as large-scale, urban factories, so industry may not have been quite the carrier of growth in the 1870 periphery that it might be in the Third World today. In any case, adding terms of trade variables to a now-standard empirical growth model and estimating that model for a nineteen-country sample between 1870 and 1940 (Hadass and Williamson, 2003), confirms that while an improving terms of trade was growth-augmenting in the center it was *growth-reducing* in the periphery. The short-run gain from an improving terms of trade appears to have been overwhelmed by a long-run loss attributed to deindustrialization in the periphery; in contrast, the short-run gain was reinforced by a long-run gain attributed to industrialization in the center.

These results imply that globalization-induced (positive) terms of trade shocks before First World War were serving to augment the growing gap between rich and poor nations. Did the same happen after 1950 when Prebisch, Singer, and other critics of conventional policy were so vocal? Maybe. Is the same true today, 50 years later? Probably not. After all, the share of manufactures in the total commodity exports in developing countries rose spectacularly from 30 to 75 percent between 1970 and 2002 (Hertel *et al.*, 2002: Figure 1.2). The Third World isn't the primary product exporter it used to be.

1.4.5 Rising inequality in the primary product exporting periphery

There were powerful global forces at work before 1913 and the Third World was very much a part of it. There was commodity price convergence within and between Europe, the newly settled non-Latin countries, Latin America, and Asia, and the price convergence was bigger in the periphery than it was in the core. The convergence was driven by a transport revolution that was more dramatic in the Asian periphery where, in addition, it was not offset by tariff intervention.

It also appears that relative factor prices converged worldwide at the same time that average living standards and income per capita diverged sharply between center and periphery.[3] The relative factor price convergence was manifested by falling wage–rental ratios in land-abundant and labor-scarce countries, and rising wage–rental ratios in land-scarce and labor-abundant countries. The convergence took place everywhere around the globe.

These events set in motion powerful inequality forces in land- and resource-abundant areas, *especially* around the pre-industrial periphery, as in Southeast Asia and the Southern Cone. Quite the opposite forces were at work in land- and resource-scarce areas, like East Asia. These distributional events in the periphery were ubiquitous and powerful (Williamson, 2002). They must have had important implications for political developments which probably persisted well in to the late twentieth century.

1.4.6 North–North and South–South mass migrations, with segmentation in between

North–North migrations between Europe and the New World involved the movement of something like 60 million individuals. We know a great deal about the determinants and impact of these mass migrations. South–South migration within the periphery was probably even greater, but we know very little about its impact on sending regions (like China and India), on receiving regions (like East Africa, Manchuria, and Southeast Asia), or on the incomes of the 60 million or so who moved. As Lewis (1978) pointed out long ago, the South–North migrations were only a trickle: like today, poor migrants from the periphery were kept out of the high-wage center by restrictive policy, by the high cost of the move, and by their lack of education. World labor markets were segmented then just as they are now.

Real wages and living standards converged among the currently industrialized countries between 1850 and the First World War. The convergence was driven primarily by the erosion of the gap between the New World and Europe, but many poor European countries also were catching up with the industrial leaders. How much of this convergence in the Atlantic economy was due to North–North mass migration?

The labor force impact of these migrations on each member of the Atlantic economy in 1910 varied greatly (Taylor and Williamson, 1997). Among receiving countries, Argentina's labor force was augmented most by immigration (86 percent), Brazil's the least (4 percent), with the United States in between (24 percent). Among sending countries, Ireland's labor force was diminished most by emigration (45 percent), France the least (1 percent), with Britain in between (11 percent). At the same time, the economic gaps between rich and poor countries diminished (Hatton and Williamson, 1998; Taylor and Williamson, 1997). What contribution did the mass migration make to that convergence? The biggest impact, of course, was on those countries that experienced the biggest migrations. Emigration is estimated to have raised Irish wages by 32 percent, Italian by 28 percent, and Norwegian by 10 percent. Immigration is estimated to have lowered Argentine wages by 22 percent, Australian by 15 percent, Canadian by 16 percent, and American by 8 percent.

This assessment suggests that in the absence of the mass migrations, real wage dispersion between members of the Atlantic economy would have *increased* by something like 7 percent, rather than decrease by 28 percent, as it did in fact. In the absence of mass migration, wage gaps between Europe and the New World would have *risen* from 108 percent to something like 128 percent when in fact they declined to 85 percent. It appears that migration was responsible for *all* of the real wage convergence before the First World War and about two-thirds of the GDP per worker convergence.

There was an additional and even more powerful effect of North–North mass migrations on "northern" income distribution. What about the large income gains accruing to the millions of poor Europeans who moved overseas? These migrants came from countries whose average real wages and average GDP per worker were perhaps only half of those in the receiving countries. These migrant gains were a very important part of the net equalizing effect on "northern" incomes of the mass migrations.

North–North mass migrations had a strong leveling influence in the North up to 1913. They made it possible for poor migrants to improve the living standards for themselves and their children. It also lowered the scarcity of resident New World labor which competed with the immigrants, while it raised the scarcity of the poor European labor that stayed home (whose incomes were augmented still further by emigrant remittances). South–South and North–North migrations were about the same size. Until new research tells us otherwise, I think it is safe to assume that South–South migrations put powerful downward pressure on real wages and labor productivity in Southeast Asia, East Africa, Manchuria, and other labor scarce regions that received so many Indians and Chinese. Since the sending labor surplus areas were so huge, it seems less likely that the emigrations served to raise labor scarcity there by much.

1.4.7 Trade policy and international income gaps: why the big regime switch?

About 30 years ago, Paul Bairoch (1972) argued that protectionist countries grew *faster* in the nineteenth century, not slower as every economist has found for the late twentieth century. Bairoch's sample was mainly from the European industrial core, it looked at pre-1914 experience only, and it controlled for no other factors. Like some modern studies (see Table 1.1), Bairoch simply compared growth rates of major European countries in protectionist and free trade episodes. More recently, Kevin O'Rourke (2000) got the Bairoch finding again, this time using macro-econometric conditional analysis on a ten country sample drawn from the pre-1914 Atlantic economy. In short, these two scholars were not able to find *any* evidence before First World War supporting the openness-fosters-growth hypothesis.

These pioneering historical studies suggest that there was a fundamental tariff-growth regime switch somewhere between the start of First World War and the end of Second World War: before the switch, protection was associated with fast growth; after the switch, protection was associated with slow growth. Michael Clemens and Jeffrey Williamson (2004a) think the best explanation for the tariff-growth paradox is the fact that: during the interwar, and led by the industrial powers, tariff barriers facing the average exporting countries rose to very high levels; and since Second World War, again led by the industrial powers, tariff barriers facing the average exporting country fell to their lowest levels in a century and a half. A well-developed theoretical literature on strategic trade policy (recently surveyed in Bagwell and Staiger 2000) predicts that nations have an incentive to inflate their own terms of trade by tariffs, but thereby to lower global welfare – a classic prisoner's dilemma. Inasmuch as favorable terms of trade translate into better growth performance and tariffs are non-prohibitive, we might expect the association between own tariffs and growth to depend at least in part on the external tariff environment faced by the country in question. After accounting for changes in world policy environment, Clemens and Williamson show that there is no incompatibility between the positive tariff-growth correlation before 1914 and the negative tariff-growth correlation since 1970.

There is growing evidence suggesting that the benefits of openness are neither inherent nor irreversible but rather depend upon the state of the world. The low-level equilibrium of mutually high tariffs is only as far away as some big world event that persuades influential leader-countries to switch to anti-global policies. The rest must follow in order to survive. Thus, today's low-tariff equilibrium is only as far away as OECD coordination in the early postwar years, and the creation of transnational institutions whose purpose was to impede a return to interwar autarky. But what sparks such shifts from one equilibrium to another? Why did it happen in the 1920s and 1950s? Could it happen again?

1.4.8 Trade policy and international income gaps: what about the pre-1940 periphery?

Were Latin America, Eastern Europe and the rest of the periphery part of this paradox, or was it only an attribute of the industrial core? Presumably, the protecting country has to have a big domestic market, and has to be ready for industrialization, accumulation, and human capital deepening if the long-run tariff-induced dynamic effects are to offset the short-run gains from trade given up. Recent work has shown that the asymmetry hypothesis wins (Clemens and Williamson, 2004a; Coatsworth and Williamson, 2004). That is, protection was associated with faster growth in the European core and their English-speaking offshoots, but it was *not* associated with fast growth in the European or Latin American periphery, nor was it associated with fast growth in interwar Asia. Indeed, before First World War protection in Latin America was associated significantly and powerfully with *slow* growth.

While policy makers in Latin America, Eastern Europe and the Mediterranean may, after the 1860s, have been very aware of the pro-protectionist infant-industry argument offered for a newly integrated (*zollverein*) Germany by Frederich List or for a newly independent (economically federated) United States by Alexander Hamilton, there is absolutely no evidence which would have supported those arguments in the periphery. We must look elsewhere for explanations for the exceptionally high tariffs in Latin America and the European periphery during the first global century.

1.5 Four lessons of history

1.5.1 Will there be South–North mass migration in our future?

It might be useful to repeat what we have learned about the mass migrations: almost all of the observed income convergence in the Atlantic economy (or North), was due to this North–North mass migration, and that same movement also generated more equal incomes in the labor-abundant sending regions. It is important to remember this fact when dealing today with the second global century.

Although the migrations were immense during the age of mass North–North and South–South migration prior to Frist World War, there was hardly any South–North migration to speak of. Thus, while the mass migration to labor scarce parts of the North played a big role in erasing poverty in the labor surplus parts of the North, it did not help much to erase poverty in the South. The same is true today. Will this world labor market segmentation break down in the near future? It all depends on policy. Certainly demographic and educational forces are contributing to the breakdown of world labor market segmentation along South–North lines. As young adult shares shrink in the elderly OECD, and while they swell in the young Third World going through demographic transitions, perhaps the pressure will become too great to resist the move to a more liberal OECD immigration policy, especially in Europe and Japan. The educational revolution in the Third World has helped augment this pressure, as potential emigrants from poor countries are better equipped to gain jobs in the OECD (Clark *et al.*, 2002; Hatton and Williamson, 2002).

The two underlying fundamentals that drove European emigration in the late nineteenth century were the size of real wage gaps between sending and receiving regions – a gap that gave migrants the incentive to move, and demographic booms in the low-wage sending regions – a force that served to augment the supply of potential movers. These two fundamentals are even more prominent in Africa today (Hatton and Williamson, 2002, 2003). Although this is no longer an age of unrestricted intercontinental migration, new estimates of net migration for the countries of sub-Saharan Africa suggest that exactly the same forces are at work driving African cross-border migration today. Rapid growth in the cohort of young potential migrants, population pressure on the resource base, and poor economic performance are the main forces driving African emigration. In Europe a century ago, more modest demographic increases were accompanied by strong catching-up economic growth in low-wage emigrant regions. Furthermore, the sending regions of Europe eventually underwent a slowdown in demographic growth serving to choke off some of the mass migration. Yet, migrations were still mass. Africa today offers a contrast: economic growth has faltered, its economies have fallen further behind, and they will undergo a demographic speed up in the near future. The pressure on African emigration is likely to intensify, including a growing demand for entrance into OECD high-wage labor markets.

This analysis for African emigation has been recently extended to US immigration by source from 1971 to 1998 (Clark *et al.*, 2002; Hatton and Williamson, 2002). Here again, the economic and demographic fundamentals that determine immigration rates across source countries are estimated – income, education, demographic composition, and inequality. The analysis also allows for persistence in these patterns as they arise from the impact of the existing immigrant stock B big foreign-born stocks implying strong > friends and neighbors = effects. Most of these Third World fundamentals will be serving to increase the demand for high-wage jobs in the OECD.

How will the OECD respond? If it opens its doors wider, the mass migrations would almost certainly have the same influence on leveling world incomes and eradicating poverty that it did in the first global century. It would help erode between-country North–South income gaps, and it would improve the lives of the millions of poor Asians and Africans allowed to make the move. And it would help eradicate poverty among those who would not move, making their labor more scarce at home and augmenting their incomes by remittances, forces that were powerful in Europe a century ago.

Inequality would rise among OECD residents, of course, just as it did in the immigrant-absorbing New World a century ago. Perhaps not as much, since the unskilled with whom the immigrants compete are a much smaller share of the OECD labor force now, but inequality would rise just the same. Are we ready to pay that price? Perhaps not. Indeed, rising inequality created an anti-global backlash a century ago, a backlash that included a retreat into immigrant restriction that *still* characterizes the OECD today.

1.5.2 Absolute or relative income? Nominal or real income?

The debate over the impact of globalization on world inequality almost always measures performance in relative terms. The questions posed are: have international income gaps between poor and rich countries widened with globalization? Has inequality within countries widened with globalization? Something is very wrong with these questions and the measures they imply. Here is a better question: if the gaps between rich and poor within countries have widened, and if globalization is the cause, is it because poor citizens have not gained by their country going global, or is it because they have actually *lost*? To the extent that policy is driven by the *absolute losses* to vocal citizens and/or vocal nations, rather than relative losses, it is all the more amazing that so many contemporary economists insist on using relative inequality measures. Economic historians know better. I offer two examples.

Historical Example 1. During the great British political debates over a move to free trade in the decades before the 1846 Repeal of the Corn Laws, predicted impact was *always* assessed *both* by reference to nominal incomes on the employment side *and* to consumption goods prices on the expenditure side. Indeed, free traders called the high duties on agricultural imports "bread taxes" (Williamson, 1990), and thought that the relative price of this wage good (grain) was central to working class living standards. And they were absolutely right! Since grain – and its derivative bread – made up such an enormous share of working class budgets, the falling relative price of this importable made a fundamental contribution to the rise in real wages and the living standards of the poor.

Historical Example 2. During the great rise in European inequality between 1500 and 1800, when Malthusian forces dominated the closed European economy (O'Rourke and Williamson, 2002, 2005), staple food and fuels became more expensive, while luxury goods, like imported exotics and domestic servants, became cheaper (Hoffman *et al.*, 2002). These relative price changes served to augment rising nominal inequality and to reduce living standards of the working poor. What happened in the nineteenth century when Europe went open? The price of imported food fell, contributing to the absolute real wage gains associated with the industrial revolution. What had been a pre-globalization inegalitarian price effect was converted into a post-globalization egalitarian price effect. And since the poor devoted such a large share of their budget to food, the poorest gained the most.

Economic historians cannot take all the credit for asking the right questions, since one can also find a few rare examples in the huge literature on the current globalization–inequality connection. David Dollar and Aart Kraay (2000b) report from late twentieth-century country cases and cross-country analysis that globalization leads to poverty reduction in poor countries, and that trade openness beneifts the poor as much as it benefits all others.[4] Of course, it may not be the poor who vote, and thus the impact of going open on their economic performance may unimportant to policy formation in poor countries and thus to the survival of global liberialism there.

The two historical examples from the first global century suggest an agenda for the second global century. If going global has had a real impact on participating economies over the past three decades, then we should see its impact on relative commodity prices in home markets: the price of importables should have fallen relative to the price of exportables and perhaps even relative to the price of non-tradables. What do the rich and poor consume in these countries? What happened to the cost of their consumption market baskets when their country went open? Did the price movements on the expenditure side serve to reinforce or offset income movements on the employment side?

Economists should be searching for modern cases where the budgets of the rich and poor are very different, the rich consuming mainly skill and capital intensive importables plus the non-traded services of the poor, and the poor consuming mainly land-intensive food and non-traded housing services. They should also search for countries that have recently switched from anti-global to pro-global policies. The best places to find both conditions satisfied are, of course, Asia and Africa.

1.5.3 Accommodating the losers with safety nets and suffrage

Any force that creates more within-country inequality is automatically blunted today – at least in the OECD, a point that is sometimes overlooked in the inequality debate. That is, any rise in the inequality of households' net disposable post-fisc income will always be less than the rise in gross pre-fisc income inequality. Any damage to the earnings of low-skilled workers is partially offset by their lower tax payments and higher transfer receipts, like unemployment compensation or family assistance. Broadening the income concept therefore serves to shrink any apparent impact of globalization on the inequality of living standards. By muting their losses, such safety nets also can mute political backlash.

So far, so good. But does globalization destroy these automatic stabilizers by undermining taxes and social transfer programs? In a world where businesses and skilled personnel can flee taxes they don't like, there is the well-known danger that governments might compete for internationally mobile factors by cutting tax rates and thus social spending. As Dani Rodrik (1997, 1998) has stressed, however, the relationship between a country's vulnerability to international markets and the size of its tax-based social programs is *positive*, not negative as a "race to the bottom" would imply. Thus, countries with greater global market vulnerability have higher taxes, more social spending, and broader safety nets. While there may be other reasons for the positive correlation between openness and social programs, there is no apparent tendency for globalization to undermine the safety nets.

While these stabilizers certainly prevail in the OECD today, one might suppose they were not common during the first global century when such safety nets were not yet in place. If one was inclined to make that assumption, one would be very wrong. Europe was globalized by 1913, and the increased market vulnerability created greater wage and employment instability. Michael Huberman by himself (2002) and with Wayne Lewchuk (2001) show that authorities responded to workers' complaints by establishing labor market regulations and social insurance programs, and by giving them the vote. Empirical analysis of 17 European countries shows that the legislation gave workers reason to support free trade. Thus, globalization was compatible with government intervention before 1913 just as it has been since 1950. And, to repeat, the first global century was also one during which the vote was extended increasingly to the previously disenfranchised. It also appears that the two were related!

The interesting question is how long it will take poor nations today to put the same modern safety nets in place and to empower all citizens in the debate over global policy choices.

1.5.4 Why do countries protect?

What better place to end this chapter than to ask: Why do countries protect? I am aware that the recent decade or so has generated a flourishing theoretical literature on endogenous tariffs. That literature is primarily motivated by recent OECD experience, thus ignoring the enormous variance over time and across regions with very different endowments, institutions, and histories.

Figure 1.3 reports the enormous variance in levels of protection for both the first global century and for the interwar years. Three big facts are revealed by Figure 1.3. First, tariffs in the independent periphery (Latin America, the non-Latin European offshoots and the European periphery) were vastly higher than

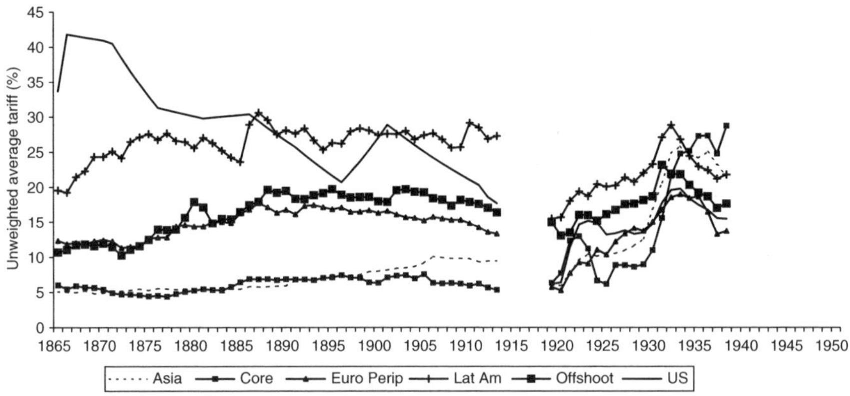

Figure 1.3 Unweighted average of regional tariffs before Second World War.

they were in the European core. Second, in an apparent – but maybe not real – globalization backlash, tariffs rose *much* more steeply in the periphery than in the European core during the first globalization century up to First World War. Third, what made the interwar years so autarkic was not a move towards protection in the periphery – since tariffs in Latin America, the European periphery, and the non-Latin offshoots were just about as high in the 1930s as they were before First World War. What made the interwar years so autarkic was the rise of protection in the European core and the United States.

Economists need to confront these facts and to offer explanations for them. When one does so for Latin America from 1820 to 1950, one finds that the motivations for protection were very complex and changed over time (Coatsworth and Williamson, 2004). Those exceptionally high Latin American tariffs were driven up by government revenue needs, strategic tariff reactions to trading partner policy (e.g. very high tariffs in the United States), Stolper-Samuelson lobbying forces, and protection of the local manufacturing industry. Before we can be confident about what causes globalization backlash today, we need to know what caused it in the past. Over the century 1820–1913, only a (perhaps small) part of the anti-global policy in Latin America was driven by development goals, by deindustrialization fears, or by the complaints of the losers. Furthermore, these determinants changed over time: revenue goals diminished in importance as Latin America became better integrated with global capital markets, as *pax Americana latina* diminished the need for and thus the financial burden of standing armies, and as these young countries developed less-distorting internal tax revenue sources. Economists need to make the same kind of assessment for the second global century if we are to understand the sources of globalization backlash better.

Notes

1 The causality is worth stressing here. While the modern globalization–inequality debate chases the causation from globalization to within-country inequality, the period

1500–1800 was characterized by population pressure on the land which raised land rents and thus the incomes of Europe's rich. Rising inequality increased the demand for imported luxuries, causing a trade boom. It also caused a boom in all well-placed European ports around the Atlantic economy, as Acemoglu *et al.* (2002) have shown, but misinterpreted.

2 For example, when Mexico joined NAFTA in 1994, its economy was only about 6 percent the size of the US. Furthermore, only about 9 percent of US trade was with Mexico, while about 75 percent of Mexican imports and 84 percent of Mexican exports involved the United States (Robertson, 2001: 1). These shares suggest that Mexico satisfied the "small country assumption" and took North American market prices as given, thus getting the full measure of terms of trade gains by going open.

3 These facts deserve stress. While there was income per capita and living standards divergence between center and periphery in the first global century, there was powerful convergence in *relative* factor prices. One wonders whether the same has been true in the second global century, and, if so, why economists haven't noticed it.

4 A more recent study by Sala-i-Matin (2002) is more descriptive, asking only what happened from 1970 to 1998, assigning no blame or applause to causes. He shows that while poverty rates have fallen since 1970, within-country inequality has increased.

References

Acemoglu, D., S. Johnson, and J. Robinson. 2002. "The Rise of Europe: Atlantic Trade, Institutional Change and Economic Growth," unpublished paper (March 28).

Bagwell, Kyle and Robert W. Staiger. 2000. "GATT-Think," *NBER Working Paper 8005*. National Bureau of Economic Research, Cambridge, MA: NBER.

Baier, Scott J. and Jeffrey H. Bergstrand. 2001. "The Growth of World Trade: Tariffs, Transport Costs, and Income Similarity," *Journal of International Economics*, 53 (February): 1–27.

Bairoch, Paul. 1972. "Free Trade and European Economic Development in the Nineteenth Century," *European Economic Review*, 3 (November): 211–245.

Bhagwati, Jagdish and Anne O. Krueger. (eds) 1973–1976. *Foreign Trade Regimes and Economic Development*, multiple volumes with varying authorship. New York: Columbia University Press for the NBER.

Boltho, Andrea and Gianni Toniolo. 1999. "The Assessment: The Twentieth Century – Achievements, Failures, Lessons," *Oxford Review of Economic Policy*, 15 (4): 1–17.

Bourguignon, François and Christian Morrisson. 2002. "Inequality Among World Citizens 1820–1990," *American Economic Review* (September): 727–744.

Chiswick, Barry R. and Timothy J. Hatton. 2003. "International Migration and the Integration of Labor Markets," in M. Bordo, A.M. Taylor, and J.G. Williamson (eds) *Globalization In Historical Perspective*. Chicago, IL: University of Chicago Press.

Clark, Ximena, Timothy J. Hatton, and Jeffrey G. Williamson. 2002. "Where Do US Immigrants Come From, and Why?" *NBER Working Paper 8998*. National Bureau of Economic Research, Cambridge, MA (June).

Clemens, Michael A. and Jeffrey G. Williamson. 2004a. "Why Did the Tariff-Growth Correlation Reverse After 1950?" *Journal of Economic Growth*, 9 (1): 5–46.

Clemens, Michael A. and Jeffrey G. Williamson. 2004b. "Wealth Bias in the First Global Capital Market Boom, 1870–1913," *Economic Journal*, 114: 311–344.

Coatsworth, John H. and Jeffrey G. Williamson. 2004. "The Roots of Latin American Protectionism: Looking Before the Great Depression," in A. Estevadeordal, D. Rodrik, A. Taylor, and A. Velasco (eds) *FTAA and Beyond: Prospects for Integration in the Americas*. Cambridge, MA: Harvard University Press.

Diakosavvas, Dimitris and Pasquale L. Scandizzo. 1991. "Trends in the Terms of Trade of Primary Commodities, 1900–1982: The Controversy and Its Origin," *Economic Development and Cultural Change*, 39 (January): 231–264.

Dollar, David and Aart Kraay. 2000a. "Trade, Growth, and Poverty," unpublished paper. Washington, DC: World Bank (October).

Dollar, David and Aart Kraay. 2000b. "Growth *Is* Good for the Poor," unpublished paper. Washington, DC: World Bank (March).

Dowrick, Steve and J. Bradford DeLong. 2003. "Globalization and Convergence," in M. Bordo, A.M. Taylor, and J.G. Williamson (eds) *Globalization in Historical Perspective*. Chicago, IL: University of Chicago Press.

Feenstra, Robert C. and Gordon H. Hanson. 1999. "The Impact of Outsourcing and High-Technology Capital on Wages: Estimates for the United States, 1979–1990," *Quarterly Journal of Economics*, 114 (August): 907–940.

Findlay, Ronald and Kevin H. O'Rourke. 2003. "Commodity Market Integration, 1500–2000," in M. Bordo, A.M. Taylor, and J.G. Williamson (eds) *Globalization in Historical Perspective*. Chicago, IL: University of Chicago Press.

Hadass, Yael S. and Jeffrey G. Williamson. 2003. "Terms of Trade Shocks and Economic Performance 1870–1940: Prebisch and Singer Revisited," *Economic Development and Cultural Change*, 51 (3): 629–656.

Hanson, Gordon. 2002. "Globalization and Wages in Mexico," paper presented to the *Conference on Prospects for Integration in the Americas*. Harvard University, Cambridge, MA (May 31–June 1).

Hanson, Gordon and Ann Harrison. 1999. "Trade Liberalization and Wage Inequality in Mexico," *Industrial and Labor Relations Review*, 52 (January): 271–288.

Hatton, Timothy J. and Jeffrey G. Williamson. 1998. *The Age of Mass Migration*. Oxford: Oxford University Press.

Hatton, Timothy J. and Jeffrey G. Williamson. 2002. "What Fundamentals Drive World Migration?" paper to be presented at the *WIDER Conference on Migration*, Helsinki (September 27–28).

Hatton, Timothy J. and Jeffrey G. Williamson. 2003. "Demographic and Economic Pressure on Emigration Out of Africa," *Scandinavian Journal of Economics*, 105: 465–486.

Hertel, Thomas, Bernard M. Hoekman, and Will Martin. 2002. "Developing Countries and a New Round of WTO Negotiations," *World Bank Research Observer*, 17 (Spring): 113–140.

Hoffman, Philip T., David S. Jacks, Patricia A. Levin, and Peter H. Lindert. 2002. "Real Inequality in Europe since 1500," *Journal of Economic History, 62* (June): 322–355.

Huber, J. Richard. 1971. "Effects on Prices of Japan's Entry into World Commerce after 1858," *Journal of Political Economy*, 79 (May/June): 614–628.

Huberman, Michael. 2002. "International Labor Standards and Market Integration Before 1913: A Race to the Top?" paper presented to the conference on the *Political Economy of Globalization*, Dublin (August 29–31).

Huberman, Michael and Wayne Lewchuk. 2001. "The Labor Compact, Openness and Small and Large States Before 1914," unpublished paper. University of Montreal (August).

Lewis, W. Arthur. 1978. *The Evolution of the International Economic Order*. Princeton, NJ: Princeton University Press.

Lindert, Peter H. and Jeffrey G. Williamson. 2003. "Does Globalization Make the World More Unequal?" in M. Bordo, A.M. Taylor, and J.G. Williamson (eds) *Globalization in Historical Perspective*. Chicago, IL: University of Chicago Press.

Maddison, Angus. 1995. *Monitoring the World Economy, 1820–1992*. Paris: OECD.

Melchior, Arne, Kjetil Telle, and Henrik Wiig. 2000. "Globalisation and Inequality: World Income Distribution and Living Standards, 1960–1998," *Studies on Foreign Policy Issues Report 6B: 2000*. Royal Norwegian Ministry of Foreign Affairs, Oslo (October).

Obstfeld, Maurice and Alan M. Taylor. 1998. "The Great Depression as a Watershed: International Capital Mobility over the Long Run," in M.D. Bordo, C. Goldin, and E.N. White (eds) *The Defining Moment: The Great Depression and the American Economy in the Twentieth Century*. Chicago, IL: University of Chicago Press.

Obstfeld, Maurice and Alan M. Taylor. 2003. "Globalization and Capital Markets," in M.D. Bordo, A.M. Taylor, and J.G. Williamson (eds) *Globalization in Historical Perspective*. Chicago, IL: University of Chicago Press.

O'Rourke, Kevin H. 2000. "Tariffs and Growth in the Late 19th Century," *Economic Journal*, 110 (April): 456–483.

O'Rourke, Kevin H. and Jeffrey G. Williamson. 1999. *Globalization and History*. Cambridge, MA: MIT Press.

O'Rourke, Kevin H. and Jeffrey G. Williamson. 2002. "After Columbus: Explaining Europe's Overseas Trade Boom, 1500–1800," *Journal of Economic History*, 62 (June 2002): 417–456.

O'Rourke, Kevin H. and Jeffrey G. Williamson. 2005. "From Malthus to Ohlin: Trade, Growth and Distribution Since 1500," *Journal of Economic Growth*, 10 (1): 5–34.

Pritchett, Lant. 1997. "Divergence, Big Time," *Journal of Economic Perspectives*, 11 (Summer): 3–18.

Robbins, Donald J. 1997. "Trade and Wages in Colombia," *Estudios de Economia*, 24 (June): 47–83.

Robertson, Raymond. 2001. "Relative Prices and Wage Inequality: Evidence from Mexico," unpublished paper. Macalester College (October).

Rodrik, Dani. 1997. *Has Globalization Gone Too Far?* Washington, DC: Institute for International Economics.

Rodrik, Dani. 1998. "Why Do More Open Economies Have Bigger Governments?" *Journal of Political Economy*, 106 (October): 997–1033.

Sachs, Jeffrey D. and Andrew Warner. 1995. "Economic Reform and the Process of Global Integration," *Brookings Papers on Economic Activity*, I. Washington, DC: Brookings Institution.

Sala-i-Matin, Xavier. 2002. "The Disturbing 'Rise' of Global Income Inquality," *NBER Working Paper 8904*. National Bureau of Economic Research, Cambridge, MA (April).

Taylor, Alan M. and Jeffrey G. Williamson. 1997. "Convergence in the Age of Mass Migration," *European Review of Economic History*, 1 (April): 27–63.

Williamson, Jeffrey G. 1990. "The Impact of the Corn Laws Just Prior to Repeal," *Explorations in Economic History*, 27 (April): 123–156.

Williamson, Jeffrey G. 1997. "Globalization and Inequality: Past and Present," *World Bank Research Observer*, 12 (August): 117–135.

Williamson, Jeffrey G. 2002. "Land, Labor, and Globalization in the Third World 1870–1940," *Journal of Economic History*, 62 (March): 55–85.

Wood, Adrian. 1994. *North–South Trade, Employment and Inequality*. Oxford: Clarendon Press.

Wood, Adrian. 1998. "Globalisation and the Rise in Labour Market Inequalities," *Economic Journal*, 108 (September): 1463–1482.

Part II

Income inequality

2 From earnings dispersion to income inequality

Anthony B. Atkinson and Andrea Brandolini

2.1 Introduction[1]

According to a widely held view, there is a straightforward explanation for the recent rise in income inequality. Since late-1970s the labour markets of industrialised countries have experienced a shift in demand away from unskilled labour. Some researchers have emphasised the bias against unskilled labour associated with technological progress. For instance, Krugman (1994) observed that

> it is surely hard not to suspect that the dramatic progress in information and communication technology over the past two decades has somehow played a central role in the increased premium on skill, and perhaps in the growth of European unemployment.
>
> (p. 71)

although he added that 'the actual linkages are, however, not at all well understood'. Other researchers have stressed the role of 'globalisation', that is, the growing world economic integration which has brought about a migration of production of labour-intensive goods to developing countries. As put by Wood (1994),

> expansion of trade has linked the labour markets of developed countries (the North) more closely with those of developing countries (the South). This greater economic intimacy has had large benefits, raising average living standards in the North, and accelerating development in the South. But it has hurt unskilled workers in the North, reducing their wages and pushing them out of jobs.
>
> (p. 1)

The impact of globalisation or skill-biased technological progress on the labour market may turn out to be different in Europe and North America. As has been described by Krugman (1994) and Wood (1994), where wages are flexible, a situation that is seen to characterise the United States, the shift in labour demand causes increased wage dispersion. On the other hand, where the widening of wage differentials is resisted by union behaviour or minimum wage provisions, as in

Continental Europe, the compensation of unskilled labour does not fall relative to that of skilled labour, resulting in a rise of unemployment among unskilled workers and little change in earnings dispersion.

Bertola and Ichino (1995) equally focus on the varying 'flexibility' of labour market institutions, but suggest that the cause of the divergent outcomes in Europe and the United States must be sought in the increasing volatility of labour demand. Technological progress or international trade may help to explain growing dispersion across skill levels in the United States, but as usually modelled they cannot account for the parallel rise of inequality within groups of workers with similar characteristics. Bertola and Ichino argue that these factors, along with many other economic and institutional developments, have led to an intensification of shocks entailing a reallocation of the labour force – producing different outcomes in different institutional environments:

> A more volatile environment requires larger wage differentials across identical workers in a flexible labor market, as the expectation of higher wages compensates the movers for mobility costs incurred when leaving firms (sectors, regions) hit by negative shocks to reach firms (sectors, regions) hit by positive ones. In a rigid economy, conversely, a more volatile environment induces more caution in hiring and, for a given wage, leads to a higher overall rate of unemployment.
>
> (p. 42)

The contrast between Europe and North America – with the United Kingdom possibly leaning towards the other side of the Atlantic – in terms of rigidity of the respective labour markets, and of the different implications for employment and wage dispersion, has become a popular theme in the public economic discourse.[2] It is part of the subtext of the Lisbon Agenda. The contrast, as described earlier, is admittedly an oversimplification, and it fails to recognise that differences across European labour markets tend to be greater than the difference between the European average and North America (Nickell, 1997). Nonetheless, it points to the need to investigate how labour market outcomes hinge on the interaction of market forces and institutional settings.

This literature has brought together a rich blend of economic theory and institutional analysis; it has drawn on a wide variety of empirical evidence, contrasting individuals, countries and time periods. The richness and variety mean, however, that (a) it is difficult to compare and contrast the different findings and (b) jumps are often made between different steps in the argument. One such jump is that indicated in our title: from earnings dispersion to income inequality. The aim of this chapter is to set out a simple analytical framework, within which we can set the different approaches and which allows us to spell out the separate stages of what is a quite complex process. For illustrative purposes, in setting out the analytical framework in Section 2.2, we adopt the Krugman–Wood perspective. We assume that the economy is formed of only two types of workers, skilled and unskilled, and that labour demand shifts relatively to the advantage of the former, because of globalisation or biased technological progress. In Section 2.3, we consider the nature of empirical evidence on earnings dispersion, distinguishing between studies where the analysis is based on individual wage equations and studies where the primitive unit is the degree of wage dispersion at a particular date in a particular country. We then survey in Section 2.4 the results from comparative studies of cross-national differences in the *level* and the *trend* of earnings dispersion. While the literature abounds with bilateral comparisons, typically the United States *vis-à-vis* some other country, we focus on studies examining three or more Organisation for Economic Co-operation and Development (OECD) countries.[3] In the second half of the chapter, we consider the link between individual earnings dispersion and the household income distribution with which many people are ultimately concerned. Section 2.5 deals with inequality in the labour market as a whole, incorporating those not employed and the trade-off between employment and wage dispersion. Section 2.6 brings in the welfare state and the interaction between redistribution and forces affecting the labour market. Section 2.7 presents evidence on the different distributions in eight OECD countries at the beginning of the twenty-first century.

2.2 Earnings dispersion in a dual labour market

In order to model the Krugman–Wood story, suppose that the population is made of only two groups of people 'skilled' and 'unskilled', and assume that the supply of skills is fixed. The Lorenz curve for this dual labour market is the broken line shown in the upper part of Figure 2.1.[4] Denote by ϕ the proportion of unskilled workers, the slopes of the two segments equal the ratio to the mean of the unskilled and skilled wages, respectively. If s is the skill premium (i.e. the skilled wage is $1 + s$ times the unskilled wage), the share of unskilled workers in total wages can be calculated as

$$\Omega = \frac{\phi}{\phi + (1 - \phi)(1 + s)}. \tag{2.1}$$

What is the effect on dispersion of a shift in the relative demand for skilled labour? As discussed earlier, the outcome hinges on the degree of rigidity of the labour market. Let us consider the two extreme cases. Where wages are fully flexible, the shift in labour demand causes increased wage dispersion, and the Lorenz curve for wages unambiguously shifts outward – see the heavy solid line in the left hand top panel of Figure 2.1 labelled 'United States'. Where wage differentials are held fixed, the unskilled wage rate does not fall relative to the skilled rate and the brunt of the adjustment is borne by the unskilled workers who become unemployed. Considering only employed workers, the impact on the earnings distribution is ambiguous. The Lorenz curve moves inwards at the top and outwards at the bottom, because the average wage rises (as fewer unskilled workers are now employed), but the ratio of the slopes of the two segments is unchanged (as the wage differential is fixed) – see the shift from P to P' in the right hand top panel of Figure 2.2 labelled 'Europe'. As the share in employment of unskilled

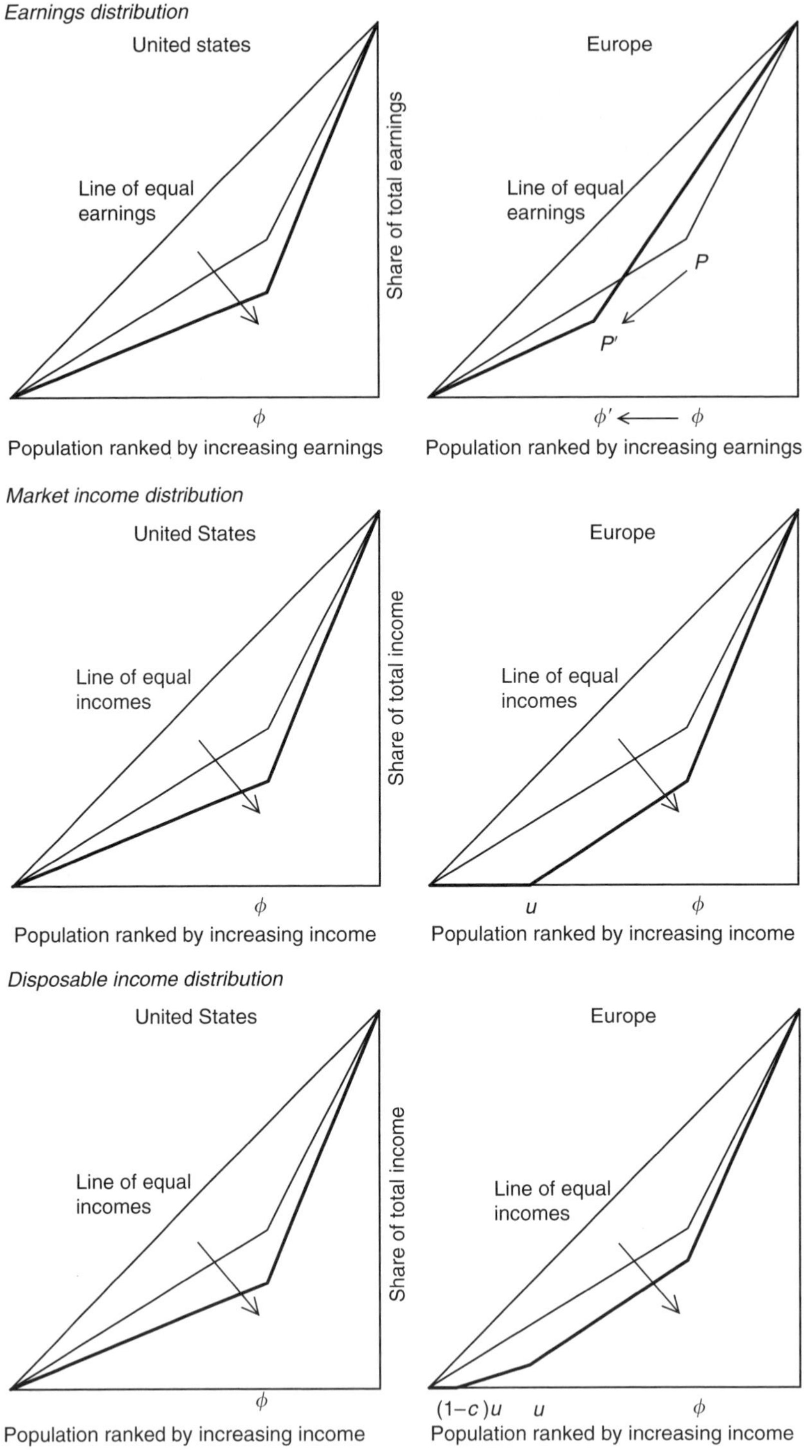

Figure 2.1 Lorenz curves for the Krugman–Wood model.

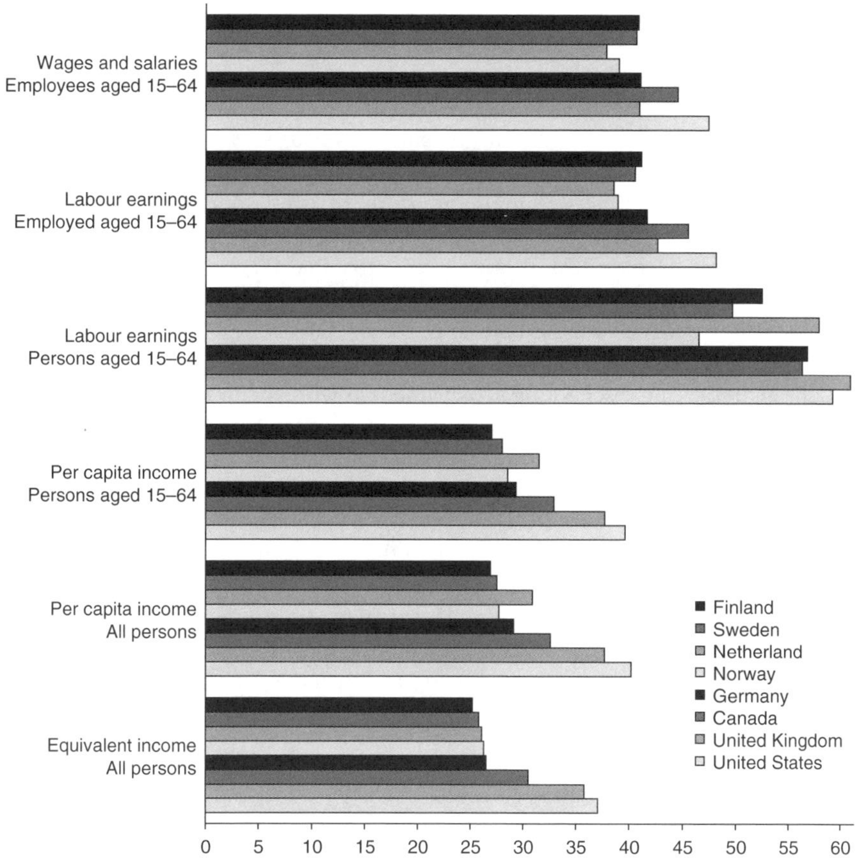

Figure 2.2 Gini index for different income variable and reference population.

Source: Authors' calculations on LIS data.

workers falls from ϕ to ϕ', dispersion can vary in either direction. When the skilled proportion is relatively low, dispersion might rise, as the top end of the distribution becomes thicker. But eventually dispersion is bound to decline. Should all demand for unskilled workers be wiped away, only skilled workers would be employed and wage dispersion would be nil.

We can summarise the distribution in a single number by computing the Gini index I, which is equal to the ratio of the area between the diagonal and the Lorenz curve to the whole triangle. In the simple case discussed here, the value of I is simply the difference between the employment share of unskilled workers, ϕ, and their share in total earnings, Ω:

$$I_{\mathrm{W}} = \phi - \Omega = \phi - \frac{\phi}{\phi + (1-\phi)(1+s)}, \tag{2.2}$$

where subscript W indicates that I refers to wages. By differentiating I_W with respect to ϕ and s, we confirm algebraically the conclusions reached by examining the movements of the Lorenz curve: dispersion I_W monotonically increases as the skill premium s goes up (the 'US' case), while it first rises and then declines as the unskilled share falls (the 'European' case).

Expression (2.2) shows that, in this simple world, wage dispersion depends on two factors: the proportion of employed unskilled workers, ϕ, and the skill premium, s. Note that the skill premium is not, by itself, a measure of inequality of the wage distribution, because it does not account for the skill composition of employment. Using (2.2), it is easy to verify that there are situations where a rise in s is associated with a decline in I_W, provided that there is an offsetting variation in ϕ – which can be both upwards or downwards.[5] The proportion of employed unskilled workers captures supply and demand factors, such as the secular increase in the schooling achievement of workers, or the need of a highly educated labour force induced by the spreading of skill-intensive technologies. On the other hand, the skill premium reflects both market forces – how wage rates respond to the net supply of educated workers – and institutional determinants. In the flexible US labour market s is free to rise as a consequence of the increasing trade with developing economies, while in the rigid European labour market s is fixed, and it is an increase in unemployment to absorb the impact of globalisation. But what is preventing s from rising? Here is where institutional variables play a role. Union behaviour, minimum wages, employment protection schemes, wage bargaining mechanisms affect the structure of earnings, and may drive diversity across countries or time periods.

2.3 Different approaches to cross-country comparisons of earnings dispersion

In the next section we review a number of empirical studies of the role of supply and demand, and of institutional variables. We make no attempt to be comprehensive in our coverage, but have brought together a variety of studies in a common format, as set out in Tables 2.1–2.3. Before examining the substance of the evidence, it may be helpful to draw some distinctions – distinctions that underlie the division of studies between the three tables.

The most basic unit of analysis is the individual i, in country c, with earnings $W_{i,c,t}$ at time t. There has been a large literature estimating earnings equations, such as

$$\ln W_{i,c,t} = \boldsymbol{\beta}_{c,t}\boldsymbol{X}_{i,c,t} + \boldsymbol{\varepsilon}_{i,c,t}, \tag{2.3}$$

where $\boldsymbol{X}$ is a vector of determinants of earnings and ε is a disturbance term. For example, with the simplest human capital model, the logarithm of earnings is a linear function of the number of years of schooling, where the coefficient on years of schooling is the rate of return. One approach to the study of the cross-country evidence is to estimate such equation using individual earnings data, where country differences appear either via different values of the $\boldsymbol{X}$ variables or via country variables. The distribution of years of education, for example, may be different in the United States from that in Scandinavia. Or the rate of return may be different. From the estimated coefficients, it is then possible to calculate the role of country differences in leading to different degrees of dispersion. If we were to take the variance of the logarithm of earnings as the measure of dispersion, then differences in the distribution of years of education would account for some fraction of the observed variance. It is this approach that underlies the four studies shown in Table 2.1.

A different approach is to take the aggregate measure of dispersion as the primitive of the analysis. Starting from equation (2.3), we can, for example, calculate the variance of the logarithm of earnings in different countries and/or at different dates, and then compare them across countries (Table 2.2) or across countries and across time (Table 2.3). More commonly employed as a measure of dispersion in the case of earnings is in fact the ratio of the top to the bottom decile, but the principle is the same: the distribution is being reduced to one number (or a few numbers). In the case of Table 2.2, the studies then compare across countries the changes over time in the summary measure(s). In the case of Table 2.3, the studies regress the resulting summary measures on variables that vary across countries and/or with time. So that we have, for example, a variable for the union density in the country at the time in question, whereas in an individual wage equation there may be a variable for individual union membership.

There are many more cross-country studies of summary measures than of individual earnings. This might be attributed to the difficulty of assembling comparable data for people in different countries. It may be attributed to the fact that the available data on individual earnings, while appropriate for estimating the coefficients $\boldsymbol{\beta}$, may not have the population coverage to give satisfactory estimates of the degree of dispersion. The data may, for example, be limited to workers in a particular age range. In contrast, there are readily accessible data on overall earnings dispersion published notably by the OECD (1993, 1996b), used in six of the studies listed in Tables 2.2 and 2.3. In our view, such an inference would be incorrect. The problems of comparability and of limited population coverage arise also with the overall earnings dispersion measures.

In Table 2.4 we document the main features of the data published by the OECD on the basis of the information reported in OCED (1996b). The degree of dispersion is affected for instance by the top-coding of earnings, as in Austria and Belgium. In the case of the United States, Burkhauser *et al.* (2004) show that changes in the top coding method ‘profoundly’ affected both the level and the trend of the measured earnings dispersion. The truncation of earnings below a certain threshold, as in Denmark or Norway, means that the dispersion is understated (or the relevant percentiles cannot be reported). For instance, using Canadian data for male workers, MacPhail (2000) finds that the Gini index in 1989 falls from 37.8 to 36.6 per cent by excluding the bottom 2 per cent of observations. The exclusion of agriculture, as in France and Portugal, is also likely to cause

Table 2.1 Selected results from studies on cross-country differences in the *level* of earnings dispersion

Study	*Publication*	*Period*	*Geographic coverage*[a]	*Number of observations on dispersion*	*Dispersion measure*	*Dispersion variable*	*Dispersion data source*	*Estimation methods*	*Results*
Blau and Kahn (1996)	*Journal of Political Economy*	1–4 years per country in the period 1980–1989	9 OECD countries, Hungary	11	Standard deviation, difference between top and bottom deciles, top decile and median, and median and bottom decile	Logarithm of hours-corrected annual or monthly, gross or net, income (from labour or total) of male employees aged 18–65	International Social Survey Programme, 3 national surveys	Decomposition based on wage equations	Greater wage dispersion in United States than in Australia and European countries: 6% due to different distribution of human capital; 15–20% due to different returns to human capital. US wage structure (i.e. returns and residual effects) widens both bottom and top distribution relative to other countries. Differences in relative net supply for skill inconsistent with relative wages by skill. Wage-setting institutions important determinant of differences in wage dispersion
Devroye and Freeman (2001)	*NBER Working Paper*	Unspecified (but 1993)	4 OECD countries	4	Coefficient of variation, standard deviation of logarithms	Annual or monthly earnings	OECD International Adult Literacy Survey[b]	Decomposition based on wage equations	Greater wage dispersion in United States than in Germany, Netherlands, Sweden: 7% due to higher dispersion in literary test scores and years of schooling; 36% due to higher returns to literacy and education

Leuven *et al.* (2004)	*Economic Journal*	1993, 1996 or 1997	10 OECD countries, Chile, Czech Republic, Hungary, Poland, Slovenia	15		Standard deviation, difference between top decile and median, and median and bottom decile	Logarithm of hourly gross or net earnings of males aged 18–65	OECD International Adult Literacy Survey[c]	Decomposition based on wage equations	One-third of relative wages by skill between countries explained by differences in relative net supply for skill, if skill measured by literary test scores instead of years of schooling and experience. Result stronger at the bottom of skill distribution
Blau and Kahn (2004)	*CESifo Working Paper* (forth-coming in *Review of Eco-nomics and Statistics*)	1 year per country in the period 1993–1997	9 OECD countries	9		Difference between top decile and median, and median and bottom decile	Logarithm of weekly earnings of full-time workers employed 26 weeks or more, exc. bottom and top earners	OECD International Adult Literacy Survey	Decomposition based on wage equations	Greater wage dispersion in United States than in European countries and, for males, in Canada: 3–13% due to the distribution of cognitive ability (literary test scores); 38–50% due to different returns to human capital (literary test scores and years of schooling). Collective bargaining coverage correlated with returns and residual effects

Notes

a ‘OECD countries’ refer to the members of the OECD as of mid-1970s: Australia, Austria, Belgium, Canada, Denmark, Finland, France, Federal Republic of Germany, Greece, Iceland, Ireland, Italy, Japan, Luxembourg, Netherlands, New Zealand, Norway, Portugal, Spain, Sweden, Switzerland, Turkey, United Kingdom and United States. Other countries are listed separately, including those which have joined the OECD since the mid-1990s: Czech Republic, Hungary, Korea, Mexico, Poland and Slovak Republic. West Germany refers to the Federal Republic of Germany until 1990 and to the Western Länder thereafter.

b Earnings data are not from the public-use file, where only earnings quintiles are reported, but from the underlying national surveys. Individual earnings are declared amounts for Sweden and the United States and estimates from 20 income intervals for Germany and the Netherlands.

c Individual earnings are declared amounts, except for Germany, the Netherlands and Switzerland where they are estimates from 20 income intervals.

Table 2.2 Selected results from studies on cross-country differences in *trends* of earnings dispersion

Study	*Publication*	*Period*	*Geographic coverage*[a]	*Number of observations on dispersion*	*Dispersion measure*	*Dispersion variable*	*Dispersion data source*	*Estimation methods*	*Results*
Green *et al.* (1992)	*Review of Income and Wealth*	2 years per country in the period 1979–1987	5 OECD countries	10	Decile shares, variance of logarithms, Gini, Theil and Atkinson indices	Annual wages and salaries of year-round full-time male heads aged 25–54[b]	Luxembourg Income Study	Comparison of time series	US experience of rising dispersion common to other industrialised countries (Australia, Canada, Sweden, West Germany). Since job creation experiences were different, a common phenomenon, such as changing technologies, was probably at work
Organisation for Economic Co-operation and Development (1993)	*Employment Outlook*	1973–1991	15 OECD countries	124	Ratios of top decile to median and median to bottom decile	Labour earnings (various definitions)	OECD Structure of Earnings Database	Comparison of time series	Mostly declining or unchanged wage dispersion over 1970s; rise only in 2 countries out of 12. Rising wage dispersion in 12 countries out of 17 over 1980s

Katz *et al.* (1995)	Freeman and Katz (eds), *Differences and Changes in Wage Structures*	1967–1990	4 OECD countries	154	Ratio of top to bottom decile	Logarithm of hourly or monthly gross earnings of full-time male and female employees	National sources	Comparison of time series	Large rise in wage dispersion in 1980s in United Kingdom and United States, moderate rise in Japan, little change in France. Relative net supply of educated workers explains in part changes in Japan, United Kingdom and United States; it is offset by collective bargaining system and minimum wage in France
Nickell and Bell (1996)	*American Economic Review Papers and Proceedings*	1980–1990	3 OECD countries	27	Ratio of top to bottom decile	Earnings of males	OECD Structure of Earnings Database[c]	Comparison of time series	Wage dispersion stable in West Germany and rising in United Kingdom and United States, but unemployment rate of unskilled workers similar in West Germany and United States and higher in United Kingdom. Explained by higher educational level of unskilled workers in West Germany

(Table 2.2 continued)

Table 2.2 Continued

Study	*Publication*	*Period*	*Geographic coverage*[a]	*Number of observations on dispersion*	*Dispersion measure*	*Dispersion variable*	*Dispersion data source*	*Estimation methods*	*Results*
Organisation for Economic Co-operation and Development (1996b)	*Employment Outlook*	1979–1995	18 OECD countries, Czech Republic	200	Ratios of top decile to median and median to bottom decile	Labour earnings (various definitions)[d]	OECD Structure of Earnings Database	Comparison of time series	Rising wage dispersion in many countries over 1980s, but no generalised trend over first half of 1990s: rise in 8 countries, no change or fall in other 8 countries. United States and United Kingdom only countries with continuation of pronounced rising trend
Gottschalk (1997)	Gottschalk *et al.* (eds), *Changing Patterns in the Distribution of Economic Welfare*	2 years per country in the period 1979–1987	7 OECD countries	14	Difference between top decile/quintile and median, and bottom decile/quintile and median	Logarithm of annual gross wages and salaries of male heads aged 25–54	Luxembourg Income Study	Comparison of time series	Greatest rise in wage dispersion in 1980s in United States, but some increase experienced by all other countries (Australia, Canada, France, Netherlands, Sweden, United Kingdom)
Bardone *et al.* (1998)	*Lavoro e relazioni industriali*	1979–1997	20 OECD countries, Czech Republic, Hungary, Korea, Poland	Not indicated (series at least 10-year long for 12 countries shown)	Ratios of top to bottom decile, top decile to median and median to bottom decile	Gross or net earnings of full-time workers	OECD Structure of Earnings Database	Comparison of time series	In only a few countries wage dispersion kept rising in 1990s: in United States and United Kingdom, and, more moderately, in Australia, Italy and Sweden. No sign that rising dispersion has become more widespread; it has basically remained confined to United States and United Kingdom

Gottschalk and Joyce (1998)	*Review of Economics and Statistics*	2 or 3 years per country in the period 1979–1992	7 OECD countries, Israel	20		Coefficient of variation, log of ratio of top to bottom decile	Annual gross wages and salaries of full-time male heads aged 25–54	Luxembourg Income Study	Comparison based on wage equations	Small increase of dispersion in some countries owing to offsetting changes in age premium, education premium, or dispersion within groups. Differences across countries in changes in age and education premiums associated with opposite changes in relative factor supplies
Peracchi (2001)	Welch (ed.), *The Causes and Consequences of Increasing Inequality*	2 years per country in the period 1974–1995	10 OECD countries, Israel, Poland, Taiwan	26		Ratio of top and bottom deciles and quartiles to median	Annual gross or net wages and salaries of full-time employees aged 25–59	Luxembourg Income Study	Comparison of time series	US experience of rising dispersion common to most developed countries, although intensity of trends differ across countries; the Netherlands and the Nordic countries are the exception

Notes

a 'OECD countries' refer to the members of the OECD as of mid-1970s: Australia, Austria, Belgium, Canada, Denmark, Finland, France, Federal Republic of Germany, Greece, Iceland, Ireland, Italy, Japan, Luxembourg, Netherlands, New Zealand, Norway, Portugal, Spain, Sweden, Switzerland, Turkey, United Kingdom and United States. Other countries are listed separately, including those which have joined the OECD since the mid-1990s: Czech Republic, Hungary, Korea, Mexico, Poland and Slovak Republic. West Germany refers to the Federal Republic of Germany until 1990 and to the Western Länder thereafter.

b Unspecified whether wages and salaries are net or gross of income taxes and employees' social contributions, but they are presumably gross.

c As published in Organisation for Economic Co-operation and Development (1993).

d See Table 2.4 for details.

Table 2.3 Selected results from time-series cross-country studies of earnings dispersion

Study	*Publication*	*Period*	*Geographic coverage*[a]	*Number of observations on dispersion*[b]	*Dispersion measure*	*Dispersion variable*	*Dispersion data source*	*Estimation methods*	*Explanatory variables, sign and significance of coefficients*[c]	
Wallerstein (1999)	*American Journal of Political Science*	1980, 1986, 1992 (or closest available year)	16 OECD countries	44 (41)	Ratio of top to bottom decile	Gross wages and salaries of full-time employees	OECD Structure of Earnings Database[d]	GLS, Fixed effects	*Table 2.3, column 2 (no fixed effects)*	
									Wage-setting centralisation	$-^{***}$
									Concentration of union membership	$-^{***}$
									Collective agreement coverage	$-^{***}$
									Cabinet share of left parties	+
									Cabinet share of right parties	$-^{**}$
									Trade openness (export + import/GDP)	$-^{***}$
									Government employment/total employment	$-^{**}$
									Government spending/GDP	$+^{**}$
									Period dummies	n.a.
Rueda and Pontusson (2000)	*World Politics*	1973–1995	16 OECD countries	217	Ratio of top to bottom decile	Gross wages and salaries of full-time employees	OECD Structure of Earnings Database	Fixed effects[d]	*Table 2.4*	
									Lagged dependent variable	$+^{***}$
									Unemployment rate	–
									Trade with less developed countries/GDP	+

										Female participation rate	$+^{**}$
										Union density	$-^{**}$
										Bargaining centralisation (Iversen index)	$-^{***}$
										Government employment/total employment	$-^{aaa}$
										Cabinet ideological balance (Cusack index)	$+^{aaa}$
Mahler (2004)	*Comparative Political Studies*	1981–2000	14 OECD countries	55		Gini index	Income (unspecified if net or gross) from wages, salaries and self-employment of households with head aged 25–55	Luxembourg Income Study	GLS	*Table 2.1, panel A*	
										Imports from developing countries/GDP	–
										Outbound investment/GDP	+
										Financial openness (Quinn-Inclán index)	$+^{**}$
										Cabinet ideological balance (Schmidt index)	+
										Electoral turnout	$-^{**}$
										Union density	+
										Wage coordination (Kenworthy index)	$-^{***}$

Notes

a 'OECD countries' refer to the members of the OECD as of mid-1970s: Australia, Austria, Belgium, Canada, Denmark, Finland, France, Federal Republic of Germany, Greece, Iceland, Ireland, Italy, Japan, Luxembourg, Netherlands, New Zealand, Norway, Portugal, Spain, Sweden, Switzerland, Turkey, United Kingdom and United States. Other countries are listed separately, including those which have joined the OECD since the mid-1990s: Czech Republic, Hungary, Korea, Mexico, Poland and Slovak Republic. West Germany refers to the Federal Republic of Germany until 1990 and to the Western Länder thereafter.

b The number in parentheses is the number of observations for the estimates reported in the last column, when it differs from the maximum number of available observations.

c Constant or country fixed effects are not reported. Significance levels are for one-tailed tests as follows: *significant at 10% level; **significant at 5% level; ***significant at 1% level.

d As published in Organisation for Economic Co-operation and Development (1996b).

Table 2.4 OECD structure of earnings database, 1996 version

Country	*Source*[a]	*Period*	*Earnings definition*	*Tax*	*Sex*[b]	*Age*	*Category*	*Excluded sectors*	*Extreme values*
Australia	Household survey	1979–1995	Weekly earnings	Gross	M, F, All	All	Full-time employees in main job	—	—
Austria	Social security archives	1980–1994	Monthly earnings (daily pay multiplied by days worked)	Gross	M, F, All	All	Wage and salary workers, some civil servants, exc. apprentices	—	Top-coded
Belgium	Social security archives	1985–1993	Daily earnings	Gross	M, F, All	All	Full-time workers	—	Top-coded
Canada	Household survey	1981–1994	Annual earnings	Gross	M, F, All	All	Full-time, full-year workers	—	—
Czech Republic	Household survey	1988–1992	Labour earnings (incl. income from self-employment)	Gross	All		Full-time workers	—	—
Denmark	Tax registers	1980–1990	Hourly earnings (annual pay divided by actual hours)	Gross	All	All	All	—	Bottom-trimmed
Finland	Household survey	1980–1994	Annual earnings	Gross	M, F, All	All	Full-time, full-year workers	—	—
France	Social security archives	1979–1994	Hourly earnings (annual pay divided by hours)	Gross	M, F, All	All	Full-time workers	Agriculture, government	—
West Germany	Household survey	1983–1993	Monthly earnings (incl. 1/12 of all benefits)	Gross	M, F, All	All	Full-time, full-year workers	—	—
Italy	Household survey	1979–1993	Monthly earnings (annual pay divided by months)	Net	M, F, All	All	Full-time, full-year employees	—	—

Japan	Earnings survey	1979–1994	Monthly scheduled earnings	Gross	M, F, All	18 and over	‘Regular’ workers in establishments with at least 10 workers	Agriculture, government, private household services	—
Netherlands	Earnings survey	1985–1994	Annual earnings (incl. overtime and occasional payments)	Gross	All	All	Full-time, full-year equivalent employees	—	—
New Zealand	Household survey	1984–1994	Weekly earnings	Gross	M, F, All	All	Full-time employees	—	—
Norway	Household survey	1980–1991	Hourly earnings (weekly/monthly pay divided by working hours)	Gross	All	19–55	All	—	Bottom- and top-trimmed
Portugal	Earnings survey	1985–1993	Weekly earnings	Gross	M, F, All	All	Full-time workers	Agriculture, government	—
Sweden	Household survey	1980–1993	Annual earnings	Gross	M, F, All	23 and over	Full-time, full-year workers	—	—
Switzerland	Household survey	1991–1995	Annual earnings	Gross	M, F, All	All	Full-time, full-year equivalent workers	—	—
United Kingdom	Earnings survey	1979–1995	Weekly earnings	Gross	M, F, All	Adult rates	Full-time employees with pay not affected by absence in reference week	—	—
United States	Household survey	1979–1995	Weekly earnings	Gross	M, F, All	25 and over	Full-time workers	—	—

Source: Organisation for Economic Co-operation and Development (1996b), Annex 3.A, pp. 100–103.

Notes

a The type of source is inferred from published information. By earnings survey we indicate information that we understand is derived from a survey of employers.

b M and F indicate males and females, respectively.

dispersion to be understated. Moreover, the difference caused by the difference in coverage is unlikely to remain constant over time; as the agricultural sector shrinks, so will the understatement. Some of the earnings data come from surveys of employers (4 out of 19 in Table 2.4), some from income tax or social security administrative records (4 out of 19), but most from household surveys (11 out of 19), which may however in turn rely on administrative sources as in Nordic countries. These sources may require care in their comparison. In fact, after discussing comparability problems, OECD (1993) concludes that: 'Differences between countries in both coverage and definition warn that these data should not be used for international comparisons of the level of dispersion' (p. 166). Yet they have been used extensively for this purpose. Even those studies that compare trends over time across countries are assuming that the data differences are constant over time, whereas there is no reason to make that assumption.

2.4 Findings of the empirical studies of earnings dispersion

The studies summarised in Table 2.1 examine cross-national differences in the *level* of earnings dispersion. Blau and Kahn (1996) study the distribution of earnings in several OECD member countries in the 1980s, using data drawn from the International Social Survey Programme and from three national surveys. Devroye and Freeman (2001), Leuven *et al.* (2004) and Blau and Kahn (2004) use instead information from the International Adult Literacy Survey conducted in several OECD countries in a year from 1993 to 1997. All four studies observe greater wage dispersion in the United States than in the other OECD countries (save for Canadian women in Blau and Kahn, 2004). After estimating standard wage equations, they decompose the difference in dispersion between the United States and (the average of) the other countries into three components: the diverse distribution of human capital variables (experience, years of schooling and, in the three recent papers, literary test scores), the different rewards of these variables, and an unexplained residual. Blau and Kahn (1996, 2004) and Devroye and Freeman (2001) calculate that the contribution of the first component is small and find that a substantial part of the difference in dispersion is due to the differential returns to schooling or cognitive ability, which in turn are seen as being strongly influenced by the wage-setting institutions. This conclusion is challenged by Leuven *et al.* (2004) who estimate that one-third of the variation in skill wage differential across countries is explained by differences in the net labour supply of skill groups, when skill is measured by literary test scores instead of years of schooling and experience.

The same juxtaposition of supply and demand factors, on one side, and institutional determinants, on the other, pervade the literature investigating *trends* in earnings dispersion. The studies listed in Table 2.2 examine a large number of OECD and non-OECD countries in different periods on the basis of a variety of sources. They tend to agree that in the 1980s a widening of the distribution of wages was common to many countries, even if with a different intensity. In the subsequent decade, the picture was more mixed, with no generalised trend. But the lack of common experience across OECD countries need not be interpreted as the result of institutions. Gottschalk and Joyce (1998), for instance, inspected the changes in the dispersion of annual earnings of full-time not self-employed prime-age male household heads in seven OECD countries and Israel. On the basis of wage regressions estimated for each country, they showed that the small increases of overall dispersion in some countries, like Finland or Sweden, could be seen as the result of offsetting changes in the returns to skill and in dispersion within groups. Since the different changes across countries in skill premiums were found to be associated with opposite variations in relative factor supplies, they concluded that 'market forces can be used to explain much of the cross-national differences that have been attributed in the literature to differences in labor market institutions' (p. 501). Conversely, DiNardo *et al.* (1996) in their study of the United States (not shown in Table 2.2) remarked that 'labor market institutions [i.e. the unionization rate and the real value of the minimum wage] are as important as supply and demand considerations in explaining changes in the U.S. distribution of wages from 1979 to 1988' (p. 1039).

Nickell and Bell (1996) contested the Krugman–Wood story. First, they estimated that the relative demand shift away from unskilled work accounted for only a modest proportion of the rise in European unemployment in the 1980s. Second, they observed that the ratio of top to bottom decile of the wage distribution remained stable in West Germany during the 1980s, while it rose in the United Kingdom and the United States. Yet, the unemployment rate of unskilled workers was not higher than in the other two countries. They suggested that this result may be partly explained by the higher educational level of German unskilled workers.

The third group of studies, summarised in Table 2.3, applies econometric techniques to a panel of countries over time. Wallerstein (1999), Rueda and Pontusson (2000) and Mahler (2004) found that the centralisation of wage bargaining had a consistently negative effect on wage dispersion in OECD countries in the last 30 years, while the evidence for union variables was less clearcut. The impact of globalisation was ambiguous: Wallerstein (1999) detected a significant and negative effect of trade openness on wage dispersion; Rueda and Pontusson (2000) found a positive, but insignificant, effect of trade with less developed countries; Mahler (2004) estimated insignificant and conflicting effects for imports for developing countries and outbound investment.

In this section, we have brought together a selection of studies seeking to explain earnings dispersion or its changes. We believe that such a confrontation of the results is necessary in order to make progress. 'Compare and contrast' is as important here as in any examination question. As may be seen from the Tables, this does not lead to tidy conclusions about the relative importance of market forces and institutions in affecting the distribution of earnings. It does however suggest some possible routes forward. Two may be highlighted here. The first is that different parts of the distribution may react differently (as may be seen from the Lorenz curves). This is recognised in the literature by the separate analysis of the ratios to the median of the top and the bottom decile, rather than the decile ratio alone. The second is that there may be important interactions between explanatory variables. As has been suggested by Rueda (2004), for example, there may be interdependence between wage bargaining and political partisanship.

2.5 Inequality in the labour market

So far we have considered the distribution of earnings among employed workers. However, the Krugman–Wood story entails that in a rigid labour market the relative demand shift hurts the unskilled workers pricing them out of job. A broader assessment of the level of inequality in the labour market could be provided by looking at the distribution of labour income amongst the whole population, which includes also jobless, and therefore wage-less, people. In this simple framework, where we have only wages, this distribution coincides with that of *market* incomes, but we should bear in mind that in real world market incomes also comprise rents, distributed profits, interest and other returns on financial assets.

Going back to Figure 2.1, we must now distinguish three groups: skilled workers, unskilled workers and the unemployed. The emergence of unemployment implies that the distribution of market incomes becomes more unequal – see the heavy solid line in the right-hand mid-panel. Mean income falls, and the Lorenz curve moves outward at the top as well as at the bottom. So while for the wage distribution across employed patterns could differ, for the distribution of market incomes among the population as a whole there is an unambiguous rise in inequality, both in Europe and in the United States. (The European Lorenz curve crosses in the top diagram because the average wage of the employed rises, and the ratio of the skilled wage to the average falls; for the market incomes, the average *falls*, so the slope of the upper segment is increased.)

In the 'US case' of flexible wages, where there is no unemployment, the Gini index for market incomes equals that for wages, which is given by expression (2.2), or in a slightly rearranged form:

$$I_{\mathrm{M}}^{\mathrm{US}} = I_{\mathrm{W}}^{\mathrm{US}} = \frac{\phi(1-\phi)s}{(1-\phi)s+1}, \tag{2.4}$$

where subscript M indicates that I refers to market income. In the 'European case' of rigid wages, the Gini index for the wage distribution can be rewritten as

$$I_{\mathrm{W}}^{\mathrm{EU}} = \frac{(\phi-u)(1-\phi)s}{(1-u)[(1-\phi)s+1-u]}, \tag{2.5}$$

which is obtained from (2.2) after replacing the share of skilled workers in total employment with its new value $\phi' = (\phi-u)/(1-u)$, where u is the unemployment rate. As shown by the previous discussion of Lorenz curve shifts, wage dispersion can move either upwards or downwards as u varies.[6] The Gini index for market income among the whole population becomes:

$$I_{\mathrm{M}}^{\mathrm{EU}} = \frac{\phi(1-\phi)s+\boldsymbol{u}(\boldsymbol{1}-\boldsymbol{u})}{(1-\phi)s+1-\boldsymbol{u}}. \tag{2.6}$$

The new terms with respect to (2.6) are shown in bold at the right of the numerator and denominator. If the effect of globalisation or skilled-biased technological progress is to raise unemployment, then (assuming that u is less than ϕ) the Gini index increases.

According to the 1996 *OECD Economic Outlook*, 'in assessing the possible distributional effects of [labour market] reforms, particularly on labour earnings at the lower end, it is important to note that greater employment will tend to reduce inequality, while a wider wage-rate distribution will tend to increase it' (Organisation for Economic Co-operation and Development, 1996a, p. 39). In our framework, there is a simple way to measure the overall impact on inequality accounting for both the 'wage effect' and the 'employment effect'. If we compare (2.5) and (2.6) it is easy to verify that

$$I_{\mathrm{M}} = u + (1 - u)I_{\mathrm{W}}. \tag{2.7a}$$

This may be seen from the fact that $(1 - I)$ is reduced by a factor $(1 - u)$. (As this relationship is true in general, we drop the superscript EU.) Expression (2.7) is a summary measure of inequality in the labour market, which assigns nil income to the unemployed and weights the Gini index of the wage distribution by the share of the employed in total population. In real world there is a distinction, which has been neglected here, between the unemployed and the jobless persons who are outside the labour force (e.g. Brandolini *et al.*, 2004). Thus, it is probably more appropriate to rewrite (2.7a) in terms of the employment rate e, that is the share of employed working-age population. This gives:

$$I_{\mathrm{M}} = 1 - e + eI_{\mathrm{W}} = 1 - (1 - I_{\mathrm{W}})e. \tag{2.7b}$$

Expression (2.7b) shows that the inequality in the labour market, as measured by the Gini index of labour earnings computed across the whole working-age population, is inversely related to the employment rate and positively associated with wage dispersion. The change over time in the Gini index, or its difference between two countries, lends itself to a simple decomposition:

$$\Delta I_{\mathrm{M}} \cong e\Delta I_{\mathrm{W}} - (1 - I_{\mathrm{W}})\Delta e. \tag{2.8}$$

In other words, with $e = 0.75$ and $I_{\mathrm{W}} = 0.4$, a 1 percentage point rise in wage dispersion would be compensated by a $1\frac{1}{4}$ percentage point increase in the employment rate.

The decomposition (2.8) may provide useful insights on the overall inequality created in the labour market in terms of income creation. But it is a partial measure: it does not cover the market incomes different from the compensation of work; in attributing nil income to the non-employed does not account for the value of leisure or non-market activities; more importantly, it does not allow for the redistributive role of the welfare states. It is to this issue that we turn in the next section.

2.6 Role of the welfare state

The last step in the story is to allow for the moderating role of the welfare state. Forcing our oversimplification even further, we assume that no redistributive institution is at work in the US economy (the Lorenz curve for disposable income shown in Figure 2.1 is the same as that for market income), but that there exists an unemployment protection scheme financed by contributions levied on wages in Europe. More precisely, we suppose that the European programme covers a proportion c (for *c*overed) of the unemployed and that each insured unemployed is paid a benefit equal to a fraction b of the net-of-tax wage of the unskilled; wage earners pay a fraction τ of their gross wage to finance the unemployment scheme. (It is assumed that $0 \leq c \leq 1$, $0 \leq \tau \leq 1$, and $0 \leq b \leq 1$.) As a consequence of these assumptions, in the European case we must distinguish four different classes of people: uninsured unemployed workers, insured unemployed workers, employed unskilled workers and employed skilled workers. The Lorenz curve consists now of the four segments shown in the bottom right-hand panel of Figure 2.1. The welfare state tempers the rise in inequality brought about by globalisation (or technological progress), but it can not offset it – as shown by the unambiguous movement of the Lorenz curve.

With regards to the Gini index, expression (2.4) also provides the value for disposable income, or $I_{\mathrm{D}}^{\mathrm{US}} = I_{\mathrm{M}}^{\mathrm{US}}$ where subscript D stays for disposable income, as no redistribution occurs in the US economy. In the European economy, introducing the welfare state gives the Gini index for the distribution of disposable income as:

$$I_{\mathrm{D}}^{\mathrm{EU}} = \frac{\phi(1-\phi)s + u(1-u) + \boldsymbol{bcuu} - \boldsymbol{bcu}(\mathbf{1} - \boldsymbol{u} + \boldsymbol{cu})}{(1-\phi)s + 1 - u + \boldsymbol{bcu}}. \tag{2.9}$$

As earlier, the new terms are shown in bold. The introduction of tax and benefit parameters means that we cannot simply differentiate I with respect to s or u to know the impact of globalisation, but we have also to consider the indirect effects through the government budget. Even where there is no change in the generosity of benefits, a rise in u adds to public spending, and this has to be financed. A policy response has to be specified. The requirement of budget balance is that

$$bc = \frac{\tau}{1-\tau}\left[\frac{(1-\phi)s + 1 - u}{u}\right]. \tag{2.10}$$

If u rises, then raising the tax rate can finance the extra spending, leaving b and c unchanged. In this case, there is no feedback effect on the Gini index: the benefit payment is scaled back in line with net wages. On the other hand, if the policy response is to cut b or c, then this will have repercussions for the level of inequality, in addition to those brought about by u and s.

Even for the very simplified distribution sketched here, the Gini indices turn out to be a rather intricate function of the macroeconomic variables s and u, and the institutional parameters b, τ and c. As just seen the impact of globalisation on inequality is mediated by the tax and benefit system: the derivative of inequality with respect to the skill premium depends on the extent of social protection as measured by b, τ and c. This consideration may appear to be fairly obvious, but it has important implications for the specification of relations to test empirically. If we were to write down an equation where the inequality I_D of disposable incomes is explained as a function of globalisation G and redistribution R, we should allow for their interaction. One simple solution would be to include a cross-term $G \times R$, but this may not be satisfactorily. If the cross-derivative is negative then $\partial I_D/\partial G$ is smaller where R is higher, suggesting that redistribution moderates the effects of globalisation. However, it also implies that the derivative $\partial I_D/\partial R$ (which is negative by construction) is even more negative when G rises, so that globalisation increases the redistributive impact of the welfare state. This underlines the importance of the theoretical framework in order to specify the relation to be estimated: as noted earlier, there may be important elements of interdependence.

The previous conclusions are derived from a rather mechanical application of the formula of the Gini index, and relate to the *impact*, or ceteris paribus, effect of changes in s or u, allowing at most for the policy response concerning b, τ and c. It is plausible, however, that this policy response will affect the behaviour of workers and employers. There are feedback effects that should be taken into account. Moreover, the response of the government may shift from simply adjusting the unemployment benefit b or the tax rate τ to introducing a wage subsidy aimed at restoring the price differential between skilled and unskilled labour faced by employers, and therefore to counteract the rise of the unemployment rate (Piketty, 1999). This second-round effect on u has to be taken into account to assess the impact on inequality. In the same vein, we may question the hypothesis that the supply of skills, hence ϕ, is fixed. In the stripped-down model just illustrated, people differ inherently in their skill. What are the origins of these differences? If skill is identified with education or training, inequality is a disequilibrium phenomenon, since any excess economic advantage from skill will over time induce people to invest in human capital formation (wages may still be different, but only by enough to compensate for the period of education). But if skill is innate, parameters like ϕ are some 'natural' constant, and then some 'original' inequality is a feature of society. This still leaves open the question of the ways in which the social and economic organisation affects the distribution of income.

To sum up, in discussing the impact on inequality of globalisation one needs to have clearly in mind the inequality of 'what'. The distribution of wages among workers has to be distinguished from the distribution of market incomes among the whole population (including the unemployed), which in turn must be distinguished from the distribution of disposable incomes. These different distributions may move differently as a result of globalisation. A levelling of the distribution of wages among the employed may come together with a widening of the distribution of disposable incomes. Second, even in highly simplified models such as the one we have discussed, the factors that determine income inequality interact in a rather complex manner. The effect of globalisation depends on the degree of redistribution and on policy responses.

2.7 Empirical evidence on individual earnings and household income

We have emphasised the importance of specifying which distribution is the object of the analysis, in particular the distribution of *what* – wages and salaries, labour earnings, market income, gross income, disposable income – and among *whom* – salaried workers, employed, working age population, persons. In this section we examine these differences using data from the Luxembourg Income Study for eight OECD countries.[7]

Table 2.5 and Figure 2.2 show the position around the year 2000 for different concepts and population definitions. As we move from left to right in the table, we make the transition from individual gross earnings to household disposable income, as highlighted in the title of the chapter. The Gini indices for all employees aged 15–64 are around 40 per cent in the European countries, 45 per cent in Canada and 47 per cent in the United States. These values may appear high, but they cover all workers, including part-time workers and part-year workers. The next column extends the population and the income concept to include the self-employed (all of their income being counted, no part being attributed to capital assets).

The third column shows the effect of bringing in those not in employment. The inclusion of zero employment incomes adds to the Gini index. As we might expect, the addition is less for those countries with high employment rates and for those with higher earnings dispersion: the difference from (2.7a) is $(1 - e)(1 - I_W)$. The impact is smaller in Scandinavia and larger in Germany, Netherlands and the United Kingdom. The fourth column moves to household total after-tax income, including transfers and capital income, attributed on a per capita basis to the same people who appeared in the third column. The Gini index is reduced by between 18 percentage points (Norway) and 28 percentage points (Germany). Adding in those aged under 15 or over 64 makes little difference to the figures, and the final stage of equivalisation reduces the Gini indices by similar amounts.

The final column ranks the countries according to the Gini index for the distribution of household equivalised disposable income among individuals. The range is from 25 per cent (Finland) to 37 per cent (the United States). How does this compare with our starting point? One could say that the first five countries have similar values for earnings and have similar values for incomes, the differences being in both cases of the same order as the sampling error. Canada and the United States are different on earnings and on income. It is the United Kingdom, European on earnings, and North American on incomes, that needs explanation.

2.8 Conclusions

Among the conclusions that we draw from this review are:

- The need to model supply and demand and institutional variables in a common framework, linked to an underlying economic model.

Table 2.5 Gini index for different income variable and reference population

Country	*Year*	*Gross wages and salaries (employees aged 15–64)*	*Gross labour earnings*		*Per capita disposable income*		*Equivalent disposable income (all persons)*
			Employees aged 15–64	*Persons aged 15–64*	*Persons aged 15–64*	*All persons*	
Finland	2000	40.8	41.1	52.4	27.0	26.9	25.2
Sweden	2000	40.6	40.5	49.6	28.0	27.5	25.8
Netherlands	1999	37.8	38.5	57.9	31.5	30.9	26.1
Norway	2000	39.0	38.9	46.5	28.5	27.7	26.3
Germany	2000	41.0	41.6	56.8	29.3	29.1	26.5
Canada	2000	44.5	45.5	56.3	32.9	32.6	30.5
United Kingdom	1999	40.9	42.6	60.9	37.7	37.7	35.8
United States	2000	47.4	48.1	59.2	39.6	40.2	37.1

Source: Authors' calculations on LIS data.

- There are different types of empirical study (individual earnings versus country summary measures).
- Differences in definitions and coverage may affect cross-country comparisons and cannot be assumed to be fixed over time.
- The findings of empirical cross-country studies of earnings need to be set alongside each other, and the differences confronted.
- The theoretical framework has demonstrated the need for care with different income concepts and different populations.
- There may be important interdependences between different explanatory variables.

Notes

1 Nuffield College, Oxford, and Bank of Italy, Economic Research Department, respectively. We are grateful for helpful comments to participants in the International Summer School at Siena in July 2003 and in the Lower conference at Seville in October 2003. The views expressed here are, however, solely those of the authors; in particular, they do not necessarily reflect those of the Bank of Italy.

2 It is implicit in most economic analyses of the performance of labour markets carried out by international organisations. See, for instance, the following remark in the *OECD Economic Outlook*.

> If only full-time workers are considered, the United States has greater disparity than the European countries examined. If the entire working-age population is considered, rather than just those in full-time work, the United States has less labour-income inequality than some European countries. The difference between these two ways of measuring inequality is essentially the employment effect.
> (Organisation for Economic Co-operation and Development, 1996a, p. 39)

3 Throughout the chapter, we use the term 'OECD countries' to refer to the members of the Organisation for Economic Co-operation and Development (OECD) as of mid-1970s: Australia, Austria, Belgium, Canada, Denmark, Finland, France, Federal Republic of Germany, Greece, Iceland, Ireland, Italy, Japan, Luxembourg, Netherlands, New Zealand, Norway, Portugal, Spain, Sweden, Switzerland, Turkey, United Kingdom and United States. Wherever necessary, we explicitly list non-OECD countries, including those which have joined the OECD since the mid-1990s: Czech Republic, Hungary, Korea, Mexico, Poland and Slovak Republic. West Germany refers to the Federal Republic of Germany until 1990 and to the Western Länder thereafter.

4 The Lorenz curve plots the share of earnings (or income) of the first $100x$ per cent of the employed (population) against x. It is drawn between 0 and 1, is convex upwards and never lies above the 45° line that represents complete equality.

5 Concentrating on the skill premium in empirical analysis may lead to ignore sizeable portions of the wage distribution. Fortin and Lemieux (1997, pp. 83–84) remark that a probable reason for the little attention paid to changes in minimum wages in the literature on rising inequality in the United States can be found in the focus on the college/high school wage differential of men working full-time, that is workers where very few earn the minimum wage.

6 Differentiating (2.5) shows that $\partial I_W/\partial u$ is positive (negative) if s is less (greater) than $[(\phi - u)^2/(1 - u)^2 - 1]$.

7 The relationship between changes over time in earnings dispersion and in income inequality are studied by Gottschalk (1997) using LIS data, and by Bardone *et al.* (1998) using time series assembled at OECD.

References

Bardone, L., M. Gittleman and M. Keese (1998), 'Causes and Consequences of Earnings Inequality in OECD Countries', *Lavoro e relazioni industriali*, No. 2, pp. 13–59.

Bertola, G. and A. Ichino (1995), 'Wage Inequality and Unemployment: United States vs. Europe', in B.S. Bernanke and J.J. Rotemberg (eds), *NBER Macroeconomics Annual 1995*, pp. 13–54, Cambridge, MIT Press.

Blau, F.D. and L.M. Kahn (1996), 'International Differences in Male Wage Inequality: Institutions versus Market Forces', *Journal of Political Economy*, vol. 104, pp. 791–837.

Blau, F.D. and L.M. Kahn (2004), 'Do Cognitive Test Scores Explain Higher U.S. Wage Inequality?', CESifo, Working Paper, No. 1139, February, forthcoming in *Review of Economics and Statistics*.

Brandolini, A., P. Cipollone and E. Viviano (2004), 'Does the ILO Definition Capture All Unemployment?', Banca d'Italia, Temi di discussione, forthcoming.

Burkhauser, R.V., J.S. Butler, S. Feng and A.J. Houtenville (2004), 'Long Term Trends in Earnings Inequality: What the CPS Can Tell Us', *Economics Letters*, vol. 82, pp. 295–299.

Devroye, D. and R.B. Freeman (2001), 'Does Inequality in Skills Explain Inequality of Earnings Across Advanced Countries?', National Bureau of Economic Research, Working Paper, No. 8140, February.

DiNardo, J.E., N. Fortin and T. Lemieux (1996), 'Labor Market Institutions and the Distribution of Wages, 1973–1992: A Semiparametric Approach', *Econometrica*, vol. 64, pp. 1001–1044.

Fortin, N. and T. Lemieux (1997), 'Institutional Changes and Rising Wage Inequality: Is There a Linkage?', *Journal of Economic Perspectives*, vol. 11, pp. 75–96.

Gottschalk, P. (1997), 'Policy Changes and Growing Earnings Inequality in the US and Six Other OECD Countries', in P. Gottschalk, B. Gustafsson and E. Palmer (eds), *Changing Patterns in the Distribution of Economic Welfare: An International Perspective*, pp. 12–35, Cambridge, Cambridge University Press.

Gottschalk, P. and M. Joyce (1998), 'Cross-National Differences in the Rise in Earnings Inequality: Market and Institutional Factors', *Review of Economics and Statistics*, vol. 80, pp. 489–502.

Green, G., J. Coder and P. Ryscavage (1992), 'International Comparisons of Earnings Inequality for Men in the 1980s', *Review of Income and Wealth*, vol. 38, pp. 1–15.

Katz, L.F., G.W. Loveman and D.G. Blanchflower (1995), 'A Comparison of Changes in the Structure of Wages in Four OECD Countries', in R. B. Freeman and L. F. Katz (eds), *Differences and Changes in Wage Structures*, pp. 25–65, Chicago, IL, University of Chicago Press.

Krugman, P. (1994), 'Past and Prospective Causes of High Unemployment', in *Reducing Unemployment: Current Issues and Policy Options*, pp. 49–80, Kansas City, Federal Reserve Bank of Kansas City.

Leuven, E., H. Oosterbeek and H. van Ophem (2004), 'Explaining International Differences in Male Skill Wage Differentials by Differences in Demand and Supply of Skill', *Economic Journal*, vol. 114, pp. 466–486.

MacPhail, F. (2000), 'Are Estimates of Earnings Inequality Sensitive to Measurement Choices? A Case Study of Canada in the 1980s', *Applied Economics*, vol. 32, pp. 845–860.

Mahler, V.A. (2004), 'Economic Globalization, Domestic Politics and Income Inequality in the Developed Countries: A Cross-National Study', *Comparative Political Studies*, vol. 37, pp. 1025–1053.

Nickell, S. (1997), 'Unemployment and Labor Market Rigidities: Europe Versus North America', *Journal of Economic Perspectives*, vol. 11, pp. 55–74.

Nickell, S. and B. Bell (1996), 'Changes in the Distribution of Wages and Unemployment in OECD Countries', *American Economic Review Papers and Proceedings*, vol. 86, pp. 302–308.

Organisation for Economic Co-operation and Development (1993), 'Earnings Inequality: Changes in the 1980s', in *OECD Employment Outlook*, pp. 157–184, Paris, Organisation for Economic Co-operation and Development.

Organisation for Economic Co-operation and Development (1996a), 'Growth, Equity and Distribution', in *OECD Economic Outlook*, No. 60, pp. 36–42, Paris, Organisation for Economic Co-operation and Development.

Organisation for Economic Co-operation and Development (1996b), 'Earnings Inequality, Low-Paid Employment and Earnings Mobility', in *OECD Employment Outlook*, pp. 59–108, Paris, Organisation for Economic Co-operation and Development.

Peracchi, F. (2001), 'Earning Inequality in International Perspective', in F. Welch (ed.), *The Causes and Consequences of Increasing Inequality*, pp. 117–152, Chicago, IL, University of Chicago Press.

Piketty, T. (1999), 'Can Fiscal Redistribution Undo Skill-Biased Technical Change? Evidence from the French Experience', *European Economic Review*, vol. 43, pp. 839–851.

Rueda, D. (2004), 'Political Agency and Institutions: Explaining the Influence of Left Government and Wage Bargaining on Inequality', Paper presented at the Conference of Europeanists, Chicago, IL, 11–13 March 2004.

Rueda, D. and J. Pontusson (2000), 'Wage Inequality and Varieties of Capitalism', *World Politics*, vol. 52, pp. 350–383.

Wallerstein, M. (1999), 'Wage-Setting Institutions and Pay Inequality in Advanced Industrial Societies', *American Journal of Political Science*, vol. 43, pp. 649–680.

Wood, A. (1994), *North-South Trade Employment and Inequality: Changing Fortunes in a Skill-Driven World*, Oxford, Clarendon Press.

3 Social mobility*

Daniele Checchi and Valentino Dardanoni

3.1 Definition

We generally define the phenomenon of social mobility as the step from one initial social positioning (the origin) to one final social positioning (the destination). This social positioning can manifest itself in different ways: it can refer to absolute positions (a typical example is the income earned by an individual that allows him or her to be positioned within the income distribution of the entire community). It can refer to relative positions (if, for example, we refer to the income portion from which an individual benefits with respect to the cumulative income of the population). It can refer to ordinal positions (typical in this case is the presence of a school degree or the belonging to a particular social class since these variables can only be ordered by means of qualitative criteria). It can also refer to nominal categories that cannot be ordered (examples are religious and political creeds or also geographical residence).

The concept of mobility closely interlaces two distinct phenomena. On one hand, the temporal evolution as the social positioning is recorded over two distinct time instances. On the other hand, the distribution of one resource (typically the socio-economical status) within a given population. We can then state that the study of social mobility is the analysis of the evolution over time of a resource distribution within a given population. If we utilize resources that can be ordered by given criteria based on socio-economical status, we can speak of vertical mobility (we study the upward and downward movement of different social statutes hierarchy); we can alternatively speak of horizontal mobility as we observe the movement within categories that cannot be ordered.

The study of social mobility pertains to the upward (or downward) movement of single individuals, single families, or entire groups (social classes, ethnic groups, work categories etc). In this context, we will primarily dwell upon vertical social mobility of individuals or families being those the predominant focus of social mobility studies. In other words, we will mean with the term 'social mobility' the change in status over time of a given individual or family. We will refer to intra-generational mobility when we analyse the social status changes of a single individual, whereas we will speak of inter-generational mobility when we refer to changes in social status within a dynasty (i.e. in the generational shift between parents and children). Since the analytical tools do not differ in the two cases, we will show the measurements problems as far as inter-generational mobility is concerned, even though these problems can be reformulated for the intra-generational mobility as well.

The object of the analysis (inter-generational mobility) once defined, can be approached from both a positive and normative viewpoint. In the first case, there are numerous studies that compared different social systems with the sole aim of providing answers to questions regarding the causes of social mobility. The reference points used in such analyses are the peculiarities of the school system and the local job market. In the second case, the normative analysis has made an attempt to suggest if and in which magnitude mobility could be deemed beneficial from a social point of view considering its redistribution effect on the opportunities of 'upward movement' for individuals of different social origins.

3.2 Why analyse social mobility?

Since 380 BC, Plato described the individuals in its *Republic* as 'golden', 'silver' and 'bronze' ones, and stated that 'golden' parents with 'bronze' children should acknowledge their sons' limits and be aware of any related risks. He thought that business conducted by 'bronze' individuals, even if coming from 'golden' families, would cause the demise of the state organization. Conversely, society should highlight the importance of 'golden' individuals, regardless of their social origins, and grant them a more privileged social status. We can reformulate this concept in a more modern light by stating that a society that guarantees an adequate social mobility is an efficient one (since the more capable individuals play more important roles and are granted a heightened social status) and, at the same time, a just one (since it guarantees equal opportunities to the capable ones).

Many centuries afterwards, analogously, Vilfredo Pareto, referring to the social mobility of occupational positions, that according to him symbolized the distribution of wealth and power, juxtaposed the concept of mobility to the one of social equilibrium stability. By doing so he meant both an economic equilibrium – the permanence of an asymmetrical income distribution, later called Pareto's law – and a political equilibrium – the elites' capability of running the government over the rest of the population. A limited mobility would not have permitted an adequate selection and cooptation of the best individuals coming from the lower strata, and at the same time, it would not have eliminated the inept individuals coming from the elites. This situation would have produced a legitimacy incapability of an aristocracy-based government, and it would have led the state towards a revolutionary toppling in the medium/long run:

> ce n'est pas seulement l'accumulation des éléments inférieures dans une couche sociale qui nuit à la société, mais aussi l'accumulation dans les couches inférieures d'éléments supérieures qu'on empêche de s'élever. Quand, à

la fois, les couches supérieures sont pleines d'éléments inférieures et les couches inférieures pleines d'éléments supérieures, l'équilibre sociale devient éminemment instable, et une révolution violente est imminente.

(Pareto 1966, p. 387, first edition 1909)

Given the evident political implications derived by the discussion on social mobility, the debates subsequent to Pareto's tended to be strongly divided into those who believed that a sufficient degree of social mobility would attenuate the disparity caused by the capitalistic development, as it would have represented a stimulus to social climbing, and those who deemed marginal the role of social mobility in a context of a strict job differentiation. Blau and Duncan, members of the first current of thought and other representatives of revisionist socialism, stated that the tendency of Western societies towards the universalism would prevent any hypothesis of transformation of revolutionary type:

> Inasmuch as high chances of mobility make even less dissatisfied with the system of social differentiation in their society and less inclined to organise in opposition to it, they help to perpetuate this stratification system, and they simultaneously stabilise the political institutions that support it.
>
> (Blau and Duncan, 1967, p. 440)

In this case, mobility was defined as occupational mobility, after ordering the occupations according to the social prestige that each one of them had. It was all about the individual or family channels through social hierarchy defined as a continuum of reachable positions.

The analyses on social stratification are found in the second school of thought, the majority of them being of Marxist inspiration. In this case, the presence of occupational mobility represented a challenge to the possibility of conceptualizing the actual notion of class based on the social division of labour:

> The greater the degree of closure in terms of mobility chances – both intergenerationally and within the career of the individual – the more this facilitates the formation of identifiable classes. The effect of closure in terms of intergenerational movements is to provide for the reproduction of common life experience over the generations; and this homogenisation of experience is reinforced to the degree to which the individual's movement within the labour market is confined to occupations which generate a similar range of material income.
>
> (Giddens, 1973, p. 107)

In more recent years, some economists, following the dictates of methodological individualism, have reproposed the analysis in terms of mobility welfare starting from the study of inequality (Atkinson, 1983a,b; Dardanoni 1993). As a matter of fact, the study of social mobility could be thought as a *dynamic analysis of inequality*. The static analysis of inequality has as a reference point the distribution of a socio-economic welfare indicator of interest in a given moment of a society. The limitations of such analysis have already been pinpointed by Milton Friedman. He stated that the inequality of a strict social system where every individual maintains his position over time is by far more worrisome than the one found in a dynamic and mobile social system:

> A major problem in interpreting evidence on the distribution of income is the need to distinguish two basically different kinds of inequality: temporary, short-run differences in income, and differences in long-run economic status. Consider two societies that have the same distribution of annual income. In one there is great mobility and change so that the position of particular families in the income hierarchy varies widely from year to year. In the other, there is great rigidity so that each family stays in the same position year after year. Clearly, in any meaningful sense, the second would be the more unequal society. The one kind of inequality is a sign of dynamic change, social mobility, equality of opportunity; the other of a status society.
>
> (Friedman, 1962)

For example, let us consider two hypothetical societies made up of only two individuals. In each one of the two societies the initial distribution of the socio-economical status is given by (1,10) where 1 represents the status of the first individual and 10 the status of the second. Let us assume now that we can observe the two societies in a subsequent period (or in the following generation) and to notice that society **A** is still characterized by the distribution (1,10) whereas society **B** is now characterized by (10,1). The simple static analysis of these two societies would reveal at every moment in both societies the presence of a high level of inequality, since every individual has a level of welfare ten times worse than the other. We would conclude that in the static analysis the same level of inequality is present in **A** and **B**. Nevertheless, if we look at the cumulative level of welfare of the two individuals (or of the two dynasties if we are observing two generations), for example by considering the average level of welfare of the two periods, we can clearly see that the two societies differ in terms of inequality: society **B** appears as a perfectly egalitarian societies in terms of average welfare, whereas society **A** maintains its initial inequality unchanged over time.

It is evident that a final judgement in terms of equality can only be formulated in reference to the causes of inequality and the ways this latter perpetuates itself over time. Even if we take into consideration that the initial distribution of the status is the result of an unequal distribution of the individual abilities, the final distribution depends on the possibilities of meritocratic competition within society. Society A (that can be characterized as *socially immobile*) returns the image of a socially closed system, where the social position remains unchanged (e.g. when the social status is transferred hereditarily) and the individual social status is determined *by attribution*. Conversely, society **B** (that we characterize as *socially mobile*) can represent the case of a socially open system, where individuals can compete among each other for the attainment of higher social position regardless of their class origin; in this case, the social status is defined *by acquisition.*

3.3 The historical evolution of social mobility

The historical evolution that started during the industrial revolution of 1800 has been one of the principal topics of discussion among the scholars of social mobility. The transformation of social systems from an agriculture-based society to an industrial one has in fact produced massive changes in the occupational structure; mass education has also enhanced the formative opportunities and opened the way to higher social positions. In addition to these two elements, the development of welfare and equal opportunities policies designed for the unprivileged minorities could also have contributed to the increase of social mobility possibilities in the last two centuries. In a recent important contribution, Erikson and Goldthrope (1992) have compared two thesis whereby the industrialization, with its inevitable implications in terms of rationality and efficient choices, can only increase the opportunities of social mobility; also, the Marxist literature exposes how the industrialization process reinforces the necessity for social stratification reproduction in order to obtain a better functioning of capitalism, thus negating the existing of mobility opportunities.

This debate is still open. Even if nowadays the Marxist analysis of capitalistic societies is not widely followed, the discussion on the effective degree of social mobility within modern societies remains open. The lack of sufficient historical data does not permit to objectively discriminate on the empiric validity of each one of the viewpoints. Exactly for this reason, many scholars preferred the approach of a comparative analysis of social mobility levels by using the United States, the most developed capitalistic society, as a reference point: in fact, since Alexis de Tocqueville's days, the United States have always been considered a nation with a high social mobility. Even Karl Marx attributed the weak presence of a communist party in the United States to the lack of a proletarian class immobile in time and without social advancement expectations. Some recent empirical studies do not reinforce this thesis: in a comparison between Italy and United States, Cecchi *et al.* (1999) find that Italy is characterized by a greater income distribution inequality, but also by a lower inter-generational mobility, not only at the income level but also on the level of education obtained. This result appears to be counterintuitive, since the Italian school system is generally free and therefore characterized by low entry barriers; nevertheless, the absence of proper incentives due to a low degree of meritocratic competition on the job market would definitely compensate this aspect and would end up in less mobility. Other studies that used the United States as a comparison showed that the United States would be socially less mobile than Germany and Sweden, thanks to an inferior school system quality and to the absence of an efficient social security system (see survey in Solon, 1999).

Conversely, the analysis of the opposite phenomenon, the presumed higher mobility in planned-economy countries, is less fashionable nowadays than it used to be towards the end of the eighties. At any rate, the empirical evidence would appear to show that, whereas in the first years following the Second World War the expansion of education and structural changes due to the rapid industrialization led the eastern-block countries towards a higher degree of inter-generational mobility, especially in comparison with Western European countries, starting at the end of the eighties the level of social mobility was nearly equivalent in the two blocks.

3.4 Some models on the determinants of social mobility

The first scientific analysis on the process of inter-generational mobility is without doubts the one by Francis Galton in 1886 found in his essay *Regression towards mediocrity in hereditary stature*.

Galton, after having analysed data on the stature of thousands of individuals and their parents concluded that 'When mid-parents are taller then mediocrity, their children tend to be shorter than they.... When mid-parents are shorter than mediocrity, their children tend to be taller than they', what Galton meant for 'mid-parent' was the average stature of the two parents after converting the female stature in the male equivalent, and for 'mediocrity' he meant the average stature of population. In modern terms, the model of inter-generational stature transmission by Galton can be written as

$$A_{t+1} = (1 - \beta)\bar{A} + \beta A_t + e_t$$

where A_{t+1} is the height of the individual, A_t the height of his/her parents, $\bar{A}$ is the average height of the population, e_t is an idiosyncratic element of the population and β is a parameter for height hereditary. If we rewrite the same relation as

$$\left(A_{t+1} - \bar{A}\right) = \beta\left(A_t - \bar{A}\right) + e_t.$$

We notice that the parameter β can be interpreted as the degree of inter-generational persistence: if a father had an above average stature (i.e. $(A_t - \bar{A}) > 0$) the son will tend to be above average as well to a degree proportional to β, not counting of course unforeseeable accidental events (the factor e_t). If the transmission model were purely deterministic ($e_t = 0$) the lower the factor β (the mean regression coefficient) the more rapidly the stature of the sons would converge towards the average stature. Galton concluded that β in the stature transmission was nearly $\frac{2}{3}$, thus representing a process with higher inter-generational persistence.

If we replace the 'stature' variable with the 'socio-economical status' variable, Galton's model can be utilized to analyse social mobility. In fact, the regression coefficient of Y_{t+1} over Y_t is a frequently used measure in mobility analyses.

Becker proposed a rationalization of this structure through an inter-generational transmission model of the status. When altruistic parents care about the welfare of their sons, they tend to donate a portion of their income with which the sons finance the acquisition of education. Since education is thought to be the principal determinant of income, inter-generational persistence in incomes will be created whenever rich parents' kids would be able to acquire more education as opposed to poor parents' kids, in the event that the latter would not find a chance of financing in the market. The principle characteristic of Becker's model is that the kids' income is determined by the rational choices for investment of the parents, thus introducing some offsetting effects: if the son independently receives one dollar (e.g. from a public education program) the parent will decrease the investment by 1 dollar: 'Public education and other programs to aid the young may not significantly better them because of compensating decreases in parental expenditures' (Becker, 1981, p. 153).

The economic system appears in this way governed by an almost mechanic law of motion that resembles Galton's model of regression to the mean. This result is the central hypothesis of the model, according to which there is a specific inter-generational transmission of non-observable characteristics (skills, intelligence): as a matter of fact, if a parent gifted with an above average intelligence operates in a world with a high persistence of intelligence transmission (i.e. where the coefficient β is close to 1) he knows that he would have, a high probability to get a son/daughter with a similar degree of intelligence. He would then tend to invest in his/her education, thus reinforcing the inter-generational persistence in the dynamic of income. Conversely, the same parent, in a world with low persistence (the coefficient β near 0) would expect his son to have an average intelligence, and would then tend to invest less; since the same reasoning is symmetrically applied to below average intelligence parents, a more rapid income convergence towards the mean in the inter-generational passage can be inferred.

Becker's model has been subsequently criticized as deemed too mechanical: it in fact assumes that the persistence in the inter-generational transmission is identical in the case of alternative consideration of intelligence, education, and individual wealth or income.

Mulligan (1997) has proposed to separately analyse the inter-generational transmission of work-based income and wealth, since the first can be transmitted through mechanisms analogous to the ones analysed by Becker (genetic transmission of intelligence and/or family financing of education) whereas the second is directly passed by inheritance. The analysis of data shows that the inter-generational correlation between work-based incomes of fathers and children is generally inferior to the correlation between social statuses (whenever this is measured on the multi-period total income of an individual, analogously to the concept of *permanent income*). Mulligan, as a matter of fact, finds that the coefficient of inter-generational correlation in the levels of permanent income (or in levels of consumption, since strictly interconnected to the multi-period income) in a representative sample of the American population is almost 0.7–0.8, whereas the same coefficient is only 0.5 in the levels of work-based income. This implies a considerable difference in the degree of inequality persistence among different generations: a correlation coefficient of 0.7 implies that if the parents of the individual i are 5 times richer (in terms of total income) than the parents of the individual j, then the individual i will be on average three times richer than the individual j. Conversely, if the correlation coefficient under examination were equal to 0.5, this would imply that in front of a difference of 5 times in the parents (i.e. the parents of the individual i earn 5 times as much as the parents of j do) a difference of only 2 times in the kids would exist (on average the individual i would earn twice as much as the individual j).

The different rapidity of transmission of intelligence/education/wealth and work-based income/socio-economical status sheds a light on the role of inter-generational transmission of wealth through inheritance in the inequalities among generations. In Becker's interpretative hypothesis, the genetic transmission of intelligence locates a degree of 'optimal' persistence accompanied by an efficient allocation of resources (the more capable individuals will receive higher investments in education from their families). Nevertheless, several obstacles to this end can be found. Among the principal ones is the inequality in wealth distribution. If, in fact, poor families cannot afford to adequately finance their sons' education with their own means, they could end up going into debt although the access to the credit market to finance education has many obstacles: poor families cannot provide real guarantees and can have their credit refused (*borrowing constraint*). In this way, the investment in education of the generation results insufficient to reach the level considered efficient. In this context, a program of free and public education, financed by the taxpayers, could simultaneously reach two objectives: on one side to promote efficiency (since it allows the deserving children coming from poor families to access the highest levels of education) on another, to improve equality (since it decreases the degree of inter-generational persistence, is in fact increasing the opportunity of equality).

Unfortunately reality is more complex than the situations described by formal models. Poor families often reduce the investment in the education of their kids not much for economical reasons but rather for cultural ones. As Checchi *et al.* (1999) pointed out, the parents' investment in the education of their kids depends on the expectations that the first ones have on the capabilities of the second ones, and those expectations are biased by the parents' experiences. A poor and/or poorly educated parent expects to have a son/daughter with characteristics similar to his/hers parents, and will be then less willing to further his/her kid's education. This will be a *self-fulfilling prophecy* insofar as that the kid with a lower education will have a lower earning income. An excellent analysis of the mechanisms of inter-generational transmission of the socio-economical inequality can be found in Pickety (2000).

3.5 Measurement problems

We will illustrate some of the problems that can be found during the analysis of social mobility. One the first methodological difficulties consists in how to precisely measure the socio-economical status of an individual. The economists tend to associate the socio-economical status to the consumption opportunities over a lifetime, that in their turn depend on the expected *permanent income* of a lifetime; for this reason, they supply measurements of social mobility based on income mobility, often utilizing multi-year averages of incomes to avoid the interference of accidental events (such as loss of job, unexpected earnings or losses, etc. – see Solon, 1999). The sociologists instead state that the concept of socio-economical status has to take into account immaterial elements such as the prestige that one has among his peers or the power wielded within a given society; they also deem the social status a resource collectively enjoyed within homogeneous social groups (*classes*) and for this reason they focus on the mobility among social classes, defined on the basis of the occupation that a given individual has (Cobalti and Schizzerotto, 1994; Erikson and Goldthorpe, 1992). The *measures of occupational prestige*, conceived on the basis of work-related income and mean (or median) level of education for each occupational group, represent a useful mediation between these two approaches: on one hand they ignore individual differences considered irrelevant in the social hierarchy (since all the individuals that have the same occupation receive the same social prestige) but on the other hand they take into account that in market-oriented societies the capability of generating income constitutes a central element (Duncan, 1961).

Let us assume then that Y_{it} represents a variable that measures the socio-economical status of an individual or a family i-th to the time t (the origin) and Y_{it+1} indicates the socio-economical status of the same individual and the same family at time $t+1$ (the destination). The study the social mobility of a society made up of n individuals (or family) will consist then in the analysis of how the vector $\mathbf{Y_t} = [Y_{1t}, Y_{2t}, \ldots, Y_{nt}]$ is transformed in the vector $\mathbf{Y_{t+1}} = [Y_{1t+1}, Y_{2t+1}, \ldots, Y_{nt+1}]$ in the examined time interval. Notice that this type of analysis can be applied to comparisons among different countries (like in the previous case of the comparison of social mobility in the United States and other industrialized countries) to inter-temporal comparisons within a given country (e.g. to see if social mobility has increased, remained the same or diminished over a given time) to comparisons among different groups within the same country (e.g. to compare social mobility according to race, sex, geographic region or other peculiar characteristics).

In the analysis of inter-generational mobility some simplifying assumptions on the nature of the analysed families are often utilized. Typically this is done by taking into consideration only male individuals (fathers and sons) to avoid the difficulties of attribution of a socio-economical status to women caused by the reduced participation of women to the job market. Therefore, we will indicate the socio-economical status of two contiguous generations with the pair of vectors $(\mathbf{Y_t}, \mathbf{Y_{t+1}})$, where $\mathbf{Y_t}$ represents the distribution of the status in the generation of the fathers and $\mathbf{Y_{t+1}}$ the one of the sons.

A second problem that arises in the empirical analysis is the one of the aggregation of individual data to obtain synthetic measures of mobility that permits the comparison among different situations. It is mandatory though to make a clear distinction between two alternative concepts of mobility, depending on whether the initial and final distributions of the status are equal or different. The sociological literature defines as *structural mobility* any mobility measure based on the level of recorded difference between the distribution of $\mathbf{Y_t}$ and the one of $\mathbf{Y_{t+1}}$. If, for instance, a country displays high growth rates (as it happens in the initial phases of the industrialization process) a change in the typology of available occupations on the market can be experienced (for instance, agricultural jobs go down and industrial ones go up, or manual occupation decreases and the intellectual one increases). In this way, the new generation experiences an array of opportunities different from the one their parents had, and the mobility process gets combined with the one of industrial transformation.

Nevertheless, this does not complete the process analysis. Let us imagine two similar societies characterized by identical distributions of the socio-economical status in the two generations. They can differ though in terms of how the two families reorder themselves in the step from one generation to the other. The name of *exchange mobility* is given to this second aspect, measured by the level of association between the parents' status and the children's one. The difficulty of empirically dissecting these two aspects causes mobility comparisons (done in contexts where the status distribution differ significantly in the inter-generational passage) to be strongly dependent on the type of indicator utilized, thus providing indications in contrast among themselves (see Chapter 6 for an illustration of this possibility).

The most intuitive analytical tool, and therefore the most utilized, for the analysis of social mobility are the *mobility matrices* (Table 3.1). When we analyse the transitions among predefined categories (social classes, occupational groups, education degrees) we can illustrate phenomena of both structural and exchange mobility; on the contrary, when we utilize categories of percentile type we can identify the phenomena of exchange mobility (this will be clarified in Tables 3.2 and 3.3). As an example, let's consider the simpler case in which the elements of vector **Y** can only take two values (example, 'proletariat' or 'bourgeoisie', or 'without mandatory education' and 'mandatory education completed', or 'manual labor' and 'intellectual labor', or finally 'below average income' and 'above average income'). In this case social mobility can be studied through a mobility table 2×2 of the type shown in Table 3.1.

Where the rows designate the origin and the columns the destination, and the coefficients $p_{ij}, i,j = a, b$ designate the individual probability of moving from state i to state j (notice that by construction we have $\sum_i \sum_j p_{ij} = 1$). This probability is deduced (but it would be more correct to say 'estimated') from the empirically observed frequencies (i.e. from the proportion of individuals that move from i to j). In the intra-generational case, p_{ij} indicates the probability that an individual in this population find himself in the state i in the period of initial reference and in the state j in the following reference period; in the inter-generational case, p_{ij} indicates

Table 3.1 A mobility matrix

Origin	*Destination*		*Marginal distribution of origins*
	Low	*High*	
Low	p_{bb}	p_{ba}	$p_{bb} + p_{ba}$
High	p_{ab}	p_{aa}	$p_{ab} + p_{aa}$
Marginal distribution of destinations	$p_{bb} + p_{ab}$	$p_{ba} + p_{aa}$	

Table 3.2 Mobility matrices for three societies with different structural mobility but similar exchange mobility

	*Society **S***		*Society **I***		*Society **U***	
	Low	*High*	*Low*	*High*	*Low*	*High*
Low	2/6	1/6	32/100	30/100	32/100	8/100
High	1/6	2/6	8/100	30/100	30/100	30/100

Table 3.3 Mobility matrices for two societies with same structural mobility but different exchange mobility

	*Society **S**′*		*Society **I**′*	
	Low	*High*	*Low*	*High*
Low	40/100	10/100	25/100	25/100
High	10/100	40/100	25/100	25/100

the probability of observing a family in which the son is in the class *j* and the father in the class *i*. The last row and the last column in the table indicate the *marginal distributions* of the origin variable and the destination one: for example, if in the inter-generational case in one society the observed marginal distribution of the status is equal to (0.3, 0.7) this implies that in this society 30 per cent of the fathers belong to the low socio-economical class and 70 per cent to the high class. Notice that by dividing every row in a mobility table with the correspondent value of the origin marginal distribution we obtain a table of *conditioned probabilities*, utilized every time the process of social mobility is analysed through a stochastic process of Markovian type.

Extreme cases of mobility matrices are, on one hand, the one of perfect immobility, in which the elements outside the principal diagonal are equal to zero: in a society characterized by this situation we can only observe families with fathers and sons that belong to the same social class. The other extreme case is given from the equality of opportunities, in which the destination status is independent from the conditions of origin; in a society characterized by a situation of this type the matrix of conditioned probabilities presents rows completely equal since every individual will face the same distribution of socio-economical success probability regardless of the family origin.

The perfect immobility and opportunity of equality cases are obviously special ones, of theoretical interest but of poor empirical relevance. From a practical point of view, the totality of empirically observed mobility matrices is 'in between' these two special cases. Let us consider for example three hypothetical societies, **S**, **T** and **U**, characterized by the following matrices of inter-generational mobility as shown in Table 3.2.

It immediately emerges from an analysis of the three matrices that while society **T** is characterized by a strong socio-economical growth in the inter-generational passage (since 62 per cent of the fathers, but only 40 per cent of sons, belong the 'low' social class) in society **U** we can notice a general impoverishment in the generational passage (60 per cent of the fathers but only 40 per cent of the sons belongs to the 'high' social class). Society **S** shows instead a situation of inter-generational equilibrium, with equal proportions of fathers and sons in the two classes. Whereas in society **S** the marginal distributions of the status have not changed during the generational passage, societies **T** and **U** are characterized by an inter-generational variation in the marginal distributions of status. It is then easy to conclude that the societies **T** and **U** are characterized by a greater structural mobility compared to society **S**. But which one of the three societies is characterized by a greater exchange mobility?

Let us consider society **S**, in which the son of a parent belonging to a 'lower class' has twice the chances of remaining in the 'lower class' than to transit in the 'higher class'. Conversely, the son of a parent belonging to a higher class has half of the chances of ending up in a lower class compared to the remaining in the same class of the father. The ratio between these two probabilities (*odds*) is called *odds ratio* and it is equal to odds ratio $= (p_{bb}/p_{ba})/(p_{ab}/p_{aa})$; in society **S** this ratio is equal to 4. The odds ratio indicates the opportunity disparity that individuals with different origins face, and it is an index of the social rigidity degree in society. It is easy to notice that the odds ratio in societies **U** and **T** is also equal to 4. Hence we could state that these three societies, although different in terms of structural mobility due to socio-economical movements of expansion and recession, are in actuality characterized by analogous social rigidity in terms of positive association between the social class of the father and the one of the son. The opposite situation is also possible. Let us consider as a matter of fact the two societies as given in Table 3.3.

It is easy to notice that both societies are characterized by equal structural mobility since the marginal distributions of the population in both societies are identical (in both societies and both generations half of the individuals belong to the higher social class and the other half to the lower class). Notice that analogous matrices to these ones are obtained whenever the economical status is defined in percentile terms, so that the marginal distributions are characterized by an equal ratio of individuals in every social class. However, whereas society $\mathbf{T}'$ is characterized by equality of opportunities (the son of a parent belonging in a higher class has the same chances of social success than the son of a parent coming from a lower class) society $\mathbf{S}'$ is characterized by a strong positive association between the father's status and the son's status, just to confirm a considerable social rigidity (it is sufficient in fact to compare the corresponding *odds ratios*).

The two examples quoted earlier show how to distinguish between the concepts of *structural mobility* and *exchange mobility* represents a crucial point in our analysis. Specifically, going back to the examples of Paragraph 3, it is agreed by many scholars that the presumed higher mobility of the USA (and the one of countries more capitalistically advanced) can be ascribed to a higher structural mobility; on the contrary, the exchange mobility seems to be very similar in various countries. The hypothesis of a substantial similarity of the exchange mobility among industrialized countries is known as the Feathermann, Jones, and Hauser hypothesis (*FJH hypothesis* – see Feathermann *et al.*, 1975). The study of the dissection of mobility matrices through parameters linked to structural mobility (typically associated to marginal distributions) and parameters linked to exchange mobility (association parameters, typically linked to the *odds-ratios*) constitutes nowadays an active area of research in the field of statistics that can be traced back to the early works of Peter McCullagh and John Nelder on the generalized linear models (see their 1989 monograph). Sobel *et al.* (1998) and Bartolucci *et al.* (2001) propose useful parameterizations of social mobility matrices that lead to an inferential analysis that allows to separate the study of structural mobility from the one of exchange mobility.

The analysis of mobility through the utilization of transition matrices has been criticized due to the fact that its results strictly depend on the categories defining the conditions of origin and destination. For this reason many scholars preferred focusing their attention on the measurement of social mobility starting from de-aggregated individual socio-economical situations, utilizing *mobility indices* that seem to be less biased by the subjective judgement of the analyst. The following chapter contains an example of the utilization of such indices for comparisons of social mobility.

3.6 An example concerning the inter-generational trend in post-war Italy

Checchi and Dardanoni (2002) consider the influence of different ways of measuring social mobility based on the results of several international and inter-temporal comparisons. They utilize mobility indices belonging to the class of distance indices studied by D'Agostino and Dardanoni (2002) based on the concept of *Euclidean distance*. The intuition behind this class of indices is that in order to measure the mobility in a given society of n individuals we can consider the distance between the effective status of the father and son for every single family and then calculate the average, after defining the effective status as a determined function of the observed status. An *absolute index of distance* is built starting from the distributions of the original variables (i.e. it is assumed that effective status is equal to the one observed) and for this reason it shows results very sensitive to structural mobility phenomena. Let's think in fact to the extreme case where there is a perfect dependence between the position of the fathers and sons; the absolute index will display a higher mobility in the presence of higher rates of incomes growth observed in the time interval elapsed between the two generations.

The *ordinal mobility indices* are on the contrary calculated in terms of the individual relative position with reference to the position of the rest of the population (*social ranking*); in other words, we assume that the effective status of each unit is completely described by the social rank of the unit itself calculated by utilizing the observed status. The index of ordinal distance measures the Euclidean distance between the social rankings' vector of the fathers and sons, and it is shown to be equivalent to the non-parametric index of correlation in social rankings known as *Spearman's Rho* (see Kendall and Gibbons, 1990); notice that this index is invariant to monotone transformations of data. For example, an economic growth that causes the following generation income to increase by maintaining constant the relative positions, would increase the absolute mobility by leaving the ordinal mobility constant; in other words, this index is strictly sensitive to the exchange mobility.

We can find the *relative mobility indices* in an intermediate position, an example of which is the *Pearson's correlation index*. This index is also based on the concept of Euclidean distance, calculated after having opportunely standardized the vectors of status. Since in relative indices the effective socio-economical status is normalized within one single generation on the basis of parameters such as average income and variance, they are less sensitive to phenomena of structural mobility that display a generalized growth or changes of inequality, whereas they stay sensitive to the exchange mobility.

Let us move now to the analysis of social mobility in post-war Italy. Our country is historically characterized by a scarce availability of data, especially the ones relative to two contiguous generations, fathers, and sons. The problems are multiplied whenever we want to know the income situation of the fathers' generation, since for a big chunk of the population that data dates back to the nineteenth century. For this reason we often resort to measures of socio-economical condition, less precise but also more easily accessible, such as occupation and school degree. It is possible to interview the individuals on their occupation and also to trace back their parents' condition through their memories. Checchi and Dardanoni (2002) utilized data collected by the Italian Central Bank over three distinct periods (1993, 1995, and 1998) for a sample of *c.*70,000 people. Some identified combinations of occupation/sector/school degree are utilized to trace back the socio-economic status, succeeding in tracing back 160 distinct possible social positions (of the type 'worker in the agricultural sector with elementary school diploma'). These social positions are then ordered in terms of income (median) of each cell. In this way we can trace back a posteriori a social hierarchy based on the occupational condition, whose relative importance depend on the capability of command on merchandises given by one's potential income. Since we do not have direct information on the incomes of the parents' generation, we resort to the simplifying hypothesis whereby the current social hierarchy of the sons is applicable to the ones of the fathers.

At this point, we are able to measure the inter-generational mobility for the Italian case by comparing the social condition reached by the fathers with the one reached by the sons. In the event that we do not feel satisfied by a social hierarchy founded on occupational incomes, we can study the mobility in the levels of acquired education. In both cases, within the span of the last century, Italy underwent deep transformations: on one hand, mass education allowed recent generations to increase their average degree of education much more than the previous generation did; on the other hand, the transformation of the productive apparatus eliminated numerous agricultural-sector-related occupations in favour of industrial and tertiary ones. Regardless of the variable of reference, we expect to experience a significant structural mobility in the period under exam, without discarding the hypothesis of experiencing a different trend in the exchange mobility. The following table shows the three indicators of mobility discussed earlier, calculated for both occupational condition and level of education. By following a recurring rule, these measures only take into account pairs of father–son data to avoid that the phenomenon could be distorted by the lack of participation in the labour market by the mothers and/or daughters. Notice that the sample has been divided into subgroups based on birth periods with the aim of verifying the temporal trends of mobility measures (Table 3.4).

We can observe by analysing the table that the absolute index of occupational mobility (based on the Euclidean distance among occupational status vectors) shows a maximum mobility for the groups of population born before Second World War and that entered the job market in the first years following the War. From that point on the phenomenon seems to decrease significantly, especially for the younger groups. On the contrary, the ordinal index (based on the correlation index of social statutes by Spearman) grows progressively up until the advent of baby-boomers born in the 1950s, to then stabilize at that level. Another different figure is finally obtained when we consider the relative mobility (calculated through the correlation index by Pearson) which takes into account the correlation (in the standardized levels, and not in social standings as in the ordinal case) between the social positions of the two generations. In this case the higher social mobility is a prerogative of the younger generations. As we discussed earlier, this seems to indicate a progressive decline in structural mobility as well as a progressive increase in exchange mobility. Obviously the answer to the question 'Has social mobility increased in Italy in the period under exam?' crucially depends on the type of mobility we choose. Notice, moreover, that if to answer this question we had used a unique mobility index, we would have obtained a univocal answer, but it would have been completely different depending on the chosen index.

On the contrary, we notice that, by considering the mobility defined by levels of education, the absolute mobility continually grows up to the people born at the end of the 1950s, which is the same generation that benefited from the unified middle school reform (1962) and from the liberalization of university enrollment (1969). Conversely, the exchange mobility seems to fluctuate through different population groups, without exhibiting a precise temporal trend.

We can then conclude that the valuation of the degree of inter-generational mobility strongly depends on the measurements adopted, that in turn are functions of the concept of mobility that we wish to describe. This underlying ambiguity is caused by the fact that the mobility measurements encompass information of composite nature. The starting point is given by the marginal distributions in each generation; such distributions supply information of static type regarding the level of inequality within each generation. If we observe the distance between the marginal distributions of two contiguous generations we can highlight the phenomena of structural mobility. If we instead observe the degree of association of the two generations we can observe the exchange mobility.

We conclude this essay by pointing out that the social mobility analysis is for its same nature of inter-disciplinary type. If, from an economic theory point of

Table 3.4 Mobility measures – Italy 1993–1995–1998 – decomposition by birth periods

Birth years	*Mobility in labour income*			*Mobility in education level*		
	Absolute index	*Ordinal index*	*Relative index*	*Absolute index*	*Ordinal index*	*Relative index*
1930–1934	0.505	0.597	0.535	0.489	0.443	0.437
1935–1939	0.547	0.575	0.563	0.473	0.418	0.437
1940–1944	0.553	0.641	0.605	0.499	0.456	0.453
1945–1949	0.502	0.674	0.659	0.530	0.487	0.501
1950–1954	0.488	0.709	0.694	0.555	0.513	0.524
1955–1959	0.453	0.726	0.695	0.562	0.525	0.547
1960–1964	0.420	0.673	0.677	0.487	0.461	0.492
1965–1970	0.344	0.699	0.704	0.448	0.488	0.522

view, it supplies useful indications on the degree of inter-temporal inequality of a population based on implications of individual rational behaviour; and if, from a statistical theory point of view, it is extremely interesting to delineate the phenomenon by distinguishing among its basic elements (structural and exchange mobility) it is still true to state that the causes of mobility are still unexplored. As Esping Andersen (2004) properly stated, the economists and statisticians' analyses pinpoint mechanical models that often ignore subtle but important phenomena, such as family upbringing in pre-school age and the transmission of role models. If the economic analysis has a tendency to focus the attention on the monetary aspects of hereditary transmission, the sociological analysis has contributed to highlight the characteristics of the socialization process, starting from the nature of formative systems to then move to strategies of matrimonial dynamics and to the functioning of different job markets. However, we still lack the comparative analyses (among countries, regions, and historical periods) that could link, with sufficient reliability, the observed mobility differences to different institutional factors.

Note

* Entry in the supplement to the Treccani Encyclopedia of Novecento–October 2002.

References

Atkinson, Anthony, 1983a, The measurement of economic mobility, in Atkinson, A.B. (eds), *Social Justice and Public Policy*, London: Wheatsheaf Books Ltd., ch. 3.

Atkinson, Anthony, 1983b, Income distribution and inequality of opportunity, in Atkinson, A.B. (eds), *Social Justice and Public Policy*, London: Wheatsheaf Books Ltd., ch. 4.

Bartolucci, Francesco, Antonio Forcina and Valentino Dardanoni, 2001, Positive Quadrant Dependance and Marginal Modelling in Two-Way Tables With Orderd Margins, *Journal of the American Statistical Association*, 96: 1497–1505.

Becker, Gary, 1981, *A Treatise on the Family*, Cambridge, MA: Harvard University Press.

Blau, Peter and Otis Duncan, 1967, *The American Occupational Structure*, New York: Wiley.

Checchi, Daniele and Valentino Dardanoni, 2002, Mobility comparisons: does using different measures matter? *Research in Inequality*, 9: 113–145.

Checchi, Daniele, Andrea Ichino and Aldo Rustichini, 1999, More equal but less mobile? Intergenerational mobility and inequality in Italy and in the US. *Journal of Public Economics*, 74: 351–393.

Cobalti, Antonio and Antonio Schizzerotto, 1994, *La mobilità sociale in Italia*, Mulino, Bologna.

D'Agostino, Marcello and Valentino Dardanoni, 2002, Mobility comparisons: a class of distance indices, mimeo.

Dardanoni, Valentino, 1993, Measuring social mobility, *Journal of Economic Theory*, 61: 372–394.

Duncan, Otis, 1961, A socioeconomic index for all occupations, in Reiss, A. (ed.), *Occupations and Social Status*, New York: Free Press.

Erikson Robert and John Goldthorpe, 1992, *The Constant Flux*, Oxford: Clarendon Press.

Esping Andersen, Gosta, 2004, What might create more equal opportunity? Money, cultural capital, and government, in Corak, M. (ed.), *Generational Income Mobility in North America and Europe*, Cambridge: Cambridge University Press.

Featherman, David, Lancaster Jones and Robert Hauser, 1975, Assumptions of social mobility in the US: the case of occupational status, *Social Science Research*, 4: 329–360.

Friedman, Milton, 1962, *Capitalism and Freedom*, Chicago, IL: University of Chicago Press.

Galton, Francis, 1886, Regression towards mediocrity in hereditary stature, *Journal of the Anthropological Institute of Great Britain and Ireland*, 15: 246–263.

Giddens, Anthony, 1973, *The Class Structure of the Advanced Societies*, London: Hutchison.

Kendall, Maurice and Jane Gibbons, 1990, *Rank Correlations Methods*, London: Edward Arnold ed.

McCullagh, Peter and John Nelder, 1989, *Generalised Linear Models*, 2nd ed., London: CRC Press.

Mulligan, Casey, 1997, *Parental Priorities and Economic Inequality*, Chicago, IL: University of Chicago Press.

Pareto, Vilfredo, 1966, *Manuel d'economie politique*, Droz, Geneve 1966 (1st edn, 1909).

Picketty, Thomas, 2000, Theories of persistent inequality and intergenerational mobility, in Anthony B. Atkinson and Francois Bourguignon (eds), *Handbook of Income Distribution*, Amsterdam: North Holland, pp. 429–476.

Sobel, Michael, Becker, Mark and Susan Minick, 1998, Origins, destinations and association in occupational mobility, *American Journal of Sociology*, 104: 687–721.

Solon, Gary, 1999. Intergenerational mobility in the labour market, in Orley Ashenfelter and David Card (eds), *Handbook of Labour Economics*, vol. 3c, Amsterdam: North Holland, 1999.

4 The size of redistribution in OECD countries

Does it influence wage inequality?

Elisabetta Croci Angelini and Francesco Farina

4.1 Introduction

Since labour is a good of a special kind (Solow, 1990), the social relationship consisting in the exchange between labour services and a wage rate requires governance institutions. The role of institutions in the wage negotiation and in the determination of the disposable income distribution is commonly portrayed as composed by two phases. First, labour market institutions, such as legislation, the government and the organisations of workers and employers, operate *ex ante* with respect to the market, mainly by ruling on labour standards, on minimum wage (either legally enforced or imposed by unions), on employment protection legislation and to the organisational level (firm, industry, private or public sector) at which labour contracts are signed, so that labour market institutions directly and indirectly influence the determination of labour contracts. Second, the government operates *ex post* with respect to the market, by stabilisation policies aimed at correcting – mainly, through unemployment benefits – the macroeconomic failure consisting in a portion of the labour force remaining unemployed, and by the monetary transfers of social protection institutions.

However, the earlier distinction of the impact of the labour market and the welfare institutions on wage inequality is carried too far. In fact, in the macroeconomic model the determination of the labour market equilibrium takes into account the subsequent appraisal of stabilisation and social policies. The workers' expectations about their well-being are not simply based on their factor income. The strategic interaction resulting in a wage contract relies on behavioural functions that are also shaped by the perception of the extent of redistribution which will be *ex post* determined both by macroeconomic policies and tax and welfare legislation.

Therefore, to determine the unions' behaviour in wage negotiations, both factor income and disposable income distributions count. Especially in those European countries where three parties (unions, employers' organisations and the government) contribute to labour market coordination, wage negotiations are conducted by setting-up expectations on the income distribution which could result – as an effect of a deliberate choice, or as a possibly undesired by-product – from the whole range of labour market and welfare institutions.[1] Similarly, the distributive features of the fiscal system as well as the monetary transfers and in kind services offered by the institutions of social protection, aimed at looking after the workers' overall well-being, enter in wage negotiations.

We agree with the strand of literature conceiving the functioning of the labour market as the interplay of technical change and a unique 'system' (Freeman, 1995) of labour market *and* redistributive institutions, also described as a sort of 'social contract' (Bénabou, 2000). The empirical investigation conducted in this chapter highlights that wage inequality in OECD countries is not only determined by technical change and the degree of labour market regulation, but also by the amount of 'risk insurance' provided by welfare institutions through redistribution, allowing factor income inequality to translate into a less unequal disposable income distribution.

The chapter is organised as follows. In Section 4.2, we argue that the political decision on the degree of redistribution by welfare institutions, is consistent with a 'risk insurance' motivation, as manifested in the aggregation of the preferences expressed by the median voter as a metaphorical agent. In Section 4.3, we regress the income inequality indicator utilized to express the political mechanism of majority voting – the median-to-mean factor income ratio – on redistribution measured by the difference between the Gini measure of inequality evaluated at the factor and the disposable income levels. We show a high degree of heterogeneity in preferences for redistribution across four clusters of different systems of social protection of OECD countries (Scandinavian, Continental, Mediterranean and Anglo-Saxon countries), where the redistributive impact of the Welfare institutions widely differs. We interpret this finding as a clue that different degrees of 'risk insurance', decided by majority voting to correct factor income inequality, reflect different cultural and psychological attitudes to the uncertainty in the market. In Section 4.4, we assess that the wage dispersion can be differently affected by skill-biased or skill-neutral technologies, respectively in combination with low and high labour market regulation, and then discuss how wage inequality stemming from labour contracts can be affected by the extent of redistribution expected by the operation of welfare institutions. In Section 4.5, the evolution of wage inequality across countries is traced back to different interactions between the degree of redistribution, the mix of technological opportunities and wage compression characterising the labour markets in OECD countries. Section 4.6 concludes.

4.2 Some empirical evidence on redistribution

Econometric tests aiming at assessing the majority voting on redistribution based on the median voter's hypothesis[2] must explicit the political mechanism channelling the political pressure for redistribution. The appropriate indicator of the impact of the majority voting political mechanism on redistribution is the most direct measure of the median voter income position relative to the average: that is the ratio between median (*Ymd*) and mean (*Ymn*) income. Since empirical evidence shows that income distribution is usually right-skewed, the median-to-mean income ratio (*Ymd/Ymn*) is lower than one. A poorer-than-average median voter is likely to endorse a political programme promoting more redistribution through the tax-and-transfers system.

The indicator designed to express the median voter's preference for redistribution, as a function of the gap between his income position and average income, is often calculated on the disposable income (DPI) after state intervention. Yet, it is apparent that the median voter preference for redistribution depends on his factor income (FI) that is, his income before the redistributive effects of the tax-and-transfers system. To compare income distribution before and after state intervention we employ Luxembourg Income Study (LIS) data, on factor income and disposable income respectively, observed in mid-1980s and mid-1990s.[3] Although a variation in the *Ymd/Ymn* value might follow any changes in the whole distribution, by comparing the *Ymd/Ymn* DPI with the *Ymd/Ymn* FI we can get an insight about the political pressure exerted by the median voter to widen the redistributive impact of welfare institutions.

By plotting the FI and DPI *Ymd/Ymn* data for the last two decades (see Figure 4.1(a) and (b)), two main tendencies appear:

1 The median income position, resulting from the operation of the market forces, deteriorates considerably from the mid-1980s to the mid-1990s. Despite a higher concentration of values around the middle of the distribution in the mid-1990s with respect to that of the mid-1980s (the standard deviation increases from 0.6 to 0.8) for virtually all countries, the second decade shows much lower FI values (the average value falls from 0.88 to 0.83) corresponding to a general rise in inequality. Although some observations could be biased by the adverse cyclical performance which characterised the early 1990s, the considerable shift in *Ymd/Ymn* FI values is a reliable clue of the median voter's income condition losing ground.
2 The amount of redistribution accruing to the median voter, shown by comparing the *Ymd/Ymn* DPI to the *Ymd/Ymn* FI, is much larger in the mid-1990s with respect to the mid-1980s and – most crucially and differently from the mid-1980s – the tax-and-transfers system operates in nearly all countries towards increasing the relative income level of the median voter. In the mid-1980s, the DPI ratio average value (0.89) is one point higher than the corresponding FI ratio. In particular, the highest redistribution captured by this indicator – the largest increases in the DPI ratio with respect to the FI ratio – often occurred in countries starting from a low *Ymd/Ymn* FI. The *Ymd/Ymn* DPI shows that especially the most unequal Anglo-Saxon countries – characterised by very low *Ymd/Ymn* FI values – after state redistribution, experience a reduction in the distance from the Continental European countries. In the mid-1990s, the redistributive effects of taxes and transfers were much larger and concerned nearly all countries. The DPI average value (0.87) is four points higher the corresponding FI ratio. In the 1990s two clusters of countries – the Scandinavian and the Anglo-Saxon – experience the most striking increases from *Ymd/Ymn* FI to *Ymd/Ymn* DPI. In particular, a major redistributive effort is undertaken by Scandinavian countries to restore a more

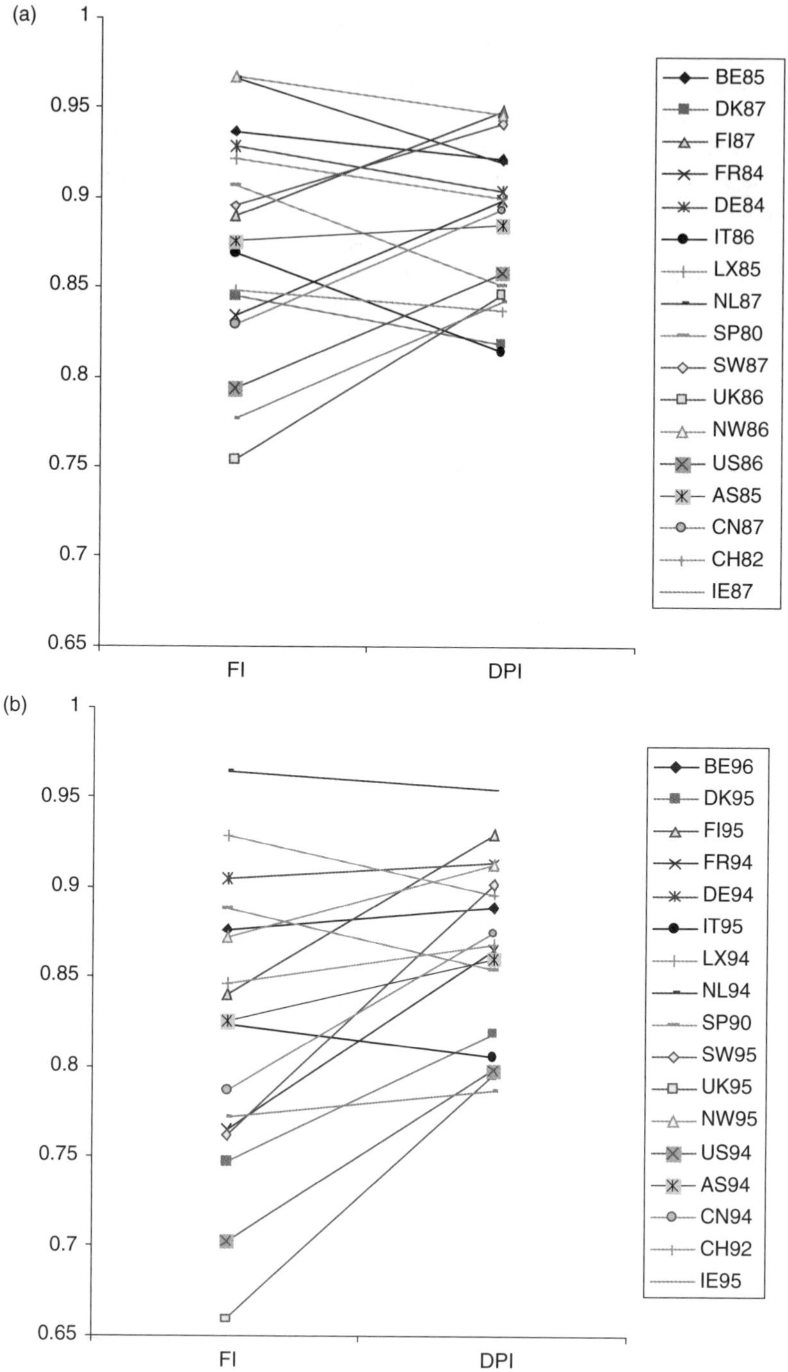

Figure 4.1 (a) *Ymd/Ymn* FI compared to *Ymd/Ymn* DPI – 1980s.
(b) *Ymd/Ymn* FI compared to *Ymd/Ymn* DPI – 1990s.

Note
For Belgium, France, Italy, Luxembourg and Spain, net income variables only.

equal income distribution, while the Benelux countries and Germany maintain high DPI *Ymd/Ymn* ratios; the United Kingdom and the United States, although experiencing a reduction in the gap with Continental Europe, keep very unequal income distributions also after a sizeable state intervention.

Figure 4.1(a) and (b) show a decline, when moving from factor to disposable income median-to-mean ratios, for seven countries in the mid-1980s and four countries in the mid-1990s. This evidence contradicts the interpretation of the median voter hypothesis implying that the bulk of redistribution should accrue to him, rather than representing the unintentional function of the individual occupying the median position.[4] This interpretation – the median voter as the self-interested utility maximisation consciously performed by the individual who occupies the median position in the income distribution – can be questioned on two grounds.

First, the identity of the person occupying the median position in the income distribution continuously changes. The median voter cannot be personally aware of his particular position, nor, consequently, of his decisiveness in determining the disposable income distribution. Consider groups of workers at different income levels hit by layoffs in the same proportion. As the newly unemployed workers with no other sources of income, will now occupy a position on the left of the median voter on the income distribution ranking, he will no longer be the median voter. The new median voter will be an individual with weaker income conditions *vis-à-vis* the former median voter.

Second, to seize the 'lion's share' of the redistribution, the median voter should be aware of the redistributive effects of welfare programmes over the whole income distribution. If a recession hits more severely the group of rich individuals, the average factor income falls and the median-to-mean income ratio goes up. The median voter may be unable to keep his disposable income at the same level of his factor income if the allocation design of the tax-and-transfers system is such that the differential effect of income redistribution across deciles allows only the poor to benefit in absolute terms from redistribution.

Since there is no deliberate motivation of a specific individual behind the median voter's preference for redistribution, the median voter's hypothesis cannot rely on a self-interest rationale related to the specific identity of the individual occupying the median position in the income distribution.

We take this clue to agree on the idea that the median voter is a metaphorical agent expressing the sense of precariousness that the majority of the electorate derives from their *ex ante* earnings, and willing to obtain 'risk insurance' by redistribution through the tax-and-transfers design.[5] The unemployment benefits, as well as the redistributive implications of a public and compulsory health insurance, public pensions and educational finance, represent a sort of *ex ante* insurance turning into *ex post* redistribution, where the poor contribute the less, and benefit the most.[6] Were a recession to decrease the median voter's earnings, he will end up belonging to the group of the low-income individuals with a higher probability of benefiting from the institutions of social protection. Thus, under a majority voting rule this metaphorical agent represents the aggregation of preferences oriented to exercise political pressure and obtain risk insurance for their 'future selves'. The majority voting in favour of redistribution can be regarded as summarising a series of factors – pressure groups, political regimes, government fragmentation, etc. – playing an important role, rather than the isolated individual occupying the median position in the electorate.

Under this perspective, the empirical evidence presented in Figure 4.1(a) and (b) could be interpreted according to a 'risk insurance' motivation, that is, the voters' coalition leaded by the median voter of the mid-1990s – with a much lower income level than the average *vis-à-vis* the income of the median voter of the 1980s – has exerted a stronger and successful political pressure so to steer the tax-and-transfers system towards a higher degree of redistribution. After the rise in factor income inequality which had occurred in the mid-1990s, the declining income in the market has been counteracted by a larger redistribution reducing the overall income dispersion.

Granted that to benefit from redistribution is not the individual occupying the median position but the group of people forming the majority voting, our attempt to measure the extent to which the desire for risk insurance succeeds in mitigating the rise in factor income inequality must choose an indicator of redistribution able to compare both factor and disposable income inequality over the whole income distribution. This indicator will be found in the difference between the Gini coefficient before and after the tax-and-transfers correction has taken place.

Furthermore, when comparing the mid-1990s with the mid-1980s observations, Figure 4.1(a) and (b) show a significant degree of heterogeneity across countries in the *Ymd/Ymn* DPI *vis-à-vis* the FI indicator. This gives a hint about the need for differentiating a wide range of preferences for redistribution across countries in conducting the econometric estimate.

4.3 Heterogeneity across Welfare State systems

In this section we estimate how the political pressure, proxied by the median voter's relative factor income position, influences income redistribution, measured by the difference between the Gini coefficients calculated on the FI and the DPI distributions. The econometric tests show that different countries may be differently keen on risk insurance, with idiosyncratic propensities towards redistribution.

On the assumption that the median voter hypothesis in principle could be ascertained irrespective of time and space (Model 1) at first all available information, which amounts to 67 observations, has been gathered into a single pooling regression model. An Ordinary Least Squares (OLS) regression (equation (4.1)) connects the extent of a country's income redistribution to the distance of the median voter income from mean income in that country.

$$\text{GiniFI}_i - \text{GiniDPI}_i = \alpha + \beta \frac{Ymd\text{FI}_i}{Ymn\text{FI}_i} + u_i \tag{4.1}$$

The dependent variable – the reduction in income inequality assessed by the difference between a country's Gini indices on factor income (GiniFI) and disposable income (GiniDPI) – accounts for the extent of redistribution. The independent variable – describing the political pressure as discussed in the previous section – that is, how much poorer-than-average the median voter is – is the median-to-mean factor income ratio (*Ymd*FI/*Ymn*FI), ranging between zero and one and signalling less inequality as its value goes up.[7]

The regression is meant to test the reliability of the postulated theoretical relationship between the income level of the median voter (relative to the mean income) and the extent of redistribution. The significant increase appearing in the average FI Gini coefficient in the mid-1990s *vis-à-vis* that for the mid-1980s, by reinforcing the findings which emerged by looking at the *Ymd/Ymn* ratios, extends to the whole income distribution the assessment of an increase in income inequality effected by the operation of market forces from the mid-1980s to the mid-1990s. To prove that the preference of a median voter hit by a decrease in his factor income level determines a wider redistribution through tax-and-transfers, one would expect a negative relationship linking the dependent to the independent variable: a decrease in the median-to-mean factor income ratio is associated to an increase in redistribution. The more distant is the income level of the median voter from the mean income, the wider the expected difference between *ex ante* (FI) and *ex post* (DPI) Gini coefficients, as redistribution should provoke a fall in the DPI Gini coefficient.

Figure 4.2 shows the scattered diagram where the abatement of the Gini coefficient from FI to DPI is on the vertical axis and the median-to-mean factor income ratio is on the horizontal axis. Although no neat relationship emerges from the whole set of observations, and a first glance observation may suggest a very mild positive relationship between the two variables, one can also appreciate four rather blurred groupings, with a somewhat similar and negatively sloping shape, which

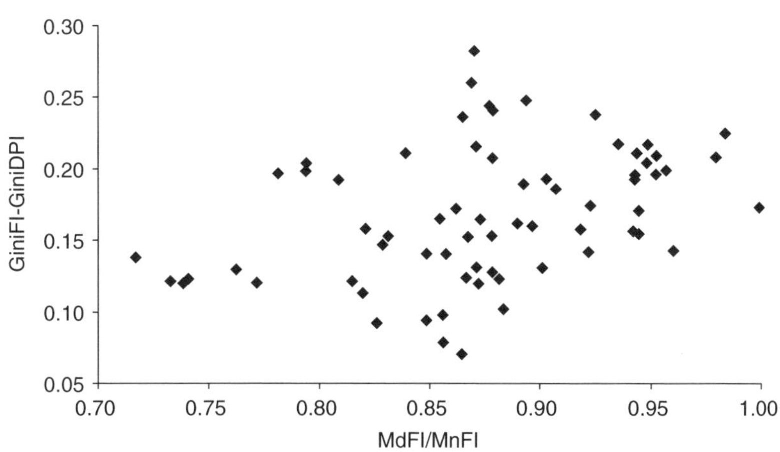

Figure 4.2 Median voter scatter diagram.

are placed in parallel to each other along the main diagonal. This finding could be traced back to the influence of different moral values and psychological attitudes of society at large in different clusters of countries. Since preferences for public goods and social insurance may sharply diverge from preferences on private goods, the range of social protection institutions and the degree of redistribution involved may be large. Market economies at the same technological level and with the same consumption model differ as for the degree of desired risk insurance. To capture this cross-country heterogeneity in the society's choice for redistribution, three dummy variables were included in the model to allow for differences across countries as for redistributive institutions.

The new specification of the regression model is therefore modified as indicated in equation (4.2):

$$\mathrm{GiniFI}_i - \mathrm{GiniDPI}_i = \alpha + \beta \frac{Ymd\mathrm{FI}_i}{Ymn\mathrm{FI}_i} + d1_i + d2_i + d3_i + u_i, \qquad (4.2)$$

where $d1$, $d2$ and $d3$ indicate the dummies added to allow for structural differences in preferences for clusters of countries characterised by different models of Welfare State. The first dummy ($d1$) is meant to single out the peculiarities of the social-democrat model in Scandinavian countries (Denmark, Finland, Norway and Sweden) and is expected to show a positive sign, so to reflect that this is the welfare state which is reputed the most generous in Europe. The other dummies cover respectively ($d2$) Catholic Mediterranean countries (France, Italy and Spain) and ($d3$) liberal Anglo-Saxon countries (Australia, Canada, Ireland, the United Kingdom and the United States). As they are all characterised by a narrower Welfare State,[8] both dummies $d2$ and $d3$ are expected to show a negative sign. The limited extent of redistribution in Mediterranean and Anglo-Saxon countries might be traced back, along with other factors, to the segmentation by which in both clusters of countries the labour market is characterised. In other words, due to the median voter's relatively higher probability of remaining an insider *vis-à-vis* the other two clusters of countries, the political pressure in favour of redistribution may be weaker. The remaining countries (Belgium, Germany, Luxembourg and the Netherlands), taken as reference countries, belong to the group of the so-called corporatist Continental Europe countries, characterised by a Welfare State with a medium redistributive impact.

Table 4.1 presents the results of the two regression models. While the first model connecting income inequality to redistribution finds a positive relation, but gives unsatisfactory results as to the quality of estimates, the second model identifies a rather strong negative relation, supported by considerably higher significance levels and explanatory power. The regression results therefore show that the median voter hypothesis is consistent with the empirical evidence: after having controlled for different institutional features characterising the four clusters of countries, all the parameters show the expected sign and are highly significant. The relevant Chi-square critical values state that for both tests – the Jarque–Bera/Salmon–Kiefer test for errors being normally distributed and the

Table 4.1 Heterogeneity across clusters of countries

		Model 1 *(all countries)*	*Model 2* *(all countries)*	*Subset 1* *(without US)*	*Subset 2* *(Europeans only)*	*Subset 3* *(no US, UK and Ie)*
α		−0.029	0.396	0.569	0.522	0.525
	t	(−0.498)	(4.152)	(5.496)	(4.587)	(3.874)
β		0.227	−0.228	−0.417	−0.366	−0.369
	t	(3.548)	(−2.179)	(−3.679)	(−2.932)	(−2.482)
$d1$ (Nw Sw Fi Dk)		—	0.027	0.032	0.030	0.030
	t	—	(2.129)	(2.617)	(2.549)	(2.414)
$d2$ (Fr It Es)		—	−0.092	−0.103	−0.100	−0.100
	t	—	(−5.692)	(−6.619)	(−6.396)	(−5.920)
$d3$ (Ie Uk As Cn Us)		—	−0.056	−0.058	−0.037	−0.066
	t	—	(−4.091)	(−4.447)	(−2.087)	(−4.560)
Adj. R^2		0.072	0.481	0.537	0.556	0.568
F		6.24	16.50	19.00	16.35	18.12
n. obs.		67	67	62	50	53
Jarque–Bera/Salmon–Kiefer		0.527	1.746	4.741	2.554	3.056
Breusch–Pagan		1.034	7.737	5.405	8.925	7.930

Breusch–Pagan test for homoskedasticity – the null hypotheses can be accepted at a very satisfactory significance level, also after the White's correction for potential heteroskedasticity.

One may observe that regressions linking such variables like income inequality and redistribution are exposed to the problem of reverse causation. The direction of causality may be ambiguous: is it a lower median-to-mean ratio to determine an increase in redistribution (the causality link implied by our estimates), or is it the variation in redistribution to determine the change in the median voter's income position? Data availability prevents the specification of the model with appropriate time lags, so to exclude reverse causation. However, the negative sign obtained by the correlation mitigates the relevance of this issue. In fact, were the direction of causality from redistribution to the median voter's relative income position one would expect a *positive* relationship – that is, more redistribution implying a higher median-to-mean factor income ratio – which is not supported by the regression results (see Table 4.1, Model 1). Moreover, in our model specification, the inequality index referred to the political mechanism is measured by the FI data, while redistribution regards the recovery in the DPI inequality with respect to FI. Hence, the possibility of a positive relationship according to a reverse causation is ruled out on theoretical grounds. In fact, it would amount to think that the independent variable – indicating income inequality *after* the tax-and-transfers reshuffling – positively feeds-back on a dependent variable represented by the income inequality *before* the tax-and-transfers reshuffling, which is clearly preposterous.

Therefore, the thesis put forward at the end of the previous section – that is, the larger the income inequality conditions experienced by the metaphorical agent expressed by the median-to-mean ratio, the larger the need for risk insurance, the larger the extent of redistribution obtained by the majority voting political mechanism – is confirmed, but at the cluster level. The regression results for the four clusters of countries support the hypothesis – conveyed by the own specific intercept of each cluster – that the negative relationship between the median voter's relative income position and redistribution is sensitive to the particular inequality aversion which is peculiar for each group. In all clusters, a change of the median-to-mean FI ratio brings about a redistributive reaction of the same size, estimated by the common β coefficient (-0.228), but with an inverse relationship – located at a different height in the plan – for each group of countries.

It is worth noting that in Model 2 the sensitivity analysis signals that the median voter model does not perform well within the group of the Anglo-Saxon countries. We have singled out heterogeneous behaviour by excluding some of these countries in the regression analysis, finding that regression results improve by doing so. In fact, all indicators improve by excluding the United States (see subset 1), where it does not seem that the median voter is particularly successful in obtaining more redistribution as his or her relative income level deteriorates. In the United States, labour market institutions let factor income inequality reach very high levels (due to the skill-premium accruing to the high-skills and to the impact of deregulation in terms of declining wage levels for the low-skills) and welfare institutions keep at low level unemployment and social protection benefits in order to prevent moral hazard behaviour in the market.[9]

Another slight improvement is obtained either by the additional exclusion of Canada and Australia (subset 2) or by excluding Ireland and the United Kingdom in addition to the United States (subset 3). All in all, one may conclude that the median voter hypothesis is proven to a stronger extent when the sample is limited to European countries, with Ireland and the United Kingdom playing an intermediate role.

4.4 The determinants of wage inequality

The recent acceleration in economic integration between developing and advanced economies is often taken as a major cause of the widening of wage inequality experienced by many OECD countries. Their increasing vulnerability to international markets due to the expanding trade with LDCs is usually alleged to impact on wage inequality through two main channels: (i) a declining demand for low-skill workers, resulting in a fall of relative prices of low-skill intensity sectors *vis-à-vis* high-skill intensity sectors; (ii) trade diversion penalising employment and wage levels of low-skill labour intensive productions, resulting in a rise in the high-skill/low-skill ratio sectors. Yet, these findings have occurred only in some productions (Acemoglu, 2002; Krugman, 1994, p. 36). The reason is that the impact of globalisation consists of many interwoven effects and the overall outcome in terms of lower employment and earnings differentiates across sectors. However, a robust correlation has been found between the advanced countries' degree of openness and the size of their social programmes aimed at shielding the weakest social groups (Rodrik, 1998). Therefore, in the regressions on wage dispersion performed in the next section, globalisation will be taken into account through the risk insurance provided by welfare institutions. The decline in both jobs and earnings, that intensified competition caused in the bottom deciles of the OECD countries' wage distribution, has been counteracted by redistribution through the tax-and-transfers system.

The literature lists the following determinants of wage inequality in OECD countries: technical change, the unions' bargaining power, and labour market regulatory institutions – such as employment protection legislation (EPL), minimum wage, labour standards. The so-called Krugman hypothesis (Krugman, 1994) offers an institution-based explanation for a much wider wage dispersion in the United States compared to Europe, where labour market institutions protect the wages of low-skill workers so determining a much lower wage and factor income inequality, but also a much higher unemployment rates and lower employment and participation rates. Acemoglu (2002, 2003) observes that wage inequality is mainly explained by skill-biased technical change (SBTC) in the United States, while the wage and employment structure has to be traced back to the interaction between technological choices and labour market regulation in Europe. Card and DiNardo (2002) claim that in many OECD countries, including the United States, institutions leading to wage compression such as minimum wage are responsible for wage inequality to a major extent than the skill-biased technical change. In the same research strand, Devroye and Freeman (2001) consider differences in the wage-setting system as the main cause of wage dispersion in the United States and wage compression in Europe. In a somewhat different vein, Piketty and Saez (2002) have both put forward the view that higher wage inequality might be traced back to a change in the value-system which took place in the last decade in some OECD countries (first of all, in the United States), whereby the prevailing social norms accept very high salaries to be paid to top job positions. In this chapter, we take for granted that in an imperfect competition labour market firms introduce technical change to generate profits, which are reduced by rents accruing to workers according to the mechanisms described in the literature, such as the insider-outsider and the efficiency-wage models.[10]

Figure 4.3(a) and (b) describe a comparative static exercise with variations in labour demand and supply occurring in a segmented labour market. Two regimes of wage and employment determination for high-skill and low-skill-workers respectively are envisaged, each one corresponding to an extreme case, that is whether SBTC or labour market institutions in turn prevail. In the first regime (Figure 4.3(a)), the labour market equilibrium is straightforwardly ruled by the introduction of technical change. Let us illustrate how the gap between high-skill (H) and low-skill (L) workers, in terms of both wage and employment levels, stems from the productivity gap created by SBTC between the two groups of workers (through the factor-augmenting technological terms A_{H} and A_{L}, with H and L indicating the high-skill and the low-skill, respectively). Consider a production function with constant elasticity of substitution (CES):

$$Y(t) = [(A_{\mathrm{L}}(t)\mathrm{L}(t))^{\rho} + (A_{\mathrm{H}}(t)\mathrm{H}(t))^{\rho}]^{1/\rho}$$

and its implicit relative demand function, expressing the skill premium:[11]

$$\frac{w_{\mathrm{H}}}{w_{\mathrm{L}}} = \frac{A_{\mathrm{H}}/A_{\mathrm{L}}}{(\mathrm{H}/\mathrm{L})^{-(1-\rho)}} = \frac{(A_{\mathrm{H}}/A_{\mathrm{L}})^{(\sigma-1)}}{(\mathrm{H}/\mathrm{L})^{-1/\sigma}}$$

Then assume that a technological innovation increases profit opportunities in the high-skill labour market, so that the increase in supply of highly educated workers (the outwards shift in the $N_{\mathrm{H}}^{\mathrm{S}}$ curve in the left graph of Figure 4.3(a) is more than matched by a more rapidly increasing labour demand oriented towards a skill-biased technical change (the shift in the $N_{\mathrm{H}}^{\mathrm{D}}$ in the right graph). Under the condition of an elasticity of substitution $\sigma > 1$,[12] an increase in the $A_{\mathrm{H}}/A_{\mathrm{L}}$ ratio higher than in the H/L ratio rises the wage rate for the more educated and more productive high-skill workers more than the wage rate for the low-skill workers. The consequent rise in the skill premium ($w_{\mathrm{H}}/w_{\mathrm{L}}$) is the augmenting effect of skill-biased technical change on wage inequality. Provided that high-skill and low-skill workers are gross substitutes, the labour force is fully employed in both segments of the labour market, but the real wage is higher in the high-skill (w_{H}) and lower in the low-skill (w_{L}) labour market, with respect to the market-clearing

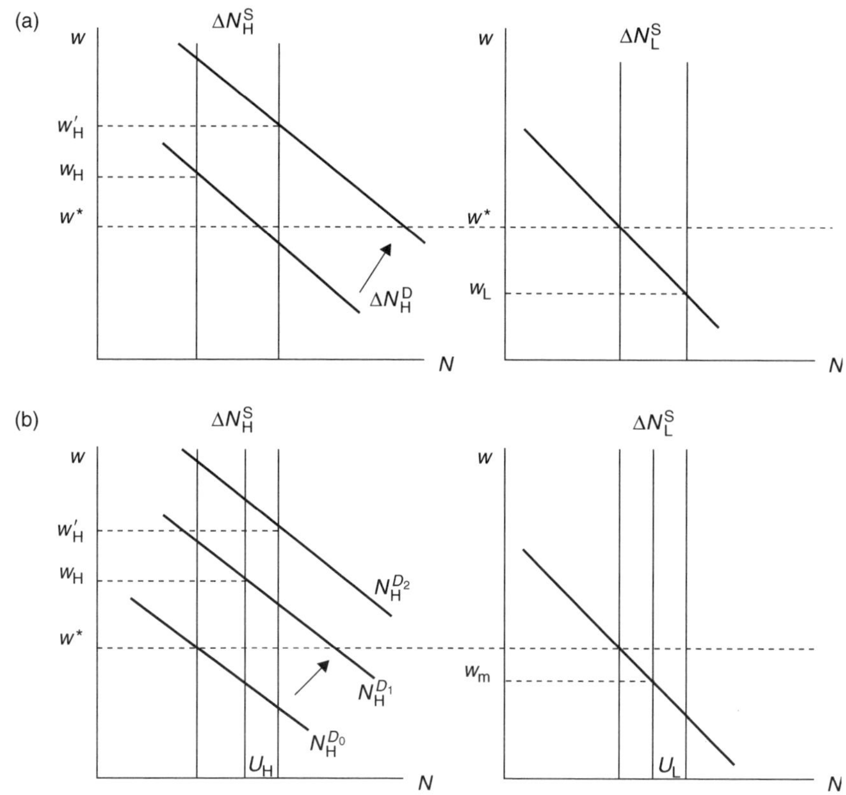

Figure 4.3 High-skill and low-skill labour markets.

level set at the wage (w^*), which we may regard as the 'natural' unemployment rate. The additional hypothesis could also be introduced whereby the acceleration in the technical change produces an 'erosion effect' on the productivity, and thus on the wage level, of the low-skill, so that the wage dispersion widens at the bottom of the distribution too (Galor and Mahov, 2000).

In the second regime (Figure 4.3(b)), labour market institutions count more, although in different combination with technical choices. Unemployment is always present in the low-skills labour market, as the higher reservation wage determined by the minimum wage (w_m) keeps the wage rigid at a level higher than the equilibrium wage, but still below the high-skills market-clearing wage. However, the wage and employment levels for each group differ depending on two alternative assumptions. When labour market institutions combine with SBTC, the more regulated is the labour market, the more firms tend to create different jobs for high-skill and low-skill workers, so that segregation equilibria substitute for pooling equilibria (Acemoglu, 1999; Bénabou, 2004). Hence, in the high-skill market, labour demand $N_H^{D_2}$ determines full employment equilibrium at the highest wage rate (w'_H), but labour demand for low-skills is stuck (the whole additional labour supply remains unemployed). In the absence of SBTC, labour market regulation endows the unions with a bargaining power in the market for high-skill workers, so that at the labour demand $N_H^{D_1}$, the real wage rate (w_H) is higher than the market-clearing level. However, the creation of more jobs is sluggish.

Suppose now the productivity level of low-skill workers be too low compared to the wage rate (w'_L) imposed by minimum wage, labour standards as an obstacle to improve the workers' effort, and very high firing costs due to EPL. Under these conditions, at the rigid wage rate (w'_L) for the low-skills, firms are forced to adopt complementary technologies based on the joint-utilisation of the high-skills and low-skills, in order to raise productivity in the workplace. The unwelcome effect is that the creation of new jobs slows down. Since firms refrain from absorbing low productivity workers, the Beveridge curve shifts rightward and vacancies diminish also for the low-skills. Hence, labour demand is unable to match labour supply and unemployment is created in both the high-skills' (U_H) and low-skills' (U_L) segments of the labour market. Empirical evidence seems to indicate that the first regime prevails not only in the United States but also in the Anglo-Saxon and Scandinavian countries, whereas the latter applies to Continental and Mediterranean European Union (EU) countries.

We put forward the hypothesis that the 'social norm' of redistribution can have a role not only by determining the disposable income distribution, but also by directly influencing the evolution of the market wage dispersion. In fact, the redistribution determined by the society's preference for risk insurance might feed-back on wage inequality, as the reshuffling operated by the tax-and-transfers system enters into the negotiation of labour contracts. Let us describe how the society's preference for redistribution can affect the interplay between technical change and labour market regulation and thus influence wage inequality.

A low labour market regulation is more favourable to the introduction of the skill-biased technical change, in that it implies an organisational move towards a more efficient combination between physical and human capital with a higher percentage of high-skill workers in the high-tech sectors. In presence of a high labour market regulation, firms are instead more likely to refrain from the adoption of skill-biased technical change and use technologies based on the complementarity between high-skill and low-skill workers, in order to improve these latter lower productivity level and equalise their rigid wage rate.[13] In the former case of SBTC, the rise in the skill premium favoured by a more flexible labour market determines an increase in the wage inequality. Depending on the degree of redistribution preferred by society, this increase is counterbalanced by a disposable income inequality lower than wage inequality determined by the labour market. In the latter case of absence of SBTC, the wage compression determined by labour market regulation will probably translate a low wage inequality in an even lower disposable income inequality, again depending on the degree of redistribution.

In turn, the correction of the wage dispersion determined by technical change brought about by the redistributive effect of welfare institutions may impinge on the unions' bargaining power on the division of rents. In modelling the interplay between the state and the market one should not forget that a relevant part of redistribution comes from social protection against unemployment spells. The disposable income distribution resulting from redistribution can then modify the unions' behaviour. A preference for high redistribution is likely to ease the degree of regulation of the labour market, improving the speed of adjustment over the cycle as to the price and the quantity of the employed labour force. In particular, redistribution stemming from social protection policies (e.g. unemployment benefits) may change incentives behind the labour supply schedule and induce rational players to modify their strategies in the market. A substitution of lower EPL with higher unemployment benefits might facilitate the switch from the second to the first regime of technical change sketched in Figure 4.3. To the extent that the leisure/work choice changes, and previously unemployed workers belonging to the low-skill group are employed, the labour supply schedule moves downward. Under high redistribution a decline in the uncertainty perceived by the *outsiders* fosters an increase in the propensity to risk which augments their labour supply allowing the shift from the second to the first regime.[14] The job search costs are positively affected and the matching of vacancies with the unemployed workers is more effective. After the increase in the employment rate of the low-skills, the wage compression is reduced and long-term unemployment tends to fall.

Overall, a less rigid labour market tends to increase a high (low) wage inequality determined by a 'skill-biased' (a 'complementary') technological regime, and a lower disposable income dispersion will finally result depending on the extent of redistribution provided by welfare institutions. Furthermore, when workers expect a high redistribution correcting for a high wage inequality and re-equilibrate the disposable income distribution, profit incentives for the skill-biased technical change more easily rise. However, this latter efficiency-enhancing effect of a less regulated labour market cannot be taken for granted. It should not be overlooked that the larger the size of the public system of social protection, the larger the tax-and-transfers income reshuffling, the wider will be the pervasiveness of tax distortions. Since the substitution effect of marginal rate of taxation may easily become higher than the income effect, the labour supply curve in Figure 4.3(b) may then shift backwards or may even not move at all, because too high an effective marginal tax rate in the lower end of the income distribution discourages the poor and the very low-skilled to enter the job market (the so-called 'poverty trap').[15]

Section 4.5 investigates the different interactions across OECD countries that the degree of labour market regulation entertains with 'skill-biased' or 'complementary' technologies and with heterogeneous welfare systems, the three factors all together impinging on the trend of wage inequality.

4.5 An econometric estimate of wage inequality in OECD countries

This section presents some econometric estimates of wage inequality, according to the models reported in Table 4.3. The heuristic model described so far indicates three main determinants of: (i) labour market regulations; (ii) the 'social norm' of redistribution, and (iii) the skill-biased or skill-neutral technology chosen by firms. Let us briefly discuss the choice of the variables representing these three determinants, to be included in the wage inequality equation.

(i) The wage dispersion produced by market forces is influenced by several factors. First, a strong bargaining power of the unions and a high union density have fostered wage compression as a direct effect. However, heterogeneity counts much. On the one hand, collective bargaining has a different influence on wage dispersion across the EU labour markets because wage bargaining at the firm and sectoral levels is not negligible in some countries. On the other hand, union density seems especially important in the United States, where the fall in union membership is alleged to be a major determinant in the widening of the skill premium. Second, job protection legislation by increasing the firms' firing and hiring costs, exerts an indirect effect on wage dispersion and negatively impacts on the employment and participation rates. In fact, the reservation wage is too high, so that hiring younger workers (as well as the re-entering into work by the laid-off) slows down, and the unemployed labour force downward pressure on the nominal wage rate is lacking. Third, a minimum wage reduces the wage spread by establishing a floor. In Europe, the minimum wage is usually established by collective contracts, as a legal level exists only in France, the Netherlands and Belgium. On the contrary, the minimum wage threshold exists in the United States, but it is too low to represent a limit to the competitive supply and demand determination of the equilibrium wage in the 'unskilled' labour market. While the minimum wage is usually deemed responsible for high reservation wages reducing the labour supply, empirical evidence from Scandinavian countries show that when complementarities are in place – such as, high levels of both coverage of collective wage contracts and union density – work incentives are not affected.[16]

Therefore, a mixed evidence is offered on how and to what extent labour market regulations (union density, collective bargaining, the enforcement of a minimum wage and employment protection legislation) impact on wage dispersion. The identification of a variable able to describe these effects in quantitative terms, and at the same time encompassing the different impacts of these various determinants across the four clusters of countries, is hard to find. However, the phenomenon one would like to address is wage compression, as this seems to be the most observed outcome of labour market regulations.

In the absence of a proper measurement of the phenomenon which is actually under analysis, a proxy variable has to be found. Three such proxy variables – the employment rate (E/P), the employment protection legislation (EPL) and the 10/50 percentile ratio on wages (ln 10/50) – have been tested to give account of the effects of labour market regulation in OECD countries, for which direct and quantified observations are unavailable. Table 4.2 compares their association to the measurement of wage inequality. As expected, wage inequality is found directly related to the employment rate (E/P) and inversely related to both the employment protection legislation (EPL) as well as to the wages 10/50 percentile ratio (ln 10/50),

Table 4.2 Proxies for wage compression

		E/P	*EPL*	*ln 10/50*
α		−1.103	0.312	0.391
	t	(−5.895)	(30.523)	(27.794)
β		0.327	−0.051	−0.057
	t	(7.292)	(−4.460)	(−10.072)
F		53.18	17.98	97.61
R^2		0.442	0.212	0.594
JB/SK		2.660	4.352	3.309
BP		2.506	4.862	0.073
N. obs.		67	64	67

and is explained by each of them to differing extents. The 10/50 percentile ratio was finally chosen as a proxy of wage compression deriving from labour market regulation for the following reasons: (i) the data source – LIS database – and the information it conveys was deemed best as to the coherence with the information available for the dependent variable, and (ii) it also favourably compared with the other possible substitutes, especially when adding the remaining variables.[17]

(ii) Societies also differ for their collective preferences about the degree of income inequality they regard as tolerable, that is for their respective preference for risk insurance. The income distribution resulting from the operating of market forces is then reshuffled not only by the correction of income inequality resulting from the labour force under-utilisation through unemployment benefits, but to a larger extent by the correction of heterogeneous well-being opportunities across individuals stemming from microeconomic failures (adverse selection, moral hazard, myopic behaviour, etc.) through the functioning of social protection institutions. A society's peculiar 'social norm' of redistribution is represented by the same indicator earlier employed in the median voter regression: the difference between the Gini FI minus Gini DPI, which measures the extent of redistribution through the tax-and-transfers system (unemployment benefits and social protection institutions, such as compulsory health insurance, public pensions, educational finance, etc.).

(iii) To investigate the role of skills in the skilled-unskilled labour market divide, a proxy measure of the 'skill premium', possibly induced by a skill-biased technical change, has been introduced by referring to an indicator of university educational attainment for each country and year.[18]

Table 4.3 shows the regression results obtained by estimating the following equation:

$$\text{Giniwages} = \alpha + \beta \ln(10/50) + \gamma(\text{GiniFI} - \text{GiniDPI}) + \delta \text{Edu}_{t-2} + d4 + \lambda(d4 \ln(10/50)) + u,$$

under four definitions which differ according to whether the skill premium (Model 2 and 4) and the dummy and drift variables (Model 3 and 4) are included.

Table 4.3 Regression results for wages inequality, redistribution and education

		Model 1	*Model 2*	*Model 3*	*Model 4*
α		0.4453	0.3747	0.4679	0.4249
	t	(15.805)	(12.314)	(16.553)	(16.312)
β		−0.0627	−0.0558	−0.0821	−0.0768
	t	(−10.096)	(−8.695)	(−11.277)	(−12.174)
γ		−0.2527	−0.2384	−0.1373	−0.1515
	t	(−2.353)	(−2.653)	(−1.931)	(−2.576)
δ		—	0.00405	—	0.00282
	t	—	(5.192)	—	(4.436)
$d4(d1+d3)$		—	—	−0.1092	−0.09988
	t	—	—	(−4.491)	(−4.991)
λ		—	—	0.0613	0.05326
	t	—	—	(6.878)	(6.931)
F		55.07	61.64	61.84	68.64
R^2		0.621	0.734	0.787	0.837
JB/SK		3.634	1.346	0.872	3.772
BP		0.066	7.682	9.309	10.374
N. obs.		67	67	67	67

At first, all observations have been pooled together irrespective of time and space, so as to find out a general relationship linking the dependent with the independent variables. Model 1 estimates the regression equation in its shortest version, which takes into account the labour market regulation and the redistributive social norm only and excludes the university education variable.

Wage compression – indicated by the 10/50 percentile ratio on the wages distribution – plus income redistribution – represented by the difference between the Gini coefficient calculated on factor and disposable income distributions – together explain a substantial part of the variability of wage inequality. Both variables show a negative sign to give account of a negative relation between wage compression and wage inequality as well as between income redistribution and wage inequality.

A better result is obtained in Model 2, by adding the proxy of the skill premium, the university educational level.[19] University education shows a positive sign, as expected, although its overall effect is far from impressive.

Our econometric investigation is completed by testing for heterogeneity across OECD countries, similarly to the approach followed in Section 4.2.

Since data show the highest levels of wage inequality in Scandinavian and Anglo-Saxon countries, a dummy ($d4$) was introduced to represent the aggregation of these two clusters of countries formerly indicated by $d1$ and $d3$, respectively. A drift variable (λ) was also added to remark the different effect wage compression may have had on these countries.

Model 3 estimates the constant and the wage compression variable as in Model 1 by distinguishing between two clusters composed of Continental and Mediterranean countries and Scandinavian and Anglo-Saxon countries, respectively.

Model 4 includes all three variables, as in Model 2, and distinguishes again between the two clusters.

In Table 4.3, column 3 and 4 show the effect of singling out these two clusters of countries. A substantial improvement follows in the first case (compare column 1 and 3) except for the redistribution coefficient (γ) showing a weak significance level. This is easily explained by the opposite 'social norm' of redistribution of these two clusters of countries, pointing to high redistribution in Scandinavian and low redistribution in Anglo-Saxon countries. However, this weakness is corrected in Model 4, where all variables are included and the significance level of the redistribution coefficient (γ) becomes satisfactory. Presumably, the introduction of education plays a role in strengthening the significativity of the parameter γ.

The econometric results with the dummy variable for the Scandinavian and the Anglo-Saxon countries are a clue that a divide might have opened between these countries and the Continental and Mediterranean countries. The relaxation of labour market regulation has recently been implemented in Scandinavian countries, while leaving unchanged the highly redistributive social protection institutions.[20] The active labour policies have improved the functioning of the labour market, thus allowing the introduction of skill-biased technical change. This positive evolution may still take place in Continental Europe, but is less likely to happen in Mediterranean Europe, where a lower degree of redistribution and weaker welfare institutions may prevent the sudden change in the level of risk insurance.

4.6 Concluding remarks

This chapter has presented a 'political economy' explanation for the increase in redistribution experienced from the 1980s to the 1990s by the OECD countries, and has shown how redistribution interacts with technology and labour market institutions in determining wage inequality. The intuition was that the amount of 'risk insurance' provided by welfare institutions through redistribution, by allowing factor income inequality to be translated into a less unequal disposable income distribution, may feedback on the labour market negotiations and thus on wage dispersion. Our econometric analysis of the political mechanism of majority voting suggests that redistribution, by lowering disposable income inequality, provides risk insurance against factor income inequality. In testing the 'risk insurance' rationale for the median voter's behaviour, different outcomes have resulted across four clusters of OECD countries following a fall in the median-to-mean factor income ratio. This heterogeneity was traced back to the political process selecting a high or a low degree of redistribution, depending on the value-system prevailing in each group of countries as expressed in the polls by the metaphorical agent identified as the median voter.

Our econometric estimates have shown that the very same heterogeneity also applies to wage inequality. We propose a possible interpretation of the regressions explaining the impact of different redistributive institutions on the interaction between labour market regulation and technological opportunities of the firms across four clusters of countries.

Anglo-Saxon countries and Mediterranean countries share a low degree of redistribution. Yet, these groups of countries differ as for the impact of their preference for 'risk insurance' on wage dispersion. In the Anglo-Saxon countries, technical change (SBTC) prevailing on regulation in the labour market determines a high wage inequality. A weak preference for 'risk insurance' prevents redistribution to substantially shrink inequality going from factor to disposable income, thus causing a lack of compensation for high wage inequality determined by the skill premium. In Mediterranean EU countries, the need to make the low-skill workers' productivity compatible with a rigid wage due to labour market regulation asks for complementary technologies. Due to a weak preference for 'risk insurance', the redistributive impact of welfare institutions is negligible, the low wage inequality and the unemployment rate stemming from a regulated labour market correspond to a high disposable income inequality.

Continental countries and Scandinavian countries share a high degree of redistribution. Again, these groups of countries differ as for the impact on wage dispersion of the preference for 'risk insurance'. In Continental EU countries, high labour market regulation together with firms sticking to traditional technologies cause high unemployment, which is counteracted by a high preference for 'risk insurance'. A large redistribution, by correcting the significant factor income inequality caused by high unemployment, allows the low wage inequality to find confirmation in a low disposable income inequality, but no relief for low employment and participation rates exists. In Scandinavian countries, a high preference for 'risk insurance' combines with a reduction in the universality of labour market regulation allowing the introduction of SBTC. Hence, a weak preference for a large redistribution seems to have an efficiency-enhancing effect, whereby the risk insurance provided by the Welfare State makes the increase in wage inequality caused by skill-biased technical change not only socially sustainable but also employment-enabling.

Acknowledgements

Financial support from the University of Siena Research Programme (PAR 2002) is gratefully acknowledged. Previous versions of this paper were presented at the XVI Workshop on 'Inequality and Economic Integration' (Certosa di Pontignano, 30 June–6 July 2003), at the Department of Economics, University of Perugia (27 April 2004), at a CHILD International Workshop (Garda, 14–16 May 2004) and at the EAEPE Annual Conference 2004 (Rethymnon, 28–31 October 2004). We thank all participants whose comments and questions this final version of the paper has benefited. The usual disclaimers apply.

Notes

1 This comprehensive approach, whereby the wage rate is negotiated within the re-organization of the system of welfare benefits, has been reported for Netherlands in Nickell and Van Ours (2000).

2 The median voter hypothesis builds upon the median voter model (Downs, 1957; Hotelling, 1929) and explains income redistribution as a consequence of the median voter decisiveness on preferences channelled by the political process through majority voting. The theoretical background is based on the analogy between voters' sovereignty on the political market for public goods and consumer sovereignty on private markets for private goods. Under majority voting procedure – if preferences can be represented along a single dimension corresponding to the issue at stake, two options are available, and vote participation is substantial – the median voter is decisive. The political process will meet the median voter's demand so that the analysis needs focus on his preferences only, rather than on preference aggregation.

3 The FI data for Belgium, France, Italy and Spain are net of taxes and contributions. While comparison between the two observations (mid-1980s and mid-1990s) related to the same country is not affected, comparisons with other countries overestimate the change in distribution which occurs in the *Ymd/Ymn* DPI *vis-à-vis* the *Ymd/Ymn* FI.

4 The self-interested behaviour of the median voter was proposed by Milanovic (2000) through econometric tests demonstrating that the middle quintiles secure the 'lion's share' of redistribution.

5 We endorse the view that the median voter 'should (. . .) be taken more as a metaphor representing the aggregation of voter's preferences than as a direct explanation of political decisions' (Atkinson, 1999a, p. 117).

6 This view is also compatible with the sympathetic concern for low income individuals, in the forward-looking expectation that the social welfare is improved by a less unequal distribution. Under this heading, two others-regarding views are worth mentioning. The view of redistribution as a 'public good' (Hochman and Rodgers, 1969), where the attitude towards redistribution in favour of the very low income is explained by the interdependency among utility functions, and the conception of redistribution as a 'local public good' (Pauly, 1973), where redistribution in lower-tier governments is traced back to a mixture of both the selfish consciousness of the negative social consequences of deprivation and a sense of compassion towards the poor.

7 Note that the indicator for the median voter's preference for redistribution – the median-to-mean income ratio – is an indicator of income inequality just as the Gini coefficient. However, a variation in the *Ymd/Ymn* ratio is regressed onto the difference between the Gini FI and DPI indicators of income inequality, so preventing spurious correlations.

8 The general reference for different Welfare State models existing in different socio-economic environments and reflecting different institutional characters as well as different preferences about the mix of private and public goods is Esping-Andersen (1999). Many studies considering different clusters of Welfare State systems in Europe, place France in the Continental group of countries. Empirical evidence casts doubts on this affiliation, by showing a surprising homogeneity among the labour market institutions of France, Italy, Spain, Portugal and Greece. These countries, usually gathered under the 'Mediterranean' heading, are characterised by a high employment protection legislation and a low percentage of individuals under social benefits (see Boeri *et al.*, 2001). This striking inverse correlation between the two main forms of labour market regulation, compared to the more mixed evidence of other European countries, suggests that the inclusion of France in the Mediterranean group is the most sensible choice. Moreover, the Eurostat Social Protection Database presents very close low values of social benefits and employment rates for Italy, Spain, Greece and France.

9 Two reasons have been put forward to explain why the preference for redistribution weakens despite the median voter becomes poorer. First, a small size of the public sector is considered a necessary condition for the market forces to develop and support a fair competition in the social processes (see Alesina *et al.*, 2001). Since the value-system is geared towards the view that effort and hard work are the main causes of economic success, the national community is devoted to the principle of 'fairness as

just reward' which raises the incentive costs of high taxation (see Alesina and Angeletos, 2003). Second, a high and positive correlation between education and earnings induces many voters to believe that social mobility will soon allow them to scale up in the income ladder from a lower to a higher percentile (see the 'prospect of upward mobility hypothesis' by Bénabou and Ok, 2001). The perception of a high probability to switch from being net beneficiaries to net payers in the tax-and-transfers system exposes the individuals in the middle quintile to the ideological influence of the very rich. Hence, this social group becomes pivotal in the polls, so that majority voting turns to voting against redistributive programmes (see Bénabou, 2000). However, rolling-back the Welfare State also implies that income inequality translates in inequality of *well-being*; this self-aggravating mechanism is the main cause of segregation in the form of huge differences in living conditions, both across ethnic groups belonging to the same area and in terms of sharp divides across jurisdictions (see Alesina and Glaeser, 2004, ch. 7).

10 Institutions create a *rent* in excess of the wage rate corresponding to the worker's 'outside option' (what the worker earns outside in an alternative employment relationship that he would immediately find in the perfect competition labour market).

11 Where $\rho \leq 1$, the skill premium depends on A_H and A_L and on the elasticity of substitution between the high-skills (H) and the low-skills (L) is $\sigma \equiv 1/(1-\rho)$ (see Acemoglou, 2002).

12 This hypothesis finds confirmation in empirical tests, which agree on an average value across OECD countries of 1.4.

13 This outcome is not warranted. The larger are educational disparities across workers, the more is likely that the complementary technologies pooling high-skill and low-skill workers will be abandoned and a separating equilibrium with technologies for the high-skills and segregation for the low-skills emerges. See Bénabou (2004).

14 'People may be willing to take risks, to retrain, and to change jobs in a society in which there is adequate social protection. Moreover, contributory unemployment insurance acts as a positive incentive for people to enter labour force. The welfare state is a system of checks and balances, not just payment checks' (Atkinson, 1999b, p. 75).

15 See Bourguignon (2001, pp. 35–44).

16 See Nickell *et al.* (2001).

17 Blau and Kahn (1996) have found that the 90/50 percentile ratios are similar across countries, while the 10/50 largely diverge between United States *vis-à-vis* the European countries. These wide differences across countries *within* the wage distribution suggest that the use of the 10/50 decile in our wage inequality equation doesn't suffer from serial correlation problems.

18 Data are supplied by De la Fuente and Domenech (2002, Table A1).

19 Data for university education have been lagged by two periods, so as to take also into account those who had obtained a university degree some 10–15 years earlier.

20 Sweden and Finland, in particular, reacted to the increasing macroeconomic instability of the 1990s by allowing for a wider dispersion in the wage distribution, just because these countries' *ex post* income redistribution by tax-and-transfers is substantial. The strategy was to gear active labour policies to the pursuit of a stronger linkage of the reservation wage to the ability of the unemployed (so to allow firms to tackle the adverse selection problem of effort) and to bridge the gap between insiders and outsiders by linking eligibility for unemployment benefits to previous employment condition, thus avoiding that high levels of the replacement rate could act as a too high 'outside option', pulling up the reservation wage.

References

Acemoglu, D. (1999), 'Changes in Unemployment and Wage Inequality: An Alternative Theory and Some Evidence', *American Economic Review*, 89: 1259–1278.

Acemoglu, D. (2002), 'Technical Change, Inequality, and the Labour Market', *Journal of Economic Literature*, 40: 7–72.

Acemoglu, D. (2003), 'Cross-Country Inequality Trends', *Economic Journal*, 113: F121–F149.

Alesina, A. and G.-M. Angeletos (2003), *Fairness and Redistribution: U.S. versus Europe*, NBER Working Paper No. 9502.

Alesina, A. and E. Glaeser (2004), *Fighting Poverty in the US and Europe: A World of Difference*, Oxford, Oxford University Press.

Alesina, A., E. Glaeser and B. Sacerdote (2001), 'Why Doesn't the United States Have a European-Style Welfare State?', *Brookings Papers on Economic Activity*, 2: 203–273.

Atkinson, A.B. (1999a), *The Economic Consequences of Rolling Back the Welfare State*, Cambridge, MA, MIT Press.

Atkinson, A.B. (1999b), 'Equity Issues in a Globalising World: The Experience of OECD Countries', in V. Tanzi, K. Chu and S. Gupta (eds), *Economic Policy and Equity*, Washington, International Monetary Fund.

Bénabou, R. (2000), 'Unequal Societies: Income Distribution and the Social Contract', *American Economic Review*, 90: 96–127.

Bénabou, R. (2004), 'Inequality, Technology, and the Social Contract', in P. Aghion and S. Durlauf (eds), *Handbook of Economic Growth*, Amsterdam, North-Holland.

Bénabou, R. and E.A. Ok (2001), 'Social Mobility and the Demand for Redistribution: The Poum Hypothesis', *Quarterly Journal of Economics*, 116: 447–487.

Blau, F.D. and L.M. Kahn (1996), 'International Differences in Male Wage Inequality: Institutions versus Market Forces', *Journal of Political Economy*, 104.

Boeri, T., A. Boersch-Supan and G. Tabellini (2001), 'Would You Like to Shrink the Welfare State? The Opinions of European Citizens', *Economic Policy*, 32: 7–50.

Bourguignon, F. (2001), 'Redistribution and Labour-Supply Incentives', in M. Buti, P. Sestito and H. Wijkander (eds), *Taxation, Welfare and the Crisis of Unemployment in Europe*, Cheltenham, Edward Elgar.

Card, D. and J.E. DiNardo (2002), *Skill Biased Technological Change and Rising Wage Inequality: Some Problems and Puzzles*, NBER Working Paper no. 8769.

De la Fuente, A. and R. Domenech (2002), *Educational Attainement in the OECD (1960–1995)*, CEPR Discussion Paper no. 3390.

Devroye, D. and R. Freeman (2001), *Does Inequality in Skills Explain Inequality of Earnings Across Countries?*, NBER Working Paper no. 8140.

Downs, A. (1957), *An Economic Theory of Democracy*, New York, Harper and Row.

Esping-Andersen, G. (1999), *Social Foundations of Postindustrial Economies*, Oxford, Oxford University Press.

Freeman, R. (1995), 'The Large Welfare State as a System', *American Economic Review, P&P*, 85(2): 16–21.

Galor, O. and O. Mahov (2000), 'Ability Biased Technological Transition, Wage Inequality and Economic Growth', *Quarterly Journal of Economics*, 115: 469–98.

Hochman, H.M. and J.D. Rodgers (1969), 'Pareto Optimal Redistribution', *American Economic Review*, 59: 542–557.

Hotelling, H. (1929), 'Stability in Competition', *Economic Journal*, 39: 41–37.

Krugman, P. (1994), 'Past and Prospective Causes of High Unemployment', *Federal Reserve Bank of Kansas City Economic Review*, 4.

Milanovic, B. (2000), 'The Median Voter Hypothesis, Income Inequality and Income Redistribution: An Empirical Test with the Required Data', *European Journal of Political Economy*, 16: 367–410.

Nickell, S. and J. Van Ours (2000), 'The Netherlands and the United Kingdom: A European Unemployment Miracle', *Economic Policy*, 30: 137–180.

Nickell, S., L. Nunziata, W. Ochel and G. Quintini (2003), 'The Beveridge Curve, Unemployment and Wages in the OECD from the 1960s to the 1990s', in M. Aghion, P. Frydman, R. Stiglitz and J. Woodford (eds), *Knowledge, Information and Expectations in Modern Macroeconomics*, Princeton, NJ, Princeton University Press.

Pauly, M.V. (1973), 'Income Distribution as a Local Public Good', *Journal of Public Economics*, 2: 35–58.

Piketty, T. and E. Saez (2002), *Income Inequality in the United States, 1913–1998*, NBER Working Paper no. 8467.

Rodrik, D. (1998), *Has Globalization Gone Too Far?*, Institute for International Economics, Washington, DC.

Solow, R. (1990), *The Labor Market as a Social Institution*, Cambridge, MA, Blackwell.

Part III

Globalization and well-being

5 Global health[1]

Simone Borghesi and Alessandro Vercelli

5.1 Introduction

The process of globalisation affects more and more the life quality of people around the world. In particular it impinges in different ways upon their health. In its turn the health of people affects the demographic and economic growth as well as their sustainability. However, notwithstanding the fundamental importance of this feedback, the nexus between globalisation, sustainable development and health has been insufficiently analysed.

This chapter aims to explore the main channels of influence through which the recent process of globalisation has affected the health of people, exerting an important influence on the sustainability of world development. To this end we try to identify the principle, direct and indirect, empirical correlations between the main features of globalisation and different indices of health; we proceed then to a preliminary discussion of their causal contents. The indirect correlations run in both directions. This feature turns out to be particularly important since the feedback between the main intermediate variables (income growth, income inequality and environmental degradation) and different aspects of health plays a crucial role in determining the sustainability of world development.

The nexus between globalisation and health is blurred by a partly spurious correlation between the indices that measure them. While globalisation spread and intensified since the early nineteenth century (with the only exception of the period 1915–1945 encompassing the two world wars), in the meantime also the indices of health improved, mainly for the extraordinary continuous progress of theoretical and applied medicine. No doubt globalisation has given a contribution of its own to the strengthening of this positive correlation by spreading updated medical knowledge, know-how, medicines and therapeutic instruments around the world and by promoting effective access to the most appropriate medical care. However, it is very difficult to disentangle the specific contribution to health of globalisation from that of scientific and technological progress, and of other economic, social, institutional factors that are in principle quite independent of, though correlated to, globalisation.

In this essay we choose to concentrate the attention on a few specific psycho-physiological and socio-economic factors of health that explain possible deviations from the long-run positive correlation between economic development (measured by per capita income), globalisation and health observed in the last two centuries or so. The study of these specific factors is important for policy because the elimination, or at least the mitigation, of the negative influences of globalisation and the corroboration of its positive influences would improve the overall positive correlation between health and globalisation.

The structure of this chapter is as follows. In Section 5.2 we try to clarify which are the main indirect influence channels between globalisation and health and argue that income growth, income inequality and environmental degradation play a crucial role in explaining the health effects of post-war globalisation. The link between inequality and health is explored in greater detail in Section 5.3 by taking into account also the underlying psychological and physiological mechanisms, whereas Section 5.4 examines the health effects of environmental degradation by distinguishing between air, water and soil pollution. Health, however, can have feedback effects on each of the three variables previously mentioned. Therefore, we then examine the inverse causality from health to income growth (Section 5.5), inequality (Section 5.6) and environmental degradation (Section 5.7). Section 5.8 investigates a few direct effects that globalisation may have on health. Some policy implications of the preceding analysis are briefly discussed in Section 5.9. A few concluding remarks follow.

5.2 Influence channels between globalisation, health and sustainable development

In this section we intend to suggest a fairly general map of the main channels of influence connecting globalisation, sustainable development and health. This map is summarised in a block diagram where the arrows express the direction of the influence between the key variables examined (see Figure 5.1).

The process of globalisation affects the sustainability of development mainly through three channels: an economic, a social and an environmental channel (Borghesi and Vercelli, 2003). The economic channel is mainly represented by the effects of globalisation on per capita income growth, the social channel by its effects on income inequality, while the environmental channel includes the consequences of globalisation on a variety of environmental degradation indices.[2]

Globalisation affects the income growth of countries according to their degree of involvement in the liberalisation of exchanges. Since the population level changes slowly in relation also to extra-economic factors, globalisation affects not only the dynamic behaviour of total income, but also that of per capita income. The rate of growth of per capita income influences, in its turn, both the environmental and social conditions of sustainability. In addition, the process of globalisation may have a direct effect on the environmental and social indices of sustainability.

This conceptual framework may help one to understand also the influence of globalisation on health. In fact, globalisation may affect the health of a population both directly and indirectly through the same channels mentioned earlier.

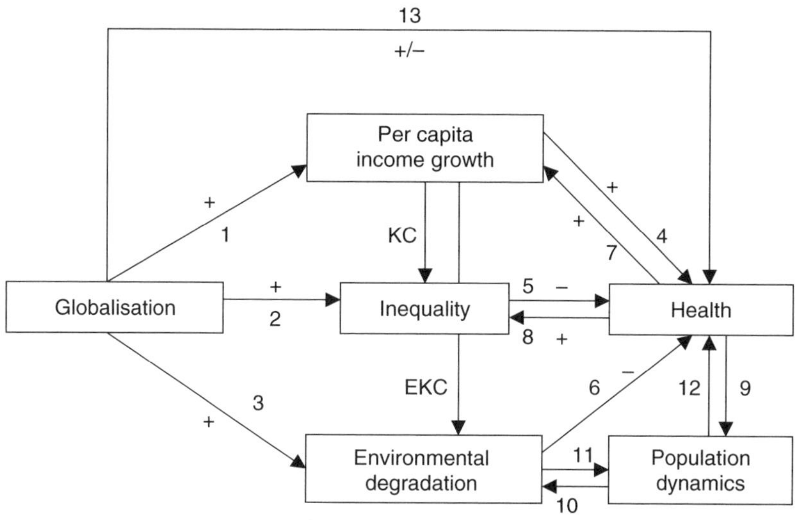

Figure 5.1 Block diagram of main causal relationships.

As to the economic channel, the average per capita income of a community (at a local, national or international level) is generally considered as a measure of its standard of living and thus also a major determinant of the average health status of the population that lives in that community. Globalisation tends to increase per capita income growth of the countries that participate actively in the process of globalisation (as shown, for example, by Lindert and Williamson, 2003), which in turn may improve their health conditions (arrow 4 in Figure 5.1). For instance, an increase in per capita income is generally accompanied by higher expenditures in health programs, better technologies that tend to improve the available therapeutic instruments and higher education levels that favour the diffusion of updated medical know-how both within and across countries.[3]

As for the social channel, it has been observed that the health of the poor has higher income elasticity than that of the rich. Cross-country evidence suggests that life expectancy increases with average per capita income in relatively poor countries, whereas this relationship tends to disappear for relatively rich countries (Preston, 1975). This can be clearly seen by looking at Figure 5.2 that shows the relationship between life expectancy and per capita Gross Domestic Product (GDP) in year 2000 based on World Bank data referring to 175 countries.[4]

Similar results emerge also in single-country studies. Using a survey on health and income in Britain, Wilkinson (1992) finds that several health indicators increase rapidly as income rises from the lowest to the middle classes of the income distribution, while no further health improvements occur at high income levels. Similarly, using data from the National Longitudinal Mortality Survey in the USA, Deaton (2001) observes that the male (age adjusted) probability of death

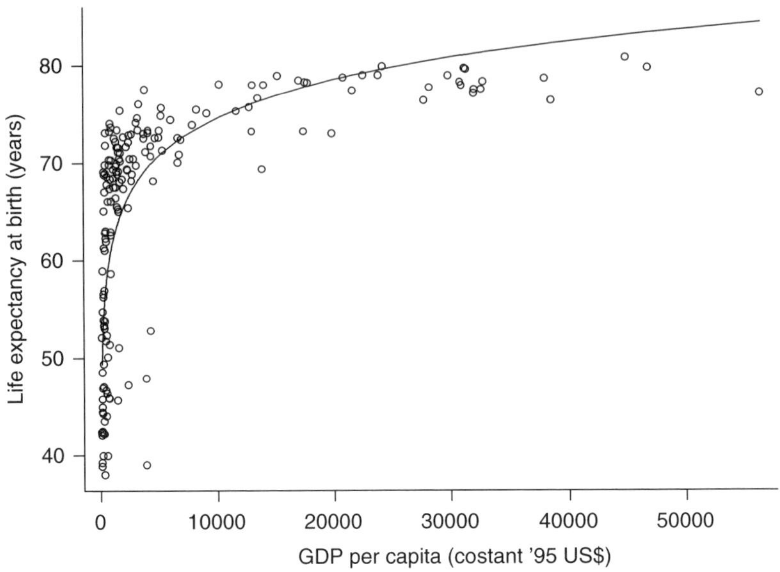

Figure 5.2 Life expectancy and per capita GDP in 175 countries in 2000.

Source: Authors' elaboration on World Bank data (World Bank, 2002).

decreases rapidly as income grows at low family income levels, while it flattens out at high family income levels. These results are relevant for policy as they suggest that redistributing income from the rich to the poor would reduce both income and health inequalities, improving the average health of the population since it benefits the health of the poor much more than it damages the health of the rich.

What we have reported so far is consistent with the traditional view that health is mainly affected by absolute income, while income inequality (both within and across countries) would have only an indirect effect on health: a reduction in income inequality would improve average health only because health indicators increase at a decreasing rate with income. In recent years, however, several studies have argued that socio-economic inequality has also a direct impact on individuals' health (arrow 5 in Figure 5.1), particularly in developed countries. A host of new evidence in different disciplinary fields clarified that, after a threshold of minimum income is reached, income inequality becomes a crucial determinant of health. Using data on nine OECD countries, Wilkinson (1992) finds evidence of a strong correlation between life expectancy and income distribution that is independent of absolute income since in this context per capita Gross National Product (GNP) has a statistically insignificant impact on life expectancy in the performed regressions.[5] As Table 5.1 shows, similar results emerge in several other studies that focused on different groups of countries and periods of time.

Table 5.1 Correlation between income inequality and health indicators in selected studies

Health indicator	*Inequality indicator*	*Correlation coefficient*	*Period*	*Countries*	*Study*
Life expectancy (years at birth)	Income share to 7th decile[a]	$0.86 (p < 0.001)$[b]	1979–1983 (single years)	9 OECD countries	Wilkinson (1992)
Life expectancy (annual rate of change)	Relative poverty[c] (annual rate of change)	$-0.73 (p < 0.01)$	1975–1985	12 European Union countries	Wilkinson (1992)
Life expectancy (annual rate of change)	Income share to 6th decile (annual rate of change)	$0.80 (p < 0.05)$	Different periods (mainly in the '70s)	7 OECD countries	Wilkinson (1992)
Life expectancy (annual rate of change)	Income share to 6th decile (annual rate of change)	$0.47 (p < 0.05)$	1979–1990	15 OECD countries	Wilkinson (1992)
Age-adjusted total mortality	Income share to 5th decile	$-0.45 (p < 0.001)$	1980	50 US states	Kaplan *et al.* (1996)
Age-adjusted total mortality	Income share to 5th decile	$-0.62 (p < 0.001)$[d]	1990	50 US states	Kaplan *et al.* (1996)
Age-adjusted total mortality (% change 1980–1990)	Income share to 5th decile in 1980	$-0.62 (p < 0.0001)$[e]	1980–1990	50 US states	Kaplan *et al.* (1996)
Age-adjusted total mortality (% change 1980–1990)	Income share to 1st decile (% change 1980–1990)	$-0.53 (p < 0.001)$	1980–1990	50 US states	Kaplan *et al.* (1996)
All-cause mortality	Robin Hood Index[f]	$0.54 (p < 0.0001)$	1990	50 US states	Kennedy *et al.* (1996)
Age-adjusted total mortality	Gini coefficient	$0.25 (p < 0.001)$	1990	282 US metropolitan areas	Lynch *et al.* (1998)
Age-adjusted total mortality	Theil Entropy coefficient	$0.21 (p < 0.001)$	1990	282 US metropolitan areas	Lynch *et al.* (1998)
Age-adjusted total mortality	90th:10th percentile income share ratio	$0.52 (p < 0.001)$	1990	282 US metropolitan areas	Lynch *et al.* (1998)

Notes

a By this we mean the proportion of income going to the least well off 70 per cent of the population. A similar interpretation applies to the other deciles in these tables.

b The correlation coefficient is $0.90 (p < 0.001)$ when controlling for GNP per head.

c Relative poverty is defined as the proportion of the population living on less than 50 per cent of the national average disposable income.

d The correlation coefficient is basically unchanged ($r = -0.59$ with $p < 0.001$) when median income is also taken into account among the explanatory variables.

e The correlation coefficient is $r = -0.51 (p < 0.002)$ when adjusted for changes in median income for each state.

f The Robin Hood Index is defined as the proportion of aggregate income that must be redistributed from households above the mean to those below it to achieve a perfectly equal distribution. Obviously, the higher the Index, the more unequal the distribution.

The same relationship, moreover, may also apply at the local level. For example, comparing the 50 states of the USA, a very weak relationship between their average income and mortality rates were found, whereas on the contrary a close relationship emerged between inequality and mortality rates (Kaplan *et al.*, 1996).[6] Analogously, among the 282 metropolitan areas of the USA the ones with the most unequal income distribution have the highest mortality rates (Lynch *et al.*, 1998). Although the regressions do not control for some potential explanatory variables and there is not yet unanimous consensus in the literature on the available evidence,[7] these results suggest that relative income, independently of absolute income, may have a crucial influence on health in these countries. More generally, the relative deprivation suffered by people in the lowest deciles of the income distribution may determine their exclusion from the social activities that promote or preserve health. Moreover, as several empirical papers have pointed out (see Section 5.3), relative deprivation may be a source of psychosocial stress, loss of self-esteem and depression that tends to damage the individuals' health. People tend to compare themselves with reference groups around them (neighbours, co-workers, friends, relatives, TV stars etc.) and may suffer chronic psychological stress from comparison with these benchmarks.[8] These psychological mechanisms can adversely affect people's health as much as the material deprivation suffered by the poor (see, for example, Brunner and Marmot, 1999; Sapolsky, 1998; Wilkinson, 2002). To the extent that these results are robust, since increasing inequality damages the average health of a population, it can be said that globalisation has indirectly contributed to deteriorate health in several countries. Empirical evidence suggests, in fact, that the process of globalisation has determined a progressive increase in income inequality between countries and within countries (see Vercelli, 2003 and the literature there cited). In particular, the evidence suggests that in the last 20 years there was a marked increase of inequality in many OECD countries including the USA and the United Kingdom (see in particular Brandolini, 2002).

The third main channel of influence of globalisation on health is the influence of globalisation on the environment. The worldwide integration process of the markets has globalised also the environmental problems and these have huge effects on health (the thinning of the ozone layer, pollution, the exhaustion of vital resources such as drinkable water, etc.). However, the influence of globalisation on environmental degradation is quite complex and ambiguous. Thus, for instance, by increasing the economic growth of the participating countries, the globalisation process may contribute to raise the scale of the production and consumption activities that damage the environment. At the same time, however, the higher economic growth that generally characterises the globalisation process may promote technological progress and thus reduce the intensity of environmental degradation. The health effect of globalisation through the environmental channel thus depends on which of these two opposite forces will tend to prevail. The increasing levels of air, water and soil pollution that have characterised most of the countries in the last decades seem to suggest that the former effect has tended to prevail so far. As in the case of inequality, therefore, globalisation may have unintentionally contributed to deteriorate health through environmental degradation. To get a deeper understanding of the complex link between globalisation and health, in what follows we will then take a closer look to the way inequality and environmental degradation may affect health.

5.3 The influence of inequality on health

Before discussing the economic mechanisms that affect health through inequality, we have to understand the psycho-physiological foundations of this influence. Though the relevance of psychosocial factors on health has been occasionally recognised since long,[9] until very recently only few observers realised that they are an important cause of global health.[10]

A reserve of (relatively liquid) financial capital is crucial to absorb economic shocks, and a reserve of natural capital to absorb environmental shocks. Analogously, it has been argued that a crucial role may be played by the intensity and quality of social relations, that is, what is often called 'social capital', in order to withstand psycho-physiological shocks. In particular, the lack of social trust was shown to be positively and significantly correlated with mortality in the USA (Kawachi *et al.*, 1997), with a correlation coefficient that ranges between 0.71 and 0.79 depending on the kind of social trust indicators used for the analysis (see Table 5.2).[11] Analogously hostility was found positively correlated with mortality. For example, Williams *et al.* (1995) estimated that mean hostility scores of ten cities in the USA were strongly and significantly correlated with their mortality rates after adjusting for race, age, gender, income and education level of the individuals (see Table 5.2). On the other hand, trust and hostility appear to be strictly correlated to inequality. Table 5.3 reports the Pearson correlation coefficients between various social capital and income inequality indicators in selected studies, with *p*-values in parentheses. As the Table shows, two commonly used indicators of social capital (civic engagement as measured by membership in groups and associations and social trust) were significantly related to inequality in the USA (Kawachi *et al.*, 1997). Similar results were obtained by Uslaner (2001), who found a high correlation coefficient ($r = -0.684$) between inequality and trust in a cross-country analysis. As the author showed, this connection between the two variables holds true also in multivariate tests that take into account economic, cultural and religious aspects that might affect the observed levels of trust and inequality in the selected countries. In particular, estimating a simultaneous equation model to test the direction of causality between trust and inequality, Uslaner (2001) found that trust has no effect on economic inequality, whereas the latter turns out to be the strongest determinant of trust among the explanatory variables (see Table 5.3). Analogously, many studies (see Table 5.3 and the survey by Hsieh and Pugh, 1993) have confirmed the existence of a close relationship between income inequality and both homicides and violent crime that can be interpreted as indirect measures of hostility and social capital.[12] Summing up, the empirical evidence suggests that inequality acts as a wedge between people that

Table 5.2 Correlation between health and social indicators in selected studies

Health indicator	*Social indicator*	*Correlation coefficient*	*Period*	*Countries*	*Study*
Age-adjusted rates of total mortality	Lack of social trust (perceived unfairness)[a]	$0.77 (p < 0.0001)$	1990	39 US states	Kawachi *et al.* (1997)
Age-adjusted rates of total mortality	Lack of social trust (perceived mistrust)[b]	$0.79 (p < 0.0001)$	1990	39 US states	Kawachi *et al.* (1997)
Age-adjusted rates of total mortality	Lack of social trust (perceived lack of helpfulness)[c]	$0.71 (p < 0.0001)$	1990	39 US states	Kawachi *et al.* (1997)
Age-adjusted rates of total mortality	Per capita group membership in voluntary groups	$-0.49 (p < 0.0001)$	1990	39 US states	Kawachi *et al.* (1997)
Mortality rates	Hostility rates[d]	$0.9 (p < 0.0001)$	1994	10 US cities	Williams *et al.* (1995)

Notes

a Perceived unfairness was measured by the percentage of respondents who agreed with the first part of the following question: 'Do you think most people would try to take advantage of you if they got a chance or would they try to be fair?'.

b Perceived mistrust was measured by the percentage of people that agreed with the second part of the following question: 'Generally speaking, would you say that most people can be trusted or that you can't be too careful in dealing with people?'.

c Perceived lack of helpfulness was measured by the percentage of respondents that agreed with the second part of the following question: 'Would you say that most of the time people try to be helpful, or are they mostly looking out for themselves?'.

d Hostility rates were based on the scores obtained through a telephone poll conducted on about 200 persons residing in each of the ten US cities taken into account.

Table 5.3 Correlation between income inequality and social indicators in selected studies

Social indicator	*Inequality indicator*	*Correlation coefficient*	*Period*	*Countries*	*Study*
Homicides/100000	Income share to 5th decile	$-0.74 (p < 0.0001)$	1989–1991	50 US states	Kaplan *et al*. (1996)
Violent crimes/100000	Income share to 5th decile	$-0.70 (p < 0.0001)$	1989–1991	50 US states	Kaplan *et al*. (1996)
Per capita group membership in voluntary groups	Robin Hood index	$-0.46 (p < 0.01)$	1990	39 US states	Kawachi *et al*. (1997)
Lack of social trust (perceived unfairness)	Robin Hood index	$0.73 (p < 0.0001)$	1990	39 US states	Kawachi *et al*. (1997)
Social trust[a]	Gini index	$-0.908 (p < 0.0001)$	1990–1993 and 1995–1996	33 countries	Uslaner[b] (2001)

Notes

a See Uslaner (2002, p. 29, footnote 22) for a description of how this variable is constructed from the data set of the World Values Study.

b The value reported in the third column for this study is the two-stage least square estimator of a multivariate regression, therefore it provides information on the partial correlation between social trust and the Gini index.

engenders mistrust and hostility with negative effects on people's health, the more so the more upper incomes are considered non-proportional to individual effort and merit.

This may explain why the most egalitarian developed countries, not the richest, tend to have the highest life expectancy.[13] A similarly close relationship between income inequality and mortality rates has been found also in time series analyses on single countries including Russia, United Kingdom and Taiwan.[14]

Income inequality may be interpreted as a measure of the intensity of relative deprivation and gap of status affecting individuals in a society. It was found that in human and non-human primates (such as baboons and macaques) the experience of a low status severely damages health producing 'obesity, glucose intolerance, increased atherosclerosis, raised basal cortisol levels and attenuated cortisol responses to experimental stressors' (Wilkinson, 2002, p. 15 and literature there cited). The physiological mechanism is based 'on the effects of sustained activation of the hypothalamus-pituitary-adrenal axis and the sympathetic nervous system. The stress response activates a cascade of stress hormones that affect the cardiovascular and immune systems' (ibid., pp. 15–16).

5.4 The influence of environmental degradation on health

In recent years numerous scientific studies have analysed the effects that individual forms of environmental degradation can have on a person's health. Some of these analyses, such as the United Nations study on the so-called Asian cloud (United Nations Environmental Programme (UNEP) and C^4, 2002), have recently received increasing attention in the mass media and on the part of public opinion for their interesting results. The World Health Organisation (WHO) has estimated that bad environmental conditions are directly responsible for about 25 per cent of all cases of preventable illness all over the world (WHO, 1997). In order to demonstrate the direct causal links between environment and health (summarised by arrow 6 in Figure 5.1), it may be useful to classify the health impacts of environmental degradation by distinguishing between atmospheric pollution, water pollution and soil pollution. These three forms of pollution are not the only ways in which environmental degradation influences a population's health status. Consider, for example, noise pollution which affects many big cities even during the night, making it increasingly difficult for people to sleep and thus reducing, by day, workers' concentration and productivity. Here we will consider three forms of pollution – those regarding air, water and food, that is, the channels through which human health is most directly exposed to environmental risks.

5.4.1 Effects of atmospheric pollution

Atmospheric pollution is considered the main cause of the large increase in cases of respiratory diseases observed in recent years. Some particularly volatile pollutants such as fine dust (PM10), nitric oxide (NO_x) and sulphur dioxide

(SO_2) – discharged by cars, for example – can penetrate as far as the bronchioles, provoking asthma, bronchitis and emphysema (Worldwatch Institute, 1990).[15] In Italy, it has been calculated (Galassi, 2002) that the number of patients with smog-related chronic coughs has doubled in the last ten years and about 20 per cent of otherwise healthy, non-smoking Italians suffer from this complaint. This is all the more worrying because it affects, in particular, individuals in the younger age groups adversely affecting the average health conditions of future generations. Children living in Italian cities, for example, have a 20 per cent higher likelihood of suffering from asthma than those living in rural or mountain areas where there is less traffic on the roads and fewer associated polluting emissions.[16] The data relating to the developing countries are even more alarming. A recent study of some Latin American capital cities reported by *The Economist* (2002a), estimates that a 10 per cent reduction in ozone and particulate emissions by 2020 could avoid 37 thousand premature deaths among the inhabitants of Mexico City and 13 thousand in San Paolo. Another study carried out in Bangladesh by the World Bank (World Bank, 2000, p. 3) estimates that the high level of atmospheric pollution in this country's towns is responsible annually for 15 thousand premature deaths and a million cases of disease, with an estimated overall cost between 200 and 800 million dollars a year. Bangladesh is one of the countries worst hit by the effects of the so-called Asian brown cloud, a thick cloud formed by carbon particles and carbon monoxide, sulphur and nitrogen gases, that stretches for about 16 million square kilometres over a large part of Asia. The cloud – caused by the continuous burning of forest areas, the activities of electrical power stations, emissions from road traffic and dust from desertified land – constitutes a new global emergency that has recently come to the fore because of the serious respiratory problems it is causing in these countries and because it could easily spread to other continents, carried by the wind.

Some authors think that the impact of atmospheric pollution on an individual's health status may be even greater than that estimated in the earlier-mentioned studies which restrict their attention to the increase in respiratory disease among the populations under consideration. Besides respiratory conditions, atmospheric pollutants are often responsible for cardiovascular disease since, once inhaled, pollutants are carried round the body in the blood. It was observed (WHO, 1997) that high concentrations of carbon monoxide in the air reduce the blood's capacity to absorb oxygen and that an increase of PM10 levels in the blood of 10 grams per square metre raises the incidence of death by cardiovascular disease by about 1 per cent.

Greenhouse gases also have other negative effects on health. As is well known, the depletion of the atmosphere's ozone layer as a result of greenhouse gases increases the population's exposure to ultraviolet rays which may account for the greater numbers of cases of skin cancer and damage to the eyes. Lastly, atmospheric pollutants can also damage health because they are deposited on water and on the soil, thus adding to the contamination of the water we drink and the food we eat. We will now deal specifically with the effects on health of water and soil pollution.

5.4.2 Effects of water pollution

One of the measures of water pollution often found in the literature is the concentration of faecal coliform bacteria in the water where there is no treatment system in place. These bacteria, which are found in human and animal faeces, give a good approximation of the quantity of pathogenic agents responsible for diarrhoea, cholera, hepatitis, typhoid and other illnesses of the digestive system. Recent studies (WHO, 1997) have estimated that these illnesses can be ascribed in 90 per cent of cases precisely to the lack of clean water and to inadequate sanitation. Those worst affected are children in the developing countries (where 95 per cent of water is untreated), thus creating a serious obstacle to the future growth of these countries and to the reduction of the gap that exists today between rich and poor countries. It has been estimated (WHO, 1997) that 88 per cent of deaths due to intestinal illnesses involve children under 15 years of age, a much higher incidence than the average number of deaths under 15 years of age due to other diseases (30 per cent).

Another factor of water pollution that has serious consequences for human health is the presence of heavy metals in the water (such as lead, cadmium, mercury, arsenic and nickel) and polluting chemical products (such as Poly-Chlorinated Biphenyls (PCB), Dichlorodiphenyltrichloroethane (DDT) and dioxins). People ingest these elements with their drinking water since they are difficult to remove under normal treatment processes, or when they eat fish where metals can accumulate. As it has been demonstrated in various studies (e.g. Conservation Foundation, 1992), some heavy metals, such as nickel, cause serious damage to the nervous system, others, such as lead, mercury and arsenic, harm the liver and the kidneys. All heavy metals and many chemical pollutants are also thought to be responsible for tumour formation. In this respect, a study on Lake Michigan (Glenn *et al.*, 1989) found that a high level of consumption of fish from this lake, polluted with high concentrations of PCB, DDT and other toxic chemical substances, increased the risk of a tumour by about 1 per cent.

A recent example of water pollution caused by heavy metals that is causing great concern is to be found in Bangladesh and the Indian region of Bengal. In well waters in these areas, used for drinking by the local population since the 1980s, the quantity of arsenic found was 50 times greater than the permitted safety level (*The Economist*, 2001). A WHO study (Smith *et al.*, 2000) estimated that the contaminated population could number between 35 and 77 million people, underlining the fact that prolonged exposure to arsenic causes skin disease (already evident in the populations of the villages concerned) and the appearance of tumours of the lung, bladder, liver and kidneys.

Furthermore, water pollution in combination with atmospheric pollution can modify the habitat of some ecosystems (temperature, humidity, vegetation density, etc.). This can encourage the survival and spreading of insects that are particularly harmful because of the diseases they carry. This is the case of the mosquito which is a vector for various diseases including malaria which is thought to be responsible for a million deaths among children aged under 5 years and which is becoming an increasingly serious problem, especially in sub-Saharan Africa where 90 per cent of the world's malaria cases are concentrated (WHO, 1977).

5.4.3 Effects of soil pollution

Many chemical, biological and radioactive pollutants tend to settle on the soil, contaminating both the crops planted there and the resultant agricultural products. This can cause serious harm to the population which can then be passed on to the next generation and last for many decades. One example is the pollution of food in Vietnam following American use, during the war, of a herbicide called 'Agent Orange' which later proved to be carcinogenic. A recent study carried out in the Bien Hoa area 30 years on from the conflict, found that 95 per cent of the resident population has extremely high levels of dioxin (sometimes as much as 200 times more than normal values) which causes damage to the liver, birth defects and the appearance of tumours (*The Economist*, 2002b).

In addition, soil pollution damages the health not only of the farmers who work the land and of any children playing there, but also of the surrounding population since dust from the polluted area can be carried by the wind. Direct contact with contaminated soil and with the numerous microbes and parasites contained in it is particularly harmful for children who are obviously more vulnerable.[17]

Not only pollution but also overworking the soil can damage the health of the population. This is particularly true for rural families in poor countries who are dependent on the food they themselves produce. The attempt to achieve a minimum level of subsistence sometimes drives rural people to over-exploit the land thus reducing its productivity. Lower productivity in turn reduces calorie and protein intake on the part of the farmers, thus reducing their own productivity and making them more vulnerable to disease. The loss of income resulting from illness and lower land and labour productivity therefore increases the indigence of the farmers thus generating a kind of vicious circle between poverty, environmental degradation and the health of the population.

5.5 The impact of health on economic growth

Recent empirical studies have shown that a country's economic growth is closely correlated to the average health conditions of its inhabitants. For a given starting income level, countries with low infant mortality rates (assumed as a proxy for a country's health conditions), grew more rapidly between 1964–1995 than those with higher mortality rates (WHO, 2001). Various empirical 'cross-country' analyses (Barro and Sala-i-Martin, 1995; Bloom and Sachs, 1998; Bhargava *et al.*, 2001) seem to confirm that good health conditions can contribute to explain economic growth (as suggested by the positive sign on arrow 7 in Figure 5.1). By introducing, besides health, some traditional explanatory variables of economic growth into the econometric model (starting income level, economic policies, and the structural characteristics of the countries), these studies found that the coefficient of the health variable is statistically significant and that a 10 per cent increase in life expectancy at birth gives a 0.3–0.4 per cent increase in a country's annual economic growth.[18]

It is possible to identify three main channels through which the health conditions prevailing in one country can influence its economic growth: through investment in the country; through the average educational level of individuals; and through individuals' productivity. In the first place, a worsening of average health conditions discourages investment in the country. High incidence of a disease like malaria, for example, increases absenteeism and turnover in the labour market, thus increasing staff training costs for companies. This makes companies less likely to invest in the country which therefore has lower growth capacity. This is what recently happened in South Africa where the incidence of Acquired Immune Deficiency Syndrome (AIDS) among workers has convinced many companies to cut their investment programmes (WHO, 2001). An epidemic or a general worsening of average health conditions can further reduce the rate of capital accumulation in a country in that it reduces the household savings rate. This can happen either because disease obliges families to face higher medical expenses, or because it reduces life expectancy and so also reduces the incentive to save for future consumption. Lastly, the accumulation of capital in a country hit by an epidemic falls, partly because the risk of contracting the disease discourages tourism in the area and related investments.

Second, as emphasised by the WHO report (WHO, 2001), the prevalence of bad health conditions in the population adversely affects not only investments in physical capital but also those in human capital. When an adult member of a family is ill, for example, this reduces the sum of money that can be spent on the children's education both because the household spends more in order to treat the illness and because disposable income is reduced. Since the incidence of disease is higher among poor families where there are already tight cash constraints, the children may be obliged to leave school early to help support their family. The low level of investment in human capital seen in countries with poor average health conditions is also the result of low life expectancy which, by reducing the temporal horizon available to an individual, makes the initial investment in education less profitable.

Furthermore, high infant mortality rates drive poor families to have many children. This reduces the amount that the family can spend on each child, leading therefore – for a given level of disposable income – to investing less on the education of each one. If the children receive less education they may repeat the same behaviour over time passing it on to successive generations. As argued by WHO (2001), the less education received by girls, the lower their future earnings will be and therefore the lower the opportunity cost of staying at home to raise their children once they reach adulthood, which means they will also have many children. What is more, the high birth rates generated by this behaviour tend to reduce the proportion of the population of working age which various studies (cf. Bloom *et al.*, 2001) find to be directly proportional to per capita income.

Lastly, the early death due to disease of many adults prevents the passing on of precious knowledge to the next generation, which also lowers the level of human capital. This aspect is particularly important in African countries hit by the spread of AIDS, where the ways of working the land are mostly passed on from father to son (WHO, 2001).

A third way in which the health status of a population influences economic growth is through individual productivity.[19] A poor state of health increases the number of sick days taken by workers and reduces both their physical and mental productivity. In addition, it reduces children's ability to learn, thus adversely affecting their future educational achievement. In this regard, many studies (see, for example, Pollitt, 2001) have found strong links between a lack of iron and vitamin A in the organism and reduced cognitive skills.

An individual's poor state of health can also have a negative spillover effect on the productivity of other family members or of people close to them. If an individual is ill, for example, other family members may have to give assistance, reducing the number of hours these carers can dedicate to their own work and often also reducing their productivity when they are at work. This productivity loss may be the result of the poor concentration and stress caused by worrying and giving assistance to their relative.

Besides the three channels described earlier (investment in physical capital, investment in human capital and individual productivity), it is also possible to hypothesise other ways in which the health of a population may influence economic growth. A worsening of average health conditions leads to an increase in government spending on health. This can generate high public deficits and an increase in public debt which cause instability harmful to economic growth in the country.

In conclusion, it can be said that the health of a population influences also the 'health' of its economy. If a population is in good health this will generally encourage economic growth in a country, especially in poor countries where the spread of diseases prevents the economy taking off, whereas the opposite occurs if the population is in bad health. In this light, health policies can promote economic growth, while the latter tends to improve health. The existence of circular relationships between health and economic growth can therefore give rise to vicious or virtuous circles according to the policies employed.

Finally, through its influence on economic growth, health can affect also inequality and environmental degradation. As argued by the vast literature on the Kuznets curve (indicated with KC in Figure 5.1) and the environmental Kuznets curve (EKC), inequality and environmental degradation (measured on the vertical axis) first rise and then decrease as per capita income grows. For those cases in which the Kuznets curves are empirically robust,[20] therefore, promoting health policies may help increase a country's per capita income (moving along the horizontal axis) and eventually reach the downward side of the two curves where inequality and environmental degradation tend to decrease.

Health, however, can also have other feedback effects on inequality and ecological degradation that are independent of income growth. We now turn to the analysis of these additional effects.

5.6 Feedback effects of health on inequality

There is a growing debate in the literature about the possible explanations underlying the observed correlation between health and inequality. In Section 5.3 we have discussed how inequality can affect health, but it seems reasonable to argue that there exists a bidirectional link between these two variables. The health status of the poor is generally worse than that of the rich since the rich enjoy higher living standards and higher access to the health care system than the poor. This fact tends to widen the gap in terms of present income and future income capacity, thus increasing the level of inequality in the country (Gwatkin, 2000). The children of poor families, in fact, generally have worse health conditions than the children of rich families, and this adversely affects their future earning possibilities as adults. It has been observed, in fact, that even when the children of poor and rich families receive the same level of education, the former may suffer inferior cognitive capacities because of the lower health conditions in which they live. For instance, several studies find a strong correlation between reduced cognitive capacity and low nutritional status, for example, lack of iron and vitamin A in the organism (Bhargava and Yu, 1997; Pollitt, 2001). Health, therefore, as many other traits (e.g. wealth, race), may explain much of the inter-generational transmission of economic status (Bowles and Gintis, 2001).

Moreover, low health conditions can increase inequality not only within countries, but also across them (WHO, 2001). Developing countries, in fact, often have poor average health conditions that hinder their ability to grow and converge towards the developed economies. Countries with high rates of infant mortality have grown more slowly during the period 1964–1995 than countries with low levels of the same variable (WHO, 2001). Thus, inequality jeopardises health and health in its turn strongly affects the earning capacity of individuals (arrow 8 in Figure 5.1). This feedback may trigger a vicious circle between bad health and inequality that risks to reinforce progressively both of them.

5.7 Feedback effects of health on the environment

The health status of a population can indirectly influence the quality of the environment as a result of two factors which have an impact on environmental degradation: economic growth and population dynamics. We have already discussed how health can affect economic growth. As to the population dynamics, population growth is influenced by the average health conditions of the population that strongly affect the birth rate. In this respect, it has been observed that the countries with the highest fertility rates are those that also have the highest infant mortality rates. A strong correlation between these two rates emerged, for example, from the analysis of 148 countries in 1995 carried out by WHO's Commission on Macroeconomics and Health (WHO, 2001, p. 36, figure 3). In general, this study found that the average number of children increased from two to six as the child survival rate fell from 95 to 75 per cent. This is because in countries with a high number of deaths in the first years of life, parents tend to have more children to ensure that at least some of them survive into adulthood. This trend is further reinforced by the fact that in many developing countries, having children is the only way parents can provide for their old age. The result is that the population with the highest infant mortality rates are also those that grow most quickly, as shown in the WHO report (2001, p. 37, figure 4), because the high rates of infant mortality are more than compensated by the high birth rates.[21] Reducing infant mortality in these countries would therefore tend to reduce population growth.

A lower population growth would have in turn a positive effect on the quality of the environment. Environmental degradation is so strongly influenced by the size of the resident population that the demographic issue holds centre stage in the sustainable development debate, right from the first contributions to be found in the literature (cf. Holdren and Ehrlich, 1974). The size of the population does, in fact, determine the amount of natural resources used to satisfy a population's consumption needs and thus also the carrying capacity of an ecosystem. Population growth can damage the environment since it is accompanied by both an increase in the demand for environmental goods and an increase in the waste coming from the production and consumption of a more numerous population.

Therefore, the causal link we have just described starts with health, moves on to population dynamics and ends with the environment, as described by arrows 9 and 10 in Figure 5.1.

Alongside this link, we can nevertheless identify another one moving in the opposite direction, starting with environmental degradation and leading to average health conditions (indicated by arrows 11 and 12 in the block diagram), making the relationship between health and environment bidirectional, mediated by variations in the population. The high level of environmental degradation in some areas of the world has, in recent years, led to increasing migratory flows of 'environmental refugees' (El-Hinnawi, 1985) who move on to escape from the pollution of their traditional habitat. There are so many cases of migration caused by environmental degradation that some authors (cf. Bates, 2002) have attempted to classify some typologies of environmental refugees to provide a theoretical framework to the fast-growing literature on this subject. Amongst the examples given is the migration of 7 million Vietnamese rural people to the cities during the war with the United States because of the destruction of the forests and harvests following the use of the previously mentioned herbicide 'Agent Orange' (Glassman, 1992). Another example is that of the 15 million people who may well be forced to leave Bangladesh by 2050 as a result of a rise in sea level (Myers, 1993).

Migration caused by environmental degradation tends to change the population's distribution over the territory which can in turn affect the health status of the population. An increase in population density in the cities, for example, can facilitate the transmission of diseases such as tuberculosis, meningitis, poliomyelitis and measles which spread rapidly, above all in the overcrowded hinterlands of large urban centres which also suffer from poor sanitation.

5.8 The direct influence of globalisation on health

After examining the indirect effects of globalisation on health through economic growth, inequality and environmental degradation and the bidirectional nature of these links, let us now move to the analysis of the direct health effects of the worldwide economic integration (arrow 13 in Figure 5.1).

Globalisation may increase the cross-border transmission of infectious diseases by augmenting the movements of people and the consequent risk of contagion. People move from the North to the South and vice versa mainly for tourism and labour, although other causes can also contribute to this sort of decisions.[22] Thus, for instance, Northern people may go on holiday to the South to enjoy unpolluted natural resources that have been depleted in their own countries by the industrialisation process. At the same time, Southern people may go to the North to find a job and enjoy higher living standards.[23]

These large multi-directional movements of people that characterise the globalisation process can spread, therefore, transmissible diseases across countries, which raises the health interdependence between developed and developing countries. Thus, for instance, large migrations from the South to the North may increase human settlements in poor areas without adequate sanitation and access to safe water (e.g. suburban areas in large Northern towns), augmenting the consequent risks of contagion throughout the Northern population. The worldwide diffusion of AIDS (apparently originated in Western Africa in the 1930s) and the transmission of multi-drug resistant tuberculosis from poor to rich countries provide other important examples of how low health conditions of the poor can have negative spill-over effects on the health status of the rich. The outbreak of Severe Acute Respiratory Syndrome (SARS) is another recent example.

As these examples show, inequality tends to strengthen the health interdependence between developed and developing countries. In a globalised world, in fact, the health of a country depends on infectious diseases that are breed by poverty in some far-distant country (Sandler and Arce, 2002).[24]

Globalisation has also a direct health effect through the consequences that international agreements can have on the health of the populations involved (Woodward *et al.*, 2001). The international agreements on food security standards and on the use of Genetically Modified Organisms (GMO), for instance, can have large positive as well as negative impacts on public health. These agreements pose important trade-offs between conflicting interests. The food security standards imposed by some developed countries, in fact, can protect the health of their inhabitants. However, this may come at the cost of a reduction in the exports of developing countries. If so, low-income countries might become even poorer, with a consequent negative impact on their average health status and on inequality between countries. Similarly, the adoption of GMO poses a delicate trade-off between the need to feed an ever-increasing population in the developing countries (that have the highest rates of demographic growth) and the unknown consequences that GMO might cause to their population in terms of health risks and variability of the agricultural production.

The recent Trade-Related Aspects of Intellectual Property Rights (TRIPS) agreements on the intellectual property rights provide another example of how the governance of globalisation can directly affect public health. Even in this case, a trade-off arises between the need to promote research in health technologies (that generally takes place in developed countries) and the need to protect public health in developing countries that cannot afford high-costs medicaments. The 'Declaration on the TRIPS agreements and public health' promulgated at the WTO meeting in Doha in November 2001 tried to find a compromise solution between the opposite interests of developed and developing countries in this field. While reaffirming the commitment of the WTO members to the TRIPS agreement, the Declaration recognised that each member has the right to grant compulsory pharmaceutical licences in case of national public health crises, especially those resulting from HIV/AIDS, tuberculosis, malaria and other epidemics that afflict many developing countries. However, most of these countries are unable to make effective use of this right since they had no manufacturing capacities in the pharmaceutical sector and wanted therefore to be allowed to import the necessary pharmaceutical medicaments from countries that can sell them at low costs. This request caused a lively debate between developed and developing countries that have reached an agreement on this issue only after several months in Geneva (August 2003). During this long bargaining process, Brazil has asked for WHO to be involved in the negotiations to safeguard its own interests, which further confirms that global governance and public health are strictly intertwined.

The international agreements on labour standards represent another important case of global governance that can affect public health, particularly in the developing countries. The possible existence of 'sweatshop' labour conditions in some multinationals that produce in developing countries and the use of children in their production process have recently attracted much attention in the public opinion. The actual extension of this phenomenon is still the object of debate.[25] However, some legitimate concerns exist on the potential impact that these labour conditions might have on the health of the population in developing countries. The exploitation of adults and children in unhealthy labour conditions could provoke diseases among the poor in the developing countries and thus reduce also the average health in these countries. If so, this would tend to raise inequality both within developing countries and across countries. On the other hand, one must be aware that imposing in the South the same labour standards of the North might increase labour costs in developing countries and reduce the incentive of Northern enterprises to invest in these countries. As the other international agreements mentioned earlier, therefore, also those on labour standards might generate a trade-off in developing countries between better health from higher labour standards and lower income (thus possibly lower health) from a reduction in investments.

Another channel through which global governance can directly affect public health is given by the international environmental agreements. The reduction in CO_2 emissions proposed by the Kyoto agreements, for instance, would largely benefit the health status of the world population, regardless of where this reduction occurs (mainly in developed countries). However, if the environmental policies required by the Kyoto Protocol had recessive effects, cutting CO_2 emissions might come at the cost of a reduction in per capita income and thus also of the average health conditions. Moreover, if the implementation of the Kyoto Protocol increases the costs of production of the firms that operate in the developed countries, these might shift their polluting activities from the North to the South with potential negative effects on the health conditions of the population living in developing countries. If so, like in the cases examined earlier, the adoption of the international environmental agreements in the North might generate a trade-off in the South between better health (from lower CO_2 emissions at the world level) and lower health (from higher concentration of polluting activities in developing countries). Although the 'pollution haven hypothesis' has found little empirical support in the past, one cannot deny that such a displacement of polluting activities might occur in the future if the environmental costs of production were to increase substantially. And this might actually occur if the countries had to respect the commitments taken in Kyoto in terms of lower CO_2 emissions, since the environmental regulations should be much stricter (and the implementation costs much higher) than the one adopted by single countries in the past.

A deeper analysis of the economic and social implications of these international agreements goes beyond the scope of the present work.[26] These few examples, however, although largely incomplete, can help to clarify the strict linkage between globalisation, health and inequality across countries. In all these examples, in fact, the governance of globalisation and its direct impact on public health raises potential trade-offs and conflicts of interests between the North and the South that are likely to increase, the higher is the level of inequality across countries.

5.9 Policy implications

As we have seen, crucial socio-economic determinants of health are poverty, inequality, social and environmental capital. Therefore, in principle, any policy that reduces the poverty and the inequality of a population and invests in its social and environmental capital also improves its health and the life quality of its members contributing to the sustainability of its economic development. We are here specifically interested in the socio-economic policies that may offset the negative implications of globalisation on health and exploit its potentialities.

As we have argued elsewhere (Vercelli, 2003), according to many researchers inequality has increased in several countries in the last two decades or so, basically because in this period redistributive policies proved unable to offset these tendencies and reduce inequality. As a matter of fact, the welfarist policies pursued in the 1950s and 1960s succeeded to some extent in this task in many countries. In principle, globalisation is fully consistent with these policies, but it raises specific obstacles to their implementation. Since the welfarist policies may increase the cost of labour, investment and production may shift to the countries where the cost of labour is the lowest, thus triggering a sort of race to the bottom in the labour markets not sheltered by the use of superior technology. Globalisation, therefore, can make welfare state policies more difficult. The higher factor mobility that characterises globalisation imposes constraints on the instruments that countries may use for redistribution, such as progressive taxation and health security systems. In a globalised world progressive taxation on capital and labour income is more likely to cause an outflow of capital and the emigration of high-income earners

(Sandmo, 2002). The same applies, in our opinion, in the case of health policies that aim to promote equality in the access to health services. Globalisation, therefore, may prevent governments from reducing income and health inequalities. Given the bidirectional link between inequality and health discussed earlier, this might be a serious problem for those developed countries where income inequality tends to increase with globalisation. Following the Heckscher–Ohlin theory, in fact, international market integration should lead rich countries to produce and export commodities that are skilled labour intensive. This tends to increase the wage differential between skilled and unskilled workers in the developed countries that, in the absence of redistributive policies, may widen also the health differential between these two categories.

The higher factor mobility that distinguishes the globalisation process may also hinder other government interventions that promote health like, for instance, the environmental policies. The 'displacement hypothesis' discussed earlier can prevent governments from implementing ecological policies that might lead some firms to move abroad to avoid the consequent reduction in the national production and employment levels. Similarly, in a globalised world, single governments have no incentive to introduce unilaterally an environmental policy that increases the cost of energy (like a carbon-energy tax), since this may induce firms to import energy from other countries where these costs are lower because of lower environmental regulations.

International financial integration provides another reason, beyond factor mobility, why globalisation can make welfarist policies in general, and health policies in particular, less viable. Financial integration, in fact, tends to raise the pressure on single countries to reduce their budget deficit, making governments increasingly unable to cope with the expensive health care programs for the poorest. In the USA, for instance, this program – named Medicaid – represents the second biggest state expenditure after education spending, corresponding to about 15 per cent of the overall USA spending (*The Economist*, 2003). In recent years, moreover, the costs of Medicaid have grown faster than any other health program, also because the number of poor people that are eligible for the program has increased over time. To cope with the stricter budget constraints imposed by financial integration, many USA states are currently cutting or planning to cut the health program for the poor (by lowering reimbursement rates to doctor that treat Medicaid patients, reducing the services covered by the program and narrowing eligibility). The same might happen in the future in the EMU countries that are currently the target of large immigration flows of poor people from the South of the world and, at the same time, must respect the Stability Pact that induce them to cut expenditures.

While factor mobility and financial integration tend to reduce the state interventions that promote health, other aspects of globalisation make such interventions more strictly needed. Thus, the existence of global environmental problems should induce developed countries to support the introduction of environmental policies and less polluting technologies also in developing countries. If not, the rising pollution intensity of the South might compromise the environmental efforts of the North and damage the health status of the Northern inhabitants. Similarly, the increasing health interdependence across countries increases the need for Northern interventions with health policies in the South of the world to avoid the potential negative feedback effects on the North of a Southern disease that spreads all over the world. This risk is currently provoking a debate on how to eradicate the risk of global diseases. Some authors (WHO, 2001) argue that the North should partially finance the health policies of the South as an investment to reduce the health risks posed by possible infectious diseases. Thus, for instance, the eradication of small-pox in 1977 was made possible in the past by large investments mainly financed by rich countries for the mass immunisation in poor countries.[27] Moreover, the existing differences in health between countries call for the transmission of new health care technologies from the North to the South of the world that can contribute to reduce both health and income inequality across countries (Sachs, 2001). In the short-run, however, the introduction of best-practice health care technologies may have ambiguous effects on the health and income distribution within the receiving country, depending on how the disease is distributed between rich and poor people in that country (Deaton, 2001).[28] The transmission of health care technologies to the South, therefore, should come along with redistribution policies that guarantee equal access to such technologies for people that equally need them, independently of their income level.[29]

5.10 Concluding remarks

In this chapter we have discussed how the process of globalisation may affect in different ways the health of people living in different areas of the globe, taking account of their economic and social status. We have seen in particular that poverty, inequality, as well as social and environmental capital, play a detectable role in affecting the health of specific individuals or groups of individuals. The health of individuals is not uniformly proportional to their per capita income but rather to poverty and to the inequality of income distribution. Poverty acts through material deprivation and inequality through relative deprivation. We have analysed in particular the impact of relative deprivation on the health of individuals independently of poverty and per capita income. Since globalisation in the last 20 years was found to be correlated with increasing inequality both between countries and within many of them, this may have induced stress and poor health in people hit by a sense of relative deprivation.

The mechanism through which chronic stress jeopardises the health of individuals is very similar to economic 'short-termism'. Energies are mobilised to obtain a desired short-term goal even at the cost of jeopardising the sustainability of the good performance in the longer term. In fact, whenever a human being has to face an emergency, the body mobilises all the resources that may be useful to face the exceptional threat preparing muscular activity for fight or flight and\or alerting the nervous system for devising a quick solution to the problems. However, the energy mobilised to face the immediate task is subtracted from the resources available for routine functions such as tissue maintenance and repair, growth, digestion and depuration of liquids and food through liver and kidneys, reproductive and immunity functions. This mechanism may be very efficient when the emergencies are brief and rare because in this case the suspension of routine functions does not produce serious damages. However, it is bound to affect health in an irreversible way when the shocks are frequent or permanent, like in the case of a worsening social status or relative deprivation. An increase in income inequality, as that induced by globalisation in the last 20 years, produced for many people exactly a reduction in social status and an increasing feeling of relative deprivation.

We have to stress the link between the physiological mechanism that explains how inequality deteriorates health and the economic mechanism that explains how certain aspects of globalisation may deteriorate the economic 'health', that is, the stability and sustainability, of the economic performance. In both cases, the pathology originates from short-termism, that is, the myopic emphasis on short-term objectives to the cost of jeopardising the achievement of longer-run objectives.

In the last two decades the globalisation process, driven by the principles of privatisation and deregulation, progressively shortened the time horizon within which decision-makers optimise their strategies. This mechanism can be seen in some more detail by focussing on three of its salient features.

The first one is the growing importance of the financial side in the balance sheets of corporations and households. Financial decisions are liable to big, often unexpected, gains and losses and must be revised almost continuously in the light of the latest available information, thus greatly contributing to the shortening of the time horizon of economic decisions. Globalisation accelerated this trend by unifying financial markets and increasing the size and velocity of 'hot money' transferred at very short notice from one sector or country to the other for speculative purposes. This greatly increased the instability of financial markets and the size of potential losses and gains of financial decisions, focusing the attention of operators on the speculative factors rather than on the long-run trends of economic fundamentals.

A second important aspect of short-termism is the growing flexibility of labour markets and industrial relations. Workers are compelled to shorten the time horizon of their decisions while the employers have the opportunity of revising their choices concerning the size and use of the labour force almost continuously on the basis of mainly speculative considerations.

The third example may be found in the field of corporate governance. Managers are evaluated and rewarded according to indices of performance calculated over increasingly short time horizon. This trend has negative implications on the sustainability of the economic performance of the firms and on its compliance with the tenets of business ethics and is a source of greater stress for the top managers and all the people affected by their decisions.

The recent phase of globalisation has greatly reinforced the three trends here briefly recalled. The increasing importance of financial capital was promoted by the radical liberalisation of the capital movements across countries. The growing flexibility of labour markets and industrial relations was enhanced by the increasing international competition based on the opportunity of shifting capital in the countries and sectors where the flexibility of labour is higher. In addition, the growing international mobility of capital and skilled labour encouraged the adoption of short-termist capital governance and reward systems.

Summing up, the growing short-termism induced by globalisation progressively increased the stress of workers, entrepreneurs, shareholders and households and this nurtured an analogously 'short-termist' physiological and psychological response that undermined their health. Of course, this effect is particularly visible and sizeable in individuals affected by absolute and relative deprivation and weakly protected by a social security network and accessible social capital. Policies that reduce poverty and inequality and invest in social capital may counteract these negative effects on health. More generally, any measure capable to curb short-termism in favour of the consolidation and diffusion of a longer-term horizon would improve global health and the sustainability of the process of globalisation.

Health policies of this kind can be interpreted as an investment that can contribute to reduce other expenditures in the longer run (e.g. by reducing poverty and thus also future health expenditures for the poor). As any other form of investment, however, health policies take time to produce their returns. Therefore, while the prevailing short-termism pushes in the direction of a further cut in health expenditures, a less myopic perspective would encourage the opposite path. In this perspective it would be particularly advisable to pursue internationally coordinated policies that exploit the potentialities of globalisation (e.g. diffusion of knowledge and human capital) to fight its negative effects (e.g. diffusion of global diseases). This consideration applies not only to health policies strictly speaking, but also to any policy that can promote or preserve good health conditions, like the environmental policies. These policies, in fact, often generate high costs in the present, but produce considerable benefits in the longer run, sometimes even well beyond the life horizon of the generation who bears the costs. The prevalence of short-termism hinders, therefore, the adoption of environmental friendly measures and calls for internationally coordinated policies to solve the current global environmental issues.

In conclusion, the deep link between psycho-physiological and economic short-termism stressed earlier suggests a further strategy of investment in health that is generally neglected in the literature. Whatever intervention may react to the growing short-termism, accelerated by the recent process of globalisation, will reduce stress, improve health and corroborate the sustainability of development. Here we limit ourselves to a few hints related to the three examples mentioned earlier. Some control of the speculative flows of capital, for example through a Tobin tax, would give a contribution in the right direction. Analogously, stopping – and possibly reversing – the process of increasing precariousness in labour relations would go in the right direction. Finally, the adoption of more rigorous and far-sighted rules of corporate governance capable to lengthen the time-horizon of managers and shareholders would provide a very important contribution to curbing short-termism. This may be obtained by adopting criteria of evaluation of managers' performance based on longer-period indicators and by strengthening the role of stakeholders in the definition and control of corporate strategies.

Notes

1 This chapter extends two previous works of the authors (Borghesi, 2002, Borghesi and Vercelli, 2004).

2 See arrows 1, 2 and 3 in Figure 5.1. The signs along the arrows in the block-diagram indicate the nature of the correlation between the variables examined.

3 The recent phase of the globalisation process has also enhanced the spread of medical knowledge through the World Wide Web. Internet, in fact, allows on-line access to specialised journals and websites that have updated information on the most recent developments in health research.

4 The regression line in the diagram describes how a logarithmic curve fits the data.

5 Regressing life expectancy on per capita GNP and on the income share going to the least well-off 70 per cent of the population, Wilkinson (1992) finds that the former variable explains less than 10 per cent of the variance of life expectancy, while the latter accounts for most of the variance. Moreover, the correlation coefficient between life expectancy and the income share to people below the seventh decile of the population is basically unchanged when controlling for per capita GNP, shifting from 0.86 to 0.90 with p-value below 0.001 in both cases.

6 Kaplan *et al.* (1996) found that the correlation coefficient between the age-adjusted mortality rates and the income proportion that goes to the least well-off 50 per cent of the population is high and basically unchanged when median income is also taken into account among the explanatory variables, shifting from 0.62 to 0.59 with $p < 0.001$ in both cases. On the contrary, the correlation coefficient between total mortality and median income is much lower and falls drastically from 0.28 ($p < 0.05$) to 0.06 ($p > 0.05$) when adjusted for income inequality.

7 Lynch *et al.* (2000) for instance, have observed that higher inequality has been related to lower mortality rates in Britain during the period 1962–1990.

8 Deaton (2001) argues that this psychological mechanism plays a crucial role in causing stress to the agents and sets up a model assuming that each individual's stress is proportional to the total amount of income that goes to richer people in the community.

9 For example, the great French sociologist Durkheim documented more than one century ago in his classical work on suicide the crucial importance of the sudden change in social status on the health of individuals (Durkheim, 1952).

10 Wilkinson (2002) claims that the psychological and social factors are 'the most important etiological factors' of health.

11 Kawachi *et al.* (1997) also take poverty into account since the latter variable can be a potential disturbance in the relationship between social capital and mortality, being related to both these variables. All the coefficients presented in this study, however, were basically unchanged when adjusted for poverty.

12 As Deaton (2001) points out, however, the link between inequality and crime is an object of debate. In principle, high inequality may coexist with little crime since very rich individuals may afford defensive expenditures to protect themselves against potential crimes (Wittenberg, 2000). However, these sorts of repressive measures are rarely sufficient to thwart the crime arising from social tension while often they foment it further.

13 For example, Wilkinson (2002, p. 14) remarks that

> the United States, although it is richer and spends more on medical care than any other country, has poorer health than almost all western European countries and comes 22nd in the international league tables of life expectancy. On the other hand, countries such as Greece, despite having just under half the level of income per head, have substantially higher life expectancy than the United States. More egalitarian countries such as Japan, Norway and Sweden have among the best health in the developed world.

14 Much of the relevant research has been collected in one volume (Kawachi *et al.*, 1999).
15 WHO (1997) estimates that atmospheric pollution is also directly responsible for 2 per cent of cases of cancer and that the highest number of deaths by tumour involve the respiratory tract (trachea, bronchi and lungs).
16 Atmospheric pollution also tends to increase the incidence of acute respiratory infections such as pneumonia which is today the main cause of infant death worldwide (WHO, 1997).
17 This may contribute to explain, for example, the high incidence of neonatal tetanus in the poorest areas of the developing countries.
18 It should be noted that life expectancy in the rich countries is today around 77 years as against 49 years in the poor countries. This difference can therefore help to explain the large and expanding gap that we find today between the economies of the North and South of the world.
19 As argued by Fogel (1997) the improvement of medical techniques and the increase in the number of calories available to workers have played an important role in supporting growth in Europe in the last two centuries.
20 Several recent contributions in the literature have cast doubts on the validity of the two relationships. See, among the others, Li *et al.* (1998) on the Kuznets curve and Borghesi (2001) on the environmental Kuznets curve.
21 The aforementioned study by WHO (2001) found that the infant mortality rate accounts for 85 per cent of the variation in the population growth rate of a country.
22 Part of the literature (e.g. Bates, 2002; Hugo, 1996) has emphasized the role of environmental degradation as a possible reason to migrate. The rise in the sea level that follows from global warming, for instance, might pose serious hazards on the future possibility to live in several islands and low lands, which induces people to migrate. Some authors (Myers, 1997) argue that these ‘environmental refugees’ might become the largest group of involuntary migrants in the near future.
23 The current level of labour mobility, however, is the object of debate. While immigration has increased in some industrialised countries such as in the European Union area, some authors (e.g. Sandmo, 2002; Woodward *et al.*, 2001) argue that labour migration is lower in the present phase of globalisation than in the previous one (1870–1914), also because developed countries have partly closed their borders to unskilled workers.
24 It is estimated that most of the infectious disease epidemics are of special relevance to sub-Saharan Africa and Asia that account for the poorest 20 per cent of the world’s population (Beaglehole and McMichael, 1999).
25 Lindert and Williamson (2003) for instance, argue that there is no positive correlation between globalisation and the use of child labour and that during the last globalisation phase (since 1950) the rates of work by children under 15 have been reducing in all member countries of the International Labour Organization.
26 See Wallach and Sforza (1999) for a thorough discussion of these potential implications.
27 Using a game theoretical model, Barrett (2003) has recently shown that global eradication of a disease, that is, its complete elimination in every country, requires international cooperation and strong international institutions.
28 Some authors (e.g. Preston and Haines, 1991) report that in some cases the transmission of health care technologies has initially widened the health and income gaps within the receiving country.
29 See van Doorslaer *et al.* (2000) for a discussion of how health care systems should be financed to ensure an equitable allocation of resources.

References

Barrett, S., (2003), ‘Global disease eradication’, *Journal of European Economics Association* (forthcoming).

Barro, R. and Sala-i-Martin, X., (1995), *Economic Growth*, New York, McGraw-Hill Inc.

Bates, D., (2002), 'Environmental refugees? Classifying human migrations caused by environmental change', *Population and Environment, Human Sciences Press Inc.*, vol. 23, no. 5, pp. 465–477.

Beaglehole, R. and McMichael, A.J., (1999), 'The future of public health in a changing global context', *Development*, vol. 42, pp. 12–16.

Bhargava, A. and Yu, J., (1997), 'A longitudinal analysis of infant and child mortality rates in developing countries', *Indian Economic Review*, vol. 32, pp. 141–151.

Bhargava, A., Dean, T., Jamison, L.J. and Murray, C.J.L., (2001), 'Modeling the effects of health on economic growth', *Journal of Health Economics*, vol. 20, pp. 423–440.

Bloom, D.E. and Sachs, J.D., (1998), 'Geography, demography and economic growth in Africa', *Brookings Papers on Economic Activity*, vol. 2, pp. 207–295.

Bloom, D.E., Canning, D. and Graham, B., (2001), 'Health, longevity and life-cycle savings', CMH Working Group Paper n.WG1: 9.

Borghesi, S., (2001), 'The environmental Kuznets curve: a critical survey', in Franzini, M. and Nicita, A. (eds), '*Economic Institutions and Environmental Policy*', pp. 201–224, Ashgate. Previosuly published as Nota di Lavoro n.85.99, 1999, Fondazione ENI Enrico Mattei, Milano.

Borghesi, S. and Vercelli, A., (2003), 'Sustainable globalisation', *Ecological Economics*, vol. 44, no. 1, pp. 77–89, Elsevier Science Ltd.

Bowles, S. and Gintis, H., (2001), 'The inheritance of inequality', *Journal of Economic Perspectives*, vol. 16, no. 3, pp. 3–30.

Brandolini, A., (2002), 'A bird's-eye view of long-run changes in income inequality'. Paper presented at the IEA World Conference in Lisbon.

Brunner, E. and Marmot, M., (1999), 'Social organization, stress, and health', in Marmots, M.G. and Wilkinson, R.G. (eds), *Social Determinants of Health*, Oxford University Press, Oxford.

Conservation Foundation, (1992), *State of the Environment 1982*, Conservation Foundation, Washington, DC.

Deaton, A., (2001), 'Health, inequality and economic development', NBER Working Paper No. 8318.

Durkheim, E., (1952), *Suicide: A Study in Sociology*, Routledge, London.

El-Hinnawi, E., (1985), *Environmental Refugees*, United Nations Environment Programme, Nairobi, 44pp.

Fogel, R.W., (1997), 'New findings on secular trends in nutrition and mortality: some implications for population theory', in Rosenzweig, M.R. and Stark, O. (eds), *Handbook of Population and Family Economics*, vol. 1a, pp. 433–481, Elsevier Science, Amsterdam.

Galassi, C., (2002), 'Fattori di rischio ambientali e disturbi respiratori nell'infanzia: i risultati dello studio SIDRA', AIST (Associazione Italiana per lo Studio della Tosse) National Congress, Bologna, 8–9 February 2002.

Glassman, J., (1992), 'Counter-insurgency, ecocide and the production of refugees: warfare as a tool of modernization', *Refuge: Canada's Periodical on Refugees*, vol. 12, pp. 27–30.

Glenn, B.S., Foran, J.A. and Van Putten, M., (1989), 'Summary of quantitative health assessments for PCBs, DDT, dieldrin and chlordane', National Wildlife Federation, Ann Arbor, MI.

Gwatkin, D.R., (2000), 'Health inequalities and the health of the poor: what do we know? What can we do?', *Bulletin of the World Health Organization*, vol. 78, no. 1, pp. 3–18.

Holdren, J.P. and Ehrlich, P.R., (1974), 'Human population and the global environment', *American Scientist*, vol. 62, pp. 282–292.

Hsieh, C.C. and Pugh, M.D., (1993), 'Poverty, income inequality, and violent crime: a meta-analysis of recent aggregated studies', *Criminal Justice Review*, vol. 18, 182–202.

Hugo, G., (1996), 'Environmental concerns and international migration', *International Migration Review*, vol. 30, pp. 105–131.

Kaplan, G.A., Pamuk, E.R., Lynch, J.W., Cohen, R.D. and Balfour, J.L., (1996), 'Inequality in income and mortality in the United States: analysis of mortality and potential pathways', *British Medical Journal*, vol. 312, pp. 999–1003.

Kawachi, I., Kennedy, B.P., Lochner, K. and Prothrow-Stith, D., (1997), 'Social capital, income inequality and mortality', *American Journal of Public Health*, vol. 87, pp. 1491–1498.

Kawachi, I., Kennedy, B.P. and Wilkinson, R.G., (1999), *Income Inequality and Health. The Society and Population Health Reader*, vol. I, New Press, New York.

Kennedy, B.P., Kawachi, I. and Prothrow-Stith, D., (1996), 'Income distribution and mortality: cross-sectional ecological study of the Robin Hood Index in the United States', *British Medical Journal*, vol. 312, pp. 1004–1007.

Li, H., Squire, L. and Zou, H., (1998), 'Explaining international and intertemporal variations in income inequality', *Economic Journal*, vol. 108, pp. 26–43.

Lindert, P.H. and Williamson, J.G., (2003), 'Does globalization make the world more unequal?' in M.D. Bordo, A.M. Taylor and J.G. Williamson (eds), *Globalization in Historical Perspectives*, pp. 227–270, University of Chicago Press, Chicago, IL.

Lynch, J., Kaplan, G.A., Pamuk, E.R., Cohen, R.D., Heck, K.H., Balfour, J.L. and Yen, I.H., (1998), 'Income inequality and mortality in metropolitan areas of United States', *American Journal of Public Health*, vol. 88, pp. 1074–1080.

Lynch, J., Smith, G.D., Kaplan, G.A. and House, J.S., (2000), 'Income inequality and mortality: importance to health of individual income, psychosocial environment, or material conditions', *British Medical Journal*, vol. 320, pp. 1200–1204.

Myers, N., (1993), 'Environmental refugees in a globally warmed world', *Bioscience*, vol. 43, pp. 752–761.

Myers, N., (1997), 'Enviromental refugees', *Population and Environment*, vol. 19, pp. 167–182.

OECD (Organisation for economic co-operation and development), (2001), *Health at a Glance*, Paris.

Pollitt, E., (2001), 'The developmental and probabilistic nature of the functional consequences of iron-deficiency anemia in children', *The Journal of Nutrition*, vol. 131, pp. 669S–675S.

Preston, S.H., (1975), 'The changing relation between mortality and level of economic development', *Population Studies*, vol. 29, pp. 231–248.

Preston, S.H. and Haines, M.R., (1991), *Fatal Years: Child Mortality in Late Nineteenth Century America*, Princeton University Press, Princeton, NJ.

Sachs, J.D., (2001), 'Tropical underdevelopment', NBER Working Paper No. 8119, Cambridge, MA.

Sandler, T. and Arce, D., (2002), 'A conceptual framework for understanding global and transnational public goods for health', *Fiscal Studies*, vol. 23, no. 2, pp. 195–222.

Sandmo, A., (2002), 'Globalization and the welfare state: more inequality – less redistribution?', Discussion Paper 4/2002, Department of Economics, Norwegian School of Economics and Business Administration. Forthcoming in D. Pieters (ed.), *European Social Security and Global Politics*, Kluwer Academic Publishers, Dordrecht.

Sapolsky, R.M., (1998), *Why Zebras Don't Get Ulcers. A Guide to Stress, Stress-Related Disease and Coping*, 2nd edn, W.H. Freeman, New York.

Smith, A.H., Lingas, E.O. and Rahman, M., (2000), 'Contamination of drinking-water by arsenic in Bangladesh: a public health emergency', *Bullettin of the World Health Organisation*, vol. 78, no. 9, pp. 1093–1103.

Uslaner, E., (2001), *The Moral Foundations of Trust*, Cambridge University Press, Cambridge.

van Doorslaer, E., Wagstaff, A. and van der, B.H. *et al.*, (2000), 'Equity in the delivery of health care in Europe and the US', *Journal of Health Economics*, vol. 19, pp. 553–583.

Vercelli, A., (2003), Globalisation and sustainable development, Discussion Paper n.399, Department of Political Economy, University of Siena.

Wallach, L. and Sforza, M., (1999), *Whose Trade Organization? Corporate Globalization and the Erosion of Democracy*, Public Citizen Foundation, Washington, DC.

WHO (World Health Organisation), (1997), Health and Environment in Sustainable Development: Five Years after the Earth Summit, Geneva.

WHO (World Health Organisation), (2001), Report of the Commission on Macroeconomics and Health, Geneva.

Wilkinson, R.G., (1992), 'Income distribution and life expectancy', *British Medical Journal*, vol. 304, pp. 165–168.

Wilkinson, R.G., (2002), Socioeconomic status and health. Studies on social and economic determinants of population health, No. 1, pp. 13–31, WHO Regional Office for Europe, Copenhagen.

Williams, R.B., Feaganes, J. and Barefoot, J.C., (1995), 'Hostility and death rates in 10 U.S. cities', *Psychosomatic Medicine*, vol. 57, no. 1, p. 94.

Wittenberg, M., (2000), *Predatory Equilibria: Systematic Theft and its Effects on Output, Inequality and Long-run Growth*, Department of Economics, University of the Witwatersrand, Johannesburg.

Woodward, D., Drager, N., Beaglehole, R. and Lipson, D., (2001), 'Globalisation and health: a framework for analysis and action, Commission on Macroeconomics and Health', Working Paper No. WG4: 10, WHO, Geneva.

World Bank, (2002), *World Development Indicators*, Washington, DC.

6 Economic integration and cross-country convergence

Exercises in growth theory and empirics

Jean-Luc Gaffard and Lionello F. Punzo

Research reported in this chapter was partly carried on within the Industrial Dynamics and European Employment (IDEE) project, with M. Amendola, B. Böhm and C. Longhi as other principal researchers. Though with the usual caveats, we thank them for letting us draw also from their contribution to such joint effort. Moreover, Punzo gratefully acknowledges the financial support of a UNISI PAR project, 2002–2004.

6.1 Preface

Substantial departures from all kinds of steady state-like behaviours by the large European countries since the mid-1970s, more recently also by Japan, in contrast with the United States, render it difficult to adhere to some of the fundamental propositions of conventional macroeconomic wisdom. We will focus upon three of them.

The first one maintains that in the long run, countries that are similar in terms of fundamentals (i.e. essentially the technology, but also preferences and the like) will eventually converge to one and the same steady state path with equal per capita and a zero rate of (labour) productivity growth if taken net of exogenous Technological Progress (TP). This proposition has proved to be un-granted, or at least in need of major qualifications, by, for example, the vast literature on *convergence* and on the integration processes going on at continental levels.

According to the second proposition, there would be a unique *model of growth* generating a single growth path, along which modern economies would travel more or less smoothly, and towards which transition economies are expected to evolve. We will argue that, on the contrary, there is a manifold (a *menu*) of such *models of growth*, suggesting that the existence of a representative economy implicit in the standard growth theory, is far from being granted.[1] Moreover, they show a tendency to get interlocked to generate observed oscillatory and more often irregular histories while the whole menu is itself varying over time as a result of structural changes. Actual economic histories can be seen as being assembled by picking up from such evolving menu. Transition and continental integration processes are likely to add to the variety.

The third and final proposition we will comment on (though briefly), asserts that, for example, the potential rate of growth of an economy is unaffected by the chains of events taking place in the shorter run. In our view, instead, forces operating on shorter time horizons may conspire with other factors in determining long-run performance. Hence they have to be taken adequately into account while policy designing.

All three propositions are of course not independent of one another. In fact, they spring from a unique view of the growth process where time fluctuations are independent of trends and this inherent stability property prevails across countries as well. We will call this, the *conventional view*, basically aggregate and long run, no room spared for fluctuations or interaction and coordination phenomena.

But the case of growth is where empirical evidence is well ahead of theory,[2] and therefore it is worth starting with the former. We are going to outline, instead, a scenario displaying cross-country heterogeneity of basically oscillatory growth behaviours. Such behaviours are more complicated than we are made to expect by either of the two conventional approaches to growth, named exogenous and endogenous, respectively. Thus, in describing cross-country and/or sector dynamics, the more general notion of *(regime) pattern* will prove to be more useful than the notions of equilibrium, steady states and the like. Moreover, there is no problem in using the notion of pattern to discuss such things as economic integration and convergence, transition and dualism resulting from integration.

To account for their peculiarities, we need to supplement that conventional view by (i) zooming into the long run performance to look at *the medium run* and (ii) articulating anew an at least sector-disaggregated representation of dynamics. In fact, it is in that little explored time span that those patterns get realized through the interaction of adjustment dynamics *and* structural change. Thus we have to consider growth fluctuations and only models exposing the economic structure behind macro aggregates can be appropriate, something that has already began to come out in the otherwise aggregate literature. This leads to set of *newer* stylized facts, supplementing the *new ones* of the recent growth empirics.[3]

For its multifaceted character,[4] we take innovation as the explanation of growth (or non-growth[5]) alternative to the production function and generally technology. As such it will play a key role in our argument, at least as much as it does in most of the post-Solow literature of recent years on convergence. Innovation will not play alone on the stage, however, as it will interact with capital accumulation in a variety of ways in determining the various growth experiences we observe.[6]

We will look at a variety of empirical experiences of growth: comparing the United States and the European Union (EU) countries, the EU countries as they grow relatively to one another, looking at integration between *un-equals* as exemplified by Mexico within the North American Foreign Trade Agreement (NAFTA), examining transition that is conceived of as a transient anomaly in growth. By conjugating broadly defined innovation, the analysis of production structure and the coordination processes of a decentralized economy, the Neo-Austrian family of models is a natural candidate for theoretical support (see Amendola and Gaffard, 1998; Amendola *et al.*, 1999). They are reviewed in the appendix as our interpretative background, together with some more technical description of our theoretical and empirical framework, multi-regime dynamics and the Framework Space.

6.2 The Golden Age and thereabout

The post-war evolution of developed economies, at least up to the 1960s, has been characterized by a very high and more or less constant growth rate, and near full employment. Moreover, pronounced cross-country similarity in average and projected performance was registered. This extraordinary performance was obtained by all economies regardless of their social and economic institutions (Böhm and Punzo, 2001; Crafts and Toniolo, 1996). It is this Golden Age that paved the way for a revival of view of growth focused on the existence of a unique, equilibrium attractor with a trend rate entirely determined by Fundamentals. Among these, it was the notion of technical progress that played the key role, whether the latter was treated as exogenous (beginning with Solow, 1956) or endogenous (with Arrow (1962) *learning by doing*, but also Kaldor (1961)), so that we can characterize this literature and the debate that it spurred as basically about the implications of sharing a production function. Output and especially productivity performance were taken to be the result of the process of absorption of technical advances into the production function, and technical change was separated from other factors affecting it. More or less at the same time, however, other studies began to mark also the existence of other, pro-growth mechanisms: commitment to demand management or liberalization of international trade. We adhere to the interpretation that sees the very success of the Golden Age as mainly due to 'an efficient coordination in the bargaining process for income distribution, leading to *high and balanced* (our italics) demand for investment and consumption, and therefore, to macro-stability, which in turn reinforced the process in a sort of virtuous circle' (Crafts and Toniolo, 1996, p. 25). The strong coordination conditions implicitly assumed in the neoclassical growth model happened to hold in reality. At the same time, human and financial constraints were being removed by virtue of a constant inflow of labour force and accommodating monetary policies. In these conditions, an easy and almost free transfer of the mass production technology developed in the US to EU economies and elsewhere, could be realized.

We all know, during the 1960s things started to change dramatically. The international system of payments based on the convertibility principle came to a collapse, this by itself generating an extraordinary monetary shock. A new monetary regime emerged, which was based on quantity controls. At the same time, shifting to new production technologies required long and costly adjustments of productive capacity. Thus, since the beginning of the 1970s up until the middle of the 1990s the evolution of the most advanced countries has been characterized by increasing levels of unemployment together with productivity slowdown. At the same time, the novelty was the emergence of deep differences even among them (not only the increase in distance from some Less Developed Countries (LDCs), differences that looked more and more of a structural, rather than conjuntural, nature.

6.3 Growth, as it looks

Growth is conventionally seen in terms of quantitative performance, measured either in terms of, for example, levels of output and employment attained, or productivity levels and growth rates or both. In other words, there is a twofold dimension to care for, extensive and intensive. Let us start with some of the more recent evidence.

After the Golden Age, a strong disparity emerges among the countries in terms of both output growth rate and labour productivity growth rate. Macroeconomic performance of the EU has been disappointing with regard to the US. Instead of growing faster than the US through assimilation of existing technologies and organizational designs as in the post-war period, the EU has achieved a lower growth rate and a higher unemployment rate than the US. Since 1970, the Gross Domestic Product (GDP) per capita gap between the EU-15 and the US has remained roughly constant. While growth in the US has been generating employment and maintaining working hours, Europe's employment performance was weak and working hours fell consistently. As a result, the steep fall in the numbers of hours worked per head of population in Europe compared to the US compensated for the rise in relative labour productivity per hour. Labour productivity, measured as GDP per hour worked, has increased faster in the EU than in the US. Labour supply in the US increased substantially because of demography and higher participation rates. While the EU population grew by a mere 0.4 per cent per annum between 1991 and 2000, that of the US increased by 1.2 per cent. At the same time, the EU employment rate (the share of population of working age actually employed) increased by only 1 percentage point while that of the US increased by 5 percentage points. With average working hours also increasing, US labour input continued to rise strongly throughout the 1990s. This has stimulated growth as well as a strong increase in labour productivity in the latter part of the decade. Then, during this period, for the first time in three decades, growth in the US labour productivity and in the Total Factor Productivity (TFP) outstripped that of the EU, while US is forging ahead.

On the other hand, within the EU, performances during the 1990s were by no means homogenous. The so-called cohesion countries exhibited higher growth rates and converged on the EU average. A slow-growth group, made up of Germany, France and Italy, had a significant impact on the overall performance because of their high weighting in the EU economy. A mixed group, composed of Finland, Netherlands and the UK exhibited a relatively high growth rate.

These facts represent something of a puzzle for empirical and theoretical reasons. For example, the increase of the rate of unemployment as well as of the Non Accelerating Inflation Rate Unemployment (NAIRU), especially severe in the countries of the European Union, can hardly be treated as a mere shortcoming of imperfections in the labour markets or else of such measures as unemployment benefits and firing restrictions. On the other hand, the slowdown in the growth of productivity in major Western economies has began as early as in the 1970s, notwithstanding the important technological advances continuously experienced at the micro levels. After having steadily decreased for nearly 30 years, the productivity gap with the US has been increasing ever since from 1975.

On the whole, it is a fact that the post-war process of convergence in macroeconomic performance (both in extensive and intensive terms) lying behind the Golden Age fast growth, got first interrupted (around 1973) and then even reversed. And this we take to deny the first proposition of standard growth theory (see the earlier paragraphs). Moreover, income variability has increased thereafter, this undermining the very existence of even country specific well-defined or smooth trends.[7] This is also further indication that we would better look at the way in which economies capture productivity gains potentially embedded in new ideas or technologies and convert them into actual performance, if we want to understand recent productivity trends. (That they be available is far from sufficient.)

This is however one among many related issues. To make way into the whole set, we need to consider country and cross-country dynamics in greater, temporal and sectoral, detail than it is normally done.

We, therefore, have to account for both the EU differences from the US as well as for differences among the EU countries. All the previous paragraphs may raise the question, do the US and the EU countries belong to distinct clubs? What is then the meaning and value of the notion of technology club? We can however address two new issues: can convergence be better re-formulated so as to take into account variability across time and across countries? Also, as productivity dynamics has been so markedly different and changing over time, can it be imputed to factors escaping the standard growth view? The dominant theoretical framework focuses mainly upon the rules and behaviours that govern the working of the markets. In this perspective, the EU would suffer from not having suitably adapted its institutions. Consistently with our interpretation of the GA, our approach focuses, instead, on the coordination failures that would prevent structural changes required by innovation processes from being realized.

To proceed to this discussion, we need to broaden the standard growth framework (with its long-run monitoring of a single state variable) to explicitly allow for the simultaneous presence of different *qualitative* behaviours across countries (*different growth models*) and over their historic experience. As explained in the Appendix, we bring in a descriptive framework (called the Framework Space (FS)) where economies need not comply to a standard model or to be stable about any specific qualitative behaviour. On the contrary, they may be seen to alternate between different regimes (or: *growth models*) defined in terms of the relative behaviours of the two intensive growth variables of standard theories (productivity and investment growth rates). A string of visited regimes defines *a (growth) pattern*.[8] Any change in regime is interpreted as an instance of structural change. Therefore, this shorter-run fluctuating view contrasts with the prevailing long-run picture of the growth phenomenon where a time-stable (average) state is sought for.[9] Of course this will make us miss the extensive dimension of the same phenomenon, which explains why we have dealt with it already, though briefly. Our focus in the sequel upon intensive features only, is meant to isolate what we believe to be qualitative properties, on which in fact growth theory concentrates when doing cross-country analysis.

6.4 Zooming into 1980–2000: growth patterns and policy choices

The central stylized fact revealed by international comparisons, is the diversity of evolution across countries which still have been confronted by the same kinds of shocks and had access to the same technology: the EU countries are markedly different from the US. Taking stock of a *mobile* panorama employment, productivity and accumulation trends; we see differences in what we will call country *growth regimes*, as well as in their dynamic patterns (i.e. *structural fluctuations*), rather than purely quantitative differences. Basically, we encounter a substantially stable investment rate, coupled with a relatively constant share of wages in the US; and, on the contrary, high fluctuations in the rates of investment and in the share of wages in the economies of continental Europe. Why so, then? These properties refer back to some, little investigated, stability property.

In fact, *regime stability*, that is, the presence of a specific *regime prevailing over time*, emerges immediately as *the* discriminating property.[10] The first finding is that in the case of the US economy (Figure 6.1), there is no clear trace of significant changes in growth regime during the last two decades, one of them in particular seems to be prevailing over time (and across sectors) exhibiting an (almost unusual) degree of stability. Quite at the opposite, most of the European countries as well as Japan exhibit wild and recurrent changes in growth regimes (Böhm *et al.*, 2001). One is naturally driven to the twofold conjecture: (i) that the higher degree of structural instability seen in the latter countries, may account for their poorer employment and productivity performance *vis-à-vis* the US, and (ii) this

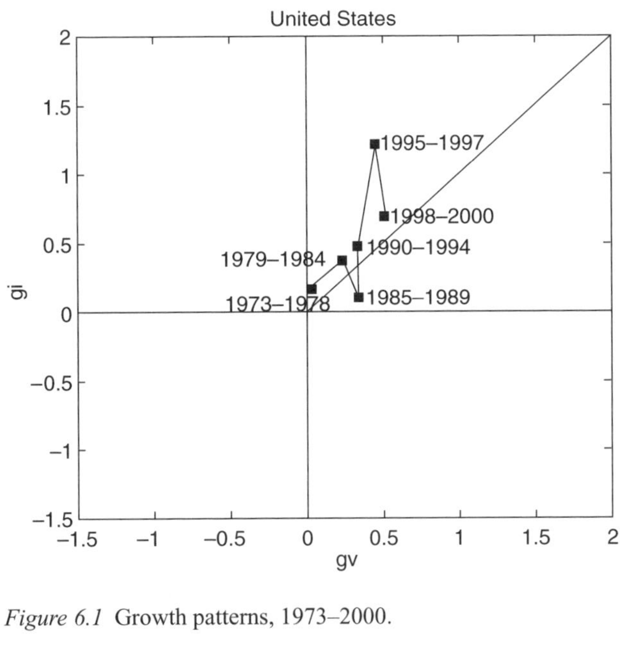

Figure 6.1 Growth patterns, 1973–2000.

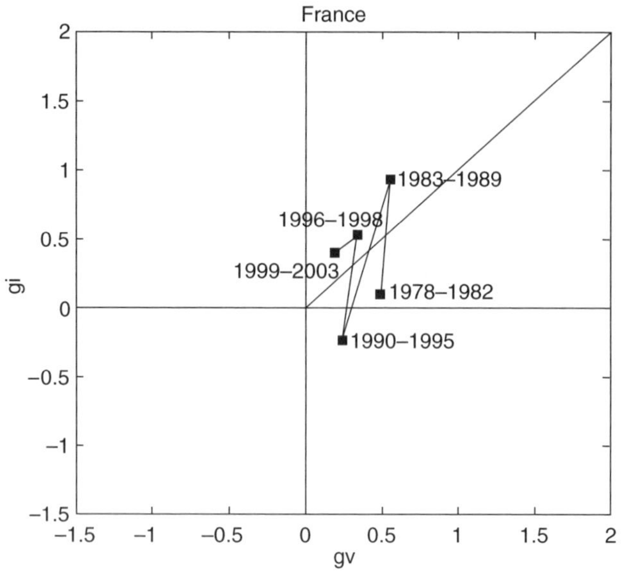

Figure 6.2 Growth patterns, 1978–2000.

may also be explained by central and commercial banks' as well as stockholders' behaviours. Some crucial episodes in the growth process of the different countries lend support to such conjecture.

Most European countries, on the other hand, and notably France, Germany and Italy, experienced fairly irregular growth from the late 1970s onwards. This took the form of alternating growth regimes (Figures 6.2, 6.3 and 6.5). In the 1980s, as the major shortcoming of coordination failures during the 1970s, among them economic policy failures, real constraints have emerged, which, being stringent, implied that recovery would generate inflation pressures, and boost inflation expectations. Hence, they seemed to suggest being restrictive on monetary policy. In reality, the lack of productive resources following the first negative (oil prices) then positive (technological) supply shocks has to be deemed to be responsible for the stagflation. Restrictive monetary policies implemented with the aim of drastically bringing down a rate of inflation already perceived too high, had the side effect of rendering the productive resource constraints even more severe. Abrupt switches in growth regimes, as appearing in the investment – productivity framework space, have been the typical outcome (Böhm *et al.*, 2001). On the whole, such structural instability factored out into a productivity slowdown and a rising NAIRU.

Later on, a stable price level and above all a strong exchange rate (particularly in France) became primary policy objectives, to be pursued with a restrictive monetary policy, and eventually a lower inflation process did prevail. During the

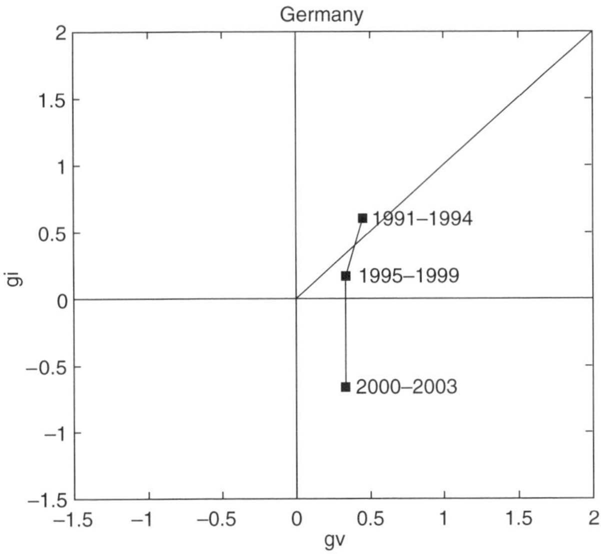

Figure 6.3 Growth patterns, 1991–2003.

1990s, share prices normalized by productivity more or less held their ground in Germany, France, Italy (and Spain), while they strongly increased in the US (Fitoussi *et al*., 2000). This confirms that liquidity constraints remained high on one side of the Atlantic, while being relaxed on the other. In the EU-area to come against the need for a more intense accumulation of capital, investment was sacrificed, with the consequence of progressively lowering the national growth rate that could be compatible with a non-accelerating inflation. Economic policies proved to be inappropriate to the point of being actually responsible for the ensuing irregular and low growth performance.

For a benchmark, the Netherlands shows instead some form of convergence towards a quasi steady state from the 1980s (Figure 6.4). Crucial episode is the long-lasting expansion began in the middle of the 1980s. Trend inflation rose from 1987 to 1991, but this did not fire any immediate, counterbalancing policy response. Thus, steady growth continued through to 1992 whereas most of the European countries went deep into recession. Inflation run-up was not permanent, at any rate. The episode is therefore significant insofar as it reveals the working of a superior coordination mechanism, whose main aspects are, on the one hand, loose banking policy with respect to the price level, and on the other hand, regulated wages' movements. As is well documented, the point of departure of this new procedure was the 1982 Wassenaar agreement on wage restraints accepted by Dutch unions. Such agreement on a concerted income policy successfully dampened the inflationary effects of final demand pressures and also allowed the central bank to implement a comparatively less restrictive monetary policy.

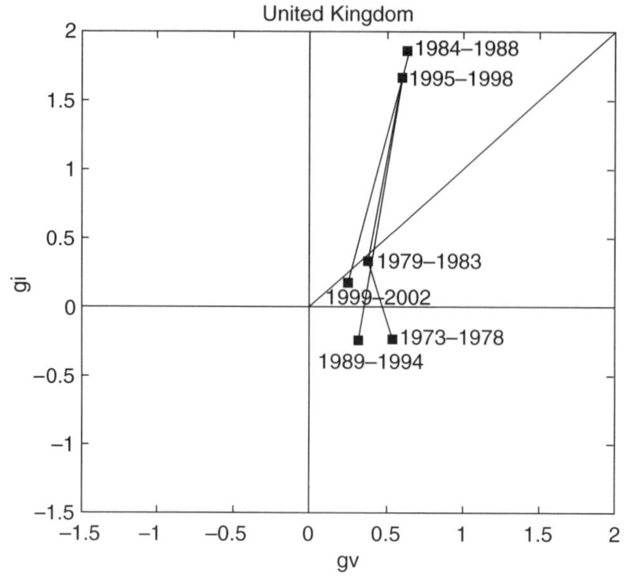

Figure 6.4 Growth patterns, 1973–2002.

On the other hand, since the early 1980s, the Netherlands has been seeing their rate of employment on the rise, which clearly mimicked the rise in share prices (normalized by productivity) (see Fitoussi *et al.*, 2000). This may lend some support to the theory of the key role of asset prices in the determination of employment determination. It may a however also be evidence in support to the conjecture, that releasing liquidity constraints[11] allow firms to fare better through transition toward new technologies and to capture thus the associated productivity gains.

Also the UK appears to have managed to steer relatively clear of the severe growth regimes instability of other countries (Figure 6.5). After experiencing a pronounced structural cycle from 1978 and 1994, similar to the one experienced by France, Germany and Italy, it seems to have returned into a stability corridor. The crucial junction in UK evolution appears to have been between the late 1980s and the early 1990s (Figure 6.6). The country began with a strong expansion in the late 1980s, the boom in borrowing being the commonly entertained explanation. Due to a lucky combination of financial liberalization, high confidence and high asset prices, this ignited and sustained a boom of both investment and consumption. At the same time, the Bank of England refrained from tightening policy immediately after inflation started to rise. Thus, the historical experience of the UK in the early 1980s can be likened to that of the US in the early 1980s: policy easing in response to the recession.

On the whole, the truly important difference between most of the European countries and the US is likely to be the following: in the US the rate of investment

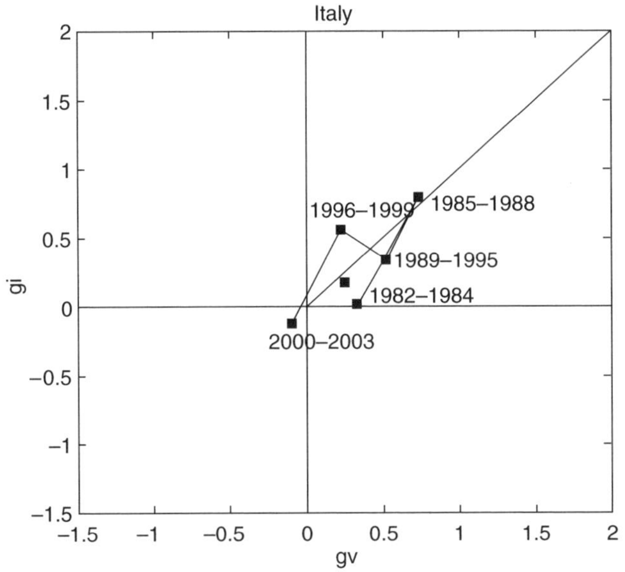

Figure 6.5 Growth patterns, 1982–2003.

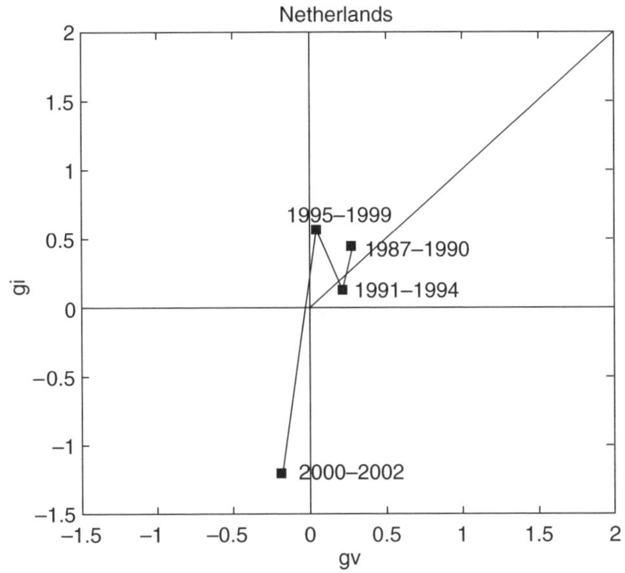

Figure 6.6 Growth patterns, 1987–2002.

has remained constant and investment levels always increased following supply shocks. This was due to the fact that 'policy has not generate bouts of severe inflation and so has not had to generate bouts of recession to control it'.[12] On the other hand, at the same time, the stock market bubble pushed capital costs down and allowed firms to carry out desired investments. As a consequence, the rate of growth consistent with price stability has risen, and the NAIRU decreased. The US economy did not experience structural fluctuations to the same extent as some other EU countries (Böhm *et al.*, 2001). However, the US investment boom in the late 1990s was unsustainable. Rise in productivity growth in the late 1990s encouraged firms to become over-optimistic about future returns. The inevitable result was over-investment in new technologies. In other words, excessively high liquidity levels favoured equally excessive investments in the new sectors. As profits start to plunge now, the evolution of share prices is going in reverse, with firms being forced to cut down on their investment plans.

The recent evolution for the Japanese economy, with the connected policy issues, easily fits into this same analytical framework (Figure 6.7). From 1991, that economy has gone through a prolonged period of slow growth leading eventually into a declared recession. Slowdown and then actual contraction have been viewed as the correction and backfiring of an unsustainable boom, where the actual growth rate would have been for a while above the potential one. Similar explanations saw the fundamental cause of the slowdown in the reduction in the rate of potential output coming from a change in the demographic as well as in the TFP trends. However, estimations of the gap between actual and potential output consistently

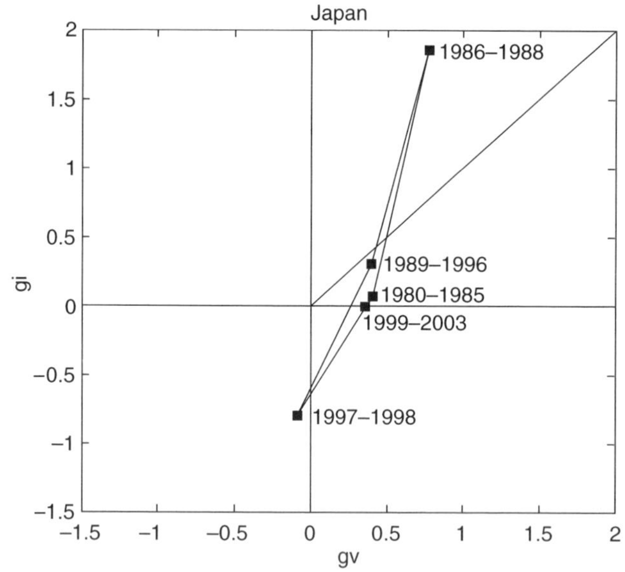

Figure 6.7 Growth patterns, 1980–2003.

conclude that it cannot exceeds 4 or 5 per cent, so that not only demand policies as they are currently advised, but perhaps to a greater extent, policies promoting a better inter-temporal coordination between supply and demand would have had an important role to play. To see why, look at the beginning of the 1990s: there was then an evident break in the inter-temporal coordination the main aspect of which was an excessively low consumption ratio while increased savings were not being converted into productive investments.[13] This resulted in dramatic switches in growth regimes and therefore structural fluctuations, to a certain extent a new experience for post-war Japan (Böhm *et al.*, 2001). To appreciate the contrast, recall that until 1985 the Japanese economy had been basically near a steady state. Thereafter, it clearly exited from its stability corridor to experience a *structural fluctuation*.

In short, the different productivity trends in Europe and the US in the 1990s support a theoretical interpretation based upon the key role of coordination failures. On the one hand the poor performance of productivity in Western Europe is the result of a slower process of accumulation (also characterized by strong fluctuations) due to tight monetary policy, and more generally to policy mismanagement. On the other hand a stable and substantial rate of investment lies behind the positive productivity trend in the US. This is an obvious explanation of the difference, but behind different accumulation processes different coordination mechanisms have also been at work, one sustaining such accumulation process, the other failing to do so.

Similarly, good coordination of the processes of capital accumulation, rather than price flexibility, is likely to be the best explanation for the more satisfactory performance of the US, though the behaviour of prices may have helped, of course. High wage flexibility associated with a pronounced increase in distribution inequality has not resulted in perturbations of the economic activity because fast growth made possible by those mechanisms led to massive job creation and hence to wage share stability. Where, like in Europe, restrictive policies were checking capital accumulation, strong policy-induced fluctuations in the wage share to GDP went on to exacerbate already existing distortions, instead of contributing to their reduction.

6.5 The empirics of cross-country convergence to structural cycles, 1970–2000

This richly diverse evolution across countries points to a relatively superior importance of idiosyncratic or endogenous factors with respect to common exogenous shocks and technologies, in determining their dynamics. Among such endogenous factors, the essential role that may have been played by monetary and financial behaviours and policies has already come to the foreground in our analysis of aggregate performance of Section 6.4. This may also explain the apparent difficulty in finding significant if any traces of convergence in the ordinary sense: that is, a (possibly conditional) approach to one and the same long run path (a single path as a point in our FS).

Key issues revolve around the nature of the various growth regimes visited by an economy in its history, the time spent there and generally their stability properties, the way they are concatenated to one another to make up the *growth pattern* in their history. Still, something can be done with the notion provided convergence is redefined in terms of regimes. Convergence is no longer required to be to, for example (a distribution around) a single path but to a prevailing regime, or else to a fairly stable sequence of regimes (a *structural cycle*), or finally to a-quasi *repeating pattern*,[14] in a succession of less and less demanding conditions.[15]

We have already found out (i) that not even such forms of weaker convergence can be taken to hold between the US and the EU countries, and likewise (ii) that theirs in any case are quite different regime histories from Japan's. We now turn to look into the EU set, where convergence has been and still is a source of political concern and the basis for the so-called structural policies. Examining convergence across European countries (and later in the NAFTA, for another example), one should bear in mind that it is being realized (if it is realized) at the same time as the process of reciprocal integration.[16] Integration implies the assembling of a new engine of growth, out of the individual engines each country had by itself, resulting of past histories and policy decisions. The key policy issue becomes, then: how is this accomplished and what will be or is expected to be the behaviour of the new engine? This answer depends upon how the convergence process is interacting with the integration process, seen in this dynamic perspective. We therefore re-define convergence in terms of regime dynamics, where the relevant concept is convergence to the (approximately) same structural cycle or fluctuation. The ordinary point state convergence implied by all standard growth analysis is, of course, the special case of this notion.[17]

To look at this newly defined convergence, and also to see the structural as basis of the diverse stability properties across the various countries,[18] we take advantage of one feature of the FS: it naturally accommodates a less aggregate descriptive statistics than the one of the previous section (and it actually was born to deal with disaggregated descriptions). So, in the following we will look at the set of Figures 6.8–6.11 showing the sectoral histories of the US, two of the EU countries and Japan.[19] Each of such figures is a *movie* with fragments taken at regular intervals (determined by the phases of the business cycle, BC) showing the distribution of growth paths of the sectors of a given economy.[20] Analysis can be made as formal or mathematical as we want, by employing the notion of distribution dynamics introduced by Quah (1993), and taking the relevant statistics, with the simple adaptation that instead of using a discrete structure on a single variable (i.e. set of intervals of values), we have to *discretize* (or coarsely partition) a two-dimensional space, the FS.[21]

A glance across the set confirms how hard it is to support analysis based upon the idea of a single attractor, both within a single country (given the high dispersion across sectors across regimes) as well as across countries, and the high time variability of the same distribution at both levels (as pointed out by Quah already in the aggregate level, Quah (1993)). Steady state like behaviours, if they

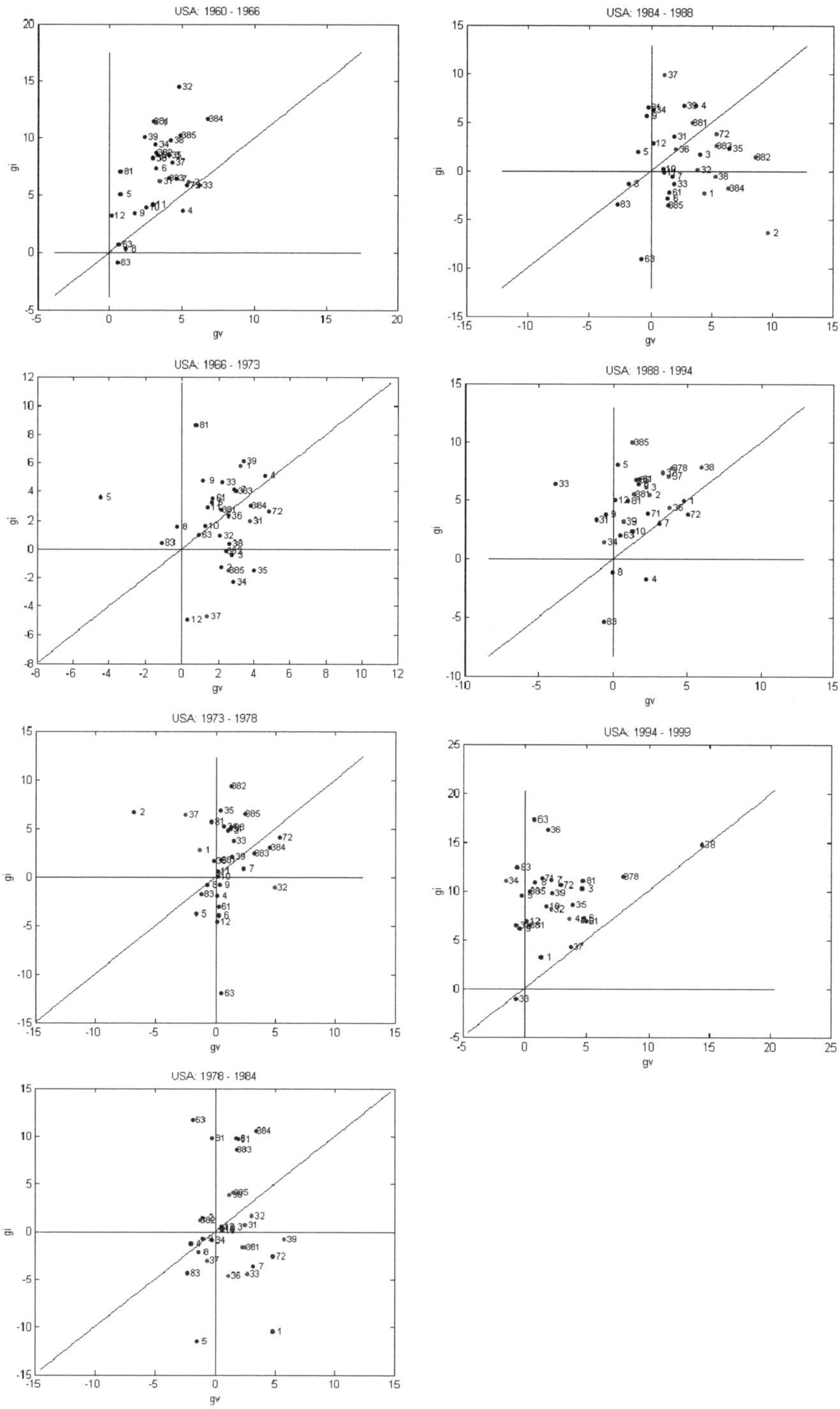

Figure 6.8 The US economy, growth cycles and regime switches, 1960–1999.

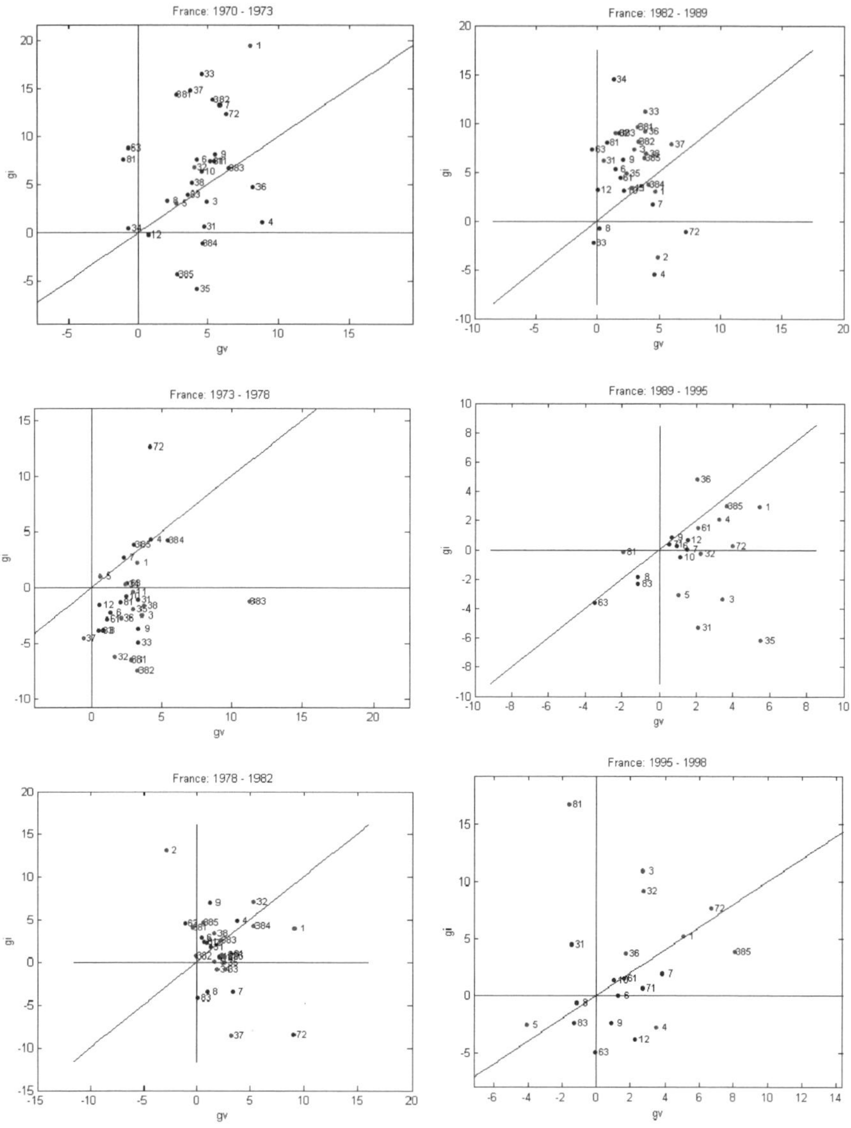

Figure 6.9 France, 1970–1998.

emerge in aggregative analysis must be the result of a twofold optical deformation, aggregation over sectors and averaging over time.

We also see confirmed the picture in the previous section with a regime stability definitely more pronounced for the US compared with the European countries, thus confirming stability in this renewed sense at the centre of our interpretative scheme.

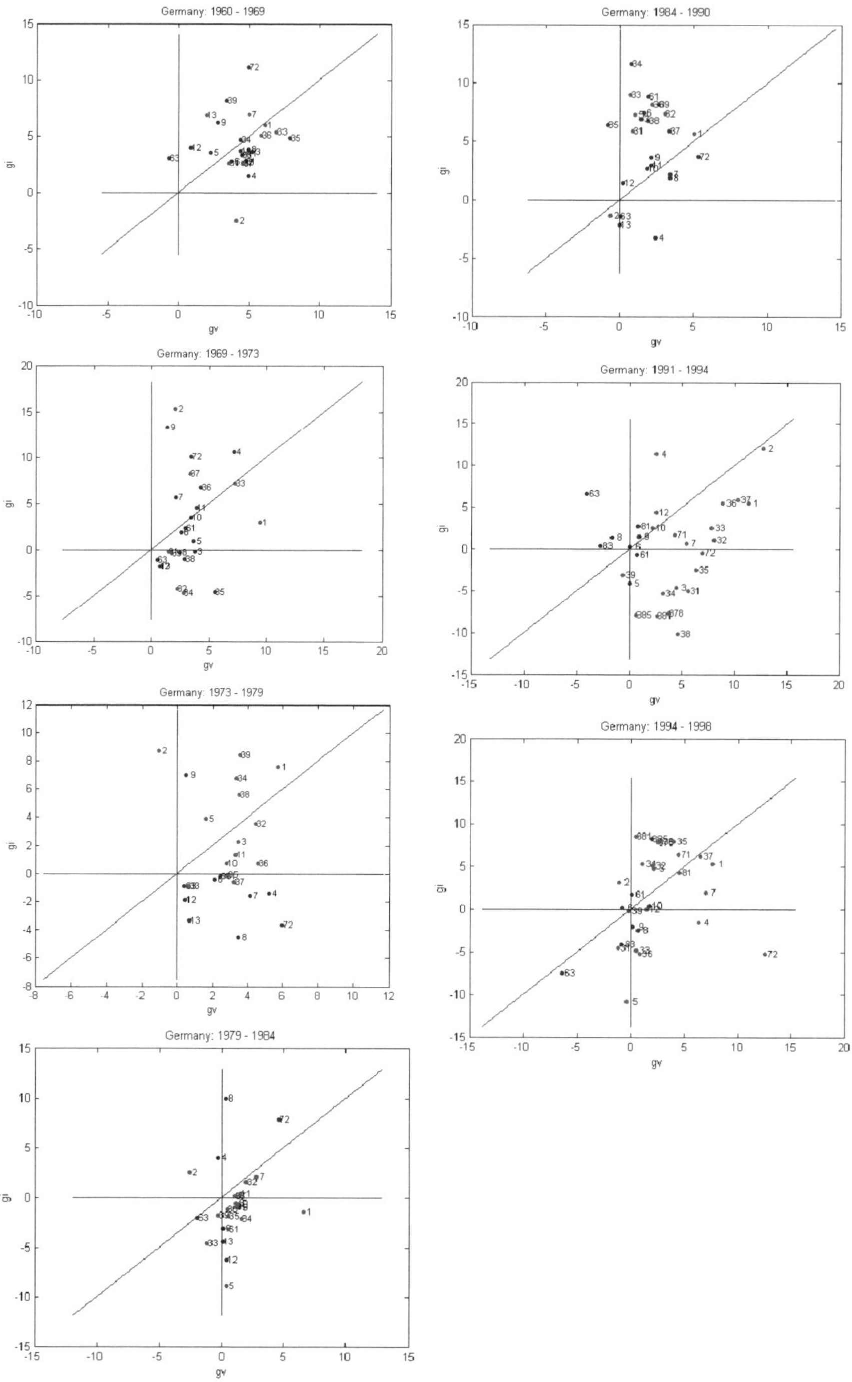

Figure 6.10 Germany, 1960–1998.

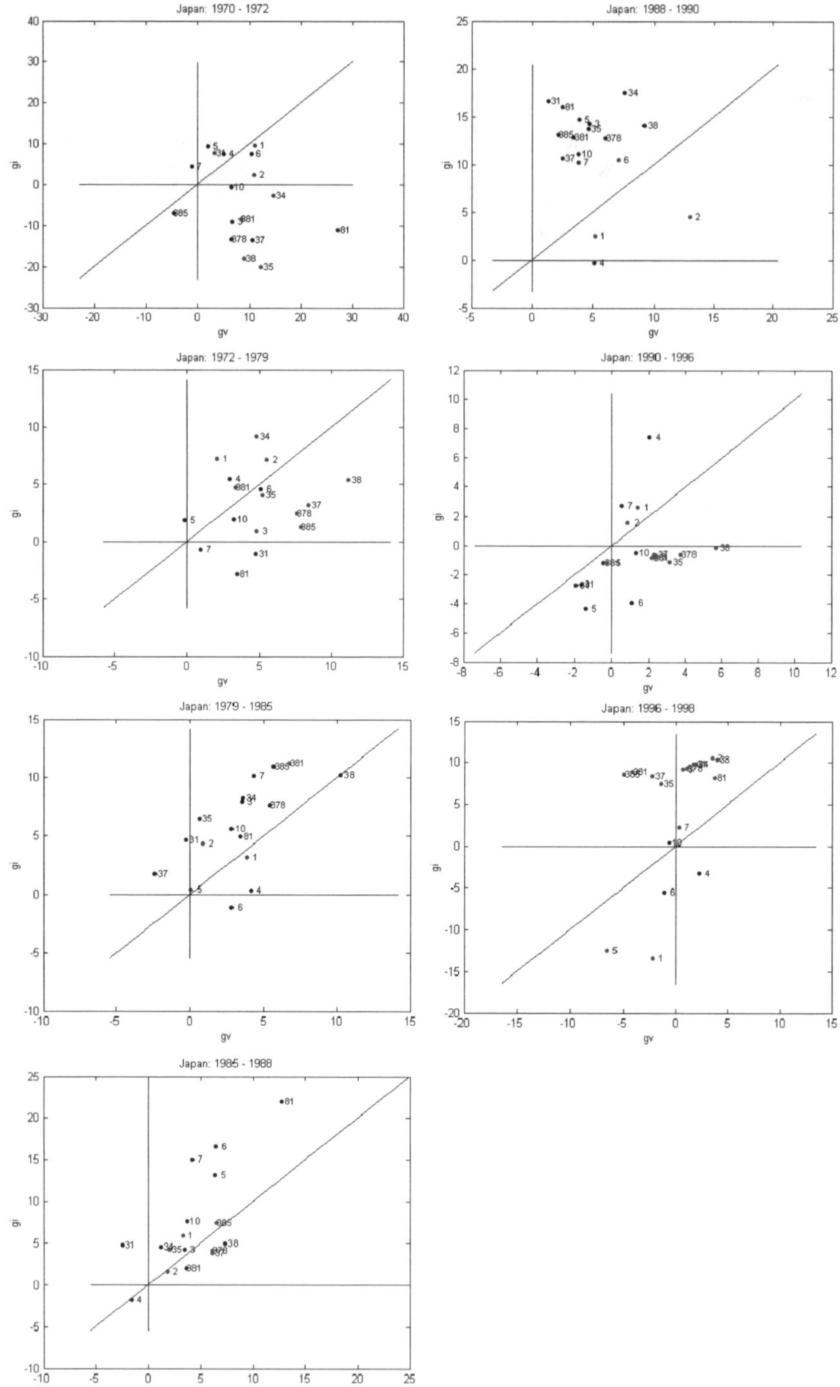

Figure 6.11 Japan, 1970–1998.

Looking in fact the movie of the US, we find a dispersion of sectoral paths that, with a moderate variability over time and special episodes, still depicts a cloud that lingers basically in the first quadrant of the FS, some episodes of sectoral invasion of the second quadrant being limited to small sets and for a limited time period. The previous aggregate pictures are good synthetic approximation therefore of such more detailed, structurally dynamic representation.

The contrast with any of the European countries' histories could not be more evident. No such behaviour is there, higher variability and greater mobility of the sectoral distribution are confirmed to lie behind the aggregate higher regime instability. This said we can address the question whether, nevertheless, there is some observed tendency among EU countries, or a subset of them, to approach (converge) to a similar dynamics, defined in the *milder sense* of regime dynamics. Then, it seems to emerge that at least for two countries, Germany and France, this seems to have been happening over the time span of the graphs, up to the end of the 1990s starting with the second half of the 1970s (in other word after the end of the Golden Age, while as said, Europe generally speaking was seeing its distance from the US increasing). Basically, taking a look at the whole cloud or sectoral distribution, after a common start, and with a phase lead by France, the two countries seem to persist on a fluctuation between accumulation (regime 6) and restructuring (regime 2), going through an intermediate phase of innovative dynamics (regime 1). Given the contrast with the US movie earlier, this can be taken as evidence of the existence of a common structural cycle with a sequence of alternating regimes, or of *convergence* in our broader sense. This seems confirmed by the harp contrast with the picture of, for example, Italy, whose regime patterns seems to exhibit entirely different properties, both as to sequence and phasing. Japan's movie adds to the variety of the regime experiences that have to be considered.[22]

6.6 New and *newer* stylized facts of growth (and structural dynamics)[23]

As is well known, Kaldor's (1961) set of stylized facts about growth across countries, basically outlined the research agenda for the following two decades. New facts have emerged from the awareness of the existence of a rich dynamics, as they are reported in, say, Durlauf and Quah (1999), and they upon the features and properties of cross-country dynamical paths, rather than upon the stability of ratios and shares. Armed with the FS language, summarized in the Appendix, a sketchy comparison of our countries leads us to add the following stylized facts of *structural dynamics*.

1 It is once again confirmed that there is no evident piling up of countries around any specific path and value of the productivity growth rate. This implies that there is no attracting steady state as implied by growth theories of one sort or the other.

2 There is not even evidence of weaker convergence that can be associated with a *prevailing regime*, rather than the single path of finite number of isolated paths of existing growth theories.[24]
3 Steady state paths are rarely observed and generally they are short lived.
4 Innovation-driven and capital accumulation-driven are not alternative growth behaviours: they are alternate regimes in basically irregular sectoral fluctuations.
5 Structural change, defined as a change in the growth model, has been the all-pervasive phenomenon throughout the period under observation, seeing repeated regime shifts in a large proportion of sectors and of economies investigated.
6 Its phasing was different across countries, which can be partially attributed to political business cycles and other related phenomena (e.g. implementation of specific economic and industrial policies).
7 Sectoral structural fluctuations seem to follow different patterns in Europe and the US compared to Japan.

   However, while the equilibria of conventional theories are basically never there to be observed, if we take average performances over the whole time span, country histories tend to look similar to each other, a fact that seems to support the hypothesis of a steady state prevailing in the long run. This also suggest, on the other hand, that those theories basically disregard important segments of the histories of observed economies, for example, the so-called *productivity paradox*.
8 Finally, some sort of limited convergence in oscillation seems to emerge but it involves a small subset of the EU countries.

All these empirical facts can be treated less intuitively and more rigorously by the aid of, for example, two techniques, developed for these and related issues, naturally descending from our approach of multi-regime dynamics. Given the finite number of regimes taken as the economy's feasible states, its two dimensional dynamics can be coded into a finite number of symbols,[25] a technique which has the advantage of synthesizing long time series (whenever available), but more so of handling (panels of) large number of country and/or sector time series and making them generally comparable (with adequate methods). Such methods are related with non-parametric statistics and information theoretic approaches, and basically produce indices of irregularity of evolution behaviour that can be taken country- and sector-wise, if we like. This makes sense of the idea that in between perfect regularity of the growth theories and the pure irregularity of the stochastic view, there is a chasm of irregular behaviours that ought to be ordered by appropriate indexing. This done, regime patterns can be compared across countries and/or sectors, other exercises being also open (see Brida and Punzo, 2003).

This produces important hints as to the direction to move on for theory and empirics. The widespread, apparently increasing instability of regimes observed across sectors, one country in comparison with others, can account for the their relative performance in terms of key variables as for instance unemployment rate. A study by Lavezzi (2003) has an ingenious extension of Quah's distribution analysis to multi-regime dynamics. Once the notion of a finite set of regimes is introduced, and a country's history is reconstructed in terms of its states as visited regimes (hence, in a coded way[26]), the two-dimensional FS state space is discretized in a way very similar to the one used in Quah's (1993) study of cross-country evolution over a discretized single state-variable. One can then address the twofold question: (i) is there one or more attracting state(s) (in our own case, *regime*[27]) or else *fluctuation*; (ii) is there a dependence between some measure of the degree of instability and other indices of macroeconomic performance (e.g. unemployment rates). Lavezzi's answers to both questions, though tentative, are positive, by showing that high regime instability across sectors makes an economy naturally candidate to exhibit high unemployment rates.

6.7 Adding to variety: dynamic dualism and transition

The picture of structural dynamics as it appears in our FS approach, can be further enriched by two more still ongoing processes: economic integration between unequals and transition of the ex-centralized countries.

6.7.1 The forbidden fruits of integration

The exemplary case of integration between unequal economies, is that of Mexico (MX) and the US as a result of the NAFTA agreements. Here (see Puchet and Punzo, 2001), again the expectation generated by conventional growth theory of at least partial convergence to some sort of common steady state, gives way to a sharply contrasting reality (see Figures 6.12–6.13). On the side of MX (1970–1997), a phase-two structural oscillation between two widely apart regimes (of high accumulation and wild restructuring) seems to emerge and this shows MX probably on the brink of persistent wild fluctuations (some of whose short-term effects have recently been seen). On the other side of the border, the US economy enjoys a much higher regime stability, consistently staying in a corridor around the 45 degree line. There, both growth rates are close to each other in values to testify regularity of growth (recall also what has been said earlier in this chapter). Moreover, one can show that Mexico's aggregate fluctuation is the result of a distribution of sectoral paths overtime stable along the accumulation axis,[28] on the contrary, the more regular, near stationary US behaviour is founded upon a distribution of paths that is confined basically to mild fluctuations in the first quadrant.[29]

The notion of *dynamic trap* indicates such patterns characterized at both the aggregate and the sectoral or structural levels by high fluctuation of investment pace to which correspond slow productivity gains (Puchet and Punzo, 2001).[30] MX and the US remain *structural divergent* with their two dynamical structures, each following distinct growth patterns. On the other hand, in the weaker of the two regions (MX, in our case[31]), the result is a dualistic structure as exhibited by the sparse scattering of sectoral paths, this being the dynamic counterpart of traditional (static) *dualism*. Far from being a stabilizer, integration can generate fluctuations, and if not properly dealt with, it initialises paths where vast resources invested do not rip the benefits expected. This complex set of dynamics eventually

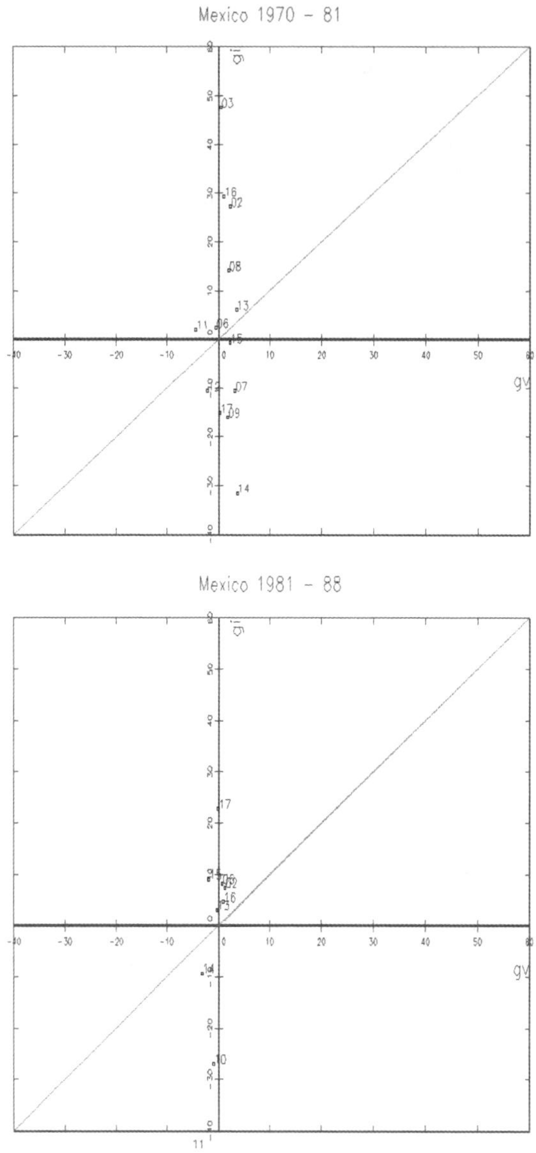

Figure 6.12 FS for the medium-run: Mexico.

prevents structurally weaker economies from landing onto that virtuous cycle of innovation and accumulation that is the greatest promise of economic integration between unequal countries.

It is the possibility of this complex *cross-layered architecture* (cross-country, cross-sectors and over various time horizons) to emerge in the actual growth

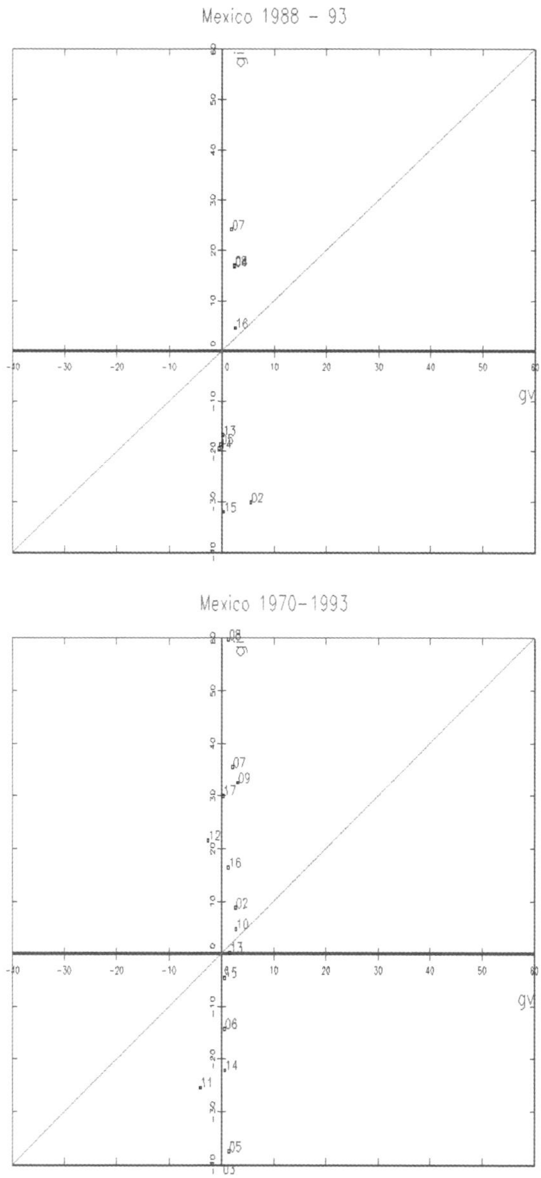

Figure 6.12 Continued.

processes, that is the *lesson* to learn from the ongoing (and possibly, future) integration processes.

First of all, as is clear, by no means economic integration brings about *necessarily* convergence in the conventional sense of equalization of standards

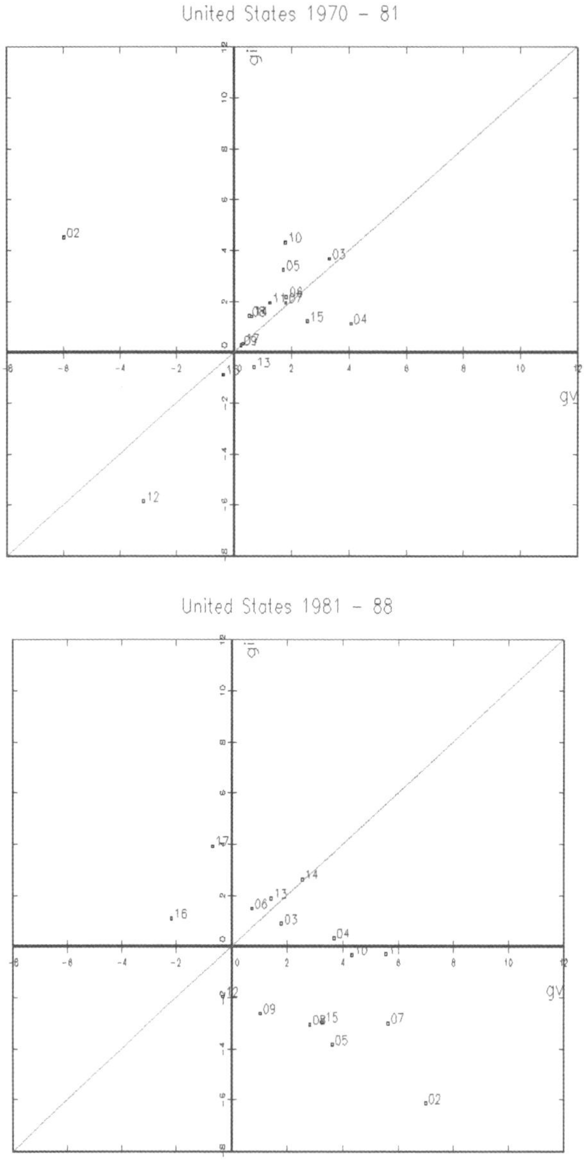

Figure 6.13 The United States.

of living or of productivity. Several regional histories in Europe (perhaps, in contrast to the US case) show this; the Italian full (political as well as) economic integration of the North and the South over some 140 years now, is one of them. Hence, fears about the outcomes of such processes are not ill founded.

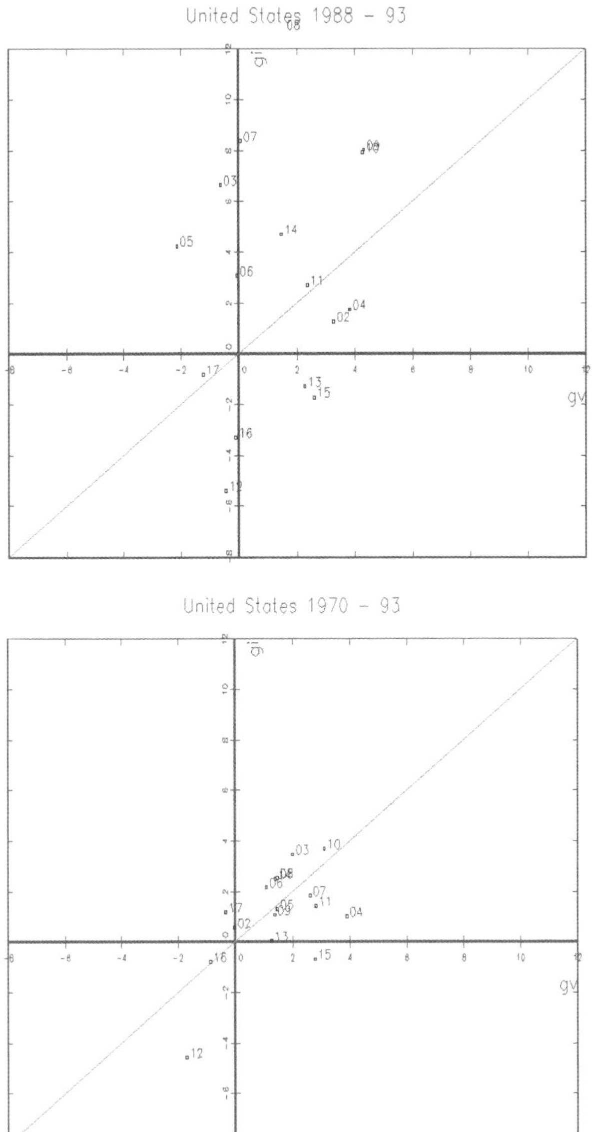

Figure 6.13 Continued.

Moreover, an important policy question is left open: do we need to have convergence first, and *then* work for economic integration? Or else can the latter be promoted under the assumption that 'it will do the job' of ensuring convergence? The issues connected with the enlargement to the Central Eastern European countries can largely be read through this problem. In the Americas, and in the NAFTA area, the idea very boldly adopted was the latter one. The structural problems, for example, the possibility of falling into a dynamic trap unveiled in Puchet and Punzo (2001), remind us that things can be more complex that they look like in an aggregative perspective.

That is why a broader notion of convergence was needed, thus increasing to at least eight the number listed by Baumol *et al.* (1994). Accordingly, there is more than one policy approach to the process of integration.

However, the notion of convergence required as a policy foundation must be based upon a deeper understanding of the structural dynamics of the economies involved and their features. The success of economic integration should be measured in terms of degree of *convergence to a common pattern of growth*. Using the 'mechanics of growth' metaphor, by the policy makers such processes should be viewed as shaping a new engine of growth by assembling existing engines, the pre-existing national or regional economies.[32] For the weaker countries, in particular, this means to find a sustainable path. The growth trap, with its unbalanced dynamics of productivity and capital accumulation, cannot be such a path. The North American market made up of two dynamically so diverse economies, has an inbuilt inconsistency that one day will have to be resolved. Here institutions are well behind markets, anti-cyclical policies still dominate the portfolio considered by governments.

6.7.2 Transition: can it mean an endless fluctuation?

Finally, the multi-regime framework can also be used to highlight the diversity of experiences among transition countries.

The transition literature was born out of the existing growth theories, the very name of transition reflecting such intellectual operation. Transition was seen as a short run *anomaly* of a growth process requiring major structural adjustments, via re-allocation of resources.[33] But it has to terminate one day, the structural adjustments to be accomplished following a certain predefined recipe. The experience of some of the countries (notably, Poland) seems to comply with that picture so well that one wonders whether the picture was taken of their specific experience.[34]

This, however, has not been happening in Romania, for instance, where, instead, GDP has followed a persistent oscillatory pattern (a W- rather than a U-shaped profile[35]) around a descending trend, at least until the end of the 1990s. In our regime framework, this goes along with a pronounced instability in terms of regimes and in particular in terms of investment rates, instability similar to an extent to the dynamic trap discussed earlier. Once again, pictures of the evolving sectoral distribution of paths over the whole time period of the transition and in a break down into its phases, confirm the image of a global process of structural change that went sour (see Figure 6.14). It also confirms that the key to its understanding lies in the relationship between broadly defined, regime stability and the rate at which productivity gains are cashed.

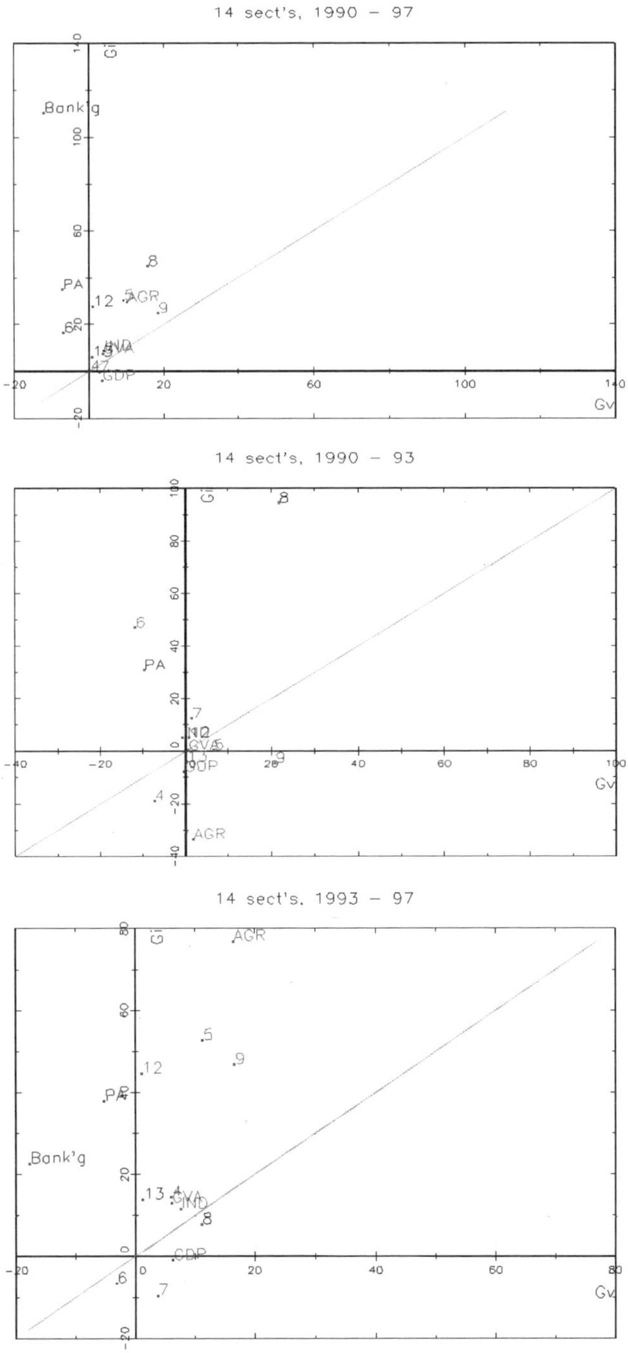

Figure 6.14 Romania.

More specifically, the seemingly erratic dynamics in Romania results from the interaction between the effects of external (unstable international demand) and domestic factors (pronounced political cycles). It will continue to be vulnerable to this dangerous mix as long as: (i) its competitiveness will be based upon lower labour and energy costs only; *and* (ii) there will be a weak domestic market. This *twofold weakness* is reflected into an atypical dynamics. I maintain that this eventually issues from the absence, in the transition phase up to now, of technological change fuelled by capital accumulation and/or innovation. The situation is worsened by the long technological stalemate of the 1980s, part of the initial conditions of Romania's transition. Thus, the *effective demand problem* in the form proposed by Romania, combines with the *investment puzzle* of a relatively fast capital accumulation, with poor productivity performance since the beginning of the transition. *Macroeconomic vulnerability* and *growth sustainability* are, therefore, two closely related issues at the macroeconomic level, reflecting deeper problems in structural dynamics.

Now that transition has been declared officially finished, the first thing one can appreciate is the diversity of *patterns* across countries. Beside the textbook case of Poland, remarkable differences (from Poland and among them) can be seen between the Czech and Slovak Republics, Hungary and say Slovenia, *success* stories all of them but different from one another if structural dynamics is considered.[36] Moreover, Romania (with other countries of South East Europe) until recently has shown the possibility of a transition path without any evident stability or convergence property, thus contradicting the very basic assumption of the whole transition literature.[37] It undermines the idea of transition as cross-country homogeneous path towards a unique model of growth (a *regime* in our words) with in-built strong attracting properties. On the other hand, as similar dynamics is shown by other countries in South East Europe, it is reasonable to conclude the existence of distinct *transition clubs*.

We think the explanation is as simple as it should be. We have three models of transition adjustments (and three different ways were implemented to handle the well known technology gap): the labour intensive in Romania (keeping high levels of employment by favouring low technology industries), the capital intensive in the Check republic (keeping large, high capital factories) and finally the Polish model where both capital and labour were adjusted, perhaps optimally. That would explain its success and justify why it represents, for many, the *ideal transition model*. The transition patterns of these countries, in the regime sense introduced in this chapter, of course look quite different.

Romania's may be an example of endless transition, endless unless adequate policies were been introduced to direct it elsewhere, away from its natural tendency to fluctuate around a negative trend. The reasonable hypothesis is that such persisting fluctuations are rooted in the kind of structural changes that have taken place, or rather *have not taken place*, at the level of production structures. These countries, too, missed the chance to catch up with the more advanced countries, by jumping into modern world technologies.

At any rate, the scenario of an un-accomplished or, even, aborted process of change from the pre-transition structure, in comparison with other experiences permits us to conclude:

1 Macrodynamics of transition can be a fluctuation, at times in apparently erratic fashion;
2 Instead of necessarily being a one-directional process, transition may end up into a persistent fluctuation, another sort of dynamic trap resulting from a structural stalemate;
3 That reallocation of resources can be a pre- or necessary (but not sufficient) condition for a 'successful transition'.

6.8 Taking care of path dependence in drawing policy implications

The productivity slowdown in the Western economies and the persistence of high unemployment rates in major European countries remain as puzzles difficult to be solved within standard macroeconomic analyses. According to the conventional story, as soon as a superior technique is available, the output associated with given inputs, and hence productivity, are to increase. So, it is hard to explain the 1970s and 1980s general slowdown in productivity in spite of tremendous technical progress, known as 'productivity paradox'. This indicates that the problems of innovation spreading can hardly be thought as purely technological, even when we think of innovation in the narrower sense of the emergence of a new technology.

In recent years there has been a substantial amount of work trying to reconcile the standard representation of technology with the observed trends in productivity and technology.

This approach relates to increases in productivity to the character of the technologies while overlooking the processes of restructuring of productive capacity associated with the introduction of a new technique. Forced to neglect them, the theory falls back to adoption lags for an explanation.

But consider the introduction of a new technology characterized by higher construction costs, as it is typically the case of the new information and communication technologies (Amendola and Gaffard, 1998). Costs come at the beginning, and hence cannot be financed out of current production. This causes a distortion of productive capacity and the dissociation in time of inputs from output, of costs from receipts, which puts a financial constraint on investment in capacity. The availability of financial resources at the right time is then essential to build a bridge over time between un-synchronized costs and revenue flows, so as to render restructuring of productive capacity viable while still on the way and unable to deliver output and revenues. If these resources are not available, necessary investment cannot be realized, which will further reduce final output and postpone (or even undermine the effective cashing of) the expected increases in productivity.

In the meantime production is lower and there is less demand for labour. Unemployment, lower revenues and the subsequent fall in final demand will further reduce receipts and financial resources. Insufficient investments will paradoxically result in excess supply, excessive productive capacity, earlier scrapping of production processes and in the aggregate, a productivity slowdown.

The scenario just drawn accounts for the fall in productivity going along with the introduction of a superior technique in terms of production coefficients. There is a divorce between the potential productivity gains of the technique, which can only take place in an economy already in the equilibrium state associated with the technique itself, and the realized productivity resulting from how the out-of-equilibrium process of transition takes place. This divorce has nothing to do with the specific character of the technique concerned; it depends on the coordination problems that arise in a transition process from an old technique to a new one.

The different productivity trends in Europe from those in the US in the 1990s and the apparent disappearance of the productivity paradox in those years confirm this scenario.

6.9 Some ideas by way of conclusion

Our foregoing analysis shifted attention away from *objective* aggregate factors of performances of the conventional growth view (i.e. the production function, technological progress, demographic factors). It focuses, instead, upon the conditions for the realization of growth potentialities implicit in those factors (and therefore on the coordination mechanisms across sectors, across firms and the interaction between the private and the public actors of the dynamics) and upon structural changes related to a broadly defined notion of innovation, and therefore induced by a number of different exogenous and endogenous forces. A much richer empirics has appeared before our eyes, then. Clearly this is just an intermediate house of a new research agenda.[38] It is therefore, hard and difficult to draw synthetic conclusions, so that we recapitulate our and related arguments under four headings.

6.9.1 Dynamics

In the proposed exercise in growth empirics, we have shown what we get by experimenting with some new notions trying to capitalize and go beyond some of more recent advances in the understanding of the growth process. Recall that Neoclassical (NC) theory examines a single economy and under the well-known assumptions on technology and production function, proves the existence of a unique steady state path. This unique equilibrium path is also a global attractor for the economy's dynamics, all other paths being transients.

It is the latter property that was re-phrased as *convergence hypothesis*, whereby, under the assumption of a common production function, countries[39] are expected to share one and the same attractor. This extension of properties of a single economy to a whole set of them can only be justified with the idea that such economy is representative. However,

> turning to the observed historical experiences of national economies in the twentieth century, what is most striking instead is how no single national

> economy is usefully viewed as representative. Rather, understanding cross-country growth behaviour requires thinking about the properties of the cross-country distribution of growth characteristics.[40]

This observation has generated a variety of amendments to the original NC analysis (e.g. the notion of conditional convergence), but also to more radical departures from it. First, it became evident that if there was any sort of convergence to a steady state with the envisioned stationarity properties, this was accomplished in groups: two (or more) convergence clubs were detected, where only members seem to share convergence to the same state. Refining previous work, Quah's statistical distribution analysis of cross countries per capita output levels showed the presence of more than one peak, an empirical property that called for interpretation. This could perhaps be a theory of clubs (as envisaged in Quah, 1993). However, this new vision of the long run admitting a finite set of attractors, can also be rationalized by an openly declared endogenous growth view (see Romer, 1986). It can also be compatible with a revised NC model, whereby the assumed production function shows non-linearities, and therefore admits of a plurality of solutions (see Durlauf, 1993; thresholds leading to poverty traps, as in Azariadis and Drazen, 1990). The set of countries originally taken into consideration can split into groups stuck in its own equilibrium. This idea has been accommodated within the conventional view in terms of the presence of multiple regimes, that is, isolated steady states.[41]

The variety of qualitatively diverse models coming to this same conclusion reveals the plurality of explanations for empirical evidence that does not seem to fit uniquely into anyone of them. However, to make the best of this idea, we need to generalize the notion of regime(s) and the idea of their multiplicity and render them *qualitative* notions. This is accomplished by defining a regime as a pair: a (growth) model *with* the set of states over which it operates. The latter contains equilibrium and non-equilibrium points, and the equilibrium set is now generalized to admit not only multiple finite equilibria but also closed curves, a-periodic but bounded fluctuations. Thus, any economy may be seen in an *equilibrium* that can be the isolated state of standard theory, or else a regular oscillations or finally an irregular but not too great fluctuation. In all such cases we can say that the economy remains within its *stability corridor*, and as that economy remains within a prevailing regime, there is regime stability (though there may not be a single attractor state). This is the property we saw for the US, in contrast to the other European countries. This is also the property we saw in MX, which was called dynamic dualism or poverty trap.

Convergence to a single attracting regime can be a property shared by a pool or club of countries, but *this is not what we have seen for the EU countries*, although it cannot be excluded for countries lying outside this empirical exercise (e.g. MERCOSUR, ASEAN). However, a given regime may be globally unstable, or *piecewise* so, so that all or certain initial conditions lead to a-periodic behaviours leading outside the regime itself. The viability condition implicit in dynamics within the stability corridor, as defined earlier, is violated and the economy is seen fluctuating across regimes, hence at the same time across distinct partitions of its state space *and* across different growth models. This *multi-regime dynamics*[42] can be very rich: for, it may contain again *structural cycles* across a (sub-)set of regimes, each returning with more or less regular periodicity, but also increasingly irregular, up to chaotic, fluctuations in regimes. Still, a group or club of countries can exhibit convergence towards the same kind of structural cycle, as a subset of European countries seems to show. But, more interestingly, an individual country or a club can show also convergence to an irregular regime dynamics, as finally it should be clear that convergence is a property of a dynamic path which has nothing to do with the stability or regularity property of the attracting path. The sketchy exercise on transition across three countries seems to support one such view.

The basic aim of such elaboration is to draw our attention to focus upon *instability*, rather than stability, of a given economy (or a group of sectors or countries). It shows that instability is to be redefined *at various levels*: the point instability of classical analysis, the set instability of more complicated dynamics of fluctuations and finally instability of multi-regime dynamics. And from a practical/policy point of view, it needs to be identified *by its degree*, not simply as stable/unstable. We have to be able to distinguish between local behaviours and structural change, which is the high instability connected with a change of the regulating dynamic model, rather than simply a change in state. It is regime instability that may reveal coordination problems at various levels, it is instability of the point type that can be assigned to exogenous shocks and local operating forces. We have seen, for instance, that there is likely to be a functional relation between regime instability and employment performance, and how this can account for the different histories of the US versus the EU countries, but also within some of them (Brida and Punzo, 2003; Lavezzi, 2003).

Detecting and understanding instability is therefore the gate to interpret past history and compare country- and sector-histories: It is also the foundation upon which to design adequate intervention policies. As a theoretical framework and a grid for empirical analysis, multi-regime dynamics redefines the very domain of policy targets: for instance, instead of being some levels of output or employment, they can be specific regimes and patterns and to control fluctuations for the cost of regime fluctuation may be too high. This leads us to the next items in these conclusions.

6.9.2 Economic integration

Of course, in the times of globalization, while several continental and regional integration processes are in competition with one another, the key story is this *integration **with** convergence*. And in fact, the twofold issue of the *possibility* the *necessity* of ‘convergence’ takes up a specific significance when considered in the perspective of the integration processes currently building EU, NAFTA (and MERCOSUR, ASEAN elsewhere), rather than in theory.

First of all, it is clear that by no means economic integration brings about *necessarily* convergence in the conventional sense. Hence, fears about the outcomes of such processes, which are entertained in Europe like elsewhere, are not ill founded, as they descend from an instinctive understanding that the attainment of the *deeper* convergence required is, as said, a recipe nobody really knows how to cook, without costs.

Moreover, that the two need to go together gives no indications as to whether we should have convergence first, and *then* economic integration, or the latter will 'do the job' automatically, so to say. The just finished debate about (the conditions of) the admission of the Central Eastern European countries can largely be read through this perspective. In the Americas, and in the NAFTA area, the idea adopted was apparently the latter one.

When, for instance, the feasibility of the European Union Enlargement or the achievements of NAFTA are being discussed, we are really asking: are the countries involved converging *already* (or are they able to converge) towards a common way of developing and growing? A question that soon will apply elsewhere in the world or in the new economic geography being designed in these days. If not, what sort of policies can be devised to help them to do so?

It has been suggested that the crucial *unifying* notion of convergence required as a policy foundation must be based upon a deeper understanding of the dynamic behaviours of the economies involved. Economic integration must 'go along' with *convergence to a common pattern of growth*. Instead, according to the expectations from the conventional view, economic integration would result in better and increasingly homogenous performance for all the countries involved provided the 'best' institutions have been set up.

However, in the multi-regime perspective, the very viability of the process of structural change demanded by, for example, integration requires specific policy interventions promoting and supporting well-working coordination procedures, that is, procedures that in particular prevent cumulative effects to pile up in wrong directions, thus generating structural instability of the type reflected in certain types of regime fluctuations. In our perspective, integration, as a synonym of free circulation of goods and services *cum* capital and labour mobility, cannot be considered as the magical solution to attain convergence. As we have tried to highlight, the recipe to success demands as basic ingredient, and goes along with, convergence in a sense that is definitely broader than envisaged by the conventional view. It is no easy recipe to cook. Not even within the EU area are countries converging all towards the same pattern of growth. Moreover, as a result of deepening dynamic interdependencies, this releases perturbations hampering the overall growth process. If this is so, institutional design ought to focus upon improving coordination among different economies, that is, a better policy mix at the *overall* level, instead of targeting specific levels of economic variables, be they GDP, employment or rates of interest.

6.9.3 A role fit for institutions

Of course, in this argument, institutions should not be ignored. However, they have to be considered not so much or uniquely in relation to the theoretical performance in the long run, as rather in relation to the adjustment processes required by qualitative or structural changes. Their role has to be altogether redefined, to be one of helping reducing the irregularity in the growth process generated by, for example, technology shocks and generally innovation, rather than in determining the growth trend. They do contribute to the latter by accomplishing the former task.

Effective institutional systems contribute to regular dynamic patterns, not those that just incorporate stronger incentives for growth. The reason is that *innovation* in its variety of forms is by its very nature a break up and implies a discontinuity: for example, a break up in the existing production structure and markets. It brings about adjustment costs and specific problems of coordination between economic activities. Depending upon the way these new problems are dealt with, an economy's growth is more or less regular and accordingly the productivity and output gains ripped out of innovation greater or smaller. The challenge is to render the technological and institutional evolution as gradual as possible. This being their appropriate role, economic policy need only go the same way.

Appendix

On the framework space

Our analytical framework is based upon variables (gross capital formation, value added and employment), which are relevant in the growth literature. They are manipulated so as to obtain growth rates from levels, often taken sectorally and/or regionally disaggregated. The rate of growth of value added and the rate of growth of gross fixed capital formation, both evaluated in terms of employee or per operative. Taken together, they are employed to index a growth path, of the economy as a whole or of a single sector, depending upon the level of data aggregation chosen. Such a path is a state in a plane endowed with axes called the Innovation and Accumulation axes, in the conventional order. On the former we write the growth rate of the GDP or sectoral value added per person employed, one of several possible indicators of productivity growth. The vertical axis records the investment pace again per person employed. The abscissa axis is the 'Innovation axis' as we can associate it with the neo-Schumpeterian and endogenous growth interpretations of productivity dynamics as basically driven by innovative activities. The Accumulation axis would be the focus of conventional aggregate theories of growth and technological progress, where accumulation of some form of capital is the driving force. In our framework, the two axes are plotted one against the other, in order to contrast the two basic views of the sources of productivity growth and welfare levels.[43]

A trajectory in this plane is a sequence of dated states: the growth paths of conventional theories. States are dated according to a certain 'clock'; this chosen, a state represents the average growth path of an economy over the corresponding date. The novelty in comparison to the conventional approaches is that a path is observed here via two variables. In addition, the dynamic evolution is reconstructed patching together a set of growth paths, and a trajectory looks like a segmented trend. Trajectories and paths coincide only if any of the latter is a stationary solution *and* an attractor.

Finally, a *regime* is a set of growth paths that are generated by the same standard model. Invoking standard explanations of growth and productivity dynamics, six such regimes can be distinguished, plus one special Harrodian generalised path, or corridor. This latter and the other semi-axes, are used to induce a partition of the coordinate plane into dynamical regimes. In the innovation regime (Regime 1), corresponding to the area below the Harrodian corridor in the first quadrant, all paths show positive productivity growth rates exceeding positive investment growth rates. The set above the corridor, where productivity falls behind investment growth, is the regime that can be associated with conventional growth theories which rely upon production functions and/or referring to capital-driven growth paths (Regime 6). With the quadrants numbered clockwise, beginning with the Innovation Regime – and observing that the positive and the negative quadrants are further subdivided by the Harrodian corridor – a classification is obtained: with no. 2 associated with 'restructuring' showing negative investment growth rates but positive productivity growth, while the remaining three regimes are mirror images of those just described. It is only when the coordinate plane is endowed with such theory-induced partition that it makes sense to call it Framework Space.[44]

One can easily show that the FS accommodates most if not all of the predictions in the existing growth literature and the related so called growth empirics. Neoclassical growth (NC) theory, for instance, predicts the long run (LR) dynamic behaviour of an economy to be a unique steady state value of $y = Y/N$, or output per capita (and assuming full employment, of labour productivity), while the LR output growth rate will be determined according to the equation: $g = n + \lambda$, where $n = \mathrm{d} \log N/\mathrm{d}t$ and λ is the rate of growth of exogenous technological progress.[45] Hence, the NC long run value of $g_y = (g - n)$ lies at the origin of the line (for $\lambda = 0$). It may not be there only when λ is positive (and of course, the zero of the line can always be shifted to such a value, whatever that is).

This shows that the implied output growth axis is basically a one-dimensional Framework Space; hence, in principle, we could introduce a regime classification there too.[46] Thus, with any given economy can be associated a steady state growth path as a pair of y (level of per capita and/or per employed output) and its productivity growth rate. Consider a pool of countries, as is often done in recent work. We can write each country's long-run level of y on a real line to get a scattered set of points, or if we like a whole distribution. Each country will be moving towards its long run value of y, going through some transient dynamics. All such paths however, if monitored through the growth rates of output per capita alone, are expected to converge to one and the same value on the growth rate line. (This of course leads straight to such issues as β- and σ-convergence.)

The first proposition of the NC model has been challenged in many ways, the principal critical idea is that there may be more than one long-run growth rate and countries need not converge to a unique long-run value of y (nor to an interval).[47] Thus, Endogenous growth theories try to explain why growth rates may apparently differ in a systematic way across countries. To account for such *population* of the growth phenomena, a single axis is simply not enough. It has to be supplemented by at least one more axis, and this leads to the present version of the FS, where the second axis is the accumulation axis.

In fact, the growth of labour productivity can be driven by innovation or by capital accumulation. Neither of these two types of paths can be found prevailing in pure form in reality, of course, for these are two extreme characterizations whose usefulness is in organizing one's ideas. One should think of them as two different growth engines because they imply economic mechanisms qualitatively rather than quantitatively different from one another. But why bother with two axes, and such a more complex structure as compared with the simplicity of the conventional growth theories? The reason is that the actual qualitative time evolution (the *phase structure*) as well as the dynamic structural dimension (the regime pattern) matter for the understanding of what has been going on to productivity and growth across countries. Performance measured by any standard index may be the same on any given time horizon. We may have that different productivity dynamics have to be explained by different underlying relations with innovative or accumulation activities (or growth engines), while the time variability of productivity growth profiles may reflect structural changes at the level of the growth mechanisms. Of course, the implications would be different, also at a policy level. To see this, take two countries having the same performance in terms of productivity. A country with a history of constantly high accumulation and therefore a relevant proportion of newer capacity would have an evolution, in terms of product and process specialization, human skills and foreign trade, quite different from a country whose development has been based upon relatively higher rates of innovation. This suggests that the notion of regime permits to discriminate qualitatively between performances that would not appear much different in a more conventional, quantity-oriented approach.

In analysing and comparing histories, the first exercise one can carry on, is to check out which of these regimes prevails, as the conventional view makes us to expect. If there is one such regime, we need to inquire as to why. If it does not exist, we have to look for *higher level* regularities, regularities that may emerge in the patterns of visited regimes: for example, structural cycles, structural fluctuations. An index can be attached to each of them, indicating the degree of irregularity embodied, according to a procedure discussed, for example, in Brida and Punzo (2003).

On the methodological approach

Conventional growth theories focus upon equilibrium behaviours, expecting them to be attractors as well. This is justification for econometric techniques that estimate attractors as time limit behaviours (e.g. long-run states implied in an unconditional experiment), and tend to or entirely overlook the shorter run. But we need to confront the issue even thought econometric box of tools may yet contain what we would need to be able and handle them. We need to keep in mind the goal: what escapes from conventional approaches is what is interesting in our observations, non-equilibrium behaviour, and with it the shorter-run.

Out of equilibrium, the dynamics of productivity is driven not only by long run, exogenous forces of technological progress and invention. It also reflects the process of transformation of the productive structure and the ability of agents and institutions to organize and to carry on a process within constraints set by economy-wide institutional features. Productivity gains generated by the introduction of a new technology, for instance, can only be reaped and recently created unemployment re-absorbed, if coordination problems are appropriately dealt with. In other words, productivity dynamics is generally the outcome of the way in which the economy is able to cope with coordination problems connected with an equilibrium displacement. This not dissimilar from what happens when the economy is forced to undergo major structural changes that are not strictly speaking of a technological nature, or begin as such.[48]

The relationship between productivity and investment characterizing a growth process is more complex than it appears in the literature. To understand it, one has to shift attention away from all convergence issues for, as we have seen, these latter spring from the un-granted assumption of the existence of a global, unique long-run attractor and a common production function. We have to acknowledge the existence of a menu of growth regimes, instead, each characterized by qualitatively different such relationships.

In this analytical framework, the rate at which an economy can grow without inflation pressures – its potential growth rate – certainly depends on the potential productivity growth. However, given the inter-temporal complementarities between production processes, the dynamics of productivity cannot be independent of investment dynamics. In other words, an economy's past and ongoing history in terms of visited growth regimes and time spent here and there, do conspire in determining its growth performance. It is the short sequence of regimes repeatedly visited, within an apparently random regime pattern that matters. When this repeats indefinitely from a point onwards, we are luckily back into the *dreamland* of the growth theorists.

Compared with the standardized settings of econometric practice, the FS is not much more than a classificatory device; nevertheless the dynamics taking place there can be associated with an interpretive scheme. Given its nature it is clear that there is no unique natural choice for this: depending upon the specific dynamics we encounter and represent in the FS (hence depending upon the history we are looking at) qualitatively different models can be good candidates for the role of interpreters. The inspiration of the construction is not so much to replicate what we already know, it is rather to look at what we do not already have in the existing theories through the lenses of *classes of theories*.[49] This is multi-regime dynamics: dynamics that may take an economy or a sector across regimes. *Adjustment* and multi-regime dynamics are coupled together to reproduce observed dynamics as a complex phenomenon. Thus, irregularity is seen as the compounded effect of those two mechanisms, working though at different paces, more than the simple reflection of stochastic disturbances. Heroically, received theories of growth separate the two from one another, and overlook dynamics induced by their coupling.[50] In the multi-regime dynamics of the FS we try to do without this twofold simplification. The notion of dynamics over a set (or *menu*) of regimes[51] rather than over individual states within a unique state space, is a way to look for regularities where they cannot be expected to emerge unless we introduce by assumption essential stochastic components.[52]

Multi-regime dynamics, on the other hand, is the privileged view of the neo Austrian approach, whose core idea is the interaction between short run adjustment with an invariant economic structure and the long-run growth process, where structure would eventually be fully adjusted (Amendola and Gaffard, 1998; Hicks, 1973). The bridge between them is provided by a theory of structural change. In one such framework, mechanisms determining output, prices and wages basically tend to amplify all imbalances in the structure of productive capacity resulting from the break up of a previous relatively regular functioning of the economy. One such break up occurs, for instance, when an attempt is made to introduce production innovations, and therefore to carry out qualitative changes at the level of the structure itself. This is to large extent at the heart of the histories of post-war economies, and more so in the recent years. This impulse triggers an out-of-equilibrium process with fluctuations in both real and nominal variables, also affecting the amount of financial resources available as well as intensity and pace of capital formation. As a consequence, investment fluctuations, at the same time as distortions in the time structure of productive capacity may become increasingly strong, and it may reach the point of threatening the very viability of the economy's path. Viability becomes the crucial analytical issue to be tackled and the appropriate objective for policy intervention.

A tendency to un-checked fluctuations becomes the typical mode in which even an exogenously impulse-triggered evolution gets realized in the FS. Consequently, fluctuations of different degrees of irregularity exhibit deep structural properties of the economy as well as showing the way they interact with one another in shaping out the response to the original impulse. This shows the view that multi-regime dynamics is basically a product of endogenous mechanisms, even though it might be initialized by exogenous shocks. It is on such out-of-equilibrium paths that an economy (or its component sectors) is (observed to be) travelling most of the time, and this is how we propose to consider actual histories (instead of zooming them into some implied long run). With this we retain irregularity that we find inbuilt into all of our time series.

Interdependence is associated with these out of equilibrium behaviours, and it takes the *twofold form* of dynamical coupling among processes/sectors and of feedback mechanisms acting over time. Different types of disequilibria can be generated in this way, which may also interact sequentially with each other. So, quite different histories may get associated even with the same kind of original impulse. Interdependence is made to account for the variety of cross-country grow experiences as well as for their evolution. Such processes cannot be tracked down uniquely, from their outset, as it would be if their historical evolution were fully determined by 'Fundamentals' alone. They are the joint outcome of all the events that happen along the way, during their unfolding. Initial conditions matter in general[53] and uncertainty is inbuilt into a path dependent process. Again, this fits well with the highly non-linear implicit in multi-regime dynamics and is needed to render endogenous the explanation of regime switches, as they result from accumulated feedback effects.

Within such processes with no predetermined direction, viability asserts itself as the key issue. Intuitively speaking, a viable economy is one that remains within the limits of its own stability corridor, a region in the state space close enough to their own steady states. There, embedded stabilizing forces allow the economy to continue functioning smoothly by absorbing even relatively large disturbances.[54] Of the paths within a given regime, an economy may follow, some may prove viable, others may not. And, of course, that menu itself may be changing over time, at least in principle. Thus, viability as a generalization of the notion of local stability is one aspect of path dependence that needs to be incorporated into our analysis in order to better account for observed histories. In a multi-regime framework stability corridors may internally structure state spaces associated with the various regimes; interesting dynamics arises when leaving a given corridor and pointing towards a different regime.

Notes

1 See Durlauf and Quah (1999, 238).

2 Also because our economists' theory may actually not be sufficient to handle the wealth of experiences history is offering. (An opinion forcefully put forward by Durlauf in his (2001) *Manifesto for Growth Econometrics*.)

3 New with respect to the classical Kaldor's stylized facts (Kaldor, 1961).

4 Be it purely technological innovation, or related with institutional changes, as in the case of integration and transition processes.

5 See Yoshikawa's (1999) for an explanation of the Japanese 1990s stagnation as a result of the lack of innovation.

6 Listed in Durlauf and Quah (1999).

7 See Quah (1993). In particular, two graphs there

> give a number of important messages. First, the data show instability in underlying long run growth patterns: thus, assuming that each country has stable growth path and then studying their cross country variation produces results that are difficult to interpret. Second, the increasing fluctuation variability suggests that important disturbances – demand and productivity – are ongoing.
>
> (pp. 428–429)

8 Record being kept of the time spent in each such regime, that defines a relative stability property (see Day, 1993, 1994, 1998). We call it a string with reference to the coded representation proposed in Brida *et al.* (2003).

9 See Appendix, also for the relations with existing growth theories and the growth empirics literature (see also Böhm and Punzo, 2001).

10 Of course, the presence of a single globally attracting equilibrium (as for example, in NC growth theory) is the strongest form of regime stability in the earlier sense. In our definition however, prevailing regime is tantamount to the presence of a dominant qualitative model of growth, which however may comprise one or more equilibria, hence attractors. On the other hand, the presence of a single attractor is sufficient (but not necessary) for the existence of a prevailing regime. This one, the most regular of all dynamic patterns, is the only pattern considered by the NC growth theory. Its alternatives and generalizations (admitting multiple steady states) in fact introduce the

possibility of patterns that in the long run admit only steady states. Our view permits the persistence of irregular patterns in the FS, and to study these we need new statistical tools (as envisaged in Brida and Punzo (2003), and in Lavezzi (2003)).

11 Here thanks to stock market bubbles that pushed capital costs down.

12 Romer (1999, 32).

13 This interpretation is consistent with the interpretation in Yoshikawa (1999). Though there it is obviously much more articulated, in particular connecting the demand slump behind the stagnation of the 1990s with the lack of innovation, and behind the latter the substantial absence of initiative of the government sector at large.

14 These will be called generally *structural fluctuations*, see Brida and Punzo (2003).

15 Beyond that we still have something to say, later in this chapter.

16 In the convergence literature on the regions of the EU, see, for example, for a recent one Baumol *et al.*'s (2002), integration has popped up also under the form of spatial dependence of regional growth, hence as determining the convergence rate. Baumol *et al.*'s use a two-macroregions model, to find out that the rate is very different. This only adds to the large literature on the topic, started by the pioneering work by Barro (1991), Barro and Sala-i-Martin (1991, 1992) and with a large section for Europe. This has offered more econometric applications than a firmer understanding of the issue at the regional levels, computed convergence rates varying dramatically with the sample and the technique.

17 Of course, if NC convergence holds, the structural cycle boils down to a single stationary state. Notice that convergence is the equivalent in cross countries analysis of stability in time series analysis for the single country. Cross-country convergence to structural cycle or fluctuations does not require stability of any cycle in the dynamic sense. It is only in the standard literature that the two go together, in the narrow sense of stability towards a point attractor, a balanced growth path. This can only lead to the wrong expectation, in particular to confusing cross-country common behaviour with stability property of a certain type of dynamics. In our case a group of countries can share a structural fluctuations which itself is chaotic, or generally without well defined periodicity.

18 In particular the peculiarity of the US economy in aggregate of spending long time around the 45 line in the FS, which can be taken to indicate paths of regular growth. Our hypothesis is that this results of a special low cross regime dispersion of its sectors, see later (see also Lavezzi (2003) for using this notion).

19 These figures are reproduced from Hamann and Longhi (2001), with the kindest permission of the authors.

20 Böhm and Punzo (2001), Hamann and Longhi (2001).

21 A more formal analysis in a discrete variable space, in the spirit of Quah's and with his tools of distribution analysis, has been used by Lavezzi (2003) in a different application of the FS approach.

22 The interdependence between sectors of a given economy can often be likened to spatial dependence among interconnected regions. It is clear that interdependence makes one expect in both cases, similar behaviours hence in this case, convergence in performance. This is not so among sectors, at least it is not always evidently so, as we are going to show. It is not so in the regional literature either, as explained in the next footnote.

23 From Böhm and Punzo (2001).

24 This of course has relevant stability implications.

25 For the technique see Brida *et al.* (2003).

26 See the reference in the previous footnote.

27 In Quah this is the existence of one or more peak of the cross-country distribution of per-capita – income, against their respective initial values. See also Durlauf and Quah (1999, p. 240).

28 While, of course, sectors would fluctuate across regimes in a fashion similar to the aggregate economy, but generally with different phases.

29 These can be called *regular fluctuations*.

30 It is *dynamic* as it is a fluctuation instead of a low-level equilibrium, as is more common in the literature (see, for example, Azariadis and Drazen, 1990).

31 But also Italy, see, for example, Lavezzi (2003).

32 See Punzo (1997).

33 This is the theory of the U-shaped curve of GDP, with an initial recession followed by the expansion driven by the productivity gains following the original massive restructuring of firms, employment and property. Implicitly the expectation of this dynamics as typical, is founded upon the acceptance of the idea that one of the growth models we have, generates a suitable attractor for the country, once the structural adjustments are accomplished (see Blanchard, 1997).

34 See, for example, Blanchard (1997).

35 See Punzo (2001).

36 A comparison can be found in Punzo (2001).

37 See Blanchard (1997). These paragraphs are based on Punzo (2001).

38 We agree that 'Numerous studies on the determinants of growth have treated the empirical evidence in a way that obscures interesting and important features'. As much as when Quah adds 'To refine these statements, to place more interpretation on the dynamics, t bring in conditional information (explanatory variables) all appear to be useful and feasible research projects' (Quah, 1993, p. 433).

39 All countries of the HS database, as in Baumol.

40 Durlauf and Quah (1999, p. 238).

41 Quah (1993) forcefully puts forward a criticism of the standard approach whereby the existence of a steady state path is assumed to justify the estimation of the average growth rate as a proxy.

42 Of course, multi-regime dynamics as defined here admits all other simpler dynamics as special cases.

43 Durlauf and Quah (1999).

44 See Böhm and Punzo (2001).

45 Such net growth rate(s) are written as coordinate value(s) on our horizontal line. The rate of growth of output per head is driven by exogenous technological progress. One can say this by saying that the endogenous growth rate of output per head $g_y = (g - n)$, and if $e = n$, of labour productivity is zero. (Let $\mathrm{d} \log E/\mathrm{d}t = e$, E being employment.) (See Böhm and Punzo, 2001.)

46 As is implicit in Durlauf and Johnson (1999).

47 See for instance Baumol *et al.*'s (1994), Durlauf, Quah, various years, and their theory of multiple local steady states for groups/clubs of countries.

48 See Amendola and Gaffard (1998, pp. 220–222).

49 Very much in the non-parameteric veiwpoint supported by the often referred to paper by Durlauf and Quah (1999).

50 This idea is creeping out in recent literature, see Lucas (1993), where interaction generates growth.

51 A regime is defined as a model with its own state spaces. Usually we assume only one model so that its domain is also the whole of the state space. This makes it easy to test theories, against alternatives. In general however we may have a partition of the state space with different local models or laws of motions. This is the notion we are using here (see Böhm and Punzo, 2001; Day, 1993, 1994, 1998).

52 Of course stochastic elements cannot be excluded. In this setting however they in principle do not supply not *the* explanation.

53 Not just for the special cases of special PF with non-convexities, see, for example, poverty traps and the like.

54 The same idea is expressed by A. Leijonhufvud who casts doubts on the capacity of economic systems for a self-regulatory behaviour. 'If the system is exposed to

disturbances of a magnitude great enough to shock it to a position (. . .) outside the equilibrium neighbourhood, it is found that its homeostatic controls are severely impaired' (1985/2000).

References

Amendola, M. and J.-L. Gaffard (1998): *Out of Equilibrium*, Oxford, Clarendon Press.

Amendola, M., J.-L. Gaffard and L.F. Punzo (1999): 'Neo-Austrian processes', *Indian Journal of Applied Economics*, 8(2): 277–279.

Arrow, K. (1962): 'The economic implications of learning by doing', *Review of Economic Studies*, XXIX: 155–173.

Azariadis, C. and A. Drazen (1990): 'Threshold externalities in economic development', *Quarterly Journal of Economics*, CV: 501–526.

Barro, R. (1991): 'Economic growth in a cross-section of countries', *The Quarterly Journal of Economics*, 407–443.

Barro, R. and X. Sala-i-Martin (1991): 'Convergence across states and regions', *Quarterly Journal of Economics*, 106(2): 407–443.

Barro, R. and X. Sala-i-Martin (1992): 'Convergence across states and regions', *Brookings Papers on Economic Activity*, 141–196.

Baumol, C., C. Ertur and J. Le Gallo (2002): 'Spatial convergence clubs and the European growth process, 1980–1995', in Fingleton, B. (ed.), *European Regional Growth, Advances in Spatial Science*, Berlin, Springer Verlag.

Baumol, W.J., R.R. Nelson and E.N. Wolff (1994): *Convergence of Productivity*, New York, Oxford University Press.

Blanchard, O. (1997): *The Economics of Post-Communist Transition*, Oxford, Clarendon Press.

Blanchard, O. (2000): 'What do we know about macroeconomics that Fisher and Wicksell did not?' NBER Working Paper No. 7550.

Böhm, B. and L.F. Punzo (2001): 'Investment–productivity fluctuations and structural change', in L.F. Punzo (ed.), *Cycles, Growth, and Structural Change*, London, Routledge.

Böhm, B., J.-L. Gaffard and L.F. Punzo (2001): 'Industrial dynamics and employment in Europe', Research Report, European Commission, Targeted Socio-Economic Research program.

Brida, G., S. Bimonte and L.F. Punzo (2001): 'Notions of regime: a review', Working Paper, University of Siena.

Brida, J.G. and L.F. Punzo (2003): 'Symbolic time series and dynamic regimes', *Structural Change and Economic Dynamics*, 14(2): 159–183.

Brida, J.G., M. Puchet Anyul and L.F. Punzo (2003): 'Coding economic dynamics to represent regime dynamics', *Structural Change and Economic Dynamics*, 14(2): 133–157.

Crafts, N. and G. Toniolo (1996): *Economic Growth in Europe since 1945*, Cambridge, Cambridge University Press.

Day, R.H. (1993): 'Non-linear dynamics and evolutionary economics', in R.H. Day and P. Chen (eds), *Non-linear Dynamics and Evolutionary Economics*, New York, Oxford University Press.

Day, R.H. (1994, 1998): *Complex Economic Dynamics*, vols 1 and 2, Cambridge, MA, The MIT Press.

Durlauf, S.N. (1993): 'Non ergodic economic growth', *Review of Economic Studies*, 60: 349–366.

Durlauf, S.N. (2003): 'Manifesto for a Growth Econometrics', *Journal of Econometrics*, 100(1): 65–69.

Durlauf, S.N. and P.A. Johnson (1995): 'Multiple regimes and cross-country growth behaviour', *Journal of Applied Econometrics*, 10(4): 365–380.

Durlauf, S.N. and D. Quah (1999): 'The new empirics of economic growth', in J.B. Taylor and M. Woodford (eds), *Handbook of Macroeconomics*, vol. 1A, Amsterdam, North Holland.

Fitoussi, J.P., D. Jestaz, E. Phelps and G. Zoega (2000): 'Roots of the recent recoveries: labor reforms or private sector policies?' *Brooking Papers on Economic Activity*, 1: 237–311.

Galbraith, J.K. (1997): 'Time to ditch the NAIRU', *Journal of Economic Perspectives*, 11: 11–32.

Hamann, E. and C. Longhi (2001): 'Growth cycles and regime switches: an analysis of structural change in Europe. Part 1: Country movies'. IDEE Working Paper 2001-9.

Hicks, J.R. (1973): *Capital and Time*, Oxford, Clarendon Press.

Kaldor, N. (1961): 'Capital accumulation and economic growth', in F.A. Lutz and D.C. Hague (eds), *The Theory of Capital*, London, Macmillan.

Lavezzi, M.A. (2003): 'Investment–productivity and distribution dynamics in a multisector economy: some theory and an application to Italian regions,' *Structural Change and Economic Dynamics*, 14(2): 185–211.

Leijonhufvud, A. (1985): 'Ideology and analysis in macroeconomics', in P. Koslowski (ed.), *Economics and Philosophy*, Tübingen, J.C. Mohr. Reprinted in A. Leijonhufvud, 2000, *Macro Instability and Coordination*, Cheltenham, E. Elgar.

Lucas, R.E. (1993): 'Making a miracle', *Econometrica*, 61: 251–272.

Puchet, M.A. and L.F. Punzo (eds), (2001): 'Structural divergence and dynamics of dualism: lessons from Mexico before and after NAFTA', in *Mexico beyond NAFTA*, London and New York, Routledge.

Punzo, L.F. (1997): 'Cyclos estructurales y convergencia durante los procesos de integracion economica', *Revista de Economia*, Segunda Epoca IV, 2, Banco Central del Uruguay.

Punzo, L.F. (2001): 'The look of stagnation: Romania's erratic transition', CIRJE, University of Tokyo; also available at www.econ-pol.unisi.it/docenti/punzo.htm

Quah, D. (1993): 'Empirical cross-section dynamics in economic growth', *European Economic Review*, 37: 426–434.

Quah, D. (1996): 'Regional convergence clusters across Europe', *European Economic Review*, 40: 951–958.

Romer, C.D. (1999): 'Changes in business cycles: evidences and explanations', mimeo, February, NBER Working Paper No 6948.

Romer, P.M. (1986): 'Increasing returns and long run growth', *Journal of Political Economy*, 94: 1002–1037.

Solow, R.M. (1956): 'A contribution to the theory of economic growth', *Quarterly Journal of Economics*, LXX: 65–94.

Yoshikawa, H. (1999, 2002): *Japan's Lost Decade*, trans. C.H. Stewart, Tokyo, International House of Japan.

7 Cultural diversity, European integration and the Welfare State

Ugo Pagano

7.1 Introduction

According to the 'American-Neoclassical' approach, stemming from the Tiebout (1956) model, the main advantage of federalism lies in the fact that individuals with similar tastes, including those related to risk-aversion and the provision of public goods, can cluster in the same jurisdictions. According to this view, federalism can favour the maximum differentiation of the characteristics of the individuals clustering in the different States. The starting point of this chapter is a criticism of this approach. While the main advantage of federalism is related to the possibility of clustering heterogeneous individuals, the assumption of costless movement from one State to the other implicitly implies that individuals are homogeneous in some of other important characteristics. For instance, the hypothesis that individuals face low mobility costs involves that they have very minor cultural and linguistic differences. This is not the case of Europe where cultural-linguistic differentiation is high and federalism is often associated to the protection of the cultural specificity of certain regions.

Cultural-linguistic standardization and the social protection given by National Welfare States can be regarded as two alternative insurance devices: the first increases the probability of alternative employment while the second provides some assistance in case of dismissal from the present employment.[1] A Europe that lacks the horizontal cultural standardization of the United States must necessarily rely more on the Welfare State than a country like the United States that is characterized by a very large market with low mobility costs. One would expect that in Europe the Welfare State should act as a substitute for low horizontal cultural homogenization – an expectation that is consistent with the more relevant role of European States in social protection.

The comparison with the United States clarifies the paradoxical problem of European integration. On the one hand, social protection is more necessary when cultural-linguistic differences make it expensive cultural standardization as a substitute for it. On the other hand, social insurance is more unlikely to be accepted when these cultural differences prevail. While a full-blown European system of Social Insurance is likely to be unfeasible, the process of economic integration makes it more difficult for the increasingly specialized national economies to insure one sector against the other and to continue to provide the type of social insurance that was traditionally supplied by National Welfare States. We argue that a possible way out is a system of mutual insurance among the European National Welfare Systems.

The chapter is structured as follows:

In Section 7.2 we contrast the 'Neo-Classical-American' view of federalism with the one that we believe to be closer to the needs of a culturally diverse Europe.

In Section 7.3 we show how economic integration and market mobility at national level were greatly favoured by 'institutional complements,' such as the existence of an undisputed dominant high culture and the loyalty to a single political unity. Similar features characterized the United States of America but cannot be taken for granted in contemporary Europe taken as a whole.

The focus of Section 7.4 is on the two instruments through which national governments insured their citizens against the risks of the mobile market society: social protection and cultural-linguistic standardization. We consider the difficult puzzle that the relations of complementarity and substitution between these two insurance devices create for Europe and how, in this respect, the European case is polar to that of United States that, unlike Europe, is characterized by high horizontal cultural homogeneity among States (and, because of many decades of immigration, by lower vertical homogeneity).

In the fifth section, we consider a possible model of 'mild European federalism', which combines some degree of cultural integration with some defence of cultural diversity and some protection against 'forced' economic mobility.

Finally, in Section 7.6, we argue that European political institutions must support National Welfare States. Their capacity to provide social insurance would otherwise be eroded by the productive specialization that is entailed by the process of European economic integration and, more generally, by globalization.

7.2 The limits to the competitive view of federalism

In the neoclassical tradition stemming from the Tiebout (1956) model, federalism is claimed to be an effective way through which citizens can get arrangements for taxes and public goods provisions that are as close as possible to their preferences. If the Welfare State is considered an insurance mechanism against the various hazards of life including health, skills redundancy and market fluctuations, federalism could solve the problems that arise from the existence of differences between tastes for State intervention and for redistribution that individuals, with different wealth and different risk aversion, are very likely to have. A Federal State offers different Jurisdictions among which the agents can choose. Thus, individuals with similar tastes for the 'degree' of intervention of the Welfare State can cluster in the same jurisdiction. According to this view, some contrasts, which characterize modern democracies, can be overcome by a market mechanism for the demand and supply of State arrangements. This view of federalism relies on the neoclassical model and, in particular, on the Tiebout (1956) model for the supply of public goods according to which people can vote with their feet. It can lead to the extreme conclusion that the different States should show little respect for their own minorities because both the majority of the community and the minority may gain if each one of them is organized in different jurisdictions according to its own community values.[2]

Market mobility guarantees the individuals against the hazards of their production activities in two ways. In the first place, individuals can find other employments if their skills become redundant where they are. In the second place, the market for jurisdictions may offer more redistributive arrangements for the most risk-averse individuals. In general, mobility and competition in both the private and public sectors can guarantee better arrangements for all the individuals.

Such a mix of neoclassical model and of some aspects of the American federalist experience can, however, be a very dangerous guide for the institutional design of the European Community. The Tiebout (1956) model relies on the idea that the costs of mobility are zero – a theoretical abstraction that can, perhaps, provide some insights for the American society where mobility costs are relatively low but it is at odds with the European situation where linguistic differences and other types of community ties make mobility very costly. In Europe federalism is often advocated by communities as a way of protecting sunk investments, such as their language and their ethnic investments, against the threats of an increasing mobile society. It is rarely seen as a means to open opportunities for people to move towards jurisdictions that are closer to their tastes.

The shortcomings of the neoclassical view of federalism for the European case are also related to some more general limitations of this model. While federalism is considered a way to enhance diversity in the population by clustering people according to their characteristics, this view relies on low mobility costs that can only hold if individuals are homogeneous in other relevant respects. For instance, if individuals are homogeneous in their linguistic characteristics, their mobility is enhanced and they could easily cluster according to the welfare provision offered by the different States. In general, the homogeneity in one dimension can favour the heterogeneous clustering in other dimensions: if the individuals are homogeneous in terms of their preference for welfare provisions their mobility among jurisdictions is enhanced in other dimensions and they can more easily cluster according to their linguistic and ethnic characteristics. State competition is rather limited; in many cases, it is possible in some spheres only because some monopoly – possibly a cultural-linguistic monopoly – has been established in some other spheres.

7.3 Cultural-linguistic standardization and individual mobility: a multiplicity of institutional equilibria

The neoclassical model can be criticized for a failure to understand the complementarities[3] existing between heterogeneity in some domains and homogeneity in some other dimensions. However, this criticism can be deepened by arguing that the traditional view fails to see the market as an institution that has required a long process of linguistic, legal and customary standardization and has, in turn, induced a further enhancement of this process. A fair degree of cultural-linguistic standardization is wrongly taken for granted while it is a crucial institutional precondition for the working of both 'political' and economic markets. Indeed, the National State has greatly helped to homogenize the individuals in important cultural-linguistic dimensions and create the conditions for a mobile market society.

Contrary to the neoclassical story the development of markets has not been associated only with increasing diversity but mostly with a great demand for standardization. Indeed, it has often come together with a growing intolerance for linguistic and cultural diversity.

Pre-market agrarian societies were very often characterized by both horizontal and vertical diversity. The dialect spoken in one village could well differ from the dialect spoken in the next village while in the same village the serf, the priest and the lord would all speak different languages. However, while linguistic diversity was itself a product of geographically and socially immobile economic relations, it enhanced their immobility stabilizing the roles that were very often peacefully transmitted from fathers to sons and from mothers to daughters: the way of speaking was enough to understand the particular slot of society where each individual should fit. Linguistic diversity and social/geographical immobility were complementary and self-reinforcing elements of a very stable institutional equilibrium. One should not be surprised at the fact that these institutions have characterized such a disproportionate share of the 'civilized' history of human kind. One should rather wonder how it was possible for such a stable equilibrium to eventually break down and for societies, characterized by linguistic and cultural homogeneity and by social and geographical mobility, to finally emerge.

Indeed, the change was only possible if and when a State (a potential National State) had spread a high culture (characterized by a written language) among the large majority of the population. Once a critical mass was reached, a different self-reinforcing process took off: increasing linguistic homogeneity favoured higher levels social and geographical mobility and, conversely, higher levels of social and geographical mobility stimulated a growing process of linguistic homogenization.

As Gellner[4] suggested, the ideal initial conditions for this process were given by situations where, as an unintended outcome of the power struggles among the political entities of agrarian societies, a single State ruled on a territory in which, despite the existence of many local dialects, there was a shared view of the dominant high culture. This was the case of England and France that were the first countries where a National State could foster the institutions of a national culture and of a national market (see case A in Table 7.1).

Germany and Italy shared with France and England the existence of a dominant high culture and language but lacked a State that could invest in their popularization and start the virtuous self-reinforcing process between cultural-linguistic homogenization and increasing market mobility. Thus, in these two countries there was strong pressure to achieve national unity that, indeed, gave them possibility to follow the development process of the early industrializers (see case B in Table 7.1).

However, the model could not be easily replicated in other parts of Europe. A symmetric case arose when more than one high culture existed within a

Table 7.1 National-state formation under alternative conditions

	Loyalty to a political unity	*No Loyalty to a political unity*
Cultural-linguistic homogeneity	(A) Early National States (England, France)	(B) Struggle for national unity (Italy, Germany)
Cultural-linguistic heterogeneity	(C) Multilingual and multicultural National States (Switzerland, Belgium)	(D) Ethnic conflict and ethnic cleansing (Yugoslavia, Turkey, Greece)

well-defined political unity that could command some loyalty from other elements; here the State could try to foster bilingualism and mutual cultural recognition as means of enhancing a virtuous circle between cultural standardization and economic mobility but the process was far from easy (see case C in Table 7.1). This type of process somehow succeeded in Switzerland and Belgium, whereas it failed in the larger scale case of the Austro-Hungarian Empire.

Even more difficult was the case of areas that had neither a clearly defined dominant language and culture nor a political unity that could command a high degree of loyalty on the population living there. In these cases the raw material was rather unfit for the coming of the modern world of cultural standardization and required often some rather brutal measures that in some most unfortunate cases took the form of ethnic cleansing (see case D in Table 7.1). According to Gellner, in these cases, 'violence and brutality seem to have been inscribed into the nature of the situation. The horror was not optional, it was predestined' (Gellner 1998, p. 54). Imposed ethnic separation (as the between Greek and Turkish or Pakistani and Indian communities) or ethnic cleansing (most recently in the former Yugoslavia) were the most evident expression of this last case.

While the transition from agrarian to industrial market mobile societies is, in general, associated with a move from an institutional equilibrium characterized by linguistic-cultural differentiation and social-economic immobility to one characterized by linguistic-cultural standardization and social-economic mobility, this move cannot be taken for granted by economic analysis and even less by policy makers. In different areas of the world the move has been more radical than in others: in Europe linguistic-cultural standardization and social-economic mobility are far more limited than in the United States. The role of market and political competition, as well as the role of social protection, can therefore be very different in these two institutional settings.

7.4 Social protection and cultural-linguistic standardization: institutional complements and alternative insurance devices

Ever since Adam Smith, the advantages of a market economy have been associated with those related to the learning-by-doing-advantages entailed by the division of labour. Market economies allow individuals to get from others most of the goods they need through exchange and allow the specialization of economic activities. However, Coase (1937) and thereby Marx well before him have convincingly argued that, even in modern industrial societies, specialized activities are coordinated by means other than market exchange.

Indeed, pre-industrial agrarian societies often have a complex division of labour and a high degree of specialization. The social immobility and the static nature of these societies can favour a high degree of specialization. By contrast, the high economic and social mobility that characterizes market societies may inhibit specialization and job specific learning by doing – a consequence that would be at odds with the traditional Smithian wisdom according to which the degree of specialization is only limited by the extent of the market. The raise of nationalism and, in particular, cultural and linguistic standardization can however greatly decrease the hazards of specialization in a mobile society by making each skill less specific and more easily employable in other occupations. In this sense cultural and linguistic standardization can act as a substitute to forms of social protection that redistribute income to the individuals made redundant by the fluctuations and structural changes that characterize the dynamic market economy. Both this kind of redistribution and cultural-linguistic standardization can act as insurance devices against the hazards of market economies and make market mobility compatible with the drive towards specialization and its related Smithian productivity advantages. The more costly the cultural-linguistic standardization process, the more convenient its (partial) substitution by forms of social solidarity.

In other respects, cultural standardization and social protection can be seen as two fundamental complementary institutions that favoured the emergence of a market economy. Nationalism favoured the dominance of a standardized high culture over a certain area and, at the same time, claimed that all the people sharing the same ethnic identity were 'brothers' linked together by a special sense of solidarity. Nationalists pushed for both cultural standardization and social protection and, moreover, the two objectives were, in many respects, mutually reinforcing. Cultural standardization reinforced the sense of solidarity and made it easier to agree to forms of social protection. In turn, social protection favoured the feeling of belonging to the same 'imagined community' and favoured the conditions under which local dialects and traditions could be abandoned for the national languages and the traditions defining the national identity. By contrast the social solidarity required by redistribution policies may suffer when there is no cultural-linguistic standardization and, vice versa, the latter may be rather difficult when there is no shared feeling of solidarity among different ethnic groups.

The relations of complementarity and substitution between social solidarity and cultural-linguistic standardization create a difficult puzzle in situations in which both factors are lacking.

On the one hand a low level of cultural-linguistic standardization make redistributive policies more important because the liquidity of the skills of the losers is low. On the other hand, the same low-level of cultural-linguistic homogeneity may inhibit social solidarity and make it difficult to implement redistributive

Table 7.2 Vertical and horizontal solidarity

	Vertical cultural homogenization	*Vertical cultural differentiation*
Horizontal cultural homogenization	(1) Social and regional solidarity (*Classic National States*)	(2) Regional solidarity without social solidarity (*United States*)
Horizontal cultural differentiation	(3) Social solidarity without regional solidarity (*Europe*)	(4) No social and no regional solidarity? (*The future Europe?)*

policies. Thus, redistributive policies are relatively more needed when they are more difficult.

In order to understand better the nature of this difficulty, one should recall that, in the case of traditional National States, social solidarity had both a vertical and a horizontal dimension (solidarity among the individuals of the same region and among regions) that were associated to the overcoming of sharp vertical cultural divides among social classes and to the elimination of pronounced horizontal cultural differences among the territories of the National State (case 1 of Table 7.2).

United States departed from the traditional National States (case 1 of Table 7.2). Horizontal homogeneity of the population of the different States (linguistic and also cultural) has gone together with a cultural vertical differentiation of the population due to ethnic division that have been associated to its immigration history. Horizontal cultural homogeneity and vertical cultural differentiation have here been associated to a solidarity among different State that has gone rather disjoint from a strong feeling of solidarity within States. In these conditions (horizontal) cultural standardization has not been complemented by social protection and has only acted as a substitute insurance device.

Europe, taken as a whole, offers a case symmetric to the United States (case 3 of Table 7.2). European Nations are culturally very heterogeneous but, until recently, European Nations have not had the vertical ethnic differentiation that has characterized the United States.[5] It is not surprising that social solidarity and social protection has been much more pronounced as an insurance device within each State but that Europe, taken as a whole, has very little redistribution among its States. Both horizontal cultural homogeneity and reciprocal protection among States are very weak and, in a way polar to that of the United States, the social protection offered by each National State is an important substitute for the lack of cultural horizontal homogenization.

The worst future scenario for Europe (case 4 of Table 7.2) may be that, while horizontal cultural homogeneity and solidarity among its Nations stay weak, immigration destroys, in a way similar to the American model, both vertical cultural homogeneity and the social solidarity existing within each State.

The mild model of European federalism, which we consider in the following section, is meant to be one possible way to give Europe a future different from the (4) scenario.

7.5 A possible model of 'mild European federalism'

Economic theories of federalism based on a mix of the American experience and neoclassical theory provide a poor guide to the understanding of the nature of the European 'mild' federalist project. While these theories consider the optimal clustering that could be obtained through the free mobility of individuals, the European project aims at a reduction of the costs of mobility and deals with all the issues related to the existence of costly mobility in situations of cultural and linguistic diversity. Federalism is a way of combining sunk linguistic and cultural investment with a common space that can be obtained by making most individuals bilingual and trilingual and/or accepting some common lingua franca: thus, in this respect, federalism is, at the same time, a way of encouraging individuals towards some limited mobility and a way of defending them against a too strong 'forced' mobility that could destroy the specific cultural and linguistic identity of a particular place. Federalism is also both a way of creating some mild European identity[6] and preserving the identity of particular nations and regions. In some ways it can be regarded as an attempt to reproduce at European level case (c) of our Table 7.1.[7]

European federalism can hardly be a sort of extension of the benefits of competition to the political market. It cannot take for granted the mobility of the individuals and must seek the creation of some minimum cultural-linguistic standardization by the way of projects such as the Erasmus exchanges for University students or the Bologna process introducing equivalent degrees in European Universities. At the same time, it must protect individuals against the excesses of mobility by some redistribution in favour of the most disadvantaged regions. Europe faces the paradox that we have just considered at the end of the last section: in absence of cultural and linguistic homogenization, costly mobility implies that redistribution is the most useful when it may be the least acceptable. Thus, in the European case, the most important issues become how to foster a self-reinforcing dynamics between some moderate cultural-linguistic standardization and some moderate mobility without upsetting regional and national identities and how to bring about some redistribution in favour of the poorest areas (that limits the need for mobility) without upsetting the slow process of creating an European solidarity. Since redistribution and cultural-linguistic standardization are both complements and substitutes, this process requires smooth and balanced progresses in both directions. By contrast, abrupt movements only towards cultural-linguistic standardization or only towards European-level redistribution are undesirable and, sometimes, dangerous.

An excessive move towards cultural and linguistic standardization can be undesirable if it is not complemented by a sense of European solidarity. Otherwise, the feelings of insecurity of the groups that are disadvantaged by the move may generate anti-European and pro-national feelings. Indeed, instead of an excessive push in this direction, redistribution policies may be preferred as a 'better substitute' for cultural and linguistic standardization in order to cope with the market uncertainties arising from specialization.

An excessive move towards redistribution policies, which is not complemented by some cultural and linguistic standardization, may also easily backfire. The 'complementary' pre-existence of a shared culture and of a shared identity may be necessary for a widespread acceptance of solidaristic policies. An excessive emphasis on these policies is also undesirable because cultural standardization could also have acted as a 'better substitute'. Indeed, beyond a certain level, some form of cultural and linguistic standardization could better achieve the same insurance results.

While, within certain limits, American federalism can take for granted conditions of horizontal cultural and linguistic standardization required by the mobility of the individuals and the competition among States, European federalism must, step by step, try to create some of these conditions. Only if these processes are successful in some dimensions, will some degree of State competition be helpful. In any case, a linguistically divided Europe will have to rely more on the protection of jobs and, in general, of welfare of the individuals in their own nations and regions. If Europe cannot provide a substantial redistribution among regions and within regions, it must at least make it possible the redistribution internal to each single National State. Knowing that there is a better employer and a better welfare protection in another region will not help much in a culturally divided Europe. Increased political and market mobility must be complemented and, sometimes, be substituted, more than in the American case, by locally based redistribution policies.

7.6 Coping with globalization: a 'European Insurance Scheme' among National Welfare States

While the National State has originated a self-reinforcing process between cultural standardization and economic development, it had opened a Pandora Box whose cultural and economic winds could hardly be contained forever within the boundaries of National States. Some National States (Britain with its Commonwealth and United States with its federal system, with its frontier and with its melting pot of different ethnic groups) developed a sense of 'global mission' and started doing to other languages and traditions what the National State had done within its boundaries.[8] The advantages of mobility and cultural standardization could now be reaped at global level.

The resistance of National States has been often unsurprisingly strong. Even when the benefits of cultural standardization were clearly greater than their costs, the cultural standard was not a matter of indifference. The National State was now often there to try to stop the further advancement of that process of cultural homogenization that had been its main task and, perhaps, the fundamental reason for its existence. Globalization meant convergence and suppressions of cultural differences in the same way in which the success of a national high culture had meant a decrease of cultural and institutional biodiversity within each country. The former cultural standardizers of the age of Nationalism have often become the victims of a historical nemesis that threatens the survival of their own traditions.

Globalization marks a new age. It is different from the Empires that had in the past unified politically the part of the world that was known. The Roman Empire and, after that, the Holy Roman Empire never posed a comparable challenge to cultural diversity. They kept the universal culture and the lingua franca as the distinctive mark of the ruling classes. Modern globalization spreads the global culture well beyond a ruling minority and, in this sense, it may help to decrease inequalities. In the ancient empires political unity was not associated to cultural unity. Modern Globalism is different: while cultural unity may be a factor putting pressure towards greater political integration,[9] political unity is rather weaker and it is mainly based on the dominance of the United States, on local processes of limited political integration such as the European Union and on some, often inadequate, governance of few international institutions.

Besides its enormously enlarged boundaries, the nature of modern Globalism is also fundamentally different from Nationalism. The politically united National State could decrease the risks of the market economy by using both universal cultural homogenization and some forms of social protection. While cultural homogenization was achieved through massive intervention in education, social protection required that the risks of the different productive sectors were not strongly correlated. Indeed, social insurance needed a production structure diversified in a considerable variety of sectors. Otherwise the Nation would have put too many eggs in too few baskets and would not be able to insure its citizens.

Globalism lacks both the social insurance programmes and the universal access to education that characterized Nation States. Moreover, it limits the capacity of National States to use either the insurance devices associated with redistribution and with the Welfare State or the insurance devices based on cultural and linguistic standardization.

In the absence of a reliable system of 'international insurance' National States should compare the gains from trade due to international specialization with the risks entailed by reduced productive diversification. The balance of these two factors should involve an 'optimal degree' of specialization. This degree of specialization will be less pronounced than the one that would be obtained by referring only to the 'gross' gains from trade according to the standard theory of comparative advantage; the 'net' gains of international specialization should also take into account the costs of supplying internal social protection that increase when the productive diversification of internationally National Economy is decreased. Unfortunately this 'optimal' level of specialization may be difficult to achieve in a globalized economy. Each single individual who moves to the sectors that have become more profitable as a result of international trade gains the full benefits of the new specialization. By contrast, she shares with all the other individuals of the same Nation the increased risk associated with the decrease of the number of productive sectors.[10] Even if National Governments realize the divergence between the private and social net benefits of specialization (and, often, they do not seem to do so!) it may well be difficult to stop the individuals from specializing according to their own private benefits. An 'international tragedy of the commons', free riding on the 'pasture' of productive diversification, may easily spread and increase insecurity in the global economy.

Also the use of cultural standardization – the other instrument by which national economies have traditionally insured their citizens against the risks of market mobility – is seriously impeded in an internationally integrated economy.

In the global economy the access to the dominant cultural standard is much more unequally distributed than in the case of national economies of the past. This inequality creates a division among workers endowed with mobile intellectual assets that are easily employable in the global economy and those that have skills that are less mobile and more specific to the national economy.[11] The first workers may find it more convenient to replace social protection with cultural standardization as a form of insurance device and get out of the mutual insurance system that characterizes national states. Like financial capital these workers may become difficult to tax. Their relatively easy exit from a national system of mutual insurance makes it even more difficult to finance the traditional forms of social protection supplied by the National State and worsens the situation of those workers who cannot use the access to the global cultural standard as a (partial) substitute for social protection (D'Antoni and Pagano 2002). Thus, in this respect, the present globalized world shows some puzzling (even, if perhaps, misleading) similarity with the ancient agrarian societies. Also here (especially in some of the countries where a language different from the Anglo-American tradition prevails) a cosmopolitan elite (but much more numerous than that existing in the agrarian societies!) speaks a new Latin that cannot be used as a working language by the majority of the population which, like in the agrarian societies, has only a limited horizontal and vertical mobility. While old forms of inequalities re-emerge in the modern globalized economy the National States, facing a shrinking tax base and increasingly correlated risks, are not able to offer to their citizens the security that they offered in the past.

The dilemma posed in the process of European integration by the 'complementarity-substitution' relation between cultural standardization and social protection can be reframed in this general framework: in many respects, the process of European integration is simply part of the process of globalization and implies that economic integration makes it more difficult for each European economy to offer social protection in a situation of increasing productive specialization. European integration may create a dangerous division between 'cosmopolitans' who are able to substitute social insurance with cultural standardization and 'provincials' who find it hard to increase the 'liquidity' of their skills. At the same time, Europe can offer some remedy for the fact that integration without forms of social insurance leads to excessively risky productive specialization.

If a European Welfare State is rather difficult to conceive in the present circumstances, Europe may try to offer mutual insurances among the Welfare States of the National Economies allowing their survival in situations in which these economies specialize within the European economic space and run increasingly correlated risks. While redistributions related to social insurance would occur within each single Nation according to its wealth, rules and political compromises, each Welfare State could receive some insurance from the other Welfare States.[12]

7.7 Conclusion

In a culturally and linguistically divided Europe, federalism cannot be considered a system based on an unfettered mobility that allows a free choice among different systems of social insurance and redistributions. It may rather require a system of mutual insurance among the different welfare systems that makes economic integration compatible with social protection (including a protection against an 'economically forced' mobility towards other states). While Europe may also promote (a limited) cultural standardization at European level, the latter can be a substitute for social protection only at an increasing cost and can cause a dangerous clash between 'cosmopolitans' and 'provincials'. Only a system of mutual insurance among National Welfare States can help the marriage between the European rich and creative cultural diversity and a process of economic and cultural integration that is not opposed to the solidaristic tradition of the European Nations.

Acknowledgement

I am grateful to the participants to the Franqui Prize Conference and Sam Bowles, Massimo D'Antoni, Michele Di Maio, Francesco Farina and Philippe Van Parijs for their useful comments and suggestions.

Notes

1 A formal model examining the roles of social protection and cultural standardization as alternative insurance devices is developed in D'Antoni and Pagano (2002) where it is also argued that Europe, taken as a whole, is likely to be very far from the optimal mix between these two policies. Bowles and Pagano (2004) develop this framework to analyse the contrasting interests of 'cosmopolitans' and 'provincials'. Arachi and D'Antoni (2003) argue that, if the risks of the workers who have made human capital specific investments in particular sectors are taken into account, the case for social insurance can get stronger as capital markets integration takes place, despite the increase in the distortionary effect.

2 This view originates from Tiebout's (1956) paper on local public goods. Some of the extreme logical consequences of this theory can be found in Alesina and Spalaore (1997). For a complete survey see Innam and Rubinfield (1997). A clear and concise analysis of this problem can be found also in Part II of Cooter (2000).

3 On the concept of Institutional Complementarity see Milgrom and Roberts (1990) and Aoki (2002). Even if they do not use the term 'institutional complementarity', according to Aoki's generous acknowledgement (2001, p. 396), Pagano (1993) and Pagano and Rowthorn (1994) are also 'two of the earliest analytical contributions to institutional complementarity'.

4 See Gellner (1983, 1998 and 1999). For an account of the important contributions of Ernest Gellner to Political Economy, see Pagano (2003).

5 Cultural class differences have often been more pronounced in Europe than the United States and, for this reason, despite ethnic differences, vertical mobility has been higher in the United States than in Europe. However, despite individual cases of amazing vertical mobility, the vertical hierarchy of the different group does not have many changes and seems, on average, to put severe constrains on the opportunities available to the members of each group.

6 To use Anderson's (1991) insightful expression Europe should become a 'new imagined community' giving 'symbolic utility' to individuals (Pagano 1995). The fact that this collective imagination is engineered by a long and somehow artificial process would not be a historical novelty but would rather make the 'creation' of Europe very similar to the process of formation of many national identities (Hobsbawn 1992; Hobsbawn and Ranger 1983).

7 This is also the case that encompasses Belgium. It is therefore not surprising that, in a very stimulating paper, Van Parijs (2003) gives a qualified positive answer to the question; 'Must Europe be Belgium?'.

8 According to Hardt and Negri (2000) the importance of the role of United States in the process of globalization has been enhanced by its differences from traditional National States that stressed the role of ethnic identity. The legitimacy of the power of the United States has rather been based on the belief in the superiority of the American way of life that would mark the boundary between the civilized world and the various realms of evil. In this sense the power of the United States is not expressed in the Imperialism typical of the traditional National States. It is rather grounded in its centrality in the Empire that should group together all the Civilized World. Since civilization should not have limits in its struggle against the forces of evil, similarly the Empire (unlike the old forms of Imperialism) should have no limits.

9 It is not inconsistent with this view that this integration may first occur among nations sharing the same civilization (common history, traditions and readings). However, it is an open issue whether this should be considered as first step for integration among these civilizations or lead to disruptive clash among civilizations (see Huntington 1997).

10 Michele Di Maio has pointed out to me that issue is not only the quantity of the sectors but also their quality. Some sectors may be characterized by more fungible core competencies than others.

11 This is the division that, according to Yael Tamir (2003) separates 'globalists' and 'communitarians' or, using a similar terminology, according to Bowles and Pagano (2004), separates 'cosmopolitans' from 'provincials'. The divide is related to the divide between the global lingua franca and the other languages that implies that many non-English-speaking countries have a differential access to the 'cosmopolitan' standard. As Van Parijs (2002, p. 72) points out 'This ubiquitous asymmetric bilingualism is arguably very efficient. But nothing guarantees that it be fair.' Redistributive justice must therefore necessarily include the issue of linguistic justice.

12 In principle, such system could make it compatible the increased specialization of each economy with stable levels of social protection. While in each country the number of sectors decreases and becomes increasingly impossible to insure each national sector with the other productive sectors, the mutual insurance among the Welfare States would allow some sort of 'indirect insurance' of each European productive sector with the other productive sectors. However, in real practice as well as in economic theory, insurance is always associated with a moral hazard problem and it is an open issue if and how a mild form of European federalism will be able to offer some indirect type of social insurance (and, at the same time, some limited common cultural standards compatible with the diversity of the European Nations and Regions).

References

Alesina, A. and Spolaore, S. (1997) 'On the Number and Size of Nations', *Quaterly Journal of Economics*, 112, 1027–1056.

Anderson, B. (1991) *Imagined Communities*. London: Verso.

Aoki, Masahiko (2002) *Towards a Comparative Institutional Analysis*. Boston, MA: MIT Press.

Arachi, G. and D'Antoni, M. (2003) 'Redistribution as Social Insurance and Capital Market Integration', *Quaderni del Dipartimento di Economia Politica*, No. 404, University of Siena.

Bowles, S. and Pagano, Ugo (2004) 'Economic Integration, Cultural Standardisation and the Politics of Social Insurance'. Forthcoming in P. Bardhan, S. Bowles and M. Wallerstein (eds) *Globalization and Redistribution*. New York: Russel Sage Foundation.

Coase, R.H. (1937) 'The Nature of the Firm', *Economica*, 386–405.

Cooter, R.D. (2000) *The Strategic Constitution*. Princeton, NJ: Princeton University Press.

D'Antoni, M. and Pagano, Ugo (2002) 'National Cultures and Social Protection as Alternative Insurance Devices', *Structural Change and Economic Dynamics*, 13, 367–386.

Gellner, E. (1983) *Nations and Nationalism*. Oxford: Blackwell.

Gellner, E. (1998) *Nationalism*. London: Phoenix.

Gellner, E. (1999) 'The Coming of Nationalism, and its Interpretation. The Myths of Nation and Class' in S. Bowles, M. Franzini and U. Pagano (eds) *The Politics and the Economics of Power*. London: Routledge.

Hardt, M. and Negri, A. (2000) *Empire*. Cambridge, MA: Harvard University Press.

Hobsbawm, E. (1992) *Nations and Nationalism since 1780*. Cambridge: Cambridge University Press.

Hobsbawm, E. and Ranger, I. (1983) *The Invention of Traditions*. Cambridge: Cambridge University Press.

Huntington, S.P. (1997) *The Clash of Civilizations and the Remaking of the World Order*. London: Simon & Schuster.

Innam, R.P. and Rubinfield, D.S. (1997) 'The Political Economy of Federalism' in D.C. Mueller (ed.) *Perspectives on Public Choice*. New York: Cambridge University Press, pp. 73–106.

Milgrom, P. and Roberts, J. (1990) 'The Economics of Modern Manufacturing: Technology, Strategy and Organization', *American Economic Review*, 81, 84–88.

Pagano, U. (1993) 'Organizational Equilibria and Institutional Stability' in Samuel Bowles, Herbert Gintis and Bo Gustafson (eds) *Markets and Democracy*. Cambridge: Cambridge University Press.

Pagano, U. (1995) 'Can Economics Explain Nationalism?' in A. Breton, G. Galeotti, P. Salmon and R. Wintrobe (eds) *Nationalism and Rationality*. Cambridge: Cambridge University Press, 173–203.

Pagano, U. (2003) 'Nationalism, Development and Integration: The Political Economy of Ernest Gellner', *Cambridge Journal of Economics*, 27(5), 623–646.

Pagano, U. and Rowthorn, R. (1994) 'Ownership, Technology and Institutional Stability', *Structural Change and Economic Dynamics*, 5(2), 221–243.

Tamir, Y. (2004) 'Class and Nation' in P. Van Parijs (ed.) *Cultural Diversity Versus Economic Solidarity*. Proceedings of the Seventh Francqui Colloquium Brussels, De Boeck.

Tiebout, C. (1956) 'A Pure Theory of Local Expenditures', *Journal of Political Economy*, 64, 416–424.

Van Parijs, P. (2002) 'Linguistic Justice', *Politics, Philosophy and Economics*, 1, 59–74.

Van Parijs, P. (2003) 'Must Europe be Belgium? On Democratic Citizenship in Multilingual Polities', forthcoming in I. Hampsher-Monk (ed.) *The Demands of Citizenship*. London: Cassel.

8 The welfare state, redistribution and the economy

Reciprocal altruism, consumer rivalry and second best

Frederick van der Ploeg

8.1 Introduction

The modern welfare state has taken centuries to develop. In early days the priest has played a crucial role to convince people to give to the poor. He had to overcome free-rider problems, since nobody likes looting and begging by the poor while each citizen would prefer others to take care of the poor (Swaan de, 1989). It is relatively easy to break down the welfare state and destroy the solidarity that may have taken centuries to build, but much harder to build up a welfare state. People are altruistic, particularly to next of kin and others closely related to them. The principle of mutual obligations underlying reciprocal altruism is important, even though people also display non-reciprocal altruism. People are more willing to help the poor if they make an effort and take risks to educate themselves and make a living. Happiness of people depends on material living standards, but also on what other people in their reference group earn and consume. This may induce a rat race in which people try to keep up with the Jones's and thus work excessively hard in order to keep up with consumption of their peers. What do these insights in and determinants of reciprocal altruism, willingness to co-operate and happiness imply for the support for redistributive taxation and the size and design of the welfare state? Are progressive taxes still a public bad? Are unemployment benefits necessarily harmful for economic activity? We attempt to investigate what these more sociological and psychological insights imply for the tax system and the welfare state and their consequences for economic performance. In particular, we are interested to examine in full political-economic equilibrium what this implies for unemployment and the purchasing power of people. We also investigate why the welfare state in Europe has evolved in a very different way from the welfare state in the US. The 'Washington consensus' maintains that liberalising markets and trimming down government is best for economic performance. We argue that this is may not be the case in societies with reciprocal altruism and rat races or when markets do not clear and unemployment is caused by trade unions, efficiency wage and/or search frictions. In that case, progressive taxes and conditional unemployment benefits may boost economic performance.

Section 8.2 discusses some empirical cross-country evidence that suggests that large welfare states do not necessarily imply worse economic performance.

Section 8.3 reviews the empirical and experimental literature on altruism, reciprocity and mutual obligations and its relevance for the welfare state. Section 8.4 applies these ideas within the context of efficiency wages to explain why higher conditional unemployment benefits may boost employment. This example illustrates the importance of mutual obligations in the design of an efficient welfare state. Section 8.5 discusses the determinants of happiness and stresses the importance of relative income positions. The resulting rat races result from consumer rivalry. Section 8.6 extends the familiar model of redistributive taxation developed by Romer (1975) and Meltzer and Richard (1981) to allow for consumer rivalry. The main insight is that, if people care about their relative income and consumption positions, taxation of labour is warranted even if there is no inequity. Since people are competing and thus working too hard in order to keep up with others, work adversely affects welfare of the others. The government corrects for this distortion by taxing labour (or subsidising labour). If there is inequality among talents and incomes, there is an additional motive for taxation. If the median voter is relatively untalented and poor, he has a selfish motive to vote for a common subsidy for all financed by a linear tax on labour. Hence, there is a Pigouvian as well as a redistributive motive for taxing labour. Section 8.7 discusses the consequences of consumer rivalry for intertemporal macroeconomics and how it might help to explain the need for counter-cyclical demand policies. Section 8.8 uses the theory of second best to give efficiency arguments for progressive taxation. It shows that with unemployment caused by trade unions, efficiency wages and/or search frictions progressive taxation induces wage moderation and can improve economic performance. Section 8.9 concludes with a summary and suggestions for further research.

8.2 International evidence on the welfare state

Taking an international perspective, Rodrik (1997) argues that markets and the state are complementary. He questions the supremacy of the idea that social policies are bad for the economy (the 'Washington consensus'). Both governments and markets have their failures but they must interact to grapple with the problems of conflicting information and offer the right incentives as first-best outcomes in the real world rarely occur. However, Dixit (1996) does not see this as proof of the inefficiency of government. Indeed, weak incentives and the various second-best constraints and prohibitions may even occur in a game equilibrium outcome. Rodrik (1997) thus stresses that the maintenance of social safety nets is not a luxury but an essential ingredient of a market economy. The welfare state has the benefit that it helps households to insure against uninsurable risks when markets fail due to moral hazard and/or moral hazard (e.g. Blanchard and Tirole, 2004; Boadway *et al.*, 2004; Sinn, 1995). Markets produce many benefits, but they also make life riskier and more insecure for many people. A reliable welfare state thus contributes to a proper functioning of the market economy. Rodrik (1998) shows that countries that are more exposed to the risks of international trade have bigger governments, possibly because governments offer social insurance to cushion the effects of exposure to external risk. De Grauwe and Polan (2003) show that countries that spend most on social security rank highest, on average, in the competitiveness leagues of Lausanne's IMD or of the World Economic Forum. They argue that causation is very unlikely to run the other way round, so that the reverse link going from strong competitiveness to a stronger economy and more funds for the welfare state is weak.

In his path-breaking historical cross-country study Lindert (2004) points out that the growth in social spending started in the late nineteenth century after the right to vote was extended to poorer men and women as well. This is in line with the median voter model discussed in section 6.1. It set the stage for Lloyd George's assault on Britain's rich just before First World War. Extending political voice led in addition to population aging and income growth to the emergence of comprehensive nation-wide social insurance programmes and more spending on public education. The growth in the post-war welfare states was particularly big in countries where the middle and bottom ranks changed places and where ethnically homogenous. Lindert also argues that there is almost no evidence of a negative effect of a substantial welfare state on gross domestic product (GDP). The net national costs of social transfers, and the taxes that finance them, are essentially zero. An important reason is that governments become more efficient as distortions of higher tax rates are proportionally much higher than lower rates. For example, countries with large welfare states tend to have a more pro-growth and regressive mix of taxes (think of high taxes on vices and low taxes on capital income). Another reason is that the unemployed caused by generous welfare states are, typically, less productive and thus the harm to national income is limited. A more fundamental reason is that in advanced market economies with developed welfare states the economics of second best apply. As we have seen in sections 4 and 8, the various distortions of the welfare state tend to wipe each other out so that the burden of the welfare state is much less than simply adding all the distortions one at a time.

The general picture that emerges from cross-country evidence is that 'laisser faire' advocates have something to explain, since neither theory nor empirical evidence suggests that social policies necessarily harm the economy. This seems particularly the case if the general public does not see redistribution as unfair. The World Values Survey suggests that people's attitudes to the rewards from effort and taking risks are quite different in the US than in Europe. Around 30 per cent of Americans believe that the poor are trapped in poverty and cannot do anything to get out of their miserable situation. Also, 30 per cent of Americans believe that luck, rather than effort or education, determines income. In contrast, these percentages are almost double in Europe. Americans are much more likely to think that the poor are lazy and that the rich have become so by hard work and effort. Europeans are much more likely to think that luck, family ties and other connections matter. Alesina and Angeletos (2003) and Bénabou and Tirole (2002) show, using different arguments, that two self-fulfilling equilibrium outcomes are possible. There is one equilibrium outcome in which there is a lot of redistribution and where people believe that people have become poor or rich by bad or good luck (Europe).

There is another equilibrium in which there is little redistribution but where people firmly believe that effort, education, hard work and taking risks pay off (the US). This explains why government spending in the US is much lower (30 per cent of GDP) than in Europe (45 per cent). This difference is remarkable, because pre-tax inequality is much higher in the US than in Europe, income mobility in the US is not much higher than in Europe and tax systems do not seem more efficient in Europe than in the US.

Alesina and Glaeser (2004) and Alesina *et al.* (2002) argue that the older welfare institutions of the US are more conservative and hostile to the welfare state whereas the proportional representation in much of Europe has led to an upsurge of communist and socialist parties. European countries are typically smaller and thus trade unions are more likely to establish powerful positions. They also argue that the US has much more racially diversity than Europe and many of the poor in the US are concentrated among non-whites. States or countries with racial diversity tend to have low government spending on poverty relief, even after correcting for differences in income per head. People are more willing to help next to kin and others that are close to them. The growing inflow of migrants in Europe will put pressure on the welfare state.

People are more prepared to sacrifice income by paying higher taxes if the proceeds go to people who are laid off, sick or disabled with no fault of their own rather than to people who are lazy or have cheated the system. Obviously, this is in line with the arguments in favour of high conditional benefits developed in section 4. To put it another way, it is much easier to build up support for a generous welfare state if the principle of reciprocity is respected, for example, Fong *et al.* (2003). Conversely, people do not mind taxing rich people as long as they got rich by luck or connections rather than by hard work.

It is important to investigate whether any of these propositions hold up empirically. Scandinavian and Dutch experience suggests it is possible to have a low unemployment rate and a generous welfare state, but this is not true for all countries. In empirical work it is worthwhile to contrast Anglo-Saxon Europe characterised by its emphasis on Beveridge social assistance of last resort for people of working age, weak unions and lots of wage dispersion with continental Europe. Continental Europe is characterised by its emphasis on extending the coverage of trade unions and the Bismarckian tradition of insurance-based non-employment benefits such as disability and old-age pensions. It may also be worthwhile to distinguish Nordic Europe with the highest levels of social protection, universal welfare provision, high tax wedges and active labour market policy with Mediterranean Europe. Mediterranean Europe has, in contrast, strong wage compression, strong unions supported by extended coverage, employment protection and early retirement provisions (Bertola and Boeri, 2001). It is no good to look for cross-country correlations between spending on social policies and unemployment rates, but one should see whether there exist correlations between the generosity of various welfare state provisions with wages and unemployment rates. To investigate this for the OECD countries is a future challenge.

8.3 Altruism, reciprocity and mutual obligations

The welfare state in many countries transfers large amounts of resources from the better off to the poorer members of society. Remarkable is that politicians have been able to do that with the support of even the better off. The theories in favour of redistributive taxation developed by economists (e.g. Meltzer and Richard, 1981; Romer, 1975) are, however, based on selfish arguments. If there is income inequality, the median voter is likely to be relatively poor and vote for populist policies of taxing the rich and subsidising the poor. However, the median voter is not necessarily selfish and many societies favour more altruistic forms of redistribution. Indeed, many of the rich support income redistribution in favour of the poor whereas a substantial number of poor people oppose redistribution. In fact, people are less willing to support the poor if they perceive that the poor are lazy and cheat the system or do not try hard enough to generate income for themselves. Conversely, people are more willing to help the poor if they have been unlucky (cf. Alesina and Angeletos, 2003; Bénabou and Tirole, 2002; Fong *et al.*, 2003; Piketty, 1995). This is related to the idea of procedural fairness and that not only *what*, but also *how* matters for utility and fairness (e.g. Frey *et al.*, 2004; Lind and Tyler, 1988). Non-instrumental determinants of utility and a sense of self are thus relevant for making welfare judgements. It is thus relevant how people perceive themselves as human beings and how others perceive them.

If people are poor due to bad luck rather than due to being lazy, society is more likely to support government redistribution. If people believe, as they do in the US, that willingness to take risks and work hard are important for improving one's economic conditions, electoral support for government redistribution is much less. If people believe that one's economic success is caused by inheritances, corruption, luck and one's (family) connections, as people do in Europe, support for redistribution and the welfare state is much larger. There will be two self-fulfilling equilibrium outcomes: one in which people believe that effort pays off and redistribution is rather less (the US) and another one where people believe that success depends on luck and redistribution is more substantial (Europe). Which equilibrium one ends up, depends on history. The fact that the US was built by immigrants, who sacrificed a lot and took great risks to build up a new life, may explain why people in the US believe that taking risks and hard work does and should pay off. To move from the inferior high-redistribution equilibrium is not easy and requires large changes in both beliefs and the welfare state.

The literature on giving and charity has stressed (impure) altruism or 'warm glow', that is, the internal satisfaction that arises from helping other people (e.g. Andreoni, 1989). However, the donors are also motivated by gift exchange considerations. Indeed, List and Lucking-Reiley (2002) illustrated that increasing seed money or introducing a refund policy led to a corresponding increase in donations to a university. Falk (2004) finds that, when a charity accompanies a request for a donation with a gift (postcards drawn by children), donations increase significantly. Numerous experiments demonstrate the importance of gift exchange and mutual obligations. Fehr and Falk (1999), Gächter and Falk (2002) and Bewley

(2004) use experimental evidence to suggest the relevance of reciprocity for the labour market. This principle has important implications for the design of the welfare state as well.

If the welfare state is based on mutual obligations and the principle of reciprocal altruism, there may be more support for a generous, yet tough welfare state (e.g. Atkinson, 1996, 2002; Ploeg van der, 2005). If welfare benefits are temporary and conditional on searching hard enough for a job, not rejecting job offers and not having been fired for misconduct, the adverse unemployment consequences may be much less – see Section 8.4. Hence, testing welfare benefits and other forms of mutual obligations reduce the dead-weight burden of the welfare state. It is tough to be kind, but also kind to be tough. Welfare state institutions that support and strengthen reciprocal altruism go a lot further than kin altruism. Europe has tried to build up a welfare state based on reciprocal altruism, whereas in the US kin altruism and help from the family has traditionally been more important. It is important to realise, however, that the human race has a millennium old tradition of sharing food among non-kin. Indeed, people have always held deeply held norms of reciprocity and mutual obligations to each other. In fact, strong reciprocity may hold which means an urge to co-operate and share with others even at cost to one self.

Experimental evidence based on, for example, dictator games and survey evidence suggests that many strangers willingly give to strangers, reward good deeds and punish violations of fairness norms by others even in anonymous one-shot encounters at significant cost to themselves (e.g. Fong *et al.*, 2003; Layard, 2003; Ridley, 1997). This form of 'true' altruism with neither present nor future economic rewards for the reciprocator is called strong reciprocity and has strong implications for the way modern societies function (Fehr and Gächter, 2000; Fehr *et al.*, 2002). Strong reciprocity cannot be explained from an evolutionary perspective by kin selection, reciprocal altruism, costly signalling or indirect reciprocity. These arguments can only explain strong reciprocity by maladaptive behaviour. In modern anonymous societies strong reciprocity does not make sense, but in small societies with repeated interactions it did. People make 'mistakes' in modern times, since they are still genetically geared up to the gathering societies of old time. However, Fehr and Henrich (2003) provide a host of anthropological, biological and experimental evidence that counters the maladaptive view of strong reciprocity.

People display true altruism and/or strong reciprocity, but also favour members of the own group over others. People are thus altruistic even to members that are not part of their own group at great cost to them selves. This is much stronger than reciprocal altruism. People are also parochial in the sense that they behave more favourably to those people closer to them than to strangers. Although altruism and parochialism each on their own do not seem to make sense from an evolutionary perspective, altruism and parochialism or alternatively love for members of the own group and hostility to outsiders may have co-evolved. This symbiotic evolution of love and hate has been demonstrated with extensive simulations (Bowles and Choi, 2003; Bowles *et al.*, 2003). Hence, smaller group sizes, strong institutions for a group and high frequencies of conflict between groups make it more likely that altruistic modes of behaviour within the own group survive. These insights have profound consequences for the welfare state. It suggests that fighting foreign enemies and curtailing immigration of foreigners go hand in hand with altruistic behaviour to unrelated members of one's own people and institutions such as 'food sharing' and the welfare state. This view on co-evolution of love and hate seems an essentially human phenomenon. Cognition, language and other capacities play an essential role in explaining the distinctive levels of co-operation among non-kin practised by humans, but one should realise that ants also display within-group co-operation at the same time as brood raiding and hostility towards neighbouring colonies (e.g. Ridley, 1997, chapter 9).

8.4 Conditional unemployment benefits may boost employment

To illustrate the point that mutual obligations matter, we demonstrate within the context of a labour market with efficiency wages that conditional unemployment benefits induce wage moderation and boost employment. In contrast, unconditional benefits always harm employment. Atkinson (2002) stresses the importance of dealing properly with the institutional details of the welfare state. It is not realistic to model unemployment benefits merely as 'leisure pay'. Benefits are neither indefinite nor unconditional 'income during unemployment'. Most countries require workers to have worked a certain period in order to qualify for benefit and do not offer benefits to people who have become unemployed after voluntary quits or misconduct. Furthermore, a claimant is only eligible for unemployment benefit if he makes a serious effort to search. Typically, one can reject job offers a number of times but eventually one must accept a job offer. The duration of unemployment benefits is often limited to a number of years. Afterwards, unemployed people may get welfare assistance, which is unrelated to the wage one once earned as an employee. In practice, most low-skilled workers benefit from welfare more or less indefinitely as eligibility conditions are seldom policed. This is especially the case in deep recessions when the chance of finding a job is very low. If eligibility conditions can be policed, conditional benefits and active labour market policies imply substantial administrative costs.

If one treats benefits as indefinite and unconditional income during unemployment, one is likely to over-estimate the adverse effects of benefits on unemployment. To understand why *conditional* rather than *unconditional* unemployment benefits may boost employment; we modify the no-shrinking theory of unemployment and moral hazard developed by Shapiro and Stiglitz (1984). Workers who have been fired for misconduct (shrinking) are not entitled to an unemployment benefit, but people who get laid off without fault of their own do qualify. We ignore taxes, since our focus is on demonstrating the importance of conditional unemployment benefits and the no-shrinking model is ill suited for addressing the effects of changes in the marginal tax rate. Unemployment arises, because the imprecise monitoring implies workers have a potential incentive to shirk (moral hazard). Firms avoid shrinking by paying more than the market-clearing wage. Let s be the exogenous probability of a worker leaving job without fault of its own and h the endogenous probability of an unemployed person finding a job. Let q be the additional probability of a worker being fired if caught shrinking. We focus on steady state, so ignore dynamics of unemployment and capital gains in the value of non-shrinking and shrinking workers. Inflow into the pool of unemployed thus equals outflow, so that $s(1 - U) = hU$ where U is the unemployment rate. The unemployment rate $U = s/(s + h)$ increases in the separation rate s and decreases with the probability of finding a job h. The (expected) value of a worker who does not shirk is given by:

$$V_{\mathrm{W}} = [W - d + (1 - s)V_{\mathrm{W}} + sV_{\mathrm{B}}]/(1 + R) = (W - d + sV_{\mathrm{B}})/(R + s),$$

where R is the interest (discount) rate and V_{B} is the value of an unemployed person who is entitled to a conditional benefit. The value of a worker equals the present value of his earnings W *minus* the disutility of work d *plus* his expected value next period. Next period he is employed with probability $1 - s$ and value V_{W} and unemployed with probability s and value V_{B}. On the one hand, the value of a shirker V_{S} is higher than that of a non-shirker because he does not suffer the disutility of work. On the other hand, the value of a shirker is lower as he has an additional probability q of being caught and dismissed and is then not entitled to the conditional unemployed benefit. The value of a shirker can thus be written as:

$$\begin{aligned} V_{\mathrm{S}} &= [W + (1 - s - q)V_{\mathrm{S}} + sV_{\mathrm{B}} + qV_{\mathrm{U}}]/(1 + R) \\ &= (W + sV_{\mathrm{B}} + qV_{\mathrm{U}})/(R + s + q), \end{aligned}$$

where V_{U} denotes the value of an unemployed person who has been dismissed for misconduct and is not entitled to a conditional benefit. To make sure that employees have on average no incentive to shirk, $V_{\mathrm{W}} \geq V_{\mathrm{S}}$, firms pay workers just enough to prevent them from shrinking:

$$W \geq RV_{\mathrm{U}} + (R + s + q)d/q - s(V_{\mathrm{B}} - V_{\mathrm{U}}).$$

The last term on the right-hand side does not appear in Shapiro and Stiglitz (1984). It shows that firms need to pay workers less to prevent them from shrinking. Effectively, denying dismissed shirkers a conditional unemployment benefit raises the penalty of misconduct. The value of somebody sacked through no fault of his known is:

$$V_{\mathrm{B}} = [B + v + hV_{\mathrm{W}} + (1 - h)V_{\mathrm{B}}]/(1 + R) = (B + v + hV_{\mathrm{W}})/(R + h),$$

where v is utility of leisure. This equals the present value of utility of leisure plus the benefit plus with probability h the value when he finds a job and with probability $1 - h$ the value when he remains unemployed next period. The value of a dismissed shirker V_U is lower than the value of other unemployed, since he is not entitled to an unemployment benefit:

$$V_U = [v + A + hV_W + (1 - h)V_U]/(1 + R)$$
$$= (v + A + hV_W)/(R + h) < V_B < V_S \leq V_W,$$

where A is the level of unconditional welfare assistance. We use the expressions for V_W, V_B and V_U and substitute them into the wage condition. If we also substitute $h = s(1 - U)/U$ from the labour-market equilibrium condition, we finally obtain the no-shrinking condition:

$$W \geq v + A + d + (R + s/U)d/q - s(B - A)/[R + s(1 - U)/U].$$

The first three terms on the right-hand side show that the wage a firm needs to pay to prevent its workers shrinking is higher if utility of leisure v, welfare assistance A and disutility of work d are high. The fourth term shows that the firm has to pay workers more to prevent them from shrinking if the job destruction rate is high, the unemployment rate is low and the additional probability of being detected and dismissed q is small. Hence, if the chance of being caught shrinking is small or the probability of finding another job is large, the firm has to pay more in order to discipline workers. The fourth term explains why the no-shrinking condition (NSC) in Figure 8.1 slopes down. Effectively, a lower wage needs to be paid if unemployment is high. The final term on the right-hand side is not in Shapiro and Stiglitz (1984). It shows that a firm pays less to prevent its employees from shrinking if the conditional unemployment benefit is high relative to the unconditional welfare payment. The unemployment benefit is granted only if the worker

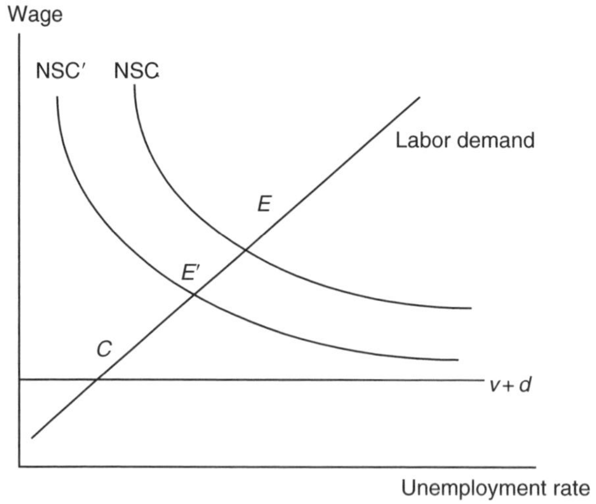

Figure 8.1 Higher conditional benefits B reduce shrinking and boost employment.

has lost his job without fault of his own. A higher sanction for misconduct, that is, a bigger gap between the conditional and the unconditional benefit, raises the effective penalty of shrinking, so firms can afford to pay workers less. Hence, a higher level of the conditional unemployment benefit boosts employment and output. Figure 8.1 shows that a higher conditional benefit B shifts the no-shrinking condition (NSC) down and thus reduces the wage, boosts employment and lowers unemployment (move from E to E'). In contrast, a higher unconditional welfare payment A shifts up the no-shrinking condition and depresses employment. Equilibrium wages are higher than in the competitive outcome C, where wages are driven down to the unconditional welfare payment plus utility of leisure plus disutility of work. Equilibrium unemployment is thus higher than in the competitive outcome. Unemployment here is akin to the Marxist idea of the need to have a reserve army of unemployed in order to discipline workers.

The drop in the unemployment rate is larger with a shift from conditional earnings-related benefit to unconditional flat-sum welfare assistance ($\mathrm{d}B = -\mathrm{d}A > 0$). The penalty for shrinking increases for two reasons now. First, dismissed shirkers do not get the conditional benefit. Second, the unconditional welfare assistance falls and thus stimulates the incentive to work. This last incentive to work also increases for people who are unemployed without fault of their own. These extra two effects make that the fall in wages and unemployment is much greater than with a straight increase in unemployment benefit. If the benefit is financed by distortionary taxes there will be offsetting adverse effects on employment and output.

Unemployment benefits are conditional in other ways as well. They typically last for a limited period and unemployed are only eligible if available for work and actively seeking a job. A 'rough-and-ready' way to capture this is to terminate with probability $p > 0$ unemployment benefits. If there is no sanction for misconduct, the benefit is the same benefit irrespective of whether people have been fired for industrial misconduct or not, $B = A$. The no-shrinking condition becomes:

$$W \geq [(R+h)/(R+h+p)]B + d + v + (R + s/U)d/q.$$

Since the unemployment benefit no longer lasts forever, the penalty for shrinking and misconduct is *increased* and thus firms have to *pay less* to prevent workers shrinking. Consequently, employment is higher and the unemployment rate lower. Alternatively, if there is a sanction and with probability $p > 0$ the conditional benefit B is terminated and replaced by the ever lasting, lump-sum welfare assistance A, the no-shrinking condition becomes:

$$W \geq v + d + A + (R + s/U)d/q - s(B - A)/[R + p + s(1 - U)/U].$$

Limiting the duration of a conditional benefit *reduces* the penalty for shrinking and misconduct and firms must *pay more* to ensure workers' discipline, hence the unemployment rate rises. Another modification is that dismissed workers have a smaller probability of finding a job than other unemployed. Since this raises the shrinking penalty, firms pay less to prevent shrinking and equilibrium unemployment is lower.

In equilibrium nobody shirks, so all unemployed receive *conditional* unemployment benefits. However, with a continuum of heterogeneous workers $i \in [0, 1]$ that differ in their disutility of work d_i, firms set a wage high enough to attract the least 'lazy' workers and more 'lazy' workers do not work:

$$\begin{aligned} d_i &\leq \{W - A - v + s(B - A)/[R + s(1 - U)/U]\}/[1 + (R + s/U)/q] \\ &\equiv d^*(W, v, A, B, U; Rq, s). \end{aligned}$$

Firms set the wage to discipline just enough workers, so that $1 - U = F[d^*(W, v, A, B, U; Rq, s)]$ where $F[.]$ is the cumulative probability density function of d_i. This yields a similar (NSC)-schedule as in Figure 8.1, so the comparative statics are qualitatively the same. However, if workers (who are not caught shrinking) enjoy protection against firing, a negative shock to labour demand after hiring has taken place induces workers with the highest disutility of work to stay on the job and shirk rather than quit. Some of them may be caught and end up on welfare rather than benefit, so the unemployment pool consists of dismissed shirkers and other unemployed who are entitled to a high benefit. A higher conditional benefit or replacement rate still reduces unemployment.

One critique of this result is that the government is unable to monitor perfectly whether the employee has been fired for misconduct or the employer and employee are using it as an attractive way to stop their relationship. If the government runs the unemployment insurance scheme, there are additional problems of moral hazard and incentives to abuse the social insurance scheme. If the firm runs the unemployment insurance scheme itself, these problems would not arise.

The result that higher conditional benefits boost employment may carry over to other settings of non-competitive labour markets (Atkinson, 2002, chapter 4). Also, redundancy payments in a dynamic no-shrinking model induce firms to fire less. This internalises the externality arising from foregone rents imposed by firms on fired workers (Fella, 2000). More generally, conditional benefits hurt employment less than unconditional benefits. With search frictions a higher benefit harms employment, since those who search for a job are less likely to accept lower-wage jobs. In dividing up the surplus of a job match a bigger part of it goes to the worker, so wages are higher and employment lower. However, if unemployment benefits are of limited duration, unemployed are more likely to accept a job for fear of not finding a job and having to fall back on the lower welfare payment. Similarly, the harmful effects on employment are attenuated in a search context if the unemployed who want to be eligible for a conditional benefit face a work test and can only reject a job offer a maximum of, say, two or three times. In fact, with search in both labour and product markets, a higher unemployment benefit induces firms to offer more high-wage jobs and may lower unemployment even if the benefit is unconditional in general equilibrium (Axell and Lang, 1990).

8.5 Rivalry and happiness: abundance and discontent

Most of neoclassical economics assumes that people are selfish and only care about income and consumption in absolute terms. Increasingly, economists have come to realise that people's happiness does not depend on money and absolute levels of consumption alone (e.g. Frey and Stutzer, 2002; Oswald, 1983, 1997; Stadt van de *et al.*, 1985; van Praag, 1993). For example, job satisfaction of a sample of 5000 British workers is only weakly correlated with absolute income, but decreases if reference wages of other comparable workers increase (e.g. Clark and Oswald, 1996). People care about fairness and the degree of relative deprivation. Also, a higher level of education requires a higher income to maintain the same level of job satisfaction. People feel better if they do better than their peers. For example, Oscar winners live four years longer than other nominees who did not win the Oscar. Conversely, people that do not score well, feel less happy. This may argue against publishing league tables or individual results of school people and students, despite the gains from competition that may result from them. There is also evidence to suggest that external rewards destroy intrinsic interest of workers so that they work less when pay stops (e.g. Frey and Oberholzer-Gee, 1997). Putting a money value to everything may diminish intrinsic motivation to do well and to help others or make sacrifices for the community.

Recently, trends in and causes of happiness in the US and Britain have been studied (Blanchflower and Oswald, 2004). Money buys happiness, but well-being of people depends on relative income as well and is badly affected by unemployment and divorce. For example, a lasting marriage rather than widowhood is estimated to be worth \$100,000 a year. Well being declines up to the age of 40 and then rises again. Happiness also depends on how friends, partners and family members assess one's well-being and biological factors such as responses to stress, headaches, digestive disorders, duration of Duchenne smiles, etc. Although happiness in Britain has been relatively stable, empirical work shows that during the last quarter century some people in the US, especially white women, have become unhappier and others, American men and blacks, have become happier. Abundance resulting from economic growth evidently makes some people unhappier and others more content. For neoclassical economics with its emphasis on selfishness it is a puzzle why abundance breeds discontent (also see Lane, 2000).

Understanding this puzzle requires one to consider habituation and the importance of relative positions for happiness (Layard, 2003). Habituation implies that people quickly adjust to higher living standards and find it difficult to adjust downwards. Hence, improvements in material living standards make people happy for a while but the effect quickly fades off. Extra money does not necessarily make people better off either, because people tend to compare their lot with others. For example, Harvard students would rather have \$50,000 a year when others get half than \$100,000 a year when others get double. People do not seem to mind having less, as long as others do not do better than themselves. If everybody works hard to get more income and spend more, they do not necessarily become happier. The extra income one earns makes other people unhappy, so this adverse externality should be corrected for by a tax on labour income. Perhaps, the more so as the same Harvard students do not display leisure rivalry. Developed societies thus have a tendency to work too hard, consume too much and enjoy too little leisure. Chasing material comforts thus does not necessarily lead to happiness (cf. Scitovsky, 1976). Humans are social creatures and are happy if relationships with their nearest and dearest are good, they live in secure communities that value trust, and they are valued by the rest of society (Putnam, 2000). Moving too much in search of a (better) job may make people unhappier, since they loose a sense of belonging. A too strong emphasis on individualism and material comforts in a society with a lot of uncertainty, geographical mobility and little job security (the 'hedonistic treadmill') destroys happiness.

The last 50 years or so much of the developing world has seen a decline in the belief in God and in religion. The associated moral code from the bible or whatever seems to have been replaced by promoting unfettered individualism and selfishness. This together with invisible hand type of arguments that self-interest is good for society has destroyed the trust and more generally the fabric of society and has led to more anxiety among ordinary people. In fact, telling people that they should behave in their self-interest seems to destroy their willingness to co-operate (Layard, 2003).

8.6 Consumer rivalry, taxation and selfish redistribution

8.6.1 Constant marginal utility of income: labour is a public bad

We first assume constant marginal utility of income and abstract from income effects in labour supply. Utility of individual i is thus linear in consumption. Since people care about their consumption relative to others, utility of individual i is given by:

$$U_i \equiv C_i - \lambda C + u(V_i), \quad 0 < \lambda < 1, \;\; u' > 0 \text{ and } u'' < 0,$$

where C_i, C and V_i denote consumption of individual i, average consumption across the population and leisure of individual i, respectively. Layard (2003) suggests that λ is about 0.3, so that people feel worse off if others are able to consume more. People differ. Some are quicker at finishing a job and enjoying leisure than others. Total time available to individuals, $1 + \theta_i$, varies across the population and can be used for leisure or labour L_i. The parameter θ_i stands for innate talent of individual i. We normalise by setting mean time available to 1. Time available to the median voter equals $1 + \theta_M$, so that $\theta_M > 0$ measures inequality in talents of different people. The government uses a linear income tax schedule to redistribute income from rich to poor individuals. The proportional tax rate is t and the uniform tax credit is denoted by A. Individual i thus chooses consumption, leisure and labour supply L_i to maximise U_i subject to its budget constraint, $C_i = (1 - t)WL_i + A$, and time constraint, $L_i + V_i = 1 + \theta_i$. The marginal rate of substitution between leisure and consumption must equal the after-tax wage,

$u'(V_i) = (1-t)W$. Leisure thus falls and labour supply increases if the after-tax wage goes up: $V_i = v((1-t)W)$ and $L_i = 1+\theta_i - v((1-t)W)$ with $v' = 1/u'' < 0$. More talented people work more hours, earn more and consume more, but they enjoy the same amount of leisure as less talented people. This follows from $L_i = L + \theta_i$, $V_i = V$ and $C_i = C + (1-t)W\theta_i$, where L, V and C denote mean labour supply, mean leisure and mean consumption.

The government balances its books, so the tax rate must be high enough to cover tax credits and government spending G. Since $tWL = A + G$, mean consumption can be written as $C = WL - G = W[1 - v((1-t)W)] - G$ and the utility of individual i as:

$$U_i = (1-t)W\theta_i + (1-\lambda)\{W[1 - v((1-t)W)] - G\} + u(v(1-t)W)).$$

The median voter maximises utility by setting the tax rate equal to:

$$t = (\theta_{\mathrm{M}}/v'W) + \lambda.$$

The level of tax credits follows residually from the government budget constraint. Any increase in government spending is fully offset by the decrease in tax credits. With constant marginal utility of money income, public goods and tax credits are thus perfect substitutes. If the distribution of talents is unequal, that is, $\theta_{\mathrm{M}} > \theta = 0$, the median voter is less talented than the voter with average ability. It is thus in the interest of the median voter to redistribute income from more talented, richer people to less talented, poorer people. The median voter engages in selfish redistribution and votes for a tax schedule with a positive tax credit for all financed by a simple proportional tax on wage income. If labour supply is very inelastic, v' is small and the tax rate is high. This is the Ramsey motive and captured by the first term in the earlier expression for the tax rate (cf. Meltzer and Richard, 1981; Romer, 1975).

The second term in the expression for the tax rate desired by the majority of the electorate says that, if people care about their relative consumption position, taxation of labour is a good thing even if talents are equally distributed, that is if $\theta_{\mathrm{M}} = 0$ (cf. Layard, 2003). Since people compete with each other to consume more than their neighbours do ('keeping up with the Jones's), they work too hard from a social perspective. It thus makes sense to correct for this externality and to tax labour to make room for a happier society with more leisure and less consumption. This suggests that the tax rate is at least 30 per cent and even higher if the median voter is relatively less well off and cares about selfish redistribution. The tax rate is thus the sum of a Pigouvian term to correct for the consumption rat race and a redistributive term to correct for talent and income inequality.

8.6.2 Non-constant marginal utility of income: the Veblen-effect

Many people seek status by trying to distinguish themselves from others and aspiring to consume as much as the rich (Bourdieau, 1979; Veblen, 1899/1934). The consumption of the rich thus affects marginal utility of consumption of the less well off (e.g. Bagwell and Bernheim, 1996; Corneo and Olivier, 1997). To allow non-constant marginal utility of income, we assume $U_i = U(C_i - \lambda C, V_i)$. Higher consumption by others in society reduces utility and increases the marginal utility of consumption. We assume homothetic preferences, so that leisure and consumption are complements ($U_{CV} > 0$). Since the marginal rate of substitution between relative consumption and leisure must equal the after-tax wage, we have $V_i = v((1-t)W)(C_i - \lambda C)$ where $v' = U_C/[U_{VV} - (1-t)WU_{CV}] < 0$. Together with the time constraint and the household budget constraint, we obtain labour supply, leisure and consumption of individual i and mean labour supply L:

$$L_i = L + \omega((1-t)W)\theta_i, \qquad V_i = 1 - L + [1 - \omega((1-t)W)]\theta_i,$$
$$C_i = \omega((1-t)W)\{(1-t)W[1 + \theta_i + \lambda v((1-t)W)C] + A\},$$
$$L = \omega((1-t)W)[1 + v((1-t)W)(\lambda C - A)],$$

where $0 < \omega((1-t)W) \equiv 1/[1+(1-t)Wv((1-t)W)] < 1$ with $\omega' = (\sigma - 1)\omega^2$ and the elasticity of substitution between leisure and consumption is defined as $\sigma \equiv -(1-t)Wv\prime/v > 0$. More talented individuals work more hours, earn more and consume more than the average individual. They also have more leisure, so they work harder and have more fun. If average consumption rises, each individual wants to keep up and consumes more as well. A higher tax credit raises income, so induces more leisure, lower labour supply and higher consumption. A higher tax rate (or lower after-tax wage) has two effects: it reduces income and induces people to work harder and it makes leisure cheaper relative to goods consumption and thus lowers labour supply. If the second effect dominates the first effect, the substitution effect is more important than the income effect and conventional labour supply slopes upward ($\sigma > 1$ and $\omega' > 0$).

The government budget constraint, $tWL = G + A$, gives the reduced-form expressions for average consumption and average labour supply:

$$C = WL - G = (W - G)/[1 + (1-\lambda)Wv((1-t)W)]$$
$$L = [1 + (1-\lambda)v((1-t)W)G]/[1 + (1-\lambda)Wv((1-t)W)].$$

Higher public spending crowds out private consumption and induces people to take more leisure and work harder on average. Utility of the median voter is given by:

$$U_M = U[(1-\lambda)C + (1-t)W\omega((1-t)W)\theta_M, 1 - L + \{1 - \omega((1-t)W)\}\theta_M].$$

Society chooses the tax rate that maximises utility of the median voter.

The effect of aggregate consumption on hours worked is positive. People work harder in order to try to emulate the consumption standards of the rich. Hence, in a world of conspicuous consumption working hours are higher if the degree of income inequality is higher. This seems to be the reflected in the data as hours worked have fallen steadily in Europe while consumption inequality has diminished (Bowles and Park, 2002). To reach a social welfare optimum with such forms of consumer rivalry may require progressive consumption taxes or subsidising the leisure of the rich. One may wonder why people try to emulate the consumption standards of the better off rather than emulate the standards of people with more leisure. Veblen suggested that the cash one needs to buy consumption is a more visible display of distinction than enjoying more leisure than others do.

8.6.3 Sociological and economic views on redistribution

Another utility specification $U_i = su(C_i - \lambda C) + (1 - s)U(C_i) + v(V_i)$, with $u', v', U' > 0$ and $u'', U'' \leq 0$, nests the 'economic' model with $s = 0$ and the 'sociological' model with $s = 1$ as special cases (Clark and Oswald, 1998). Large values of s capture the idea that human beings have a deep wish to conform to others in their consumption patterns, but do not wish to emulate the leisure afforded by others. This sociological element suggests that humans constantly compare themselves to others and feel good when they out-perform their peers. With small values of s preferences are private and selfish and people do not look that much over their shoulders to see what others are up to. It can be shown that consumption of any individual goes up after a rise in the consumption of others if $v'' < 0$, that is if the utility function of relative consumption is concave. Hence, comparison-concave utility is required for people to mimic other people's consumption patterns. Conversely, if $v'' > 0$, consumption declines if consumption of others goes up. This obviously leads to deviant behaviour. If $v(.)$ is linear, people's consumption patterns are independent of those of others. If utility is linear in own consumption, that is, $U'' = 0$, consumption of any individual follows consumption of any other individual one for one.

8.7 Consumer rivalry in intertemporal macroeconomics

In dynamic economies it is important to be precise about the nature of consumer externalities. Typically, utility of any individual depends positively on its own consumption but also on some reference or aspiration level of consumption. This reference or aspiration level of consumption may simply be average consumption in the population (or consumption of 'other people') or, alternatively, may be a geometric average of past levels of average consumption. Dupor and Liu (2003) define two basis types of consumption externalities. The first one is based on jealousy effects, which requires that the utility of an individual drops if other people consume more. The second relates to keeping up or catching up with the Jones's and requires that the marginal utility of consumption of an individual increases if other people consume more. The latter is particularly important for asset price consideration and in theories of economic growth, while jealousy effects are crucial for consumption allocations. Many studies use utility functions that display both envy and keeping up with the Jones's. Most of these studies show that such consumption externalities require the government to step in with the use of distortionary taxes in order to reach the first-best optimum (e.g. Abel, 2003; Boskin and Sheshinski, 1978; de la Croix and Michel, 1999; Ljungqvist and Uhlig, 2000).

8.7.1 *Keynesian demand management and catching up with the Jones's*

Consumer externalities are prevalent in the real world and have drastic implications for inter-temporal macroeconomics. Since households fail to internalise the adverse effects of consuming more themselves on other households who have to engage in a rat race to keep up consumption, competitive markets fail to yield the first-best outcome and there is a need for government intervention. Consider an inter-temporal macroeconomic model with consumption externalities and driven by technology shocks, but without capital accumulation. Ljungqvist and Uhlig (2000) show that, if consumer externalities take the form of catching up with the Jones's, counter-cyclical demand management is needed to restore the first-best outcome in competitive equilibrium. The instrument to correct for the consumer externality is a pro-cyclical tax on labour. The labour tax rate is increased to cool down an over-heated economy caused by a positive productivity shock. In a boom households chase each other into a rat race where they work and consume too much, so the government must step in to end this rat race. In contrast, in a depression the tax rate on labour should be cut in order to bolster consumption when households are caught together in a negative spiral. Despite a purely competitive, market-clearing general equilibrium framework, there is nevertheless a role for counter-cyclical Keynesian demand management to correct for the external effects caused by catching up with the Jones's. All households are assumed to be the same, so there is no need to consider redistributive taxation. Let expected utility of household i be given by

$$E_0 \sum_{t=0}^{\infty} \beta^t \{[C_{ti} - X_t)^{1-\gamma} - 1]/(1-\gamma) - \nu L_{it}\}$$

where $0 < \beta < 1$ is the discount factor and $\nu > 0$ stands for the disutility of work. The aspiration level of consumption X is a geometric average of past average consumption levels:

$$X_t = \lambda(1-\phi)C_{t-1} + \phi X_{t-1}$$

where $0 \le \lambda < 1$ and $0 \le \phi < 1$. Each household faces a tax rate on labour income of t and receives a lump-sum transfer A of the government. The government budget is balanced each period. In symmetric equilibrium $C_{it} = C_t$ and $L_{it} = L_t$. Output is proportional to average labour input, that is $Y_t = \theta_t L_t$, and productivity θ_t follows the stochastic process:

$$1/\theta_t = [(1-\psi)/\bar{\theta} + \psi/\theta_{t-1}](1+\varepsilon_t)$$

where $0 \leq \psi < 1$ and ε_t is i.i.d. with zero mean and bounded below by $\varepsilon_t > -1$. The stochastic process is approximately the same as an AR(1) process for $\log(\theta_t)$. Households consume a lot if the aspiration level of consumption in society is high, the tax rate is low, productivity is high and their dislike of work is low:

$$C_t = X_t + [(1-\tau_t)\theta_t/\upsilon]^{1/\gamma}.$$

Ljungqvist and Uhlig (2000) show that the first-best allocation and consumption level

$$C_t^* = X_t + [\nu(1-\beta\phi)/\bar{\theta}(1-\delta) + \nu(\theta_t^{-1} - \bar{\theta}^{-1}(1-\beta\phi\psi)/(1-\delta\psi)]^{-1/\gamma}$$

can be achieved by the following tax rate:

$$\tau_t/(1-\tau_t) = [\beta\lambda(1-\phi)/(1-\delta\psi)][\psi + (1-\psi)\theta_t/(1-\delta)\bar{\theta}],$$

$$\delta \equiv \beta[\phi + \lambda(1-\phi)] < 1$$

The steady-state tax rate is given by $\tau_\infty = \lambda\beta(1-\phi)/(1-\beta\phi)$. It follows that the optimal tax policy impacts the economy counter-cyclically via pro-cyclical taxes. The tax rate varies positively with productivity. This counter-cyclical form of Keynesian demand management corrects for the externalities induced by catching up with the Jones's.

Ljungqvist and Uhlig (2000) also study consequences of nonlinear forms of catching-up-with-the-Jones's effects as used by Campbell and Cochrane (1999). Since the surplus consumption ratio exhibits increasing returns to scale, the social planner can increase the well being of individuals by generating welfare-enhancing consumption cycles in otherwise stationary environments. They find that the parameter values of Campbell and Cochrane (1999) suggest very high tax rates on labour. Lettau and Uhlig (1995) show that introducing catching-up-with-the-Jones's in economies with capital accumulation has the implication that consumption is excessively smooth in competitive equilibrium.

8.7.2 PAYG and capital income taxes in OLG economies with consumer rivalry

Liu and Turnovsky (2002) show in a framework of neoclassical growth with infinitely-lived households and inelastic labour supply that the steady-state return on capital is unaffected by consumption externalities. This result is not robust and does not hold in economies with overlapping generations and finitely-lived households. Abel (2003) therefore analyses a dynamic competitive economy with overlapping generations and capital formation and also introduces a benchmark level of consumption into the utility function of individuals. The socially optimal balanced growth path is characterised by the same modified golden rule as in standard neoclassical growth models. However, the concern for consumption relative to the benchmark or aspiration level of consumption imposes an optimality condition on the allocation of consumption across generations that are simultaneously alive. Without consumption externalities the first-best optimum in the standard neoclassical economies with overlapping generations can be obtained with a balanced-budget lump-sum inter-generational transfer scheme. A pay-as-you-go form of social security can thus be used to achieve the appropriate level of saving and the modified golden rule. If consumers also care about a benchmark level of consumption, the government needs an additional tool to achieve the first-best optimum. This requires a distortionary tax on capital income. When the social planner is more patient than individual households, the transfer scheme typically transfers from the current young to the current old (Abel, 2003). In that case, the optimal rate on capital income must be positive. This is surprising, since one would expect a more patient social planner to subsidise capital in order to raise the capital-labour ratio. However, a more patient social planner also favours later, that is, younger, generations and can do this by taxing capital income at a positive rate.

8.7.3 Equity premium riddles explained by consumer rivalry

Catching up with the Jones's and various forms of consumer rivalry have been the focus of considerable attention in the asset pricing literature (e.g. Abel, 1990). Such envy effects may explain the equity premium puzzle of Mehra and Prescott (1985). The idea is to allow one's own marginal utility from an additional unit of consumption to be higher if one observes that other people consume more. This can happen immediately, that is, keeping up with the Jones's (e.g. Gáli, 1994), after a lag, that is, catching up with the Jones's (cf. Campbell and Cochrane, 1999), or using a variant based on habit formation (e.g. Constantinides, 1990). All variants rely on the by now familiar consumption externality, so that households do not take account of the unhappiness they cause to others if they themselves consume more. Through this route one can shed new light on the puzzle that equity seems to consistently demand a much higher rate of return than bonds than would be warranted by any reasonable degree of risk aversion.

8.8 Merits and costs of progressive taxation

Increasingly, economists have come to realise that people's happiness does not depend on money and absolute levels of consumption alone – see section 5. If everybody works hard to get more income and spend more, they do not necessarily become happier. The extra income one earns makes other people unhappy, so this adverse externality should be corrected for by a progressive tax on labour income. People engage in wasteful rat races which leave less room for leisure and provide additional grounds for progressive taxes (Akerlof, 1976). Developed societies have a tendency to work too hard, display rat races, consume too much and enjoy too little leisure. Efficiency can be improved with a progressive tax system – see section 8. This is interesting, because the neo-liberal agenda (the 'Washington Consensus') stresses the harmful effects of progressive taxes on incentives and economic activity.

8.8.1 Unemployment and progressive taxation

Economies experience 'real' unemployment, not leisure or holidays disguised as unemployment. Involuntary unemployment is prevalent in capitalist societies. Markets fail or disappear if there are legal restrictions, institutional rigidities, high transaction costs, external effects, adverse selection and moral hazard problems arising from asymmetric information, and/or imperfect competition. In the real world prices do not equal marginal costs and labour is paid more than its marginal product. Rents are shared between employers and employees. Wages are typically set by trade unions, by firms or in negotiations between workers and firms rather than as the outcome of clearing labour markets. In such a second-best world reducing one distortion does not necessarily improve welfare. The distortion arising from a more progressive tax system may offset the distortions from imperfect labour markets.

Substantial parts of the labour force are unionised. In some countries trade union agreements are legally extended to all workers, thus making the power of trade unions even stronger. Monopoly trade unions have sufficient monopoly power to set wages for its members given knowledge of the labour demand curve. Firms subsequently take the wage set by the monopoly union as given when maximising profits. With right to manage, unions bargain with firms over the wage, but not the employment level. This does not change results very much, because the outcome is still on the labour demand curve. We assume middle-sized trade unions, big enough to set wages but too small to internalise adverse effects of higher wages on prices and purchasing power of members. The unions are also too small to bargain with the government over taxation, benefits, childcare, pensions, training and other matters that may concern employees. Unions thus do not internalise the government budget constraint. Their welfare is captured by a utilitarian welfare function.

Firms face a concave production function $Y = F(L)$, where Y denotes output and L employment. Profit maximisation implies firms set marginal productivity of labour to the real producer wage, $F'(L) = (1 + T_L)W$ where T_L is the employers' tax rate. Demand for labour decreases with the producer wage. The union operates under a Rawlsian 'veil of ignorance' and maximises $Lv(W_A) + (N - L)v(B)$, subject to the labour demand curve, where $v' > 0$, $v'' < 0$, B is the unemployment benefit, $N - L$ the number of unemployed and W_A the after-tax wage. This yields the union wage mark-up:

$$[v(W_A) - v(B)]/[W_A v'(W_A)] = S/\varepsilon_D,$$

where $S \equiv (1 - T_M)/(1 - T_A)$ is the measure of residual income progression, T_A the average income tax rate, T_M the marginal income tax rate and ε_D the wage elasticity of labour demand. The left-hand side gives the difference in utility of an employed and an unemployed union member, converted from utility into production units, and expressed as fraction of the after-tax wage. The right-hand side indicates that, given the unemployment benefit, the mark-up is particularly large and unemployment high if the wage elasticity of labour demand ε_D is low.

Also, given the unemployment benefit, the mark-up falls and employment rises if the tax system becomes more progressive (lower S). With a unit coefficient of relative aversion the union mark-up is $W_A = \exp(S/\varepsilon_D)\ B$. The unemployment benefit sets a 'floor' in the after-tax wage, so higher benefit immediately translates into a higher wage and lower employment. For a given degree of tax progression, a higher average income tax rate T_A leaves the after-tax wage unaffected and thus the pre-tax wage rises. The after-tax wage displays real wage rigidity, hence the full burden of the labour income tax is borne by firms. A higher payroll tax also leaves the after-tax wage unaffected, so labour costs rise and employment falls.

If unemployed union members do not rely on unemployment benefit, but have probability $1-U$ of finding a job and probability U of being on the dole with U the unemployment rate, then expected outside income, $W_O = (1-U)W_A + U(B+I)$, is the relevant alternative income and not the benefit B. Here I stands for (utility of leisure or) untaxed informal income. Since $W_A - W_O = U(W_A - B - I)$, the income differential of a union job increases if the differential between the after-tax wage and the benefit plus informal income is high and if the chance of falling back on the dole is high (i.e. if unemployment is high). With risk-neutral preferences we obtain the equilibrium unemployment rate:

$$U = (S/\varepsilon_D)/[1 - (B/W_A) - (I/W_A)].$$

Equilibrium unemployment is high if replacement ratios for benefits $\rho \equiv B/W_A$ and informal incomes are high, the tax system is not so progressive and labour demand is fairly inelastic.

If benefits are indexed to after-tax wages and informal incomes are indexed to before-tax wages, $\rho_I \equiv I/W$, the equilibrium unemployment rate $U = (S/\varepsilon_D)/[1-\rho-(\rho_I/(1-T_A)]$ rises if the replacement rates for benefits and informal incomes rise and the average tax rate rises. If benefits or informal incomes are not indexed to after-tax wages, the earlier gives a wage setting equation in which the wage rises with both the level of employment and the benefit. Together with the labour demand curve, one can solve simultaneously for employment and the wage. Although cuts in payroll taxes do not affect the unemployment rate if benefits are indexed to after-tax wages and informal incomes are absent, they raise the wage, boost employment and reduce the unemployment rate if benefits are not indexed (cf. Bovenberg and van der Ploeg, 1994; Pissarides, 1998). Hence, if benefits are not indexed to after-tax wages or the unemployed enjoy untaxed, informal income, the wage setting equation is flatter and payroll taxes boost employment by cutting the replacement rate and increasing the incentive to work – see Figure 8.2. Another way of putting it is that the effects of a higher average labour tax depend on whether the unemployed escape the burden of taxation. There is no increase in unemployment if the unemployed share fully in the higher tax burden, that is, if the outside option is fully taxed and the net replacement rate is not increased. Of course, it is then debatable whether this is a very social policy. In practice, it is unlikely that the unemployed share fully in the tax burden. Unemployed people

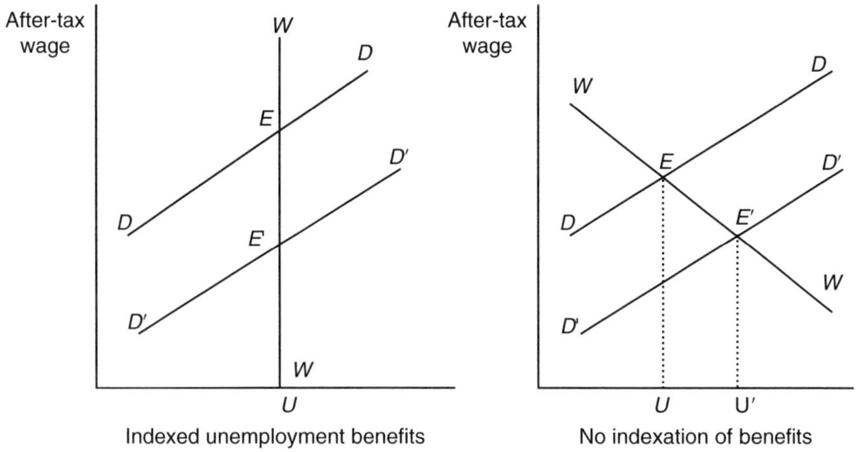

Figure 8.2 Indexation of benefits and incidence of taxes in non-competitive labor markets.

enjoy untaxed leisure and income in the informal economy, so that a higher average tax rate on labour destroys jobs.

The result that with a fixed after-tax replacement rate a more progressive tax system moderates wages and boosts employment and output also holds with 'right to manage' where the wage follows from a Nash bargain between unions and firms and employment is subsequently set by firms. The ratio of the wage bargaining outcome to outside income is again high if labour demand is fairly inelastic and the degree of tax progression is small. In addition, the wage is high if the 'ability to pay' (as measured by the share of profits relative to that of wages) is high and the bargaining power of firms relative to that of unions is relatively weak. Also, imperfect competition in product markets lowers the wage elasticity of labour demand and bolsters the power of trade unions. Koskela and Vilmunen (1996) extend the results to efficient Nash bargaining between firms and unions.

If unemployment benefits are indexed to after-tax wages and unemployed people share fully in the tax burden, changes in labour taxes do not affect unemployment and are fully borne by workers. However, Graafland and Huizinga (1999) give evidence for the Netherlands that the tax rate adversely affects unemployment even after correcting for the effects of changes in the net replacement rate. Also, Daveri and Tabellini (2000) provide empirical evidence that changes in labour taxes are strongly correlated with changes in unemployment rates, particularly for European countries with substantial unionisation and less so for the Nordic European countries with centralised trade unions. One reason is that unemployed people also enjoy untaxed, informal incomes and enjoy utility of untaxed leisure. In that case, the *true* replacement rate is not constant and a higher tax wedge boosts unemployment even if productivity growth must be consistent with stationary unemployment (Bovenberg, 2003; Bovenberg and Ploeg van der, 1994, 1998;

Sørensen, 1997). These insights also hold for an open economy with international capital mobility and constant returns to scale in production. With interest rates set on world markets the producer wage is pinned down by the factor price frontier. A higher replacement rate or less progressive tax system then reduces the demand for capital from abroad and the demand for labour but leaves the producer wage unaffected. The end result is the same: more unemployment.

With efficiency wages firms pay relatively high wages to recruit, retain and motivate workers. Abilities and effort of workers are hard to monitor for a firm. However, by paying a bit more than elsewhere, firms counteract adverse selection by improving the average quality of the workforce. Paying a 'fair' wage also reduces work disruption and raises morale and work effort. When effort by workers in firm i depends on differences in indirect utility in work and out of work,

$$E_i = [v(W_{Ai}) - v(W_O)]^{\varepsilon} \quad \text{with}$$
$$W_O \equiv U(B+I) + (1-U)W_A = \{1 - [1 - (B+I)/W_A]U\}W_A,$$

where $\varepsilon > 0$, W_{Ai} is the after-tax wage of a worker in firm i, relative wages matter. Effort increases if the chance of unemployment and a large drop in income is high, that is if the unemployment rate U is high and replacement rate low. Output of firm i, $Y_i = E_i L_i$, rises with efficiency and volume of labour. Firm i sets its wage to maximise profits, $[E_i - (1 + T_L)W_i]L_i$, This yields:

$$[v(W_{Ai}) - v(W_O)]/[W_{Ai}v'(W_{Ai})] = \varepsilon S.$$

Firm i sets relatively high wages if the efficiency wage or leapfrogging effect ε is strong and the tax system is not very progressive. Less risk-averse workers require firms to pay more to recruit, retain and motivate workers. Again, more tax progression reduces the wage mark-up. Firms have in the margin less incentive to offer higher wages if the government grabs a bigger slice of the wage rise. With risk-neutral preferences we obtain in symmetric equilibrium:

$$U = \varepsilon S/[1 - \rho - \rho_I/(1 - T_A)].$$

$\rho \equiv B/W_A$ and $\rho_I \equiv I/W$. More leapfrogging (higher ε), a higher replacement rate, a less progressive tax system (higher S) and, with untaxed informal income, a higher average labour tax rate induce higher unemployment. More risk aversion among workers also lowers unemployment. More tax progression boosts employment and output and reduces unemployment, since it is less attractive to pay high wages and to leapfrog other firms and for workers to do their best. Hence, labour productivity and the pre-tax wage fall. This contrasts with competitive labour markets, where more progressive taxes destroy incentives to work more hours and lower employment and output. Indeed, if we allow for optimal choice of hours worked and efficiency wages, a more progressive tax system lowers labour supply per household (i.e. reduces hours worked per job) which generates upward wage pressure. Total demand for labour will not rise as much and may even fall.

The number of jobs will rise albeit that each job has shorter working hours. Of course, the size of the national income need not necessarily rise.

If unemployment benefits are indexed to after-tax wages (ρ fixed) and informal income is absent, a higher average income tax rate T_{A} or payroll tax T_{L} does *not* affect unemployment again. However, if benefits or informal incomes are not indexed to after-tax wages, the unemployment rate decreases as after-tax wages rise and one needs

$$\log(W) = [1/(1-\varepsilon)][\varepsilon\{\log(S) - T_{\mathrm{A}}\} - T_{\mathrm{L}}] \quad \text{and}$$
$$\log(W_{\mathrm{A}}) = [1/(1-\varepsilon)][\varepsilon \log(S) - T_{\mathrm{A}} - T_{\mathrm{L}}],$$

to assess the incidence of taxes and the effects on unemployment. A rise in taxation keeping the degree of tax progression unchanged, raises marginal and average tax rates together and lowers the pre-tax wage. After-tax wages fall by more than 100 per cent and thus workers bear more than 100 per cent of the tax burden. These results differ from under a monopoly union, since there firms rather than workers carried the burden of labour income taxation as now firms rather than unions set wages. If unemployed benefits are not indexed to after-wages or the unemployed enjoy untaxed income, a higher average labour income or payroll tax depresses after-tax wages more than 100 per cent, raises the replacement rate and thus increases the unemployment rate. The beneficial effects of a more progressive tax system, that is, wage moderation and a lower unemployment rate, are less if benefits are not indexed to after-tax wages, because then the replacement rate is pushed up by the fall in after-tax wages. Clearly, the welfare state components can not be seen in isolation.

More generally, we show that, if the unemployed do not escape the burden of taxation, changes in the average labour tax rate do not affect the unemployment rate or the producer wage. However, if unemployment benefits are not fully indexed to after-tax wage income or the unemployed enjoy untaxed, informal income, the unemployed escape part of the burden of taxation. In that case, a higher tax rate on labour pushes up unemployment and wages. In non-Walrasian settings there is a surplus to be divided between firms and workers. Progressive taxes then tilt the balance in favour of less purchasing power and more jobs. This explains why in many econometric estimates of wage equations higher average tax rates give rise to upward wage pressure while higher marginal tax rate induce downward wage pressure (e.g. Lockwood and Manning, 1994).

8.8.2 Other efficiency grounds for progressive taxation

In the presence of trade union power, efficiency wage and/or search frictions, a more progressive tax system thus tends to moderate wages and boost employment (e.g. Bovenberg, 2003; Ploeg van der, 2005). The boost to the number of jobs may be enhanced, since a more progressive tax system typically reduces the number of hours worked per employee. Sørensen (1999) shows that a union, concerned with employment of its members, restricts working hours below the level which the individual employed member would prefer at the going after-tax wage. Since tax progression drives an additional wedge between the marginal disutility of work and the marginal productivity of labour, hours worked per worker falls and labour supply is further distorted. Wage moderation boosts employment, that is, the total hours of labour demanded by firms. Together with the induced shorter working week this boosts the total number of jobs in the economy. Labour supply effects thus remain important in non-Walrasian labour markets and, *a priori*, it is not clear what happens to unemployment. We need to closely examine the evidence from micro-econometric studies, since some agents may face high marginal tax rates and exhibit elastic labour supply (Bovenberg, 2003). In any case, it is better to focus on the employment effects, which also seems more relevant in the analysis of problems arising from ageing of the population. Cross-country comparisons of employment are also easier for statistical reasons.

Many politicians are concerned about the unequal distribution of labour within the family. Men typically work more hours on the labour market than women, but do less shopping, childcare and other household chores. A more progressive tax system has, if the tax system is individualised, the added benefit that the partner who works most hours is stimulated to work less while the other partner is encouraged to work more hours on the labour market. Hence, a more progressive tax system can contribute to a more equal distribution of labour between men and women in the family.

Failing capital and insurance markets may also provide efficiency grounds for progressive taxation (e.g. Ewijk van *et al*., 2003). Future labour income is usually not accepted by commercial banks as a guarantee for a loan, since people cannot be forced to work and pay back in future. Problems of adverse selection imply that good risks do not borrow, thus the bad risks remain. As a result, interest rates go up and credit is rationed (Stiglitz and Weiss, 1981). People thus are unable to borrow when they are young and to smooth consumption over their life cycle. Progressive taxes redistribute incomes from people that are old and earn a lot to people that are young and do not earn a lot. In this sense, a progressive tax system acts as an implicit credit market and alleviates some of the distortions of rationed credit markets (Hubbard and Judd, 1986). Rationing of credit particularly hurts students with poor parents. This is bad for society, since the full potential of human capital remains underdeveloped. Since a progressive tax system also redistributes from rich to poor parents, it partially alleviates adverse effects of credit rationing on schooling (Jacobs, 2003).

Insurance markets fail to fully insure the risks of loosing income if people become ill, disabled or unemployed. People typically have a better knowledge of their own chances of becoming ill, disabled or unemployed than insurance companies. The good risks thus leave the market and the insurance companies are left with the bad risks. Insurance premiums go up; some insurance markets may stop functioning altogether (Rothschild and Stiglitz, 1976). As a result, people engage in less risk jobs and activities. Since a progressive tax system also redistributes income from people with good luck to people with bad luck, it also corrects to a certain extent for failing insurance markets (cf. Sinn, 1995). A progressive tax system also encourages risk-averse people to invest in risky studies (e.g. Eaton and Rosen, 1980).

We have given a large number of arguments why social policies and redistributive taxation may alleviate non-tax distortions in second-best economies, but social policies such as progressive taxation also exacerbate non-tax distortions and may reduce output. They distort markets, reduce the incentive to work and can exclude many people from the labour markets. If unemployment benefits are taxed or the unemployed enjoy untaxed, informal income, tax progression raises the *effective* net replacement rate and can thus induce wage pressure and destroy jobs. If labour supply is endogenous, the effect of progressive taxation on employment is ambiguous. The effects on wage moderation and on hours worked typically work in opposite directions. Tax progression may harm the incentive to invest in training and human capital, so that it may lower the productivity of the economy. Tax progression also encourages tax evasion, reduces working hours, lowers productivity by reducing the employers' optimal efficiency wage relative to the level of unemployment benefit, and lowers the efficiency of the job matching process by reducing workers' expected marginal return to job search. Even if employment rises with more tax progression, output may fall and finance of a generous welfare state may become more difficult. Conversely, a by-product of a less progressive tax system is that some low-wage earners may face higher average and marginal tax rates. Since low-wage earners are likely to have relatively elastic labour supplies, OECD (1995) argues that the efficiency costs of taxation may actually increase rather than decrease.

Sørensen (1999), Røed and Strøm (2002), and Bovenberg (2003) point out that there is an optimal degree of tax progression. It is an empirical matter to find out whether the efficiency grounds for social policies dominate the costs of market distortions. However, the case for social policies is greater in economies plagued by many non-tax and non-benefit distortions.

8.9 Concluding remarks

Countries with large welfare states and substantial redistribution do not seem to have much worse economic performance. This is a puzzle for advocates of the 'Washington consensus'. We stressed reciprocal altruism, mutual obligations and second-best as important factors to bear in find when designing the welfare state and redistributive tax schemes. In particular, we provided an example of an economy with efficiency wages where higher conditional unemployment benefits boosted job growth while higher unconditional benefits (welfare) depressed job growth. We also showed that more tax progression induces wage moderation in non-competitive labour markets with trade unions and/or efficiency wages. Effectively, modern market economies with large welfare states are riddles with distortions. Many of these distortions cancel out against each other, so the economics of second best applies. Also, welfare is hardly ever given unconditionally. Governments understand the principle of reciprocity and mutual obligations. They also know how to deal with problem of second best when they design the welfare state. These are the reasons why there is no empirical evidence that large welfare states make countries poorer in the sense of lowering national income per head of the population. Another reason is that countries with large welfare states typically introduce many pro-growth policies such as low taxes on capital, special treatment for corporations and more education subsidies.

Social interactions and the effects of neighbours on individual behaviour are just as important for understanding the causes of unemployment (Akerlof, 1980; Klundert van de, 1990) and welfare stigma (e.g. Besley and Coate, 1992; Lindbeck *et al*., 1999). These insights are crucial for the design of an efficient welfare state. It is a mistake to think that all interactions between people are mediated through the price and wage mechanism alone. The individual's voluntary choice between living on welfare and working depends very much on social norms and interactions. In a very interesting paper Åberg *et al.* (2003) study the social and psychological costs of involuntary unemployment empirically and within the context of a search-theoretic model of the labour market. Examining the behaviour of young people in Stockholm, they find evidence that these costs are low if people live in a neighbourhood where many people are unemployed and vice versa. Consequently, there are ratchet effects in unemployment. If unemployment is high in an area, psychological costs of unemployment are low and thus people search less intensively for a new job and are more likely to become and remain unemployed themselves. Conversely, if unemployment is low, psychological costs of unemployment are low, people search harder for a new job, and unemployment is more likely to remain low. This work emphasises the importance of communities and of social norms in understanding unemployment and in the design of the welfare state.

It also matters for the welfare state what people believe are the rewards of effort, hard work and risk taking. If people think these activities lead to economic success, there is much less support for redistribution and the welfare state. If people are down and out after having tried to get a job and search for income, there is much more support for redistribution. Fairness implies that society is much more willing to help those with bad luck than lazy people. Since many people care about relative incomes and are engaged in rat races, it makes sense for governments to have a higher tax rate and more redistribution simply to correct for the adverse externality of working too hard. Also, societies with a lot of inequality end up with populist governments who redistribute more than more equal societies. In the process such unequal societies end up with higher tax rates, higher unemployment, lower output and higher inflation. In sum, reciprocity, mutual obligations, sociological considerations, beliefs, procedural fairness, consumer rivalry and the theory of second best matter for a better understanding of the effects of the welfare state on employment and output. This has important implications for public finance and promises exciting venues for future research.

Acknowledgements

Based on my lecture at the Sienna Summer School, XVIth Workshop on 'Inequality and Economic Integration', 2–6 July 2003, and my lecture at the CRISS First

Annual Young Economists' Workshop, University of Rome 'La Sapienza', 31 May 2004. I thank Samuel Bowles for helpful discussions.

References

Abel, A.B. (1990). Asset prices under habit formation and catching up with the Joneses, *American Economic Review*, 80(2), 38–42.

Abel, A.B. (2003). Optimal taxation when consumers have endogenous benchmark levels of consumption, Working Paper No. 10099, NBER, Cambridge, MA.

Åberg, Y., P. Hedström and A.-S. Kolm (2003). Social interactions and unemployment, mimeo., Nuffield College, Oxford and Uppsala University.

Akerlof, G. (1976). The economics of caste and of the rat race and other woeful tales, *Quarterly Journal of Economics*, 90(4), 599–617.

Akerlof, G. (1980). A theory of social custom, of which unemployment may be one consequence, *Quarterly Journal of Economics*, 84, 749–775.

Alesina, A. and G.-M. Angeletos (2003). Fairness and redistribution: U.S. versus Europe, NBER Working Paper 9502, Cambridge, MA.

Alesina, A. and E. Glaeser (2004). *Fighting Poverty in the US and Europe: A World of Difference*, Oxford University Press, New York.

Alesina, A., E. Glaeser and B. Sacerdote (2002). Why doesn't the US have a European-type welfare state?, *Brookings Papers on Economic Activity*, 2, 187–277.

Andreoni, J. (1989). Giving with impure altruism – applications to charity and Ricardian equivalence, *Journal of Political Economy*, 97, 1447–1458.

Atkinson, A.B. (1996). *Incomes and the Welfare State*, Cambridge University Press: Cambridge.

Atkinson, A.B. (2002). *The Economic Consequences of Rolling Back the Welfare State*, Munich Lectures in Economics, CES and MIT Press: Cambridge, MA.

Axell, B. and H. Lang (1990). The effects of unemployment compensation in general equilibrium with search unemployment, *Scandinavian Journal of Economics*, 92, 531–540.

Bagwell, L.S. and D.B. Bernheim (1996). Veblen effects in a theory of conspicuous consumption, *American Economic Review*, 86, 349–373.

Bénabou, R. and J. Tirole (2002). Belief in a just world and redistributive politics, mimeo.

Bertola, G. and T. Boeri (2001). EMU labour market reforms two years on: microeconomic tensions and institutional evolution, in M. Buti and A. Sapir (eds), *EMU and Economic Policy in Europe: The Challenge of the Early Years*, Edward Elgar: Aldershot.

Besley, T. and S. Coate (1992). Understanding welfare stigma: tax payers resentment and statistical discrimination, *Journal of Public Economics*, 48, 165–183.

Bewley, T. (2004). Fairness, reciprocity, and wage rigidity, Discussion Paper No. 1137, IZA, Bonn.

Blanchard, O. and J. Tirole (2004). The optimal design of unemployment insurance and employment protection: a first pass, NBER Working Paper 10443, Cambridge, MA.

Blanchflower, D. and A. Oswald (2004). Well-being over time in Britain and the USA, *Journal of Public Economics*, 88, 1359–1386.

Boadway, R., M. Leite-Monteiro, M.G. Marchand and P. Piestieau (2004). Social insurance and redistribution with moral hazard and adverse selection, Discussion Paper No. 4253, CEPR, London.

Boskin, M. and E. Sheshinski (1978). Optimal redistributive taxation when individual welfare depends on relative income, *Quarterly Journal of Economics*, 92(4), 589–601.

Bourdieau, P. (1979). La Distinction – Critique Sociale du Jugement, Editions de Minuit, Paris.

Bovenberg, A.L. (2003). Tax policy and labor market performance, CESifo Working Paper No. 1035, Munich.

Bovenberg, A.L. and F. van der Ploeg (1994). Effects of the tax and benefit system on wage setting and unemployment, Center, Tilburg University.

Bovenberg, A.L. and F. van der Ploeg (1998). Tax reform, structural unemployment and the environment, *Scandinavian Journal of Economics*, 100(3), 593–610.

Bowles, S. and J.-K. Choi (2003). The co-evolution of love and hate, mimeo.

Bowles, S. and Y. Park (2002). Emulation, inequality, and work hours: Was Thorsten Veblen right?, mimeo.

Bowles, S., J.-K. Choi and A. Hopfensitz (2003). The co-evolution of individual behaviours and social institutions, *Journal of Theoretical Biology*, 223, 135–147.

Campbell, J.Y. and J.H. Cochrane (1999). By force of habit: a consumption-based explanation of aggregate stock market behaviour, *Journal of Political Economy*, 107(2), 205–251.

Clark, A.E. and A.J. Oswald (1996). Satisfaction and comparison income, *Journal of Public Economics*, 61(3), 359–381.

Clark, A.E. and A.J. Oswald (1998). Comparison-concave utility and following behaviour in social and economic settings, *Journal of Public Economics*, 70, 133–155.

Constantinides, G.M. (1990). Habit formation: a resolution of the equity premium puzzle, *Journal of Political Economy*, 98(3), 519–543.

Corneo, G. and J. Olivier (1997). Conspicuous consumption, snobbism, and conformism, *Journal of Public Economics*, 66, 55–71.

Daveri, F. and G. Tabellini (2000). Unemployment, growth, and taxation in industrial countries, *Economic Policy*, 15, 30, 49–104.

De Grauwe, P. and M. Polan (2003). *Globalisation and Social Spending*, Working Paper No. 885, CESifo, Munich.

De la Croix, D. and P. Michel (1999). Optimal growth when tastes are inherited, *Journal of Economic Dynamics and Control*, 23(4), 519–537.

Dixit, A.K. (1996). *The Making of Economic Policy: A Transaction-Cost Politics Perspective*, CES and MIT Press, Cambridge, MA.

Dupor, B. and W.-F. Liu (2003). Jealousy and equilibrium overconsumption, *American Economic Review*, 93(1), 423–428.

Eaton, J. and H.S. Rosen (1980). Taxation, human capital, and uncertainty, *American Economic Review*, 70, 705–715.

Ewijk, C. van, B. Jacobs, R. de Mooij and P. Tang (2003). Tien doelmatigheidsargumenten voor progressive belastingen, *Tijdschrift voor Openbare Financiën*, 1, 30–35.

Falk, A. (2004). Charitable giving as a gift exchange – evidence from a field experiment, Presented at the CESifo Area Conference on Public Economics, Munich.

Fehr, E. and A. Falk (1999). Wage rigidity in a competitive incomplete contract market, *Journal of Political Economy*, 107, 106–134.

Fehr, E. and S. Gächter (2000). Fairness and retaliation: the economics of reciprocity, *Journal of Economic Perspectives*, 14, 159–181.

Fehr, E. and J. Henrich (2003). Is strong reciprocity a maladaptation? On the evolutionary foundations of human altruism, CESifo Working Paper No. 859, Munich.

Fehr, E., U. Fischbacher and S. Gächter (2002). Strong reciprocity, human cooperation and the enforcement of social norms, *Human Nature*, 13, 1–25.

Fella, G. (2000). Efficient wages and efficient redundancy pay, *European Economic Review*, 44(8), 1473–1490.

Fong, C.M., S. Bowles and H. Gintis (2003). Reciprocity and the welfare state, mimeo.

Frey, B.S. and F. Oberholzer-Gee (1997). The cost of price incentives: an empirical analysis of motivation crowding-out, *American Economic Review*, 87(4), 746–755.

Frey, B.S. and A. Stutzer (2002). *Happiness and Economics: How the Economy and Institutions Affect Human Well-Being*, Princeton University Press: Princeton, NJ.

Frey, B.S., M. Benz and A. Stutzer (2004). Introducing procedural utility: not only what, but also how matters, *Journal of Theoretical and Institutional Economics*, 160(3), 377–401.

Gächter, S. and E. Falk (2002). Reputation and reciprocity: consequences for the labour relation, *Scandinavian Journal of Economics*, 104, 1–26.

Graafland, J.J. and F.H. Huizinga (1999). Taxes and benefits in a non-linear wage equation, *De Economist*, 147, 39–54.

Hubbard, R.G. and K.L. Judd (1986). Liquidity constraints, fiscal policy, and consumption, *Brookings Papers on Economic Activity*, 1, 1–50.

Jacobs, B. (2003). Optimal taxation of human capital and credit constraints, Discussion Paper No. 044/2, Tinbergen Institute, Amsterdam and Rotterdam, The Netherlands.

Klundert, Th. van de (1990). On socioeconomic causes of 'wait unemployment', *European Economic Review*, 34(5), 1011–1022.

Koskela, E. and J. Vilmunen (1996). Tax progression is good for employment in popular models of trade union behaviour, *Labour Economics*, 3, 65–80.

Lane, R.E. (2000). *The Loss of Happiness in Market Economies*, Yale University Press: New York.

Layard, R. (2003). Lectures on happiness (income and happiness: rethinking economic policy; What would make a happier society?), Lionel Robbins Memorial Lectures 2003, Centre for Economic Performance, London School of Economics.

Lettau, M. and H. Uhlig (1995). Can habit formation be reconciled with business cycle facts, Center discussion paper 9554, Tilburg University.

Lind, E.A. and T.R. Tyler (1988). *The Sociological Psycology of Procedural Justice*, Plenum Press: New York.

Lindbeck, A., S. Nyberg and J. Weibull (1999). Social norms and economic incentives in the welfare state, *Quarterly Journal of Economics*, 114(1), 1–35.

Lindert, P.H. (2004). *Growing Public – Social Spending and Economic Growth Since the Eighteenth Century*, Cambridge University Press: Cambridge.

List, J.A. and D. Lucking-Reiley (2002). The effects of seed money and refunds on charitable giving: experimental evidence from a university capital campaign, *Journal of Political Economy*, 40, 611–619.

Liu, W.-F. and S.J. Turnovsky (2002). Consumption externalities, production externalities, and the accumulation of capital, University of Washington, Seattle.

Ljungqvist, L. and H. Uhlig (2000). Tax policy and aggregate demand management under catching up with the Joneses, *American Economic Review*, 90(3), 356–366.

Lockwood, B. and A. Manning (1993). Wage setting and the tax system: theory and evidence from the United Kingdom, *Journal of Public Economics*, 52, 1–29.

Mehra, R. and E. Prescott (1985). The equity premium puzzle, *Journal of Monetary Economics*, 15, 145–161.

Meltzer, A. and S. Richard (1981). A rational theory of the size of government, *Journal of Political Economy*, 89, 914–927.

OECD (1995). *The OECD Jobs Study. Taxation, Employment and Unemployment*, Paris.

Oswald, A.J. (1983). Altruism, jealousy, and the theory of optimal nonlinear income taxation, *Journal of Public Economics*, 20, 77–87.

Oswald, A.J. (1997). Happiness and economic performance, *Economic Journal*, 107(445), 1815–1831.

Piketty, T. (1995). Social mobility and redistributive politics, *Quarterly Journal of Economics*, 110, 551–584.

Pissarides, C.A. (1998). The impact of employment tax cuts on unemployment and wages: the role of unemployment benefits and tax structure, *European Economic Review*, 42, 155–183.

Ploeg, F. van der (2005). Do social policies harm employment?, Second-best effects of taxes and benefits on employment, in J. Agell and P. Sørensen (eds), *Tax Policy and Labor Market Performance*, CESifo and MIT Press, Cambridge, MA (to appear).

Praag, B.M.S. van (1993). The relativity of the welfare concept, in M. Nussbaum and A. Sen (eds), *The Quality of Life*, Clarendon Press: Oxford, pp. 363–392.

Putnam, R. (2000). *Bowling it Alone*, Simon & Schuster: New York.

Ridley, M. (1997). *The Origins of Virtue*, Penguin Books: London.

Rodrik, D. (1997). The 'paradoxes' of the successful state, *European Economic Review*, 41(3–5), 411–442.

Rodrik, D. (1998). Why do open economies have bigger governments? *Journal of Political Economy*, 106, 997–1032.

Røed, K. and S. Strøm (2002). Progressive taxes and the labour market: is the trade-off between equality and efficiency inevitable? *Journal of Economic Surveys*, 16(1), 77–110.

Romer, T. (1975). Individual welfare, majority voting and the properties of a linear income tax, *Journal of Public Economics*, 7, 163–188.

Rothschild, M. and J.E. Stiglitz (1976). Equilibrium in competitive insurance markets, *Quarterly Journal of Economics*, 90, 629–649.

Scitovsky, T. (1976). *The Joyless Economy: An Inquiry into Human Satisfaction and Consumer Dissatisfaction*, Oxford University Press: Oxford.

Shapiro, C. and J.E. Stiglitz (1984). Equilibrium unemployment as a worker discipline device, *American Economic Review*, 74, 433–444.

Sinn, H.-W. (1995). A theory of the welfare state, *Scandinavian Journal of Economics*, 97, 495–526.

Sørensen, P.B. (1997). Public finance solutions to the European unemployment problem?, *Economic Policy*, 25, 223–264.

Sørensen, P.B. (1999). Optimal tax progressivity in imperfect labour markets, *Labour Economics*, 6, 435–452.

Stadt, H. van de, A. Kapteyn and S. van de Geer (1985). The relativity of utility: evidence from panel data, *Review of Economics and Statistics*, 67, 179–187.

Stiglitz, J.E. and A. Weiss (1981). Credit rationing in markets with imperfect information, *American Economic Review*, 71(3), 393–410.

Swaan, de A. (1988). *In Care of State: Health Care, Education and Welfare in Europe and the US in the Modern Era*, Oxford University Press, Oxford.

Veblen, Th. (1899/1934). *The Theory of the Leisure Class*, Modern Library: New York.

Part IV

Multidimensional inequality

9 Social welfare, priority to the worst-off and the dimensions of individual well-being

Marc Fleurbaey

9.1 Introduction

Measuring social welfare is considered a difficult, if not impossible, task. The theory of social welfare is rather well developed for the favorable case when there exists an accepted interpersonally comparable measure of individual well-being and the difficulty is confined to the issue of aggregating a vector of individual levels of well-being into a synthetic measure. The main ethical issue in such aggregation is the degree of preference for equality (or aversion to inequality) embedded in the social welfare function, and there is some consensus that some strict preference for equality is warranted, although there is much less agreement about whether this preference for equality should go all the way down to the extreme maximin criterion.

The case when there is no interpersonally comparable measure of individual well-being is much more confused in welfare economics. Some controversial approaches in cost–benefit analysis do rely on ordinal notions of willingness-to-pay and expenditure functions, and some discussion of ideally efficient and equitable allocations is made in the theory of fair allocation on the sole basis of individual non-comparable preferences. But orthodox social choice theory argues that an essential impossibility, revealed in Arrow's theorem (Arrow, 1951), plagues the whole aggregation exercise. This difficulty is thought to create a dilemma for theories of justice such as Rawls' and Sen's, which rely on multidimensional notions of primary goods or functioning, and apparently have to choose between imposing a uniform and perfectionist index (of primary goods, or capabilities) which neglects individual preferences, or coming back to the welfarist idea of measuring individual utility in an interpersonally comparable way.

In Section 9.2, the "easy" one-dimensional case is briefly examined, and some recent results (and generalizations thereof) are presented about how to introduce inequality aversion in social preferences, in relation to variants of the famous Pigou–Dalton principle of transfer. This preliminary section is useful in order to introduce basic notions, and also in order to highlight the contrast between the one-dimensional and the multidimensional case. The importance and relevance of the multidimensional case, where one has at best individual non-comparable preferences about the various dimensions of well-being, is examined in Section 9.3, and the apparent dilemma between perfectionism and welfarism, which may affect theories like Rawls', is explained in Section 9.4. The rest of the chapter is devoted to showing that such a dilemma is non-existent, and to present an approach which does construct a social welfare function on the sole basis of individual ordinal non-comparable preferences.

Sections 9.5 and 9.6 explain basic results which derive relevant consequences from fundamental principles of Pareto efficiency, Pigou–Dalton preference for equality, and informational parsimony. Two key points are, first, that the Pareto conditions are rather constraining, although they are compatible with some degree of non-welfarism; second, that the maximin criterion appears to be much more compelling in the multidimensional setting than in the one-dimensional case. Sections 9.7 and 9.8 illustrate how this approach can be applied to concrete issues of tax, transfers and low-income support, in the context of recent Welfare State reforms and globalization. Some simple criteria (exactly three, which leaves some room for political disputes) are uncovered in Section 9.7, which make it possible to derive clear social welfare conclusions from an immediate examination of individual budget sets. Section 9.8, however, points out that there may be phenomena which standard statistics fail to describe accurately and which may be important to assess recent evolutions of social welfare.

In order to give the reader a good intuition about the results, simple sketches of the proofs are provided for every result.

9.2 Priority to the worst-off in one dimension

In a one-dimensional setting, the situation of every individual i is measured by a real number $x_i \in \mathbb{R}$. The situation of a population with n individuals is then described by an n-dimensional vector $(x_1, \ldots, x_n)$. Social welfare may be measured by a function W, so that $W(x_1, \ldots, x_n) \in \mathbb{R}$ is a synthetic evaluation of the population's situation. For simplicity, we restrict our attention to the case of separable and impartial social welfare functions, that is, to the case when W can be written

$$W(x_1, \ldots, x_n) = u(x_1) + \cdots + u(x_n),$$

for some "utility" function u. Notice that u need not be interpreted as measuring the individual utility of i, but is better viewed as representing the social utility of x_i. The role of u is mainly to appropriately aggregate the population's heterogeneous situation into one synthetic measure.

A central principle in this context, in relation to inequality aversion, is the so-called Pigou–Dalton principle of transfer. It is useful to define the notion of a Pigou–Dalton transfer before coming to the principle itself.

Definition 9.1 (Pigou–Dalton transfer). *Consider a vector $(x_1, \ldots, x_n)$, and two individuals i and j such that $x_i < x_j$. A Pigou–Dalton transfer consists in* *transferring a positive amount δ from j to i, without altering the ranking:*

$$x_i + \delta \leq x_j - \delta,$$

and without changing any other individual's situation.

The notion of a Pigou–Dalton transfer is rather demanding in terms of informational content of the individual index x_i. This index must measure individual well-being so that levels and differences of well-being can be interpersonally compared. Such informational requirements are easily satisfied when x_i is a resource, like income, but would appear more demanding if x_i measured subjective satisfaction.

The Pigou–Dalton transfer principle is sometimes defined in terms of inequality measurement, but we will focus here on its application to social welfare.

Axiom 9.1 (Pigou–Dalton principle). *Consider two vectors $(x_1,\dots,x_n)$ and $(y_1,\dots,y_n)$. If the latter is obtained from the former by a Pigou–Dalton transfer, then $W(x_1,\dots,x_n) < W(y_1,\dots,y_n)$.*

There are two ways of relating this principle to inequality aversion in the social welfare function W. The first way focuses on a given function W, and examines under what conditions W obeys the Pigou–Dalton principle. The basic result, the origin of which can be traced back to early welfare economics, is the following.

Proposition 9.1. *W satisfies the Pigou–Dalton principle on X^n, where $X \subset \mathbb{R}$ is an interval, if and only if u is strictly concave over X.*

Proof. The interesting part is the implication from Pigou–Dalton to strict concavity. If W satisfies the Pigou–Dalton principle on X^n then for any $x, x' \in X$ with $x < x'$, one has

$$W(x,x',x,\dots,x) < W\left(\frac{x+x'}{2},\frac{x+x'}{2},x,\dots,x\right),$$

which after simplification and rearrangement reads

$$\frac{u(x)+u(x')}{2} < u\left(\frac{x+x'}{2}\right),$$

and this inequality is satisfied for all $x, x' \in X$ if and only if u is strictly concave over X. □

The second approach focuses on two given vectors $(x_1,\dots,x_n)$ and $(y_1,\dots,y_n)$, and examines under what conditions a whole family of inequality-averse social welfare functions unanimously considers one vector to be better than the other one.

The following result is a variant of a part of the celebrated Hardy–Littlewood–Polya theorem (1952).[1]

Proposition 9.2. *Let* $(x_1,\ldots,x_n)$ *and* $(y_1,\ldots,y_n)$ *be such that* $x_1 \leq \cdots \leq x_n$ *and* $y_1 \leq \cdots \leq y_n$. *Then the two following statements are equivalent:*

(i) $(y_1,\ldots,y_n)$ *is obtained from* $(x_1,\ldots,x_n)$ *by a finite number of increments*[2] *and Pigou–Dalton transfers;*
(ii) $u(x_1)+\cdots+u(x_n) < u(y_1)+\cdots+u(y_n)$ *for all continuous, increasing and strictly concave functions* $u : X \to \mathbb{R}$, *where* X *is any interval containing* $x_1,\ldots,x_n,y_1,\ldots,y_n$.

Proof. The interesting part is the implication from (ii) to (i). Although this is a classical result, intuitive proofs are scarce in the literature.[3]

Let $u_k(x) = \min\{x, x_k\}$. This is a continuous, non-decreasing and concave function over X, which is arbitrarily close to a continuous, increasing and strictly concave function. Therefore

$$u_k(x_1)+\cdots+u_k(x_n) \leq u_k(y_1)+\cdots+u_k(y_n),$$

for all k. For $k=1$, one has

$$x_1+\cdots+x_1 \leq \min\{y_1,x_1\}+\cdots+\min\{y_n,x_1\},$$

which can be written

$$x_1 \leq \min\{y_1,x_1\}+(\min\{y_2,x_1\}-x_1)+\cdots+(\min\{y_n,x_1\}-x_1),$$

and since necessarily

$$\min\{y_1,x_1\}+(\min\{y_2,x_1\}-x_1)+\cdots+(\min\{y_n,x_1\}-x_1) \leq y_1,$$

one deduces $x_1 \leq y_1$. By a similar reasoning, for any k, one obtains $x_1+\cdots+x_k \leq y_1+\cdots+y_k$. From (ii), at least one of these n inequalities must be strict. In other words, $(y_1,\ldots,y_n)$ dominates $(x_1,\ldots,x_n)$ according to the generalized Lorenz criterion.

Let $x'_n = x_n + \sum_{i=1}^n (y_i - x_i)$. If $x'_n > x_n$ this means that the vector $(x_1,\ldots,x_{n-1},x'_n)$ is obtained from $(x_1,\ldots,x_n)$ by a simple increment. One has $x_1+\cdots+x_{n-1}+x'_n = y_1+\cdots+y_n$. If $(x_1,\ldots,x_{n-1},x'_n) = (y_1,\ldots,y_n)$ then no transfer needs to be done. Otherwise, a sequence of transfers may be simply constructed as follows.

Let any agent i, in any vector $(z_1,\ldots,z_n)$, be said to be "R" (like "recipient") if $z_i < y_i$, "D" (like "donor") if $z_i > y_i$, and "N" (like "neutral") if $z_i = y_i$. Similarly, a group G may be said to be R, D or N depending on the comparison of $\sum_{i\in G} z_i$ and $\sum_{i\in G} y_i$.

These inequalities prove that, in vector $(x_1,\ldots,x_{n-1},x'_n)$, every group $\{1,\ldots,k\}$ is either N or R. As a consequence, in the ordered list $1,\ldots,n$, the first non-N agent in $(x_1,\ldots,x_{n-1},x'_n)$ must be R. Since $x_1+\cdots+x_{n-1}+x'_n=y_1+\cdots+y_n$, there must be a D agent.

Let i be the first R and j the first D in $(x_1,\ldots,x_{n-1},x'_n)$. Since i is the first non-N agent, one has $i<j$, so that $y_i \leq y_j$. Therefore,

$$\delta_1 = \min\{y_i - x_i, x_j - y_j\},$$

is a possible Pigou–Dalton transfer from j to i :

$$x_i + \delta_1 \leq y_i \leq y_j \leq x_j - \delta_1.$$

Let z^1 be the new vector obtained from $(x_1,\ldots,x_{n-1},x'_n)$ by this transfer.

Consider the status of agents in z^1. Either i or j is now N, and no other agent has changed his status, so that the subset of N agents has expanded by at least one unit. Notice that if i is not N, he remains R.

Moreover, it is still true in z^1 that every group $\{1,\ldots,k\}$ is either N or R.[4] Indeed, for $k<i$ and $k\geq j$, the sum is unchanged:

$$z_1^1+\cdots+z_k^1 = x_1+\cdots+x_k$$

so that the comparison to $y_1+\cdots+y_k$ is unaltered. For $k=i:\{1,\ldots,i\}$ cannot be D since i, like $\{1,\ldots,i-1\}$, is N or R in z^1. For $i<k<j$: all agents a such that $i<a\leq k$ are R or N (recall that j is the first D in $(x_1,\ldots,x_{n-1},x'_n)$), like $\{1,\ldots,i\}$, so that $\{1,\ldots,k\}$ is either N or R.

As a consequence, if z^1 differs from $(y_1,\ldots,y_n)$ one can iterate and make a second Pigou–Dalton transfer from the first[5] D to the first R in z^1, so that at least one of them becomes N after the transfer. After at most $n-1$ iterations of this kind, the set of N agents contains the whole population, which means that the sequence of transfers has produced $(y_1,\ldots,y_n)$. □

There is a logical link between the less interesting parts of these two propositions. The fact that the implication (i) ⇒ (ii) holds for all $(x_1,\ldots,x_n)$ and $(y_1,\ldots,y_n)$, in the latter proposition, is equivalent to saying that a social welfare function with strictly concave u does satisfy the Pigou–Dalton principle. But there is no logical link between the interesting parts of these two propositions.

Both propositions highlight the fact that the Pigou–Dalton principle does not imply a substantial degree of inequality aversion. A strictly concave u may be arbitrarily close to being affine or linear, so that, for instance, the utilitarian social welfare function $x_1+\cdots+x_n$ is just on the boundary of the family of social welfare functions epitomized in these propositions. This raises the question of how to modify these notions and results in order to accommodate a stronger preference for equality.

In a Pigou–Dalton transfer, the recipient gets exactly what the donor gives away. This means that the Pigou–Dalton principle is silent about "leaky-bucket" transfers in which the recipient receives less. A more egalitarian transfer principle should be able to express a definite endorsement of some such transfers. Moreover, one can argue that the wider the gap between donor and recipient, the more tolerant one should be about the size of the loss during the transfer.

Along these lines, Fleurbaey and Michel (2001) have proposed considering proportional transfers, in which the size of the transfer is proportional to the agents' positions. Then, the rich donor gives more, and the poor recipient gets less. Moreover, the tolerated loss during the transfer increases with the gap between donor and recipient. They consider two versions of this idea, depending on whether one focuses on the agents' initial or final positions when assessing proportionality of the transfer. When the transfer is proportional to *ex ante* positions, one gets the following transfer principle:

Axiom 9.2 (Proportional transfer principle). *Consider a vector* $(x_1, \ldots, x_n) \in \mathbb{R}^n_{++}$, *two individuals i and j, and a positive number* δ. *If the vector* $(y_1, \ldots, y_n)$ *is such that for all* $k \neq i, j$, $y_k = x_k$ *and*

$$y_i = x_i(1+\delta) \leq y_j = x_j(1-\delta),$$

then $W(x_1, \ldots, x_n) < W(y_1, \ldots, y_n)$.

This principle endorses transfers in which the loss, relative to the donor's gift, equals

$$\frac{\delta(x_j - x_i)}{\delta x_j} = 1 - \frac{x_i}{x_j},$$

an amount which is increasing in the donor's x_j and decreasing in the recipient's x_i.

When the proportions are computed with respect to the post-transfer levels of well-being, instead of the pre-transfer levels as earlier, one gets the following condition:

Axiom 9.3 (Proportional *ex post* transfer principle). *Consider a vector* $(x_1, \ldots, x_n) \in \mathbb{R}^n_{++}$, *two individuals i and j, and a positive number* δ. *If the vector* $(y_1, \ldots, y_n)$ *is such that for all* $k \neq i, j$, $y_k = x_k$ *and*

$$y_i = x_i + \delta y_i \leq y_j = x_j - \delta y_j,$$

then $W(x_1, \ldots, x_n) < W(y_1, \ldots, y_n)$.

The relative loss in the transfer, in proportion to the donor's gift, is then

$$1 - \frac{y_i}{y_j},$$

and a new feature here is that it decreases with the size of the transfer, and at the limit, when the *ex post* levels of consumption are close to being equal, no loss is allowed. Notice that the loss is smaller here than the previous one, which means that the latter principle expresses a weaker tolerance to losses, that is, a weaker preference for equality than the former.

The following proposition rephrases Proposition 9.1 for the two proportional transfer principles.

Proposition 9.3. *W satisfies the proportional transfer principle (resp. the proportional* ex post *transfer principle) over $\mathbb{R}^n_{++}$ if and only if there is a strictly concave function $v : \mathbb{R}_{--} \to \mathbb{R}$ such that $u(x) = v(-1/x)$ (resp. there is a concave function $v : \mathbb{R} \to \mathbb{R}$ such that $u(x) = v(\ln x)$).*

Proof. Again we focus on the necessity parts of the proposition. Let W satisfy the proportional transfer principle. One can define a function v by $u(x) = v(-1/x)$. Consider $0 < x_i < x_j$ and $\delta > 0$ such that

$$x_i(1+\delta) = x_j(1-\delta).$$

One has

$$\delta = \frac{x_j - x_i}{x_i + x_j},$$

implying

$$x_i(1+\delta) = \frac{2x_ix_j}{x_i + x_j},$$

By the proportional transfer principle

$$u(x_i) + u(x_j) < 2u(x_i(1+\delta)),$$

which also reads

$$v\left(-\frac{1}{x_i}\right) + v\left(-\frac{1}{x_j}\right) < 2v\left(-\frac{x_i + x_j}{2x_ix_j}\right)$$

or equivalently, denoting $z_i = -1/x_i$, $z_j = -1/x_j$:

$$\frac{v(z_i) + v(z_j)}{2} < v\left(\frac{z_i + z_j}{2}\right),$$

which can only be satisfied for all $z_i < z_j < 0$ if v is strictly concave.

Let W satisfy the proportional *ex post* transfer principle. One can define a function v by $u(x) = v(\ln x)$. Consider $0 < x_i < x_j$ and $\delta > 0$ such that

$$y_i = x_i + \delta y_i \leq x_j - \delta y_j = y_j.$$

One computes

$$y_i = \frac{x_i}{1-\delta}, \quad y_j = \frac{x_j}{1+\delta}.$$

The transfer principle requires

$$u(x_i) + u(x_j) < u\left(\frac{x_i}{1-\delta}\right) + u\left(\frac{x_j}{1+\delta}\right),$$

or equivalently

$$v(\ln x_i) + v(\ln x_j) < v\left(\ln \frac{x_i}{1-\delta}\right) + v\left(\ln \frac{x_j}{1+\delta}\right).$$

When δ is small, this approximates into

$$v(\ln x_i) + v(\ln x_j) \leq v(\ln x_i + \delta) + v(\ln x_j - \delta).$$

This inequality is satisfied for all $0 < x_i < x_j$ and all $\delta > 0$ small enough only if v is concave. □

It is convenient to remember what such results mean for the family of Constant Elasticity Substitution (CES) social welfare functions

$$W_\varepsilon(x_1, \ldots, x_n) = \frac{1}{1-\varepsilon} \sum_{i=1}^{n} x_i^{1-\varepsilon}, \quad \text{for } \varepsilon \geq 0, \ \varepsilon \neq 1,$$

and adopting the convention that the case $\varepsilon = 1$ corresponds to

$$W_1(x_1, \ldots, x_n) = \prod_{i=1}^{n} x_i.$$

One then has that the Pigou–Dalton principle is satisfied whenever $\varepsilon > 0$, the proportional transfer principle is satisfied whenever $\varepsilon > 2$, and the proportional *ex post* transfer principle whenever $\varepsilon \geq 1$.

Aboudi and Thon (2003) examine how to rephrase Proposition 9.2 for the families of social welfare functions highlighted in this last result. They notice that a simple change of variables, from x to $-1/x$ or $\ln x$, makes it easy to obtain the following result.[6]

Proposition 9.4. *Let* $(x_1, \ldots, x_n) \in \mathbb{R}^n_{++}$ *and* $(y_1, \ldots, y_n) \in \mathbb{R}^n_{++}$ *be such that* $x_1 \leq \cdots \leq x_n$ *and* $y_1 \leq \cdots \leq y_n$. *Then the two following statements are equivalent:*

(i) $(y_1, \ldots, y_n)$ *is obtained from* $(x_1, \ldots, x_n)$ *by a finite number of increments and of "hyperbolic" (resp. "logarithmic") transfers such that*

$$y_i = \frac{1}{(1/x_i) - \delta} \leq y_j = \frac{1}{(1/x_j) + \delta}, \quad \text{for } \delta > 0$$

(resp. such that

$$y_i = x_i\delta \leq y_j = x_j/\delta, \quad \text{for } \delta > 1);$$

(ii) $v(-1/x_1)+\cdots+v(-1/x_n) < v(-1/y_1)+\cdots+v(-1/y_n)$ *(resp.* $v(\ln x_1)+\cdots+v(\ln x_n) < v(\ln y_1)+\cdots+v(\ln y_n)$*) for all continuous, increasing and strictly concave functions* $v : \mathbb{R} \to \mathbb{R}$.

Proof. The formula

$$y_i = \frac{1}{(1/x_i) - \delta} \leq y_j = \frac{1}{(1/x_j) + \delta}$$

also reads

$$-\frac{1}{y_i} = -\frac{1}{x_i} + \delta \leq -\frac{1}{y_j} = -\frac{1}{x_j} - \delta,$$

so that one just has to apply Proposition 9.2, replacing x, y by $-1/x$, $-1/y$.

The formula

$$y_i = x_i\delta \leq y_j = x_j/\delta$$

also reads

$$\ln y_i = \ln x_i + \delta' \leq \ln y_j = \ln x_j - \delta',$$

so that one just has to apply Proposition 9.2, replacing x, y by $\ln x$, $\ln y$. □

The transfers obtained in Proposition 9.4 are different from proportional transfers, and one cannot obtain the analogue of Proposition 9.4 with proportional transfers. Indeed, one computes that when

$$y_i = \frac{1}{(1/x_i) - \delta} \quad \text{and} \quad y_j = \frac{1}{(1/x_j) + \delta},$$

the relative loss in the transfer is equal to

$$1 - \frac{x_i}{x_j}\frac{y_i}{y_j} \geq 1 - \frac{x_i}{x_j},$$

which means that the loss is greater than allowed by a proportional transfer. This proves that when $v(-1/x_1) + \cdots + v(-1/x_n) < v(-1/y_1) + \cdots + v(-1/y_n)$ for all strictly concave functions $v : \mathbb{R} \to \mathbb{R}$, it is not necessarily the case that $(y_1, \ldots, y_n)$ is obtained from $(x_1, \ldots, x_n)$ by a finite number of proportional transfers. Transfers with greater losses may be required.[7] As a consequence, when there is a strictly concave function $v : \mathbb{R}_{--} \to \mathbb{R}$ such that $u(x) = v(-1/x)$, the social welfare function satisfies not only the proportional transfer principle, as stated in Proposition 9.3, but also a principle of hyperbolic transfers which is even more "egalitarian." The same kind of conclusion obtains when one compares proportional *ex post* transfers to logarithmic transfers.

There is no difficulty to generalize Proposition 9.4 in the direction of greater preference for equality, by considering "more concave" transformations. It also possible to generalize Proposition 9.3. One has the following result, in particular.

Proposition 9.5. *W satisfies the k transfer principle over $\mathbb{R}^n_{++}$, which is defined by the formula*

$$y_i = x_i(1+\delta)^{1/k} \leq y_j = x_j\,(1-\delta)^{1/k},$$

if and only if there is a strictly concave function $v : \mathbb{R}_{--} \to \mathbb{R}$ such that $u(x) = v(-1/x^k)$.

Proof. The formula

$$y_i = x_i(1+\delta)^{1/k} \leq y_j = x_j(1-\delta)^{1/k}$$

also reads

$$(y_i)^k = (x_i)^k(1+\delta) \leq (y_j)^k = (x_j)^k(1-\delta),$$

so that one just has to apply Prop. 9.3, replacing x, y by x^k, y^k. □

With such transfers, the relative loss in the transfer is equal to

$$1 - \frac{x_i}{x_j}\frac{(1+\delta)^{1/k} - 1}{1 - (1-\delta)^{1/k}}.$$

an expression which is increasing in k, indicating an increasing tolerance to losses, and therefore a greater preference for equality.

The kinds of transfers obtained by changes of variables (Propositions 9.4 and 9.5) are less intuitive than the traditional Pigou–Dalton transfers or the proportional transfers. It remains an open question to see how one can find intuitive sorts of transfers which are more egalitarian than proportional transfers and can be related unambiguously to a family of inequality-averse social welfare functions.

9.3 Multidimensional well-being

The assumption that individual well-being can be measured synthetically and read on the scale of real numbers is convenient, but must be considered as a dangerous simplification. It raises more issues than it solves. Take, for instance, the application of the theory of social welfare functions, some elements of which have been summarized in Section 9.2. How should x_i be interpreted, empirically?

In most applications to inequality issues, x_i is simply taken to be income. But it is usually recognized that income is a poor measure of individual well-being. In particular, there is a problem with taking account of how income is used within households of different sizes. This issue is often tackled by computing adult-equivalent income, on the basis of equivalence scales, but there are disputes about the empirical and ethical foundations for the determination of equivalence scales. Another important issue is leisure and earning ability. The same income may be earned with different labor times, and this is an important aspect of inequality between households with one or two breadwinners.

In an important tradition of welfare economics, x_i must instead be interpreted as measuring subjective satisfaction (individual utility). This tradition has been shaken by the many difficulties occurring when one tries to measure subjective utility in an interpersonally comparable way. Many economists believe, following Robbins (1932), that there is actually no way to perform such measurement without introducing essential value judgments about distributive justice. Individual utility, in this line of reasoning, tends to melt with social utility. It is then the task of the social planner (a misleading name for the democratic decision-body inspired by public debates) to define x_i as a function of the various dimensions of the individual situation.

Multidimensionality has also acquired an additional degree of importance in the non-welfarist theories of justice which propose to measure individual situations in terms of resources, primary goods (Rawls) or of functionings and capabilities (Sen). The theories put forth by Rawls and Sen do not offer precise lists of relevant dimensions, nor methods for trading-off the various dimensions, but they bring this kind of issue to the top of the agenda.

9.4 An indexing dilemma?

Commentators of Rawls' theory have argued that the construction of an index of primary goods is plagued by a fundamental difficulty. A primary good is, as defined by Rawls (1971, 1982), an all-purpose resource which any person will rationally desire, whatever his particular goals in life. This includes basic rights and freedoms, prerogatives of responsibility positions, income, and wealth. Some individuals may happen to be rich in one dimension and poor in another, and this calls for a synthetic measure. Rawls argues that there are two sources of simplification in the construction of an index. First, some primary goods, namely basic rights and freedoms, have absolute priority, and can be maximally and equally granted to all, which reduces the weighting problem to the remaining primary goods. Second, according to the difference principle (maximin), only the worst-off matter, and the worst-off are often disadvantaged in many dimensions simultaneously. Nonetheless, even in this favorable context, weighting the various dimensions remains important, in particular when seeking the most appropriate institutional structure. Concretely, should the basic structure of society be conceived so as to provide the worst-off with more autonomy and responsibility, more income, or more wealth?

Rawls suggests that the index of primary goods should take account of people's preferences, but severely limits this idea by proposing to consider a "representative individual," and to retain only "rational" preferences. In Sen's theory (1987, 1992), primary goods are replaced by "capabilities," which are the sets of various functionings to which individuals have access. Since this is still a multidimensional approach, similar considerations appear, and individual preferences are also granted some role. A difference with Rawls' theory is that, in Sen's view, subjective satisfaction is a relevant functioning among others, whereas the primary goods in Rawls' approach are only external resources. In Sen's theory, then, interpersonal comparisons of subjective utility may be required. Sen's approach therefore combines the difficulty of measuring subjective utility with that of weighting the various functionings, including subjective utility.

The indexing dilemma, identified by commentators such as Arneson (1990), Arnsperger and van Parijs (2000), is the following. If the index contains a unique set of weights, applied uniformly to all individuals, then it fails to respect individual preferences, leading to violations of the Pareto principle, and it conveys a perfectionist view of the good life. On the other hand, if it faithfully espouses individuals' preferences in all their diversity, then the index of primary goods is just a utility function representing those preferences, and the theory comes back to the welfarist tradition. This dilemma, clearly, can be opposed not only to Rawls' approach but also to Sen's, and to similar theories such as one proposed in Fleurbaey (1995), which relies on basic functionings instead of capabilities. In brief, the indexing exercise apparently forces one to choose between perfectionism and welfarism, two loathsome perspectives in the Rawlsian tradition.

Can one respect individual preferences and avoid the problem of interpersonal comparisons of subjective satisfaction? In a famous comment, which is implicitly based on his impossibility theorem of social choice, Arrow declares this to be impossible:

> consider the haemophiliac who needs about $4000 worth per annum of coagulant therapy to arrive at a state of security from bleeding at all comparable to that of the normal person. Does equal income mean equality? If not, then, to be consistent, Rawls would have to add health to the list of primary goods; but then there is a trade-off between health and wealth which involves all the

> conceptual problems of differing utility functions. (...) So long as there is more than one primary good, there is an index-number problem in commensurating the different goods, which is in principle as difficult as the problem of interpersonal comparability with which we started.
>
> (Arrow, 1973, p. 254)

Kolm makes a similar assessment:

> maximizing a bundle of goods is a priori undefined. Rawls says we should choose weights and maximize the weighted sum. But he does not say how we should make this choice. (...) On the contrary, the maximin is well-defined with "fundamental preferences".
>
> (Kolm, 1996, pp. 176–177)

Interestingly, Rawls rejects the notion of "fundamental preferences":

> The notion of a shared highest-order preference function is plainly incompatible with the conception of a well-ordered society in justice as fairness. For in the circumstances of justice citizen's conceptions of the good are not only said to be opposed but to be incommensurable.
>
> (Rawls, 1982, p. 179)

Rawls also insists on the fact that the index of primary goods is meant to solve the problem of resource sharing, and not to measure a theoretical quantity such as subjective well-being:

> To an economist (...) an index of primary goods may seem merely ad hoc patchwork not amenable to theory. (...) The economist's reaction is partly right: an index of primary goods does not belong to theory in the economist's sense. It belongs instead to a conception of justice which falls under the liberal alternative to the tradition of the one rational good. Thus the problem is not how to specify an accurate measure of some psychological or other attribute available only to science. Rather, it is a moral and practical problem.
>
> (Rawls, 1982, pp. 184–185)

This idea that the choice of index may reflect distributive principles rather than substantive views on well-being will find an illustration in the method developed in the next sections.

A different kind of comment is made by Roemer, who also examines the indexing dilemma. "Finding an index is a problem that Rawls does not solve, and (...) it is a key problem in Rawls's theory, for on it hangs Rawls's claim that his theory is non-welfarist" (Roemer, 1996, p. 167). Contrary to the other authors, Roemer rejects the idea that welfarism is unavoidable if the index respects individual preferences:

> Arneson is (...) not right to conclude that the Rawlsian view must dissolve into welfarism – in particular, into equalizing (or maximinning) welfare.

> There may be room for a theory which chooses indices of primary goods which are ordinally equivalent to welfare (...). Such a theory would not be welfarist, as these indices need not be recoverable from information on welfare levels. The task for a Rawlsian must be to find such indices which are justifiable without appeal to a perfectionist standard or to the inherent superiority of some life plans over others.
>
> (Roemer, 1996, pp. 171–172)

Roemer, however, does not propose a concrete method in order to define a non-welfarist Paretian index. One such method is the topic of the next sections. It circumvents the problem of interpersonal comparisons by allowing the social criterion to take account of more information about individual preferences than usual in the theory of social choice. This approach has roots in Samuelson (1977, 1987) and Pazner (1979) and has been recently rekindled by Fleurbaey and Maniquet (1996, 2001, 2005).[8]

9.5 The power of Paretianism

From now on we assume that x_i is multidimensional: $x_i \in \mathbb{R}^l$, where l is the number of relevant dimensions in x_i. The dimensions of x_i may be ordinary commodities, primary goods, functionings, etc. We assume that, like income, every component is measured on cardinally measurable and interpersonally comparable scale. Vector inequalities are denoted $\geq, >, \gg$. Individual preferences about x_i are described by an ordering $\succeq_i$ defined on a relevant set X. The associated strict preference relation is denoted $\succ_i$, and indifference is denoted $\sim_i$.

Respect for individual preferences may be expressed by the following Pareto condition:

Axiom 9.4 (Pareto). *Consider two vectors $(x_1, \ldots, x_n)$ and $(y_1, \ldots, y_n)$. If for all i, $x_i \prec_i y_i$, then $W(x_1, \ldots, x_n) < W(y_1, \ldots, y_n)$. If for all i, $x_i \sim_i y_i$, then $W(x_1, \ldots, x_n) = W(y_1, \ldots, y_n)$.*

The first part is usually called the Weak Pareto condition, and the second part the Pareto Indifference condition. The essence of the results in the rest of this paper would be obtained with Weak Pareto, and Pareto Indifference is added here in order to simplify the presentation.

This Pareto axiom is quite demanding, and imposes serious limits on non-welfarist evaluations of individual situations. This can be seen in particular when one tries to formulate an adapted Pigou–Dalton transfer principle in this new setting.[9]

Axiom 9.5 (Pigou–Dalton principle). *Consider two vectors $(x_1, \ldots, x_n)$ and $(y_1, \ldots, y_n)$. If the latter is obtained from the former by a Pigou–Dalton transfer,* *defined by the formula*

$$y_i = x_i + \delta \leq x_j - \delta = y_j,$$

for $\delta \in \mathbb{R}^l_+ \setminus \{0\}$, *then* $W(x_1, \ldots, x_n) < W(y_1, \ldots, y_n)$.

In the literature on multidimensional inequality, surveyed in Weymark (Chapter 12, in this volume), it is common to consider Pigou–Dalton transfers alternatively defined by the formula

$$y_i = \lambda x_i + (1 - \lambda)x_j, \quad y_j = (1 - \lambda)x_i + \lambda x_j,$$

for $\lambda \in [0, 1]$. No requirement is made about $x_i < x_j$, so that these complex Pigou–Dalton transfers may go in opposite directions for different dimensions. For instance, if $x_i = (1, 3)$ and $x_j = (3, 1)$, a complex Pigou–Dalton transfer, in which i is a recipient in the first dimension and a donor in the second, may yield $y_i = y_j = (2, 2)$. But since it may happen that $x_i \succ_i y_i$ and $x_j \succ_j y_j$, such transfers may go against unanimous individual preferences. Another problem, noted by Dardanoni (1995) and discussed in Weymark (Chapter 12, in this volume), is the following. Imagine that there is another agent at $(1, 1)$, and that all agents have the same preferences $\succeq$ such that $(1, 1) \prec (3, 1) \sim (1, 3) \prec (2, 2)$. Then the transfer does not go against i's and j's preferences, but clearly increases the inequality in well-being since the well-being of the worst-off stays put while the well-being of the best-off increases.

The earlier axiom avoids the two problems, since

$$x_i < y_i \leq y_j < x_j,$$

guarantees that there is an unambiguous donor whose well-being is negatively affected by the transfer, and a clear recipient who gains in well-being. As shown later, however, a clash with individual preferences, as defended by the Pareto axiom, is not avoided.

The Pigou–Dalton principle can indeed be interpreted as a non-welfarist condition, since it advocates transfers of resources without looking at the agents' preferences. The idea that conditions of this kind clash with the Pareto principle has been voiced by Gibbard (1979) and Brun and Tungodden (2004). Fleurbaey and Trannoy (2003) have shown the following result.

Proposition 9.6. *Let* $X = \mathbb{R}^l_+$, *and consider any profile* $(\succeq_1, \ldots, \succeq_n)$ *of continuous, strictly monotonic and convex preferences, with at least two individuals having different preferences. Then* W *cannot satisfy Pareto and the Pigou–Dalton principle.*

Proof. If i and j have different preferences, one can find

$$x_i < y_i \leq y_j < x_j,$$
$$y'_j < x'_j \leq x'_i < y'_i,$$

such that $y_i - x_i = x_j - y_j, y'_i - x'_i = x'_j - y'_j$, and

$$x_i \sim_i x'_i, y_i \sim_i y'_i,$$
$$x_j \sim_j x'_j, y_j \sim_j y'_j.$$

The proof that such a construction is possible is omitted here. It is illustrated in Figure 9.1.

For all agents $k \neq i,j$, let $x_k = x'_k = y_k = y'_k$. By Pareto, $W(x) = W(x')$ and $W(y) = W(y')$. By Pigou–Dalton, $W(x) < W(y)$ and $W(x') > W(y')$, a contradiction. □

The assumptions that preferences are strictly monotonic and convex are inessential to the result and are just meant to show that the result does not depend on the consideration of non standard preferences.

If one wants to retain the Pareto condition, the Pigou–Dalton principle must be abandoned, or at least weakened. Notice that the conflict between the two axioms, as illustrated in Figure 9.1, is due to the possibility of making Pigou–Dalton transfers between agents of different preferences, and in any portion of the space. This suggests two ways of weakening the Pigou–Dalton principle. The first one consists in restricting application of the transfer principle to the case when the contemplated agents have identical preferences.

Axiom 9.6 (Preference-restricted Pigou–Dalton principle). *Consider two vectors $(x_1, \ldots, x_n)$ and $(y_1, \ldots, y_n)$. If the latter is obtained from the former by a*

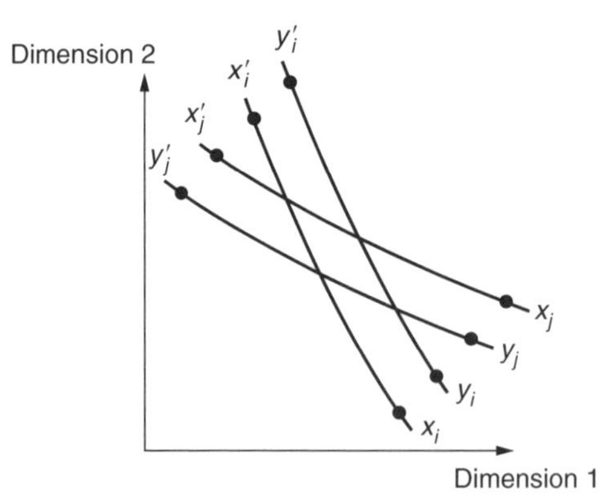

Figure 9.1 Conflict between Pigou–Dalton and Pareto.

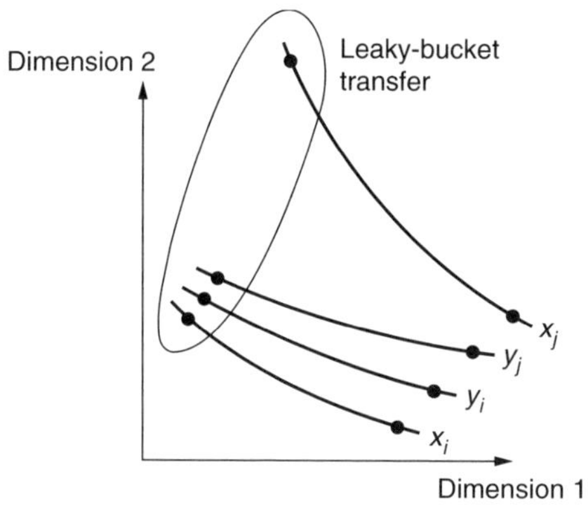

Figure 9.2 Justifying a leaky-bucket transfer.

Pigou–Dalton transfer, defined by the formula

$$y_i = x_i + \delta \leq x_j - \delta = y_j,$$

for $\delta \in \mathbb{R}^l_+ \setminus \{0\}$ *and* i,j *such that* $\succeq_i \; = \; \succeq_j$, *then* $W(x_1,\ldots,x_n) < W(y_1,\ldots,y_n)$.

Combined with Pareto, this condition still has strong implications. For some preferences it may justify leaky-bucket transfers, since a Pigou–Dalton transfer on one side of the space X may be Pareto equivalent to a leaky-bucket transfer, with an arbitrarily high rate of loss, on another side of X, where indifference curves have different slopes. See Figure 9.2. This consequence will be examined in Section 9.6.

The second weakening consists in restricting application to a subspace of X^n. There are several possibilities, and one is presented here, as an illustration. Let $\Omega \in \mathbb{R}^l_+$ be a given vector.

Axiom 9.7 (Space-restricted Pigou–Dalton principle). *Consider two vectors* $(x_1,\ldots,x_n)$ *and* $(y_1,\ldots,y_n)$ *such that all* x_i *and all* y_i *are proportional to* Ω. *If the latter is obtained from the former by a Pigou–Dalton transfer, defined by the formula*

$$y_i = x_i + \delta \leq x_j - \delta = y_j,$$

for $\delta \in \mathbb{R}^l_+ \setminus \{0\}$, *then* $W(x_1,\ldots,x_n) < W(y_1,\ldots,y_n)$.

Again, combining this condition with Pareto demonstrates the power of Pareto conditions. Indeed, for individuals with different preferences and intersecting indifference curves, this condition may justify transferring from a poor to a rich, if

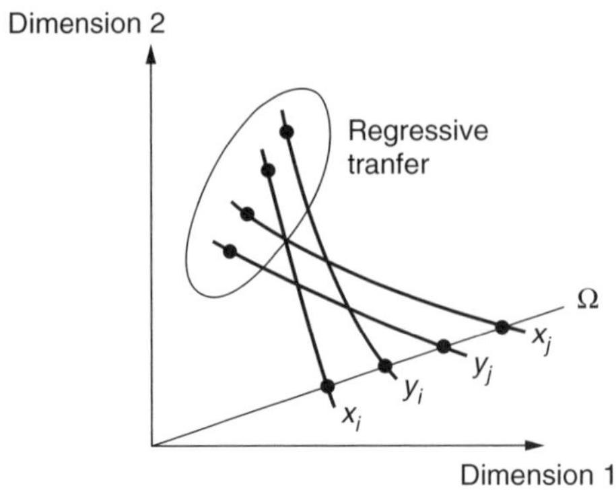

Figure 9.3 Justifying a regressive transfer.

this regressive transfer is Pareto equivalent to a Pigou–Dalton transfer on the ray to Ω (see Figure 9.3).

9.6 The maximin vindicated

When preferences $\succeq_i$ are identical and representable by a utility function u, with non-increasing increments, i.e. such that $U(x + \delta) - u(x) \leq u(y + \delta) - u(y)$ whenever $x \geq y$ and $\delta \geq 0$, then

$$W(x_1, \ldots, x_n) = u(x_1) + \cdots + u(x_n)$$

satisfies Pareto and the Pigou–Dalton principle. The degree of inequality aversion may thus be very low when u can be chosen close to an affine function.

When preferences $\succeq_i$ are different but are still representable by utility functions u_i, with non-increasing increments and such that $u_i = u_j$ whenever $\succeq_i \; = \; \succeq_j$, then

$$W(x_1, \ldots, x_n) = u_1(x_1) + \cdots + u_n(x_n),$$

satisfies Pareto and the preference-restricted Pigou–Dalton principle. Again, the degree of inequality aversion may be very low in some cases.

Now, when one looks at various normative approaches which are based on individual preferences, such as cost–benefit analysis (using the criteria of sums of compensating and equivalent variations) or the theory of fair allocation, one sees that the information retained about preferences in order to evaluate a given allocation is limited to the indifference curves of the population at the contemplated allocation. It would indeed be strange to make the evaluation of a social situation depend on the particulars of preferences at alternatives which are radically different in terms of individual well-being. This justifies the following independence condition, due to Hansson (1973), which stipulates that the comparison of two social situations should depend only on the population's indifference curves at the two situations. The axiom refers to upper and lower contour sets, in order to accommodate cases of discontinuous preferences or discrete space of alternatives.

Axiom 9.8 (Independence). *Let W and W' be the social welfare functions associated to the profiles $(\succeq_1, \ldots, \succeq_n)$ and $(\succeq'_1, \ldots, \succeq'_n)$, respectively. Consider two vectors $(x_1, \ldots, x_n)$ and $(y_1, \ldots, y_n)$, such that for all i,*

$$\{z \in X \mid z \succeq_i x_i\} = \{z \in X \mid z \succeq'_i x_i\},$$

$$\{z \in X \mid z \succeq_i y_i\} = \{z \in X \mid z \succeq'_i y_i\},$$

$$\{z \in X \mid z \preceq_i x_i\} = \{z \in X \mid z \preceq'_i x_i\},$$

$$\{z \in X \mid z \preceq_i y_i\} = \{z \in X \mid z \preceq'_i y_i\}.$$

Then $W(x_1, \ldots, x_n) \leq W(y_1, \ldots, y_n)$ if and only if $W'(x_1, \ldots, x_n) \leq W'(y_1, \ldots, y_n)$.

It is hard to consider weakening this condition, because it would mean that the comparison of two social situations could depend on preferences of the population at situations with entirely different levels of satisfaction. Combined with Pigou–Dalton and Pareto, however, this condition has strong consequences. Consider the following axiom, which is a maximin version of the preference-restricted Pigou–Dalton principle, and is an adaptation of Hammond's (1976) equity axiom.

Axiom 9.9 (Preference-restricted Hammond equity). *Consider two vectors $(x_1, \ldots, x_n)$ and $(y_1, \ldots, y_n)$. If the latter is obtained from the former by an inequality reduction between i and j, such that*

$$x_i \prec_i y_i \preceq_i y_j \prec_i x_j,$$

and $\succeq_i = \succeq_j$, then $W(x_1, \ldots, x_n) < W(y_1, \ldots, y_n)$.

This condition is very strong in terms of inequality aversion, since it sanctifies this inequality reduction even when the gain from x_i to y_i is very small and the loss from x_j to y_j is huge. This condition is satisfied only by social welfare functions of the maximin (or leximin) kind. Now, one has the following result, which states that under Independence and Pareto, the Pigou–Dalton principle does not allow less inequality aversion than Hammond equity in standard economic domains.[10]

Proposition 9.7. *Let $X = \mathbb{R}^l_+$ and let the domain of preferences contain all profiles of continuous, strictly monotonic and convex preferences. If W satisfies Pareto, preference-restricted Pigou–Dalton and independence, then it satisfies preference-restricted Hammond equity.*

Proof. Consider two allocations $(x_1,\ldots,x_n)$ and $(y_1,\ldots,y_n)$ and two agents i,j such that $\succsim_i \; = \; \succsim_j$,

$$x_i \prec_i y_i \preceq_i y_j \prec_i x_j,$$

and $x_k = y_k$ for all $k \neq i,j$. Figure 9.4(a) illustrates the situation, considering an example where the gain for i is small and the loss for j is more important, so that Pigou–Dalton transfers cannot justify the conclusion that $W(x_1,\ldots,x_n) < W(y_1,\ldots,y_n)$.

Consider the case when i and j's preferences are $\succsim_i' \; = \; \succsim_j'$, with indifference curves as in Figure 9.4(b), and let W' denote the related social welfare function. The indifference curves at x_i, y_i, y_j, x_j are the same as those for $\succsim_i \; = \; \succsim_j$.

Consider bundles z_i^k, z_j^k, for $k = 1,\ldots,4$, as in Figure 9.4(b). In particular, one has

$$z_i^1 < z_i^2 < z_j^2 < z_j^1 = z_j^2 + \left(z_i^2 - z_i^1\right),$$
$$z_i^3 < z_i^4 < z_j^4 < z_j^3 = z_j^4 + \left(z_i^4 - z_i^3\right).$$

such preferences $\succsim_i' \; = \; \succsim_j'$ and such bundles cannot always be constructed, but the other cases are dealt with similarity. This is omitted here.

By Pareto,

$$\begin{aligned} W'(x_1,\ldots,x_n) &= W'(x_1,\ldots,z_i^1,\ldots,z_j^1,\ldots,x_n), \\ W'(x_1,\ldots,z_i^2,\ldots,z_j^2,\ldots,x_n) &= W'(x_1,\ldots,z_i^3,\ldots,z_j^3,\ldots,x_n), \\ W'(y_1,\ldots,y_n) &= W'(x_1,\ldots,z_i^4,\ldots,z_j^4,\ldots,x_n). \end{aligned}$$

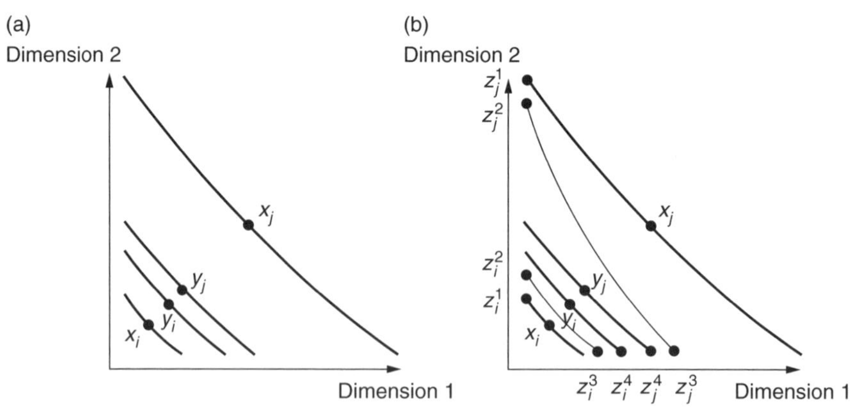

Figure 9.4 Illustration of the proof of Proposition 9.7.

By preference restricted Pigou–Dalton,

$$W'(x_1, \ldots, z_i^1, \ldots, z_j^1, \ldots, x_n) < W'(x_1, \ldots, z_i^2, \ldots, z_j^2, \ldots, x_n),$$
$$W'(x_1, \ldots, z_i^3, \ldots, z_j^3, \ldots, x_n) < W'(x_1, \ldots, z_i^4, \ldots, z_j^4, \ldots, x_n).$$

As a result, one concludes that

$$W'(x_1, \ldots, x_n) < W'(y_1, \ldots, y_n).$$

Recall that indifference curves at x_i, y_i, y_j, x_j are the same for $\succeq_i = \succeq_j$ and for $\succeq_i' = \succeq_j'$. By independence, then,

$$W(x_1, \ldots, x_n) < W(y_1, \ldots, y_n). \qquad \square$$

Informally, the intuition for this result is that if one wants to accept Pigou–Dalton transfers in all portions of the space, one must be ready to accept leaky-buckets transfers as well. Under Pareto and Independence, leaky-bucket transfers (such as the transfer leading from x to y in Figure 9.4(a) can always be rendered equivalent to sequences of Pigou–Dalton transfers in other parts of the space (such as the two transfers from z^1 to z^2 and from z^3 to z^4 in Figure 9.4(b).

In summary, in the multidimensional setting it is very hard not to adopt a social welfare function W of the maximin kind. This shows that, in terms of inequality aversion, there is much less flexibility in the multidimensional case than in the one-dimensional case. The maximin criterion may be viewed as representing an extreme degree of egalitarianism, but it has been defended by prominent authors like Rawls (1971), Kolm (1972) and others. It has very often been studied in the theory of optimal taxation (see for example, Atkinson, 1973, 1995; Choné and Laroque, 2001; Tuomala, 1990). It is then interesting to see that the multidimensional setting provides an additional argument in favor of it.

9.7 Wages, labor and the Welfare State

An interesting domain of application of this approach is the two-dimensional setting in which individual positions are described by a quantity of labor and a net income. In this setting, one can evaluate the social consequences of tax redistribution, various forms of income support, and changes in wage rates in the labor market.

Let $X = [0, 1] \times \mathbb{R}_+$, with $x_i = (l_i, c_i)$, where $l_i \in [0, 1]$ denotes a quantity of labor and c_i is net income. The domain of preferences contains all profiles of preferences which are continuous, strictly monotonic in c_i. Preferences are not required to be monotonic (negatively) in l_i, because some individuals may actually be willing to pay for the possibility to spend some time in their job. Convexity could be assumed without altering the results, but this additional condition is not introduced here, in order to accommodate the fact that in reality, individuals may not always satisfy it.

This section draws a lot from Fleurbaey and Maniquet (2002, 2003, 2005), but provides variants of the results which allow for a synthetic and simple presentation. An important difference is that, here, the individuals are characterized only by their preferences and not by the wage rate they earn on the market. This makes it possible to extend Fleurbaey and Maniquet's analysis in two directions. First, it enables us to study the effect of changes in the market wage rates on social welfare, for a given population. Second, the current setting is also applicable to the case when individuals have unearned income in top of their wages, since the sources of net income are not explicitly described. But this particular way of proceeding has an ethical implication as well. Since individual i is distinguished only by her preferences $\succeq_i$ and the allocation is described only by bundles like x_i, no individual is given any preferential treatment in virtue of her wage rate or her unearned income. In other words, skill differentials, which are typically reflected in wage inequalities, are not considered a legitimate source of inequalities, and the same can be said about unearned income. As far as skills are concerned, this is justifiable if one considers that, in the current situation of modern societies, differences in skill acquisition are mostly due to unequal opportunities (due to innate talent and social background) across pupils and students rather than to different choices.[11] Regarding unearned income, a similar argument can be developed for the differences in unearned income which are due to inheritance and investment luck. Admittedly, it is more questionable to say that inequalities in unearned income due to different saving behavior are also illegitimate. A satisfactory analysis of this issue requires an intertemporal framework. This is left for future research.

In this context, the axioms of Pareto, preference-restricted Pigou–Dalton and independence can be retained without any difficulty. In this particular setting, however, a more intuitive version of the Pigou–Dalton axiom may be used, which considers only transfers of net income, between individuals with identical preferences and identical amounts of labor. It is indeed more intuitive to think about transfers of income than about transfers of labor.

Axiom 9.10 (Preference-restricted Pigou–Dalton principle). *Consider two vectors* $((l_1, c_1), \ldots, (l_n, c_n))$ *and* $((l_1, c_1'), \ldots, (l_n, c_n'))$. *If the latter is obtained from the former by a Pigou–Dalton transfer, defined by the formula*

$$c_i' = c_i + \delta \leq c_j - \delta = c_j',$$

for $\delta \in \mathbb{R}_{++}$ *and* $\succeq_i = \succeq_j$, $l_i = l_j$, *then* $W(x_1, \ldots, x_n) < W(y_1, \ldots, y_n)$.

Notice how this axiom confirms that skill differentials are not a legitimate source of inequalities. Indeed, it means that the socially ideal situation for two individuals with the same preferences is to end up on the same indifference curve, whatever their difference in skill and wage rate.

Space-restricted Pigou–Dalton axioms may also be quite appealing in this particular setting. We will actually consider weak versions of space-restricted egalitarianism, that is, weaker than Pigou–Dalton transfer principles. The kind of egalitarian condition which will be introduced below says that the egalitarian distribution

$$\left(\frac{1}{n}\sum_{i=1}^{n} a_i, \ldots, \frac{1}{n}\sum_{i=1}^{n} a_i\right),$$

which puts every individual at the average level, is at least as good as the unequal distribution $(a_1, \ldots, a_n)$. This can be viewed as a minimal form of egalitarianism.

Consider an allocation in which individuals have net incomes which do not depend on their labor, as if their productivity was nil. In this situation, some individuals would choose not to work, while others would still work some time because they enjoy it. In such a context of fixed incomes, how could unequal incomes be justified? When incomes are equal, every individual is then equally able to practice his favorite activity (work or leisure) and it is hard to imagine on what grounds some individuals would deserve to receive a greater income than others. The following axiom formalizes this intuition. Let $B_{\succeq_i}(A)$ denote the subset of best elements for $\succeq_i$ in any given set A.

Axiom 9.11 (Minimal egalitarianism of fixed incomes). *Consider two vectors* $(x_1, \ldots, x_n)$ *and* $(y_1, \ldots, y_n)$. *If for all i,*

$$x_i \in B_{\succeq_i}\left(\{(l, c) \in X \mid c \leq I_i\}\right),$$

$$y_i \in B_{\succeq_i}\left(\left\{(l, c) \in X \mid c \leq \frac{1}{n}\sum_{j=1}^{n} I_j\right\}\right),$$

then $W(x_1, \ldots, x_n) \leq W(y_1, \ldots, y_n)$.

This condition is intuitively quite appealing. One may complain, however, that it refers to a very unusual situation. It is more familiar to examine allocations where people have a positive wage rate. It is indeed simple to generalize the above axiom in order to allow for positive wage rates.

Axiom 9.12 (Minimal egalitarianism among $\tilde{w}$-earners). *Consider two vectors* $(x_1, \ldots, x_n)$ *and* $(y_1, \ldots, y_n)$. *If for all i,*

$$x_i \in B_{\succeq_i}\left(\{(l, c) \in X \mid c \leq I_i + \tilde{w}l\}\right),$$

$$y_i \in B_{\succeq_i}\left(\left\{(l, c) \in X \mid c \leq \frac{1}{n}\sum_{j=1}^{n} I_j + \tilde{w}l\right\}\right),$$

then $W(x_1, \ldots, x_n) \leq W(y_1, \ldots, y_n)$.

When $\tilde{w} = 0$, minimal egalitarianism among $\tilde{w}$-earners is equivalent to minimal egalitarianism of fixed incomes. Notice that it would be impossible to satisfy this

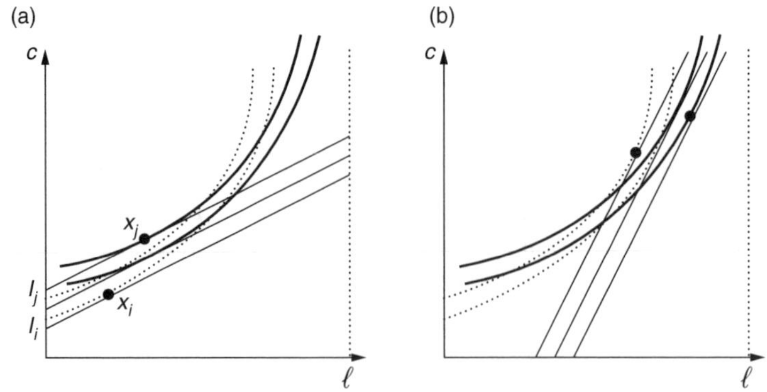

Figure 9.5 Equalizing budgets versus Pareto.

axiom for several values of $\tilde{w}$ at the same time and jointly with Pareto. This has been noted by Gibbard (1979), and is formally very close to the impossibility stated in Proposition 9.6. Figure 9.5 illustrates this for a simple case with two individuals. On Figure 9.5(a) an equalization of budgets is displayed, but Figure 9.5(b) shows that it is Pareto-equivalent to the reverse operation for a different wage rate.

As a consequence, the axiom of minimal egalitarianism among $\tilde{w}$-earners must be retained only for one precise value of $\tilde{w}$. The choice of $\tilde{w}$ will be discussed later.

Yet another variant of space-restricted egalitarianism is given by a third condition, which considers equalizing wage rates when the population works at various wage rates.

Axiom 9.13 (Minimal egalitarianism of wage rates). *Consider two vectors* $(x_1, \ldots, x_n)$ *and* $(y_1, \ldots, y_n)$. *If for all* i,

$$x_i \in B_{\succeq_i}\left(\{(l,c) \in X \mid c \leq w_i l\}\right),$$

$$y_i \in B_{\succeq_i}\left(\left\{(l,c) \in X \mid c \leq (\frac{1}{n}\sum_{j=1}^{n} w_j)l\right\}\right),$$

then $W(x_1, \ldots, x_n) \leq W(y_1, \ldots, y_n)$.

How should one go about choosing between these variants of space-restricted egalitarianism? In order to understand the underlying ethical stakes, consider two individuals at positions where their indifference curves cross, as in Figure 9.6. Ann has a flatter curve than Bob, which means that she is less averse to work. The problem is to determine which of these two individuals is worse-off and should therefore receive social help.

This figure illustrates three possible ways in which the same configuration of indifference curves may arise. In Figure 9.6(a), incomes are fixed, and both

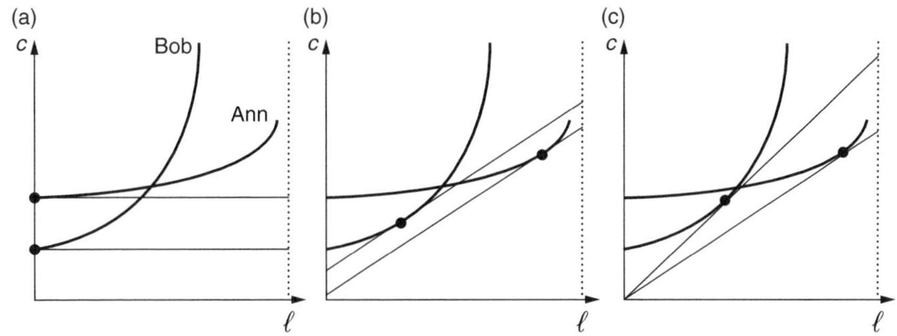

Figure 9.6 Comparing Ann's and Bob's situations.

individuals choose not to work. According to the axiom of minimal egalitarianism of fixed incomes, Bob is worse-off and it would be acceptable to equalize their incomes by a transfer from Ann to Bob. In Figure 9.6(b), they earn a positive wage rate, and Bob has a greater unearned income, so that now equalization would go the opposite way, penalizing Bob and benefiting Ann. The same occurs in Figure 9.6(c), where Bob has a greater wage rate.

The choice of the suitable axiom depends on which of the three cases seems to warrant equalization in the most compelling way. Consider Figure 9.6(c). Is it obvious that Bob should be taxed at the benefit of Ann? It is true that, as discussed earlier, the fact that he has a greater wage rate does not convey any notion of superior merit. But notice that Bob does not really take advantage of his more favorable budget set and that he earns less than Ann. It may be that his high aversion to work is due to the greater difficulty of his job, which is not compensated adequately by the wage rate differential, and that may be the reason why he decides to work less than Ann. If this were the case, then it would be questionable to tax him and redistribute in favor of Ann. On the other hand, if his aversion to work simply reflected the fact that, for instance, he is keen on outdoor activities, then he would indeed appear to be better-off than Ann. In summary, the axiom of minimal egalitarianism of wage rates implicitly relies on the ethical assumption that individuals may be held responsible for their apparent laziness. In particular, it pinpoints as fully ideal the situation in which all individuals have the same wage rate, and work at their convenience without tax and transfer.[12] Those who prefer to work little and earn little, then, receive no special attention and are considered just as well-off as the others. This neutrality about individual choices is justified when individual preferences are a pure matter of taste.

Now compare Figure 9.6(a) and (b). When Ann and Bob have the same wage rate and it is sufficiently high, as in Figure 9.6(b), then Bob is again considered better-off, whereas the opposite conclusion obtains when the wage rate is low, as in Figure 9.6(a). This shows that when the axiom of minimal egalitarianism among $\tilde{w}$-earners is adopted, for a high $\tilde{w}$, the agents with high aversion to labor

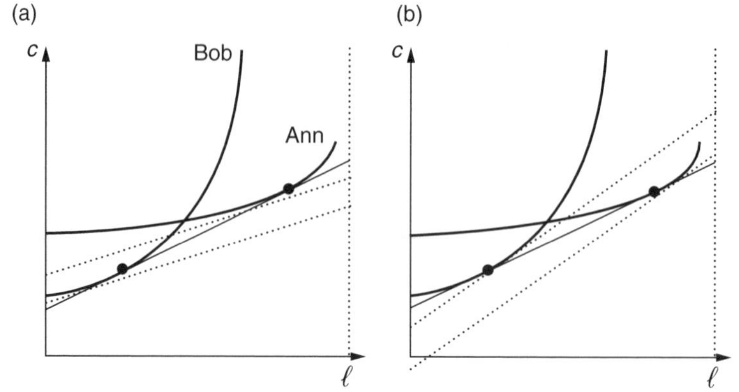

Figure 9.7 Choice of $\tilde{w}$ and interpersonal comparisons.

are easily considered better-off, and therefore are not favorably treated. On the contrary, the axiom of minimal egalitarianism of fixed incomes offers maximal protection to individuals with high aversion to labor. In summary, the choice of $\tilde{w}$ is linked to the protection against poverty granted to the apparent lazy. The lower $\tilde{w}$, the greater the protection. More precisely, under minimal egalitarianism among $\tilde{w}$-earners, social preferences express a bias *in favor of* apparent laziness for individuals whose wage rate is *greater* than $\tilde{w}$, and *against* apparent laziness for individuals whose wage rate is *less* than $\tilde{w}$. Consider Figure 9.7, in which Ann and Bob have the same budget, with the same wage rate w. If the situation is evaluated by looking at the Pareto-equivalent situation in which they earn $\tilde{w} < w$ (dotted lines in Figure 9.7(a)), the lazy Bob is deemed worst-off and equalization will proceed in his favor. The reverse occurs if $\tilde{w} < w$ (Figure 9.7(b)).

Two salient values of $\tilde{w}$ are therefore worth considering. First, $\tilde{w} = 0$, which, as just explained, gives full protection to apparent laziness. Second, $\tilde{w} = w_m$, where w_m is the smallest wage in the population (presumably, the legal minimum). This is the only value which avoids any bias against apparent laziness of the low-skilled and which also avoids displaying a pro-laziness bias at all prevailing levels of skill.

For the choice of space-restricted egalitarianism, then, the key issue is how favorably one wants to treat individuals with low or high aversion to labor, in relation to considerations about whether individuals may be held responsible for their preferences or not. In the sequel we retain the three following axioms, which provide an array of reasonable ethical attitudes: (i) Minimal egalitarianism of fixed incomes, which grants maximal protection against apparent laziness; (ii) Minimal egalitarianism among w_m-earners, which has the smallest degree of pro-laziness bias under the constraint of avoiding any anti-laziness bias; (iii) Minimal egalitarianism of wage rates, which is neutral about individual preferences for any level of wage rate, among individuals who have the same skill (and no unearned income).

These three axioms give us the choice between three kinds of social criteria, as stated in the following proposition.

Proposition 9.8. *Let W satisfy Pareto, preference-restricted Pigou–Dalton and independence. If, in addition, it satisfies minimal egalitarianism of fixed incomes (resp. among w_m-earners, of wage rates), then $W(x_1,\ldots,x_n) < W(y_1,\ldots,y_n)$ whenever* $\min_i U_i(x_i) < \min_i U_i(y_i)$, *for*

$$U_i(x_i) = I \text{ such that } x_i \sim_i B_{\succeq_i}(\{(l,c) \in X \mid c \leq I\})$$

(resp.

$$U_i(x_i) = I \text{ such that } x_i \sim_i B_{\succeq_i}(\{(l,c) \in X \mid c \leq I + w_m l\}),$$

$$U_i(x_i) = w \text{ such that } x_i \sim_i B_{\succeq_i}(\{(l,c) \in X \mid c \leq wl\})).$$

Proof. We focus on minimal egalitarianism of fixed incomes and on a simple case with two individuals. Consider two allocations x, y with

$$U_1(x_1) > U_1(y_1) > U_2(y_2) > U_2(x_2),$$

as illustrated on Figure 9.8. In order to clarify the figures, indifference curves for 1 are thick, while those for 2 are thin. We want to show that $W(y) > W(x)$.

Suppose that, on the contrary, $W(y) \leq W(x)$. By Pareto, one then has $W(y') < W(x)$, for y' defined as on Figure 9.9.

By Independence, one still has $W^a(y') < W^a(x)$ for the profile $\left(\succeq_1^a, \succeq_2^a\right)$ with indifference curves as on Figure 9.10 (because indifference curves at x, y' are the same as in the initial profile).

A new allocation x^a is defined on Figure 9.10. By Pareto, one has $W^a(x) < W^a(x^a)$, and therefore $W^a(y') < W^a(x^a)$. By Independence again, one still has $W^b(y') < W^b(x^a)$ for the profile $\left(\succeq_1^b, \succeq_2^b\right)$ with indifference curves as on

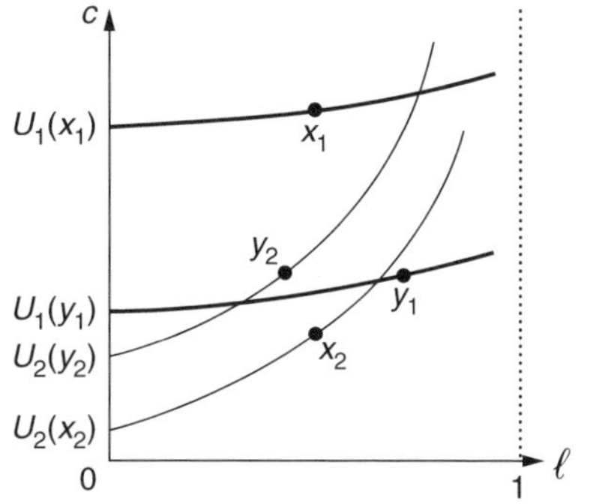

Figure 9.8 $U_1(x_1) > U_1(y_1) > U_2(y_2) > U_2(x_2)$.

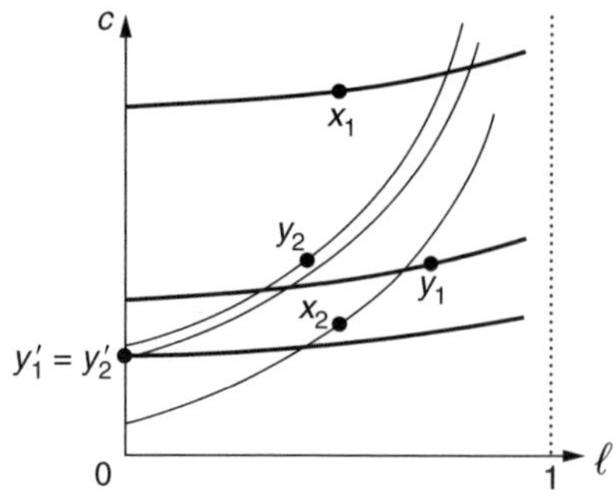

Figure 9.9 Definition of y'.

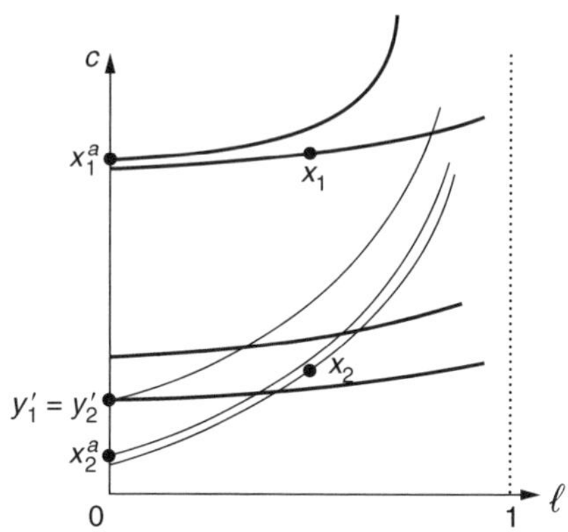

Figure 9.10 Profile $(\succeq_1^a, \succeq_2^a)$.

Figure 9.11 (because indifference curves at x^a, y' are the same as in profile $(\succeq_1^a, \succeq_2^a)$).

New allocations x^b and x^c are defined on Figure 9.11. By Pareto, one has $W^b(x^a) = W^b(x^b)$, and therefore $W^b(y') < W^b(x^b)$.

Consider a profile $(\succeq_1^c, \succeq_2^c)$ with $\succeq_1^c = \succeq_2^c$ and indifference curves as on Figure 9.12. By preference-restricted Pigou–Dalton, $W^c(x^b) < W^c(x^c)$, and by Independence, $W^b(x^b) < W^b(x^c)$, since indifference curves at x^b and x^c are the same in both profiles $(\succeq_1^b, \succeq_2^b)$ and $(\succeq_1^c, \succeq_2^c)$. As a consequence, $W^b(y') < W^b(x^c)$.

New allocations x^d and x^e are defined on Figure 9.13, with

$$x_1^e = x_2^e = \frac{x_1^d + x_2^d}{2}.$$

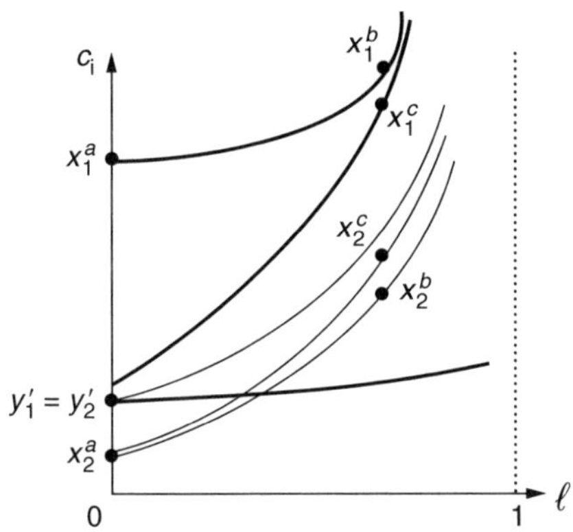

Figure 9.11 Profile $\left(\succeq_1^b, \succeq_2^b\right)$ and x^b, x^c.

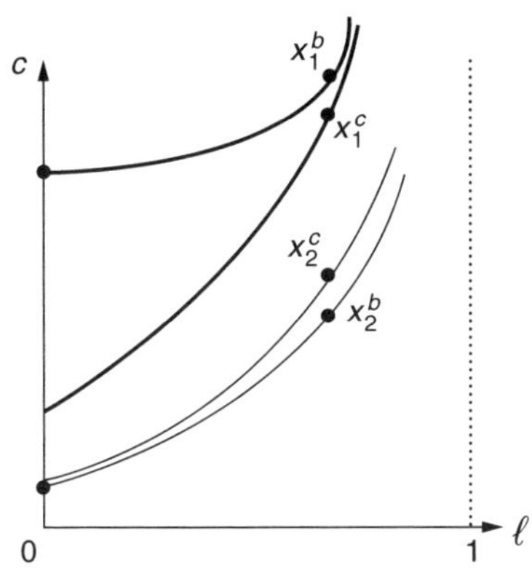

Figure 9.12 Profile $\left(\succeq_1^c, \succeq_2^c\right)$.

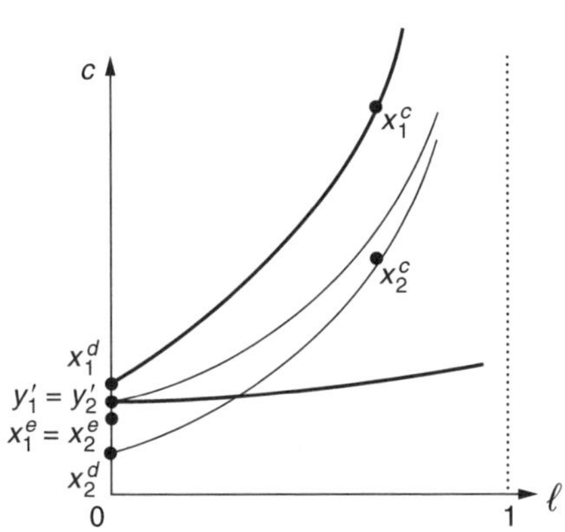

Figure 9.13 Allocations x^d, x^c.

By Pareto, one has $W^b(x^d) = W^b(x^c)$, and therefore $W^b(y') < W^b(x^d)$. By minimal egalitarianism of fixed incomes, $W^b(x^d) \leq W^b(x^e)$, so that $W^b(y') < W^b(x^e)$. But by Pareto $W^b(y') > W^b(x^e)$, a contradiction. □

This proposition illustrates Rawls' argument (see Section 9.4) that the index will reflect distributive principles rather than a conception of well-being. Indeed, the three possible U_i functions pinpointed earlier derive from the distributive judgments embodied in the three axioms of minimal egalitarianism, not from an inquiry into the nature of individual well-being.

As could be expected from Propostion 9.7, all three criteria are of the maximin kind. In order to get an intuitive understanding of these three criteria, consider that they evaluate the situation of any individual by asking her the following question.

First criterion (the "rente criterion"): "What income would be enough for you, in replacement of your current situation, if you did no longer have to earn it?"

Second criterion (the "rente + minimum wage criterion"): "What unearned income would be enough for you, in replacement of your current situation, if your net wage rate were equal to w_m and you could adjust your amount of work as you wished?"

Third criterion (the "wage rate criterion"): "What net wage rate would be enough for you, in replacement of your current situation, if you could adjust your amount of work as you wished?"

Proposition 9.8 provides a partial description, not a full definition of W, but this partial description is quite sufficient to derive precise conclusions about tax and transfer policies. Indeed, let us consider the application of the three criteria to the context when individual gross income is $g_i = r_i + w_i l_i$, where r_i denotes unearned income, and gross income is transformed into net income c_i by a tax function τ:

$$c_i = g_i - \tau(g_i).$$

When $\tau(g_i) < 0$, it is a subsidy. When $g_i = 0$, net consumption equals the basic income: $c_i = -\tau(0)$.

Individuals are free to choose their quantity of labor under this budget constraint. We are then in a standard setting of taxation with incentive constraints. The difference with the traditional Mirrlees (1971) approach to optimal taxation is that we consider the possibility that individuals differ not in one but in several dimensions: their wage rate w_i, their unearned income r_i, and their preferences $\succeq_i$.

We focus here on minimal tax functions, namely, on tax functions τ such that whenever τ', under incentive constraints, yields the same allocation as τ, then $\tau' \geq \tau$. This is not restrictive for large populations. A tax function which would not be minimal would be such that a significant tax cut could be implemented without changing the final allocation. We also restrict attention to tax functions such that net income $g - \tau(g)$ is non-negative and non-decreasing in g. This is standard, but justified only if individual preferences are negatively monotonic in l. The analysis can be easily generalized to the case when $g - \tau(g)$ may be decreasing (which happens to be the case over small intervals of earnings in some countries; see for example, Fleurbaey *et al.* 1999).

We also assume that preferences in the population are sufficiently diverse so that it never happens to the distribution of gross income that over some subinterval of $[0, w_m]$, only agents with wage rate $w > w_m$ appear. Such a situation would be rather peculiar and it is sensible to exclude it. More precisely, we make the following assumption, which implies that whenever an agent is willing to earn $g_i \leq w_m$, there is an agent with wage rate $w_i = w_m$ and unearned income $r_i = 0$ who is willing to earn the same amount. Formally, let $uc((g_i, c_i), w_i, r_i, \succeq_i)$ denote the closed comprehensive upper contour set for $\succeq_i$ at (g_i, c_i), in the space of gross income and net income:

$$uc((g_i, c_i), w_i, r_i, \succeq_i) = \left\{ (g, c) \in [0, r_i + w_i] \times \mathbb{R}_+ \mid \left(\max\left\{ \frac{g - r_i}{w_i}, 0 \right\}, c \right) \succeq_i \left(\frac{g_i - r_i}{w_i}, c_i \right) \right\}.$$

This set contains all (g, c) such that either i weakly prefers (g, c) to (g_i, c_i), or $g < r_i$ and without working the individual is as well off as with (g_i, c_i).

Assumption (Low-skill diversity): For every agent i, and every (l, c) such that $r_i + w_i l \leq w_m$, there is an agent j such that $w_j = w_m$, $r_j = 0$ and $uc((r_i + w_i l, c), w_j, r_j, \succeq_j) \subseteq uc((r_i + w_i l, c), w_i, r_i, \succeq_i)$.

This assumption guarantees that if i is willing to choose (l, c), such that $r_i + w_i l \leq w_m$, out of her budget set

$$\{(l, c) \in X \mid c \leq r_i + w_i l - \tau(r_i + w_i l)\},$$

then individual j, with $w_j = w_m$ and $r_j = 0$, will also accept to choose (l, c) out of his own budget set

$$\{(l, c) \in X \mid c \leq w_m l - \tau(w_m l)\}.$$

It turns out that, under this assumption, we obtain very simply criteria to evaluate different tax policies.

Proposition 9.9. *If W satisfies the conditions of Proposition 9.8, then a tax function τ is strictly preferable to another tax function τ' whenever*

$$\tau(0) < \tau'(0)$$

(*resp.*

$$\max_{g\in[0,w_m]} \tau(g) < \max_{g\in[0,w_m]} \tau'(g),$$

$$\max_{g\in[0,w_m]} \frac{\tau(g)}{g} < \max_{g\in[0,w_m]} \frac{\tau'(g)}{g}).$$

Proof. Consider a minimal tax function τ. In the space (g,c), the graph of $g-\tau(g)$ coincides with the envelope curve of individuals' indifference curves at the incentive-compatible allocation $(x_1,\ldots,x_n)$ produced by τ.

1 Rente criterion: Let $U_i(x_i) = I_i$ such that $x_i \sim_i B_{\succeq_i}(\{(l,c)\in X \mid c\leq I_i\})$. Let $(l_i^*,c_i^*)\in B_{\succeq_i}(\{(l,c)\in X \mid c\leq I_i\})$. One has $U_i(x_i)=c_i^*$. Since $g-\tau(g)$ is non-decreasing, $c_i^*\geq -\tau(0)$. Moreover, since the graph of $g-\tau(g)$ coincides with the envelope curve of individuals' indifference curves, there is some i for whom $c_i^* = -\tau(0)$. Therefore, $\min_i U_i(x_i) = -\tau(0)$.

2 Rente+minimum wage criterion: Let $U_i(x_i) = I_i$ such that

$$x_i \sim_i B_{\succeq_i}(\{(l,c)\in X \mid c\leq I_i + w_m l\}).$$

Let $(l_i^*,c_i^*)\in B_{\succeq_i}(\{(l,c)\in X \mid c\leq I_i + w_m l\})$. One has $U_i(x_i) = c_i^* - w_m l_i^*$. By incentive compatibility, $c_i^* \geq r_i + w_i l_i^* - \tau(r_i + w_i l_i^*)$, so that

$$U_i(x_i) \geq r_i + w_i l_i^* - \tau(r_i + w_i l_i^*) - w_m l_i^*.$$

For any agent i such that $w_i \geq w_m$, since $g-\tau(g)$ is non-decreasing,

$$U_i(x_i) \geq r_i + w_i l_i^* - \tau(r_i + w_i l_i^*) - w_m l_i^* \geq w_m l_i^* - \tau(w_m l_i^*) - w_m l_i^* = -\tau(w_m l_i^*).$$

By Low-skill diversity, the graph of $g-\tau(g)$ coincides over $[0,w_m]$ with the envelope curve of the closed upper contour sets of individuals with $r_i = 0$ and $w_i = w_m$. Therefore there is j in this subpopulation such that

$$U_j(x_j) = w_m l_j^* - \tau(w_m l_j^*) - w_m l_j^* = -\tau(w_m l_j^*) = \min_{l\in[0,1]} -\tau(w_m l).$$

In conclusion, $\min_i U_i(x_i) = \min_{l\in[0,1]} -\tau(w_m l) = -\max_{g\in[0,w_m]} \tau(g)$.

3 Wage rate criterion: Let $U_i(x_i) = w_i^*$ such that

$$x_i \sim_i B_{\succeq_i}\left(\{(l,c)\in X \mid c\leq w_i^* l\}\right).$$

Let $(l_i^*,c_i^*)\in B_{\succeq_i}\left(\{(l,c)\in X \mid c\leq w_i^* l\}\right)$. One has $U_i(x_i) = c_i^*/l_i^*$. By incentive compatibility, $c_i^* \geq r_i + w_i l_i^* - \tau(r_i + w_i l_i^*)$, so that

$$U_i(x_i) \geq \frac{r_i + w_i l_i^* - \tau(r_i + w_i l_i^*)}{l_i^*}.$$

For any agent i such that $w_i \geq w_m$, since $g - \tau(g)$ is non-decreasing,

$$U_i(x_i) \geq \frac{r_i + w_i l_i^* - \tau(r_i + w_i l_i^*)}{l_i^*} \geq \frac{w_m l_i^* - \tau(w_m l_i^*)}{l_i^*}$$
$$= w_m \left[1 - \frac{\tau(w_m l_i^*)}{w_m l_i^*} \right].$$

By Low-skill diversity, the graph of $wl - \tau(wl)$ coincides over $[0, w_m]$ with the envelope curve of the closed upper contour sets of individuals with $r_i = 0$ and $w_i = w_m$. Therefore there is j in this subpopulation such that

$$U_j(x_j) = \frac{w_m l_j^* - \tau(w_m l_j^*)}{l_j^*} = w_m \left[1 - \frac{\tau(w_m l_j^*)}{w_m l_j^*} \right]$$
$$= w_m \min_{l \in [0,1]} \left[1 - \frac{\tau(w_m l)}{w_m l} \right].$$

In conclusion,

$$\min_i U_i(x_i) = w_m \min_{l \in [0,1]} \left[1 - \frac{\tau(w_m l)}{w_m l} \right] = w_m \left[1 - \max_{g \in [0, w_m]} \frac{\tau(g)}{g} \right].$$

□

In summary, the upshot is that the "rente" criterion implies that the minimum income should be as high as possible; the "rente+minimum wage" criterion implies that income support to incomes below w_m should be as high and uniform as possible; the "wage rate" criterion implies that the rate of subsidy to low incomes should be as high as possible. Figure 9.14 illustrates how the three criteria can be simply applied to the graph of the net income function $g - \tau(g)$. In the figure, the small arrow, for each case, points to the value of $\min_i U_i(x_i)$ under each criterion.

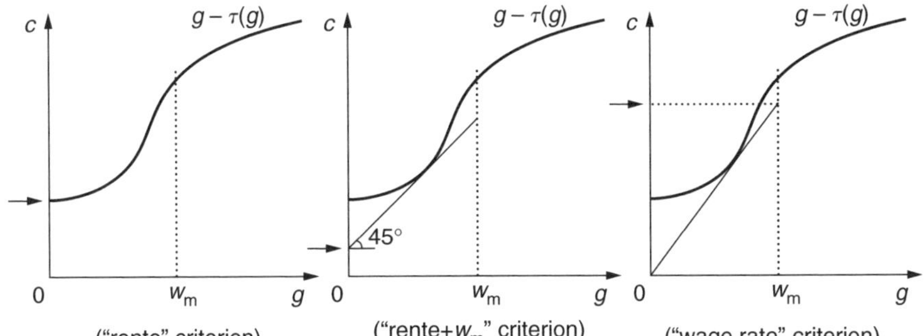

Figure 9.14 Applying the three criteria.

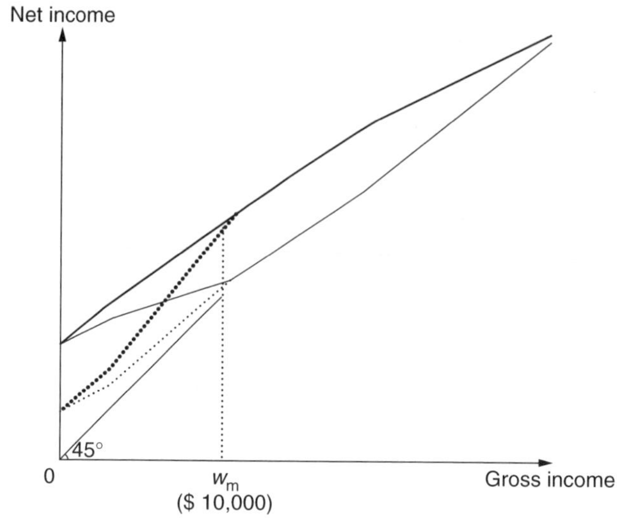

Figure 9.15 Income support and tax in the United States.

Source: Brewer (2000).

Such criteria can easily be applied to the evaluation of policies. Figure 9.15 displays the budget set, in the space of gross income and net income, for a lone parent with two children, in the United States. The full thick line is the budget set resulting from the addition of food stamps, Temporary Assistance for Needy Families (TANF) and Earned Income Tax Credit (EITC). The thick dotted line is the budget after removal of TANF (which is temporary, and is limited to at most 60 months). The corresponding thin lines are hypothetical budgets without EITC.

The figure also features a 45° line which helps in applying the "rente+ minimum wage" criterion (one must slide such a line upward until it is tangent to the budget line). One sees on the figure that removing TANF is clearly bad for the "rente" criterion, and is also bad for the "rente+minimum wage" criterion in presence of EITC. This suggests that the fact that TANF is temporary, contrary to the former Aid to Families with Dependent Children (AFDC), is problematic for social welfare. The removal of TANF does not affect social welfare for the "wage rate" criterion only (it is also neutral for the "rente+minimum wage" criterion in absence of EITC). Finally, note that removing EITC would be neutral for the "rente" criterion, and bad for the other two criteria (without or without TANF).

This example only deals with the case of lone parents with two children. This theoretical analysis was formulated for a population of individuals, and can easily be extended to a population of homogeneous households if one adopts the unitary view of households according to which a household can be analyzed just like an individual. When the whole population contains households of different sizes, the analysis can be applied separately to each subpopulation of households of the same type (as done earlier for the subpopulation of lone parents with two children). The earlier simple criteria then determine $\min_i U_i(x_i)$ over every subpopulation. It then remains to compare the values of $\min_i U_i(x_i)$ across households of different types. A priori, this cannot be done by a simple computation of equivalence scales without a thorough justification, and it requires a specific exploration, which should also, presumably, try to avoid the pitfalls of the unitary approach. This is an important field for future research.

9.8 Measuring the stress of globalization

The analysis made in Section 9.7 has focused on the evaluation of redistributive policies, and has not shed much light on the evaluation of the impact of economic shocks, such as those due to globalization. Although there is much disagreement on the empirical assessment of the consequences of globalization, it is at least considered possible that, in developed countries, globalization has adverse consequences on low-skilled workers and even on other parts of the work force. Such consequences may include: downward pressure on low-skilled wages; increased unemployment; increased volatility of incomes and uncertainty; reduced quality of jobs. The latter phenomenon has to do not only with the reduced reliability of labor contracts, in the general development of labor market flexibility, but also with the fact that management of labor in firms submitted to the effects of globalization and increased competition has evolved toward more individualistic and more stressful forms of incentives, responsibilities, and constraints.

Let us consider these various effects in turn. A reduction in low-skilled wages does not affect the evaluation of social welfare for the three above criteria as long as redistributive policies and the minimum wage w_m are unaltered. If the minimum wage is reduced, this does not affect the "rente" criterion, which focuses on minimum income. But the other two criteria will typically record a decrease in social welfare. For the "wage rate" criterion, social welfare equals

$$w_m \min_{wl \in [0, w_m]} \frac{wl - \tau(wl)}{wl},$$

an expression which is non-decreasing in w_m for any function τ such that $wl - \tau(wl)$ is non-decreasing.[13] The "rente+minimum wage" criterion is less easily used for the comparison of social situations with different minimum wage, since it involves a reference to the minimum wage in the computation of $U_i(x_i)$. This criterion satisfies Pareto only if this reference is kept fixed in comparisons of allocations. Suppose for instance that w_m changes to $w'_m < w_m$, and that the criterion is computed with reference to w_m. Then social welfare ex post equals

$$\min_{wl \in [0, w'_m]} wl - \tau(wl) - \frac{w_m}{w'_m} wl,$$

an expression which is non-decreasing in w'_m for any function τ such that $y - \tau(y)$ is non-decreasing.[14]

The issue of uncertainty is famously hard in welfare economics. But the fact that our social welfare criteria are of the maximin kind may provide a great deal of simplification. Let us assume that our criteria are applied to ex post allocations, where all uncertainty is resolved. Then, by application of the maximin, one focuses not only on the worst off agents, but also on the most unlucky among them. Therefore, in no way can such criteria, when applied ex post, be criticized for failing to take account of the risks suffered by the agents. On the contrary, they can be criticized for failing to take account of the agents' *ex ante* willingness to take risks. But in the context of basic economic situations described in terms of income and labor, it is probably not a terrible drawback if social policies are more precautionary than agents would spontaneously be. The conclusion then is that increased uncertainty due to globalization is not neglected but is evaluated only through its impact on the fate of the worst-off. Increased risk imposed on middle-class individuals is not directly registered by the social criteria at hand, simply because they focus on those at the lower end of the social scale.

Job quality has no *prima facie* impact on social welfare, according to the three criteria, because it does not directly affect the agents' budget sets. But this result obtains only when one assumes, as this has been done so far, that individuals are free to choose their amount of work between zero and one. Assume, in another extreme case, that agents only have the choice between no work, half time and full time jobs, and for some of them, only between no work and a full time job. Then a worsened atmosphere at work may have a negative impact on social welfare, because it may make indifference curves rotate counterclockwise, representing an increased labor disutility. Individuals would be willing to work less hours on the continuous budget set, but are prevented from doing so by restrictions on working time. The difficulty is that social welfare can then no longer be measured directly on budget sets, and depends on how more strenuous jobs affect labor disutility. Figure 9.16 illustrates this for an individual who works full time, and has choice only between working full time in a similar job or quitting the labor market (the two black circles in the figure). A degradation of labor conditions may alter his indifference curve as shown in the figure, and the apparent budget set, as well as the observed behavior of this individual, fail to record this worsened situation.

It is hard to conceive of any direct economic measure of this effect, and one probably has to rely on indirect evidence (e.g. morbidity, turnover) or questionnaire surveys in order to get any information about it.

A job with different working conditions or different management is actually a different job, and a more rigorous way of analyzing this issue consists in distinguishing the various kinds of jobs that any given individual may perform. The normative study of unemployment also requires a similar move, because to be unemployed is not the same as to have full-time leisure. Therefore the model has to enriched, by redefining l_i as being a multidimensional description of the various

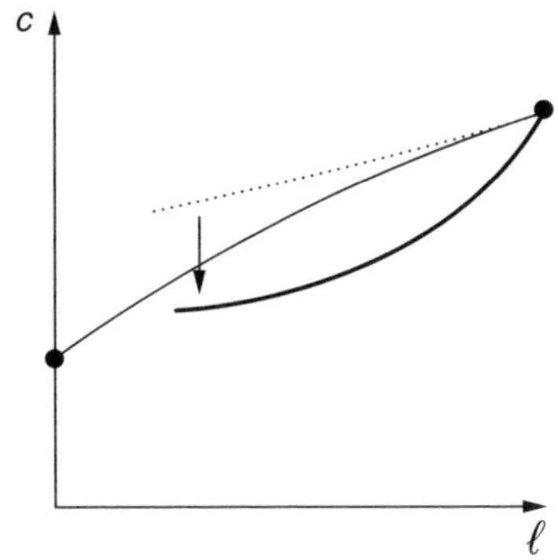

Figure 9.16 Degradation of labor conditions.

activities of work or job search performed by i in the relevant time span. Let a be the number of different activities, and l_{ik} be the time spent by i in activity k. The consumption set X will be redefined as

$$X = \left\{ (l_i, c_i) \in [0,1]^a \times \mathbb{R}_+ \mid \sum_{k=1}^{a} l_{ik} \leq 1 \right\}.$$

This new setting may be useful not only to describe the variety of possible jobs, but also to take account of intertemporal issues. The vector $l_i = (l_{i1}, \ldots, l_{ia})$ may be interpreted as describing the various activities successively performed by the individual over several months or years.

Typically, a given individual is not able to perform all a activities, and following the same ethical approach as earlier we do not record this as a morally relevant characteristic of the individual. Notice that typically individuals are strongly averse at practising activities for which they are not competent.

Individual preferences over the various activities may be influenced not only by the intrinsic rewards and pains attached to the activities, but also by extrinsic social rewards or stigmas. For instance, unemployment may be dreaded not only because job searching is unpleasant, but also because it undermines self-respect.

There is no problem in applying Pareto, preference-restricted Pigou–Dalton and independence to this richer setting. Space-restricted egalitarianism may be adapted by adding the possibility of choosing the activity to the possibility of choosing the quantity of labor. Minimal egalitarianism of fixed incomes can be retained without any change, and the other two are slightly modified as follows.

Axiom 9.14 (Minimal egalitarianism among $\tilde{w}$-earners). *Consider two vectors* $(x_1, \ldots, x_n)$ *and* $(y_1, \ldots, y_n)$. *If for all i,*

$$x_i \in B_{\succeq_i}\left(\{(l,c) \in X \mid c \leq I_i + \tilde{w}\sum_{k=1}^{a} l_k\}\right),$$

$$y_i \in B_{\succeq_i}\left(\{(l,c) \in X \mid c \leq \frac{1}{n}\sum_{j=1}^{n} I_j + \tilde{w}\sum_{k=1}^{a} l_k\}\right),$$

then $W(x_1, \ldots, x_n) \leq W(y_1, \ldots, y_n)$.

Axiom 9.15 (Minimal egalitarianism of wage rates). *Consider two vectors* $(x_1, \ldots, x_n)$ *and* $(y_1, \ldots, y_n)$. *If for all i,*

$$x_i \in B_{\succeq_i}\left(\{(l,c) \in X \mid c \leq w_i\sum_{k=1}^{a} l_k\}\right),$$

$$y_i \in B_{\succeq_i}\left(\{(l,c) \in X \mid c \leq \frac{1}{n}\sum_{j=1}^{n} w_j\sum_{k=1}^{a} l_k\}\right),$$

then $W(x_1, \ldots, x_n) \leq W(y_1, \ldots, y_n)$.

The ethical implications of adopting one or the other of the above variants of space-restricted egalitarianism are similar as in Section 9.7. Proposition 9.8 is reworded as follows.

Proposition 9.10. *Let W satisfy Pareto, preference-restricted Pigou–Dalton and independence. If, in addition, it satisfies minimal egalitarianism of fixed incomes (resp. among* w_m*-earners, of wage rates), then* $W(x_1, \ldots, x_n) < W(y_1, \ldots, y_n)$ *whenever* $\min_i U_i(x_i) < \min_i U_i(y_i)$, *for*

$$U_i(x_i) = I \text{ such that } x_i \sim_i B_{\succeq_i}(\{(l,c) \in X \mid c \leq I\})$$

(resp.

$$U_i(x_i) = I \text{ such that } x_i \sim_i B_{\succeq_i}\left(\{(l,c) \in X \mid c \leq I + w_m\sum_{k=1}^{a} l_k\}\right),$$

$$U_i(x_i) = w \text{ such that } x_i \sim_i B_{\succeq_i}\left(\{(l,c) \in X \mid c \leq w\sum_{k=1}^{a} l_k\}\right)).$$

Proof. The adaptation of the proof of Proposition 9.8 to this generalized setting involves no special complication. □

If every individual could freely choose his job and quantity of work, then the application of such social criteria could be made with the help of the same simple budget criteria as in Section 9.7 (the adaptation of Proposition 9.9 is left to the reader). But an important feature of the labor market is that, in addition to the stark constraints felt by the unemployed who do not find a suitable activity, many workers do not work in their most preferred kind of job. Let us call this general phenomenon, which encompasses unemployment as a particular case, "job constraint." As already shown in Figure 9.16, the budget set then fails to provide sufficient information about social welfare. With unemployment, the situation can even be worse than in Figure 9.16, as we now show. Let us consider an example in which there are only two activities, job and unemployment. Figure 9.17 shows how a graphical representation of this situation may be constructed.

In Figure 9.17(a) one sees a budget set such that the individual is forced to spend some time in unemployment. The dotted curves correspond to parts of the budget possibilities which have been unaccessible. This may be an accurate description of the ex post situation of an individual who has kept seeking a job in hope of finding one soon. But his unemployment spell may have been much longer than expected, in which case, as shown in Figure 9.17(b), his indifference surface may, in the subspace of job and consumption, fall *entirely* below his apparent budget set (the thick dotted curve on the right of the figure). In other words, if he had known *ex ante*, this individual would have preferred never entering the job market. This example is rather extreme, but it shows how complex the empirical evaluation of social welfare is in presence of job constraints.

Figure 9.18 illustrates a different situation in which an individual is forced to spend two thirds of her working time in a bad job which gives the same wage rate as the good job, but has a lower quality. Again one sees that her indifference surface may lie below her apparent budget set (the thick dotted curve on the right of the figure), including at the point corresponding to her quantity of work.

These examples strongly suggest that the priority goal for social policies should be to reduce job constraints and especially unemployment. Nonetheless, the

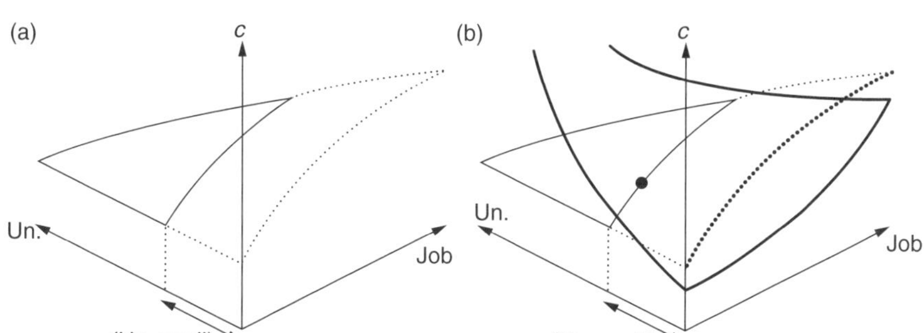

Figure 9.17 Budget and preferences over consumption, job and unemployment.

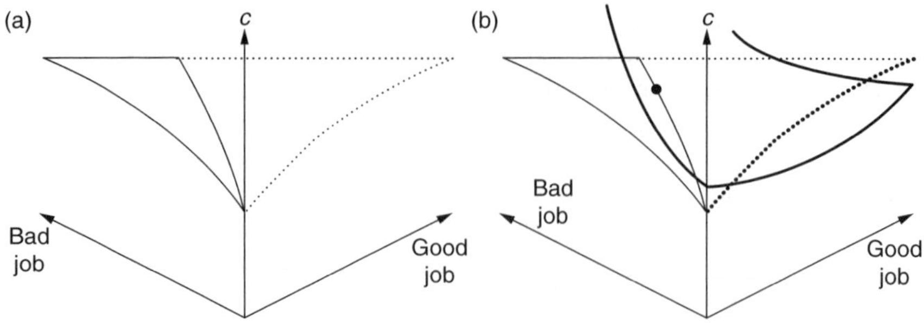

Figure 9.18 Good job and bad job.

determination of a proper empirical method for the measurement of social welfare, as it is defined in Proposition. 9.10, remains to be imagined.

Another topic which would deserve more exploration, including at the theoretical level, is the comparison between job constraints and low skills. Just like job constraints, having a low skill bars access to gratifying jobs. In this perspective, education policies may be powerful instruments for the improvement of social welfare. In the current model, preferences about various activities are influenced by skills (being competent at an activity makes it more pleasant), so that it is not simple to evaluate the impact of policies like education, because they alter individual preferences of this kind. Such analysis probably has to rely on more fundamental individual preferences about types of jobs (e.g. one may dream of being a pilot while being afraid of taking command of a plane because of one's current lack of skill).

9.9 Conclusion

In conclusion, let us just briefly recapitulate various points, touched upon in this chapter, which call for further research.

1 In the one-dimensional setting, Pigou–Dalton transfers and proportional transfers provide just a sample of possible principles of transfers. Many other interesting transfer principles which have not yet been formulated probably lie just below the surface, and their relationship with families of social welfare functions would provide good insight in the ethical properties of these functions.
2 In the multidimensional setting the maximin criterion is easily obtained out of lenient Pigou–Dalton transfer principles, under Pareto and Independence. This specific and rather striking argument in favor of the maximin deserves more scrutiny. Can one avoid the maximin result by restricting the domain of admissible individual preferences or by weakening Independence in a sensible

way? It also remains to study if a similar result can be obtained with a discrete set of alternatives (Propostion 9.7 relies heavily on continuity of preferences).

3 The main topic of application, in this chapter, has been the labor-consumption trade-off. But several other dimensions of well-being have been mentioned briefly. Savings and intertemporal choices, in particular, deserve a full-fledged analysis. This topic raises delicate ethical issues, such as whether individual preferences can be fully trusted for intertemporal choices, due to myopia.

4 Heterogeneity of households in size and composition is another important topic to be studied, especially in the perspective of empirical applications.

5 Education is a third dimension to be analyzed thoroughly in the future. It has implications for the discussion of individual educational choices, but also and maybe more importantly with respect to the opening of opportunities permitted by higher skills, with a related change in preferences about different activities.

6 Proposition 9.9 has shown how the social welfare criteria proposed here can in some cases be empirically applied by a simple examination of budget sets. Section 9.8 has shown, however, that such simple methods are not appropriate when job constraints hinder individual choices of activities. It remains to find empirical methods for the measurement of well-being for constrained individuals. Methods in use in cost-benefit analysis may prove useful in this perspective.

Acknowledgment

This chapter has benefitted from discussions with F. Farina, F. Maniquet, A. Trannoy, J. Weymark, and from detailed comments by E. Savaglio. The usual disclaimer applies.

Notes

1 One can find it in Aboudi and Thon (2003) and Marshall and Olkin (1979, p. 123).

2 An increment changes a vector $(x_1, \ldots, x_n)$ into $(x_1, \ldots, x_{i-1}, x_i + \delta, x_{i+1}, \ldots, x_n)$, with $\delta > 0$.

3 The proofs in Hardy *et al.* (1952, pp. 47–48) and Fields and Fei (1978) are involved, and the proof in Marshall and Olkin (1979, pp. 21–22) lacks an argument at some point. On the history of this result and comments on various proofs, see Foster (1985).

4 This part of the proof is not sufficiently explicit in Marshall and Olkin (1979, p. 22).

5 That is, the first in the ordered list $1, \ldots, n$. Notice that $z_1^1 \leq \cdots \leq z_n^1$ need not hold. This would have been guaranteed if, instead of taking the first R agent for the first transfer, we had taken the last R before the first D (as in the proof of Hardy *et al.*). But this precaution is useless for the result.

6 The idea of using a change of variable to generalize results about second-degree stochastic dominance was already exploited in Meyer (1977). From his results one can obtain criteria which extend generalized Lorenz dominance for social planners with a lower (or upper) bound on inequality aversion.

7 The rigorous proof goes by considering one hyperbolic transfer and checking that it cannot be implemented by a finite number of proportional transfers. A key argument is that cutting a proportional transfer into a sequence of sub-transfers entails less losses (for a given donation, the recipient gets more) than the initial transfer. Since the hyperbolic

transfer has more loss than a proportional transfer, a fortiori it entails more loss than any sequence of proportional transfers.

8 The relation between the possibility results obtained with this approach and the tradition of impossibility results in the theory of social choice is examined in Fleurbaey (2003), Fleurbaey and Hammond (2004), Fleurbaey and Maniquet (2001, 2005), Fleurbaey *et al.* (2005a,b).

9 One may wonder what a transfer means if x_i is a vector of functionings rather than commodities. One cannot transfer a nutrition level from one individual to another as easily as a banana. But the Pigou–Dalton principle is not about practical transfers. It simply compares various situations and makes a judgment for situations which can be related by hypothetical transfers. (Similarly, in the one-dimensional context, the Pigou–Dalton transfer can be applied to cardinally measurable and interpersonally comparable welfare levels, not just income levels, even though welfare is not directly transferable.)

10 This particular result appears in late versions of Fleurbaey and Maniquet (2001). Earlier variants of this result appeared in Fleurbaey (2005) and Maniquet and Sprumont (2004).

11 Presumably, every young individual tries to reach the highest skill under the constraint of his learning and financial possibilities. This does not mean that they try to maximize their earning abilities, since different skills may require the same amount of studies but command unequal wages in the market. Therefore wage differentials across individuals may indeed partly reflect their different preferences in the learning process. But one can defend the view that individuals do not have to bear the full consequences of wage gaps between specializations.

12 This is closely related to an axiom of "laisser-faire" studied in Fleurbaey and Maniquet (2002).

13 Let $w'_m < w_m$. For any $\alpha \in [0, w'_m]$, one obviously has

$$w'_m \min_{wl \in [0, w'_m]} \frac{wl - \tau(wl)}{wl} \leq w_m \frac{\alpha - \tau(\alpha)}{\alpha},$$

and for any $\alpha \in [w'_m, w_m]$, since $wl - \tau(wl)$ is non-decreasing,

$$w'_m \min_{wl \in [0, w'_m]} \frac{wl - \tau(wl)}{wl} \leq w'_m - \tau(w'_m) \leq \alpha - \tau(\alpha) \leq w_m \frac{\alpha - \tau(\alpha)}{\alpha}.$$

14 Let $w'_m < w''_m < w_m$. For any $\alpha \in [0, w'_m]$,

$$\min_{wl \in [0, w'_m]} wl - \tau(wl) - \frac{w_m}{w'_m} wl \leq \alpha - \tau(\alpha) - \frac{w_m}{w'_m}\alpha \leq \alpha - \tau(\alpha) - \frac{w_m}{w''_m}\alpha,$$

and for any $\alpha \in [w'_m, w''_m]$, since $wl - \tau(wl)$ is non-decreasing,

$$\min_{wl \in [0, w'_m]} wl - \tau(wl) - \frac{w_m}{w'_m} wl \leq w'_m - \tau(w'_m) - w_m \leq \alpha - \tau(\alpha)$$
$$- w_m \leq \alpha - \tau(\alpha) - \frac{w_m}{w''_m}\alpha.$$

References

Aboudi, R. and Thon, D. (2003) "Transfer principles and inequality aversion," *Mathematical Social Sciences* 45: 299–311.

Arneson, R. (1990) "Primary goods reconsidered," *NOÛS* 24: 429–454.

Arnsperger, C. and van Parijs, Ph. (2000) *Ethique économique et sociale*, Paris: La Découverte.

Arrow, K.J. (1951) *Social Choice and Individual Values*, New York: Wiley.

Arrow, K.J. (1973) "Some ordinalist-utilitarian notes on Rawls's theory of justice," *Journal of Philosophy* 70: 245–263.

Atkinson, A.B. (1973) "How progressive should income tax be?" in M. Parkin and A.R. Nobay (eds), *Essays in Modern Economics*, London: Longmans.

Atkinson, A.B. (1995) *Public Economics in Action*, Oxford: Clarendon Press.

Brewer, M. (2000) "Comparing in-work benefits and financial work incentives for low-income families in the US and the UK," Institute for Fiscal Studies WP #00/16.

Brun, B.C. and Tungodden, B. (2004) "Non-welfarist theories of justice: Is the 'intersection approach' a solution to the indexing impasse?" *Social Choice and Welfare* 22: 49–60.

Chone, P. and Laroque, G. (2001) "Optimal incentives for labor force participation," INSEE-CREST mimeo.

Dardanoni, V. (1995) "On multidimensional inequality measurement," in C. Dagum and A. Lemmi (eds) *Income Distribution, Social Welfare, Inequality, and Poverty*, Stamford: JAI Press.

Fields, G.S. and Fei, J.C. (1978) "On inequality comparisons," *Econometrica* 46: 303–316.

Fleurbaey, M. (1995) "Equal opportunity or equal social outcome?" *Economics and Philosophy* 11: 25–55.

Fleurbaey, M. (2003) "On the informational basis of social choice," *Social Choice and Welfare* 21: 347–384.

Fleurbaey, M. (2005) "The Pazner–Schmeidler social ordering: a defense," *Review of Economic Design* 9: 145–166.

Fleurbaey, M. and Hammond, P.J. (2004) "Interpersonally comparable utility," in S. Barbera, P.J. Hammond, and C. Seidl (eds), *Handbook of Utility Theory*, Dordrecht: Kluwer (forthcoming).

Fleurbaey, M. and Maniquet, F. (1996) "Utilitarianism versus fairness in welfare economics," in M. Salles and J. A. Weymark (eds), *Justice, Political Liberalism and Utilitarianism: Themes from Harsanyi and Rawls*, Cambridge: Cambridge University Press (forthcoming).

Fleurbaey, M. and Maniquet, F. (2001) "Fair social orderings," mimeo, U. of Pau and U. of Namur.

Fleurbaey, M. and Maniquet, F. (2002) "Fair income tax," *Review of Economic Studies* (forthcoming).

Fleurbaey, M. and Maniquet, F. (2003) "Help the low-skilled or reward the hardworking? A study of fairness in optimal income taxation," mimeo, U. of Pau and U. of Namur.

Fleurbaey, M. and Maniquet, F. (2005) "Fair orderings with unequal production skills," *Social Choice and Welfare* 24: 93–128.

Fleurbaey, M. and Michel, Ph. (2001) "Transfer principles and inequality aversion, with an application to optimal growth," *Mathematical Social Sciences* 42: 1–11.

Fleurbaey, M. and Trannoy, A. (2003) "The impossibility of a paretian egalitarian," *Social Choice and Welfare* 21: 243–264.

Fleurbaey, M., Hagneré, C., Martinez, M., and Trannoy, A. (1999) "Les minima sociaux en France: entre compensation et responsabilité," *Economie et Prévision* 138–139: 1–25.

Fleurbaey, M., Suzumura, K., and Tadenuma, K. (2005a) "Arrovian aggregation in economic environments. How much should we know about indifference surfaces?," *Journal of Economic Theory* 124: 22–44.

Fleurbaey, M., Suzumura, K., and Tadenuma, K. (2005b) "The informational basis of the theory of fairness," *Social Choice and Welfare* 24: 311–342.

Foster, J.E. (1985) "Inequality measurement," in H.P. Young (ed.), *Fair Allocation*, Providence: American Mathematical Society.

Gibbard, A. (1979) "Disparate goods and Rawls's difference principle: a social choice theoretic treatment," *Theory and Decision* 11: 267–288.

Hammond, P.J. (1976) "Equity, Arrow's conditions, and Rawls' difference principle," *Econometrica* 44: 793–804.

Hansson, B. (1973) "The independence condition in the theory of social choice," *Theory and Decision* 4: 25–49.

Hardy, G.H., Littlewood, J.E., and Pöyla, G. (1952) *Inequalities*, Cambridge: Cambridge University Press.

Kolm, S.C. (1972) *Justice et equité*, Pariss: Ed. du CNRS.

Kolm, S.C. (1996) *Modern Theories of Justice*, Cambridge, MA: MIT Press.

Maniquet, F. and Sprumont, Y. (2004) "Fair production and allocation of an excludable nonrival good," *Econometrica* 72: 627–640.

Marshall, A. and Olkin, I. (1979) *Inequalities : Theory of Majorization and Its Applications*, New York: Academic Press.

Meyer, J. (1977) "Second degree stochastic dominance with respect to a function," *International Economic Review* 18: 477–487.

Mirrlees, J. (1971) "An exploration in the theory of optimum income taxation," *Review of Economic Studies* 38: 175–208.

Pazner, E. (1979) "Equity, nonfeasible alternatives and social choice: a reconsideration of the concept of social welfare," in J.J. Laffont (ed.), *Aggregation and Revelation of Preferences*, Amsterdam: North-Holland.

Rawls, J. (1971) *A Theory of Justice*, Cambridge, MA: Harvard University Press.

Rawls, J. (1982) "Social unity and primary goods," in A.K. Sen and B. Williams (eds), *Utilitarianism and Beyond*, Cambridge: Cambridge University Press.

Robbins, L. (1932) *An Essay on the Nature and Significance of Economic Science*, London: Macmillan.

Roemer, J.E. (1996) *Theories of Distributive Justice*, Cambridge, MA: Harvard University Press.

Samuelson, P.A. (1977) "Reaffirming the existence of 'reasonable' Bergson–Samuelson social welfare functions," *Economica* 44: 81–88.

Samuelson, P.A. (1987) "Sparks from Arrow's anvil," in G.R. Feiwel (ed.), *Arrow and the Foundations of the Theory of Economic Policy*, New York: New York University Press.

Sen, A.K. (1987) *On Ethics and Economics*, Oxford: Blackwell.

Sen, A.K. (1992) *Inequality Re-examined*, Oxford: Clarendon Press.

Tuomala, M. (1990) *Optimal Income Tax and Redistribution*, Oxford: Oxford University Press.

10 Three approaches to the analysis of multidimensional inequality

Ernesto Savaglio

10.1 Introduction

The standard objective of the economic literature concerning inequality measurement is to compare single-dimensioned welfare indicators, such as income. However, in order to evaluate the social state of an individual, more than one criterion often needs to be applied, since economic disparity does not arise from the distribution of income alone. People are different in income, education, health, etc. and we must take several individual characteristics into account if we want to answer to the two questions posed by Sen (1997): "*Why inequality?*" and "*Inequality of what?*". As was stressed by Sen (1980), Kolm (1997), Maasoumi (1986) and many other scholars, analysis of different individual attributes is crucial to understand and evaluate inequality between people. Unfortunately, inequality in the context of more than one variable has seldom been studied and indeed the literature on multidimensional inequality comparisons is rather sparse. Since, the problem is inherently complex, it is difficult to extend the ranking principles and measures from the univariate to the multivariate case. The main reason for this difficulty regards the interaction between income and non-income attributes.

In this chapter, our aim is to survey the main results on multidimensional analysis of economic inequality. We first discuss the relations among inequality criteria in a unidimensional setting. In Section 10.3, we explain basic definitions and notation of multidimensional inequality, analytically as well as intuitively. Section 10.4 reviews the three main approaches to the study of inequality in economics when individuals differ in several characteristics besides income. We first survey assessment of well-being associated with a multivariate distribution by means of social welfare functions. We then show the pros and cons of measuring multidimensional inequality, adopting alternative classes of indices, followed by a survey of measurement of multidimensional inequality, using tools of convex analysis. Section 10.5 concludes with remarks on future research in this unexplored field.

10.2 Unidimensional majorization

Early last century, economists became interested in measuring how income or wealth distributions might be compared in terms of inequality. The first statement of this kind of which we are aware was due to Lorenz (1905), who introduced what has become known as the *Lorenz curve*.

Consider a population of n individuals and let x_i be the wealth of individuals i, $i = 1, \ldots, n$. Order the individuals from poorest to richest to obtain $x_{(1)}, \ldots, x_{(n)}$. Now plot the points $(k/n, S_k/S_n)$, $k = 0, \ldots, n$, where $S_0 = 0$ and $S_k = \sum_{i=1}^{k} x_{(i)}$ is the total wealth of the k poorest individuals in the population. Join these points by line segments to obtain a curve connecting the origin with the point $(1, 1)$. Let $x_1, \ldots, x_n$ represent the wealth of individuals for the distribution of total wealth T, similarly let $y_i, \ldots, y_n$ be an alternative distribution of T. Then according to the idea of Lorenz:

Definition 10.1. $(x_1, \ldots, x_n)$ *represents a more even distribution of wealth than does* $(y_i, \ldots, y_n)$ *if and only if*

$$\sum_{i=1}^{k} x_{(i)} \geq \sum_{i=1}^{k} y_{(i)} \quad k = 1, \ldots, n-1, \tag{10.1}$$

Of course,

$$\sum_{i=1}^{n} x_{(i)} = \sum_{i=1}^{n} y_{(i)} = T. \tag{10.2}$$

Relations 10.1 and 10.2 are a way of saying that x is *more spread out* than (or dually is majorized by) y, denoted as $x \preceq y$.

The set $\mathbb{R}^n$ of all income distributions of a population of n individuals, an *inequality criterion* $\preceq$, such as the Lorenz one, is generally a binary relation defined on a subset $\mathcal{A}$ of $\mathbb{R}^n$, satisfying:

(Reflexivity) $x \preceq x$ for all $x \in \mathcal{A}$

(Transitivity) $x \preceq y$ and $y \preceq z$ implies $x \preceq z$ when $x, y, z \in \mathcal{A}$

(Antisymmetry) $x \preceq y$ and $y \preceq x$ implies $x = y$

A binary relation $\preceq$ with these three conditions is called a *partial ordering*.[1] When two income distributions $x, y \in \mathbb{R}^n$ satisfy $x \preceq y$, we say that y is more unequal than x.

Later Dalton (1940) noted that:

> If there are only two income-receivers and a transfer of income takes place from the richer to the poorer, inequality is diminishing, respecting the limiting condition that the transfer must not be so large as to more than reverse the relative positions of the two income receivers.

Formally, this means that if $y_i < y_j$ with y_k the income of individual k for $k = 1, \ldots, n$ and an amount δ of income is transferred from individual j to i, then income inequality is diminished provided $\delta \leq y_j - y_i$.

Muirhead (1903) had already discussed what Dalton calls a transfer. He proved that if the components of x and y are non-negative integers, then the following conditions are equivalent:

(i) x can be derived from y by a finite number of transfers (each satisfying Dalton's restriction);
(ii) the sum of the k largest components of x is less than or equal to the sum of the k largest components of y, $k = 1, \ldots, n$, with equality when $k = n$.[2]

Indeed, Muirhead (1903) noticed that if y_i and y_j were replaced by $y_i + \delta$ and $y_j - \delta$ in $\delta \leq y_j - y_i$, then it amounted to the replacement of y_i and y_j by averages. If $0 \leq \alpha = \delta/(y_j - y_i) \leq 1$ and $\overline{\alpha} = 1 - \alpha$, then

$$y_i + \delta = \overline{\alpha} y_i + \alpha y_j \quad \text{and} \quad y_j - \delta = \alpha y_i + \overline{\alpha} y_j. \tag{10.3}$$

Repeated averages of two incomes at a time are then equivalent to obtaining distribution x from y through a finite number of transfers. Hardy *et al.* (1934, 1952) (henceforth HLP), subsequently showed that operation 10.3 produces the same result as replacement of x_i from y_i through an arbitrary average of the form:

$$\begin{cases} x_i = y_1 p_{1i} + \ldots + y_n p_{ni}, & i = 1, \ldots, n \\ \text{where } p_{ij} \geq 0, & \text{for all } i, j, \text{ is such that:} \\ \sum_{i=1}^{n} p_{ij} = 1 & \text{for all } j, \quad \text{and} \sum_{j=1}^{n} p_{ij} = 1 \quad \text{for all } i. \end{cases} \tag{10.4}$$

They also showed that operation 10.4 is tantamount to post-multiplying a vector y by a doubly stochastic matrix $P = (p_{ij})$, namely a square matrix where all entries are non-negative and the sums of all rows and columns are equal to one. In words, this elegant result means that if $x \preceq y$, then x can be derived from y by a finite number of transfers (each satisfying the restriction of the Dalton principle), if and only if:

$$x = yP \quad \text{where } P \text{ is a } n \times n \text{ doubly stochastic matrix.}$$

Remark 10.1. Note that permutation matrices, namely square matrices such that each row and column has a single unit, and all other entries are zero, are particularly interesting examples of doubly stochastic matrices. Birkhoff (see Marshall and Olkin, 1979) showed that permutation matrices constitute the extreme points of the (convex) set of doubly stochastic matrices and that the set of doubly stochastic matrices is the convex hull of the permutation matrices.

HLP (1934, 1952) showed that a special kind of linear transformation called T-*transform*, whose matrix has the form

$$T = \lambda I + (1 - \lambda)Q$$

where $\lambda \in [0, 1]$ and Q is a permutation matrix that just interchanges two coordinates, is tantamount to one transfer in the sense of Dalton. As yT has the form:

$$\begin{aligned} yT =& (y_1, \ldots, y_{j-1}, \lambda y_j + (1 - \lambda)y_k, y_{j+1}, \ldots, y_{k-1}, \lambda y_k \\ &+ (1 - \lambda)y_j, y_{k+1}, \ldots, y_n), \end{aligned}$$

they show that if x is a more even distribution than y, according to the Lorenz criterion, then x can be derived from y by successive applications of a *finite* number of T-transforms. As a T-transform is a doubly stochastic matrix and the (finite) product of doubly stochastic matrices is a doubly stochastic matrix, HLP provided the following equivalence:

$$x = y \prod_{i=1}^{k} T_i = yP.$$

In words, a sequence of Muirhead–Dalton transfers (i.e. P) can be decomposed in a finite number of elementary transfers, namely transfers where just two coordinates are involved (i.e. T). This is a major result in the study of economic inequality theory. It suggests to taking $n = 2$ without loss of generality to prove some of the main results reviewed in this section.

Although the notion of "equality" is quite intuitive, it was only made precise recently by the work of Schur (1923) on Hadamard's determinants of a positive semi-definite Hermitian matrix. Schur's results are the starting point to a variety of inequalities. In fact, Schur (1923) discovered what are known as order-preserving functions or in economics, (social) evaluation functions. Analytically, let $\preceq$ be any preordering defined on some set $\mathcal{A} \subseteq \mathbb{R}^n$,

Definition 10.2. *A function $\varphi : \mathcal{A} \subseteq \mathbb{R}^n \to \mathbb{R}$ is said to be order-preserving (or isotonic) if*

$$x \preceq y \quad \textit{implies} \quad \varphi(x) \leq \varphi(y), \quad x, y \in \mathcal{A}.$$

Since the research of Schur (1923) is a pioneer and systematic study on order-preserving functions, in Schur's honor such functions are now said to be "convex in the sense of Schur," "Schur-convex," or "S-convex," as opposed to "convex in the sense of Jensen," or simply "convex." We define a function φ, convex in the sense of Schur, as follows:

Definition 10.3. *A function $\varphi : \mathcal{A} \subseteq \mathbb{R}^n \to \mathbb{R}$ is S-convex if $f(Bx) \leq f(x)$ for all $x \in \mathcal{A}$ and all $n \times n$ bistochastic matrices B and it is strictly S-convex if the inequality is strict when B is not a permutation matrix.*

According to Schur's work, if φ is differentiable and if

$$\varphi_{(k)}(z) = \partial\varphi(z)/\partial z_k$$

is the partial derivative of φ with respect to its k-th argument, the following theorem characterizes the class of *S-convex* functions:

Theorem 10.1 (Schur, 1923; Ostrowski, 1952). *Let $\mathcal{A} \subset \mathbb{R}$ be an open interval and let $\varphi : \mathcal{A}^n \to \mathbb{R}$ be continuously differentiable. Necessary and sufficient conditions for φ to be Schur-convex on $\mathcal{A}^n$ are*

$$\varphi \text{ is symmetric on } \mathcal{A}^n$$

and

$$\varphi_{(i)}(z) \text{ is increasing in } i = 1, \ldots, n \quad \text{for all } z \in \mathbb{R} \cap \mathcal{A}^n,$$

where $\mathbb{R} = \{(x_1, \ldots, x_n) : x_1 \leq \cdots \leq x_n\}$ is an ordered field.

Alternatively, φ is Schur-convex on $\mathcal{A}^n$ if and only if φ is symmetric and for all $i \neq j$,

$$(z_i - z_j)[\varphi_{(i)}(z) - \varphi_{(j)}(z)] \geq 0 \quad \text{for all } z \in \mathcal{A}^n. \tag{10.5}$$

Condition 10.5 is often called *Schur's condition*. Note that, in proving that a function φ is Schur-convex, it is sufficient to prove that $\varphi(x) \leq \varphi(y)$ when $x \preceq y$ and x and y differ in only two components. This is a consequence of the fact that if $x \preceq y$, then x can be derived from y by a finite number of T-transforms.

The result of Schur in useful to identify the class of functions consistent with a given ordering. Indeed, Theorem 1 means that if a distribution x is more spread out than y, according to a preordering (such as the Lorenz one), then the inequality associated with y will be greater than the inequality associated with x by a class of real-valued (social) evaluation functions φ (such as the class of S-convex ones).

Since the work of Schur (1923), mathematical research in the field of inequality theory has flourished. On the contrary, in economics, it was not until the beginning of the seventies, that interest in the issues of inequality measurement revived with the pioneer papers of Kolm (1969) and Atkinson (1970). Atkinson justified use of Lorenz curves as a tool for measuring income inequality in a utilitarian framework. He showed that if a social evaluation function is additively separable and is the sum of individual utility functions (the same function for each individual), then the partial ordering of income distributions obtained using the Lorenz dominance criterion is tantamount to the ordering implied by the social evaluation function, where individual utility functions are concave.

This result relies on the following more general proposition:

Theorem 10.2 (HLP, 1934). *For $x, y \in \mathbb{R}^n$, the following conditions are equivalent:*

(i) $x \preceq y$;
(ii) $x = yP$ *for some doubly stochastic matrix* P;
(iii) $\sum_1^n g(x_i) \leq \sum_1^n g(y_i)$, *for any strictly concave function* g.[3]

Theorem 10.2 is the cornerstone of all economic literature on inequality theory. It shows that ranking (income) distributions in terms of inequality has both a descriptive and normative content. Indeed, condition (i) represents the Lorenz ordering (a descriptive condition); condition (ii) is the Muirhead–Dalton criterion of transfers (normative); and condition (iii) is an evaluation function (normative) or, dually, the measurement of the degree of inequality of a distribution (descriptive).

10.3 Multidimensional majorization

We now review the abstract problem of modeling and measuring multidimensional inequality. Let us suppose that the components of the two distributions x and y are points in $\mathbb{R}^m$, that is column vectors. In this case x, y become matrices that we denote with capital letters:

$$X = (x_1^n, \ldots, x_m^n),$$

where x_i^n are all column vectors of length n. Recalling the notion of *T-transform*, the following definition expresses the idea that X is *more spread out* than Y:

Definition 10.4. *Let X and Y be $n \times m$ matrices. Then X is said to be chain majorized by Y, written $X \prec\prec Y$, if $X = PY$ where P is a product of finitely many $n \times n$ T-transforms.*

In other terms, the idea of transfer introduced by Muirhead (1903) and Dalton (1920) also applies if the components of x and y are vectors. In fact, if we replace y_i and y_j by x_i and x_j in order to obtain a new vector x from y, under the constraints:

(i) x_i, x_j lie in the convex hull of y_i, y_j;
(ii) $x_i + x_j = y_i + y_j$.

then:

Definition 10.5. *If X and Y are two $n \times m$ matrices, then X is said to be majorized by Y, written $X \prec Y$, if $X = PY$, where P is an $n \times n$ doubly stochastic matrix.*

Because a product of *T-transforms* is doubly stochastic, then *chain majorization* implies *majorization,* $Y \prec\prec X \Rightarrow Y \prec X$ and when $n = 1$, as when $m = 2$, the converse is also true. In general, for $n \geq 2$ and $m \geq 3$ *majorization* does not imply *chain majorization*. This is the first major difference with respect to the univariate case, where, as we said earlier, a bistochastic matrix can be decomposed as a finite product of T-transforms. Definition 10.4 simply says that the average is a smoothing operation, that makes the components of X more *spread out* than those of Y.

If we define the convex hull of a generic matrix Y denoted

$$H = co\{(y_i^1, \ldots, y_i^n), \ i = 1, \ldots, m)\},$$

as the convex combination of the row vectors of the matrix, then an equivalent definition of the *majorization* $\prec$ is as follows:

Definition 10.6. *Let $X, Y \in \mathbb{R}^{n \times m}$ be two matrices, then we say X contains a lower level of inequality with respect to Y, if X lies in the convex hull of all permutation of Y.*

In a multidimensional setting, a result corresponding to Theorem 10.2 is unknown, and little is known about functions that preserve the ordering $\prec$. The difficulty in characterizing functions preserving $\prec$ lies in the fact that there is no stepwise path result like Muirhead's condition (i) quoted above (p. 271). Rinott (1973) characterized the class of functions preserving the ordering $\prec\prec$. Finally, we know that if $X \prec Y$, then $\sum_1^n \varphi(x_i^C) \leq \sum_1^n \varphi(y_i^C)$ for all continuous concave functions $\varphi : \mathbb{R}^m \to \mathbb{R}$, where z_i^C is a column vector of length m (see Marshall and Olkin (1979), chapter 15). Not much more than this is known about multivariate order-preserving functions.

Another notion of matrix majorization, important in economics, is that of *price majorization*. It was proposed by Marshall and Olkin (1979) as an open problem. Formally:

Definition 10.7. *For two matrices X and Y, X is said to be price (or directionally) majorized by Y, written $X \prec_d Y$, if $aX \prec aY$ for all $a \in \mathbb{R}^n$.*

Marshall and Olkin (1979) showed that $X \prec Y$ implies $X \prec_d Y$, in a more general setting, where $X \prec_d Y$ means $XA \prec YA$ for all $A \in \mathbb{R}^{m \times k}$ (for fixed k). They posed the open question whenever $X \prec_d Y$ implies $X \prec X$. In an important paper, Bhandari (1988) gave the sufficient conditions under which directional majorization implies multivariate majorization, by showing the following:

Theorem 10.3. *Suppose every column vector of $Y \in \mathbb{R}^{n \times m}$ is an extreme point in the convex hull generated by the columns of X, which has r-dimensional positive volume, and at least $(m - r + 2)$ of these column vectors are co-planner.*[4] *Then $X \prec_d Y$ implies $X \prec Y$ for all X. Moreover, $XP \prec YP$ for all $P \in \mathbb{R}^{m \times k}$ implies $X \prec Y$.*

What Bandhari (1988) called directional majorization is called *majorization through linear combination* by Joe and Verducci (1993) and *price majorization* by economists such as Kolm (1977). Indeed, when a distribution X is more equal than distribution Y, that is $X \prec Y$, each Lorenz curve of X lies nowhere under that of each one of Y for all price vectors p (which can be restricted to nonnegative prices), and if they are not permutations of each other. This implies that all the properties reviewed above for the unidimensional case hold between income distributions derived from Y and X, that is, $pX \prec pY$, whatever the prices used for this aggregation.

The notion of price majorization is very useful for comparing nonmonetary quantities. In such a case, we evaluate the disparity associated with the matrices with qualitative components (e.g. health, education, etc.), simply by assigning a price to all the entries. Unfortunately, individual characteristics are thus reduced to monetary quantities, losing information.

In order to express the idea of multidimensional inequality in an economic framework, we now consider the rows of a matrix to represent individuals endowed with several attributes (the columns), which describe the welfare of a society. Comparison of matrices according to an inequality criterion is how economic literature provides solutions to the problem of measuring inequality in a multivariate context.

10.4 Measuring multidimensional inequality in economics

We now consider the case in which attributes other than income (e.g. health, education, talent, capabilities, etc.) characterize a population of individuals. The classical literature on inequality measurement, that depicts the disparity of an attribute in a given population, considers income as a useful proxy of individual welfare. Nevertheless, Kolm (1977), Atkinson and Bourguignon (1982) and many others have shown that this kind of approach is very unsatisfactory, because people differ in many aspects besides income. To rank individuals who differ in many attributes, the economic literature has historically followed two different trends. The first ranks different multivariate distributions according to a social welfare function (typically Atkinson and Bourguignon, 1982 and Kolm, 1977). The second uses evaluative summary inequality statistics (Gajdos and Weymark, 2005; Maasoumi, 1986; Tsui, 1995), measuring individual attributes with a utility function. In this way, it obtains an univariate distribution vector of utilities that are valued using an inequality index. Both approaches present certain problems, as pointed out by Dardanoni (1992). More recently, a third elegant approach was developed by Koshevoy and Mosler (1995, 1998, 1999, 1996), who introduced some tools of 'convex analysis' to evaluate the inequality of a multidimensional distribution. In what follows, we review the main results of these three approaches.

10.4.1 Ranking matrices by means of social welfare functions

As individuals vary in income, needs, education, sex, age, ability etc., welfare comparisons must be based on application of evaluation functions expressing the multiattribute endowments of people. We start by considering the seminal paper of

Kolm (1977), who introduced the question: "When is one multivariate distribution more spread out than another one?" into economics. Kolm records the notion of multidimensional inequality by means of a social welfare function (SWF)

$$W : \mathbb{R}_{+}^{n\times m} \rightarrow \mathbb{R},$$

defined on the set of all semi-definite rectangular matrices. In our terminology, a SWF is an order-preserving function with certain properties. Kolm also introduced the notion of majorization $\prec$ and proposed another notion of matrix majorization.

Let us consider a generic matrix X with rows $x_1^R, \ldots, x_m^R$:

Definition 10.8. *For each $X, Y \in \mathbb{R}_{+}^{n\times m}$, X is said to be row-wise majorized by Y, denoted $X \prec_{\text{row}} Y$ if and only if there exists a doubly stochastic matrix P such that $x_i^R = y_i^R P$ for $i = 1, \ldots, n$.*

$X \prec_{\text{row}} Y$ can also be written:

$$(x_1^R, \ldots, x_n^R) = (y_1^R, \ldots, y_n^R) \begin{bmatrix} P & 0 & \ldots & 0 \\ 0 & P & \ldots & 0 \\ . & . & . & . \\ 0 & 0 & \ldots & P \end{bmatrix}. \tag{10.6}$$

This implies that:

$$x_i^R \preceq y_i^R \quad \text{for each} \quad i = 1, \ldots, n, \tag{10.7}$$

where majorization $\preceq$ is in the sense of Definition 10.1. As P may be the product of a finite number of *T-transforms*, *$\prec$-majorization* presumably implies 10.6 and 10.7, however it only implies that there exist doubly stochastic matrices $P_1, \ldots, P_m$ such that $x_i^R = y_i^R P_i, i = 1, \ldots, m$. It does not guarantee that $P_i = P_j \forall i \neq j$, (see Marshall and Olkin, 1979, chapter 15).

The main criticism to the approach based on SWF for evaluating multidimensional disparity relies on the fact that the results obtained in this setting generally hold for the case in which interrelations between welfare components are assumed to be irrelevant for inequality comparisons. To the contrary, these interrelations are very important, as Atkinson and Bourguignon (1982) and Rietveld (1990) have shown.

Atkinson and Bourguignon (1982) studied the inequality comparisons by means of stochastic dominance. They concentrated on the two-dimensioned case in particular and applied some results on multivariate stochastic dominance for portfolio theory to the measurement of inequality.[5] Generalizing the results on unidimensional Lorenz ordering, they analyzed how different forms of deprivation (such as low income, low education, low standard of living, etc.), tend to be associated. They used a SWF[6] to evaluate the welfare associated with different *named vectors* x^i,[7] that is, vectors that represent the percentage of the total quantity of the i-th commodity allocated to the j-th individual, and investigated the implications of different assumptions about the form of the SWF and the different degrees of interdependence between the elements of x^i.

Rietveld (1990) deals with (issues of) inequality decompositions of income factor components. He investigates correlations between the various components of income by means of the Lorenz criterion. Indeed, he shows that if we define the Lorenz curves for each component of individual income characteristics, we find that inequality in total income is no greater than that of the most unequal component. It follows, in general, that the Lorenz curve of total income is above the weighted mean of Lorenz curves of income components. Hence, there exists a sort of *aggravation effect* caused by considering a correlation between different components of income. Moreover, measuring the inequality of a (given) distribution by a function $f : \mathbb{R}^n \to \mathbb{R}$ homogeneous and Schur-concave, Rietvield shows that joint consideration of income components leads to a *mitigation* of inequality of total income for a broad class of inequality measures, homogeneous of degree 0, which can be written as the sum of concave functions. However, this does not hold in general. If we consider, for example, the Gini coefficient, it is possible to show that it has the inequality mitigation property, but it cannot be written as a sum of concave functions. Rietveld claims that homogeneity and Schur-concavity are not sufficient conditions for the inequality mitigation property in a multidimensional context. He therefore concludes that interrelations between welfare components are relevant for inequality comparisons.

In the literature on measurement of multidimensional inequality via SWF, the work of Mosler (1991) is of interest. Mosler considered several attributes in describing individual social states as well as several criteria of evaluation. Welfare comparisons are based on simultaneous application of a set of social evaluation functions, depending on the multiattribute endowments of individuals. Mosler used social evaluation functions which can be represented as the sum of evaluation functions of individual states, in order to compare individual welfare levels in a purely ordinalistic framework. The approach is axiomatic and some partial multidimensional welfare orderings are introduced and a selected class of social evaluation functions is shown to be coherent with such orderings. The originality of this work lies in its new approach to multidimensional welfare orderings. Since social states have limited comparability under an ordinalistic setup, Mosler proposed comparison of individual endowments with respect to a critical level, that is, a minimum endowment in commodities (a sort of threshold).

10.4.2 Multidimensional inequality indices[8]

We now study the properties of multidimensional evaluative inequality statistics. According to this approach, people are first represented by an aggregate utility function of all attributes (they received by chance). A univariate distribution of utilities is thus obtained. A standard inequality index is then applied to the utility distribution to obtain a multidimensional inequality evaluation.

Definition 10.9. *A multidimensional inequality index can be written as a function of the real valued vector* $U_1(x_1), \ldots, U_n(x_n)$, *where* $U_i(\cdot) : \mathbb{R}^m \to \mathbb{R}$ *denotes an individual utility function and* x_j *a row of the* $n \times m$ *matrix* X.

This exercise involves two issues. First we have to choose a utility function. This is an arbitrary choice. To select one function rather than another means stressing the preferences of certain individuals and disregarding other evaluative spaces that could be very important. Secondly, we have to aggregate the vector of individual utilities into a real-valued inequality index, which means loss of information.

Appealing to a criterion from information theory, Maasoumi (1986) argued that when the distribution of welfare is the primary concern of the analysis, the class of functions of Generalized Entropy (whence many of the popular utility functions employed in economics), is the best solution to the first issue mentioned earlier. Following Kolm's approach (1977), he considers a matrix Y that represents a society of n individuals, endowed with m commodities.[9] Multiplying a matrix Y by a bistochastic matrix P, he obtains a new matrix X that should be declared more equal on the basis of any summary inequality index. This claim is based on an argument discussed by Kolm (1977), who noticed that a doubly stochastic transformation is a necessary and sufficient condition for unambiguous improvement in the welfare of a multivariate distribution. However, as Dardanoni (1992) noticed, in a multidimensional context, the effects of bistochastic transformation are sometimes ambiguous. In fact, he showed that rearranging components of a 3×3 matrix, (i.e. 3 individuals endowed with 3 attributes):

$$Y = \begin{bmatrix} 100 & 1 & 1 \\ 1 & 90 & 100 \\ 90 & 100 & 90 \end{bmatrix},$$

by means of a doubly stochastic matrix, we could obtain a new matrix:

$$Y' = \begin{bmatrix} 1 & 1 & 1 \\ 90 & 90 & 90 \\ 100 & 100 & 100 \end{bmatrix},$$

the rows of which represent an uneven allocation of attributes. Unfortunately, this is not the conclusion reached by application of any multivariate inequality index. There are SWF, belonging to Maasoumi's General Entropy class of functions, which show a decreasing inequality after an unfair rearrangement of this type. Dardanoni (1992) shows that a social welfare function must be additively separable in its utility components, if we want it to be decreasing from Y to Y'. However, as Fishburn (1988) has shown, this is not a suitable representation of individual preferences, and such a requirement is in contradiction with the evaluation of individual welfare when there are correlations between attributes of a distribution.

The Maasoumi's two-stage approach to designing a class of multidimensional inequality measures is also used by Tsui (1995, 1999) to axiomatically characterize the class of Atkinson-Kolm-Sen inequality indices and that of Shorrocks (1984). Gajdos and Weymark (2005), who generalize the class of Gini indices to a multidimensional context, reverse Maasoumi's procedure by first aggregating the distributions of each attribute and then aggregating the values, obtained in the first step, into an overall evaluation.

10.4.3 Multivariate Lorenz majorization and Gini index

The joint work of Koshevoy and Mosler warrants a special mention. Using the approach of Rado (1952), they introduced *convex analysis* into the field of multivariate majorization. In his seminal paper, Koshevoy (1995) considered a population with n agents among which a set of goods is distributed, and a distribution matrix $X = (x_{ij}) \in \mathbb{R}_+^{n \times m}$ which assigns its annual vector of goods to the i-th agent. He (1995) poses the following question: "*Given two distribution matrices X and Y, which one contains the lower level of disparity?*". To answer the question, Koshevoy generalizes the notion of Lorenz curve through that of convex body, that is, a convex polyhedron in $\mathbb{R}_+^m$, which constitutes a Lorenz curve in the $m + 1$ dimensional space. The multivariate generalization of the Lorenz curve is called *Lorenz zonotope*, and denoted as LZ (X). The multivariate Lorenz criterion is thus:

Definition 10.10. *Let X and Y be two matrices, then X is said to be Lorenz majorized by Y, denoted as* $X \preceq_{LO} Y$, *if* $\mathrm{LZ}(X) \subseteq \mathrm{LZ}(Y)$.

Koshevoy (1995) shows that the notion of Lorenz majorization is equivalent to that of price majorization. According to Bhandari [3], as price majorization $\prec_d$ is equivalent to majorization $\prec$, we should expect that majorization $\prec$ is tantamount to Lorenz majorization $\prec_{\mathrm{LO}}$. But this is not true. Majorization $\prec$ implies Lorenz majorization, but in the multidimensional case, the contrary does not hold, because multivariate Lorenz is not consistent with the assumption of separability across attributes. Adopting an argument similar to that of Dardanoni (1992) to criticize Maasoumi's two-stage approach, Koshevoy notices that $X \preceq_{\mathrm{LO}} Y$ does not hold when we restrict our attention to any submatrix of X and Y characterized by fewer attributes than m. In words, $X \preceq_{\mathrm{LO}} Y$ does not imply $X^M \preceq_{\mathrm{LO}} Y^M$, with Z^M any submatrix of n rows and s columns with $s < m \in M = \{1, \ldots, m\}$, the set of all attributes considered.

In (1998), Koshevoy extends the notion of Lorenz zonotope through that of cone ordering[10] by developing a geometric approach to the study of the multidimensional inequality. By interpreting the coordinates of a direction in a cone as the weights (prices) of individual attributes, the cone extension of multidimensional Lorenz majorization can be shown to be equivalent to the cone extension of the price majorization, where a distribution is said to be cone price majorized by another if the expenditures of households at any price in a cone with the first distribution are less dispersed than with the other. This geometric approach to multidimensional inequality has the advantage that the set of matrices majorized by a given matrix can be described by a finite number of inequalities using the notion of cone ordering. In the case of a cone with a finite number of extreme rays, checking for cone price majorization is therefore equivalent to verifying univariate dispersion of household expenditure for a finite number of prices (directions).

Koshevoy and Mosler (1999) studied extensions of the Gini mean difference and Gini index to the measurement of disparity of populations endowed with several attributes. They investigate two approaches, one based on a notion of distance, the other on the volume of a convex set in $(m + 1)$-space. They (1999) showed that several properties, that hold for the univariate case, follow easily from the definitions of distance Gini mean difference and distance Gini index for the multivariate case. This result is important since the Gini index is the most widely used measure of unidimensional inequality.

Finally, Koshevoy and Mosler (1996) extended the notions of Lorenz curve and Lorenz order to several attributes of multivariate *empirical* distributions. They generalized the usual Lorenz curve to the multivariate situation, using the notion of zonoid, namely the set of all points between the graph of the dual multivariate Lorenz function and the graph of the multivariate Lorenz function. The Lorenz zonoid is a closed convex subset of the unit hypercube in $\mathbb{R}^{m+1}$. It is a convex polytope for a discrete distribution. Two multivariate empirical distributions are therefore ranked by the inclusion of Lorenz zonoids. The set inclusion criterion of Lorenz zonoids is equivalent to a well-defined notion of price majorization between multidimensional empirical distributions.

10.5 Conclusion and further possible extensions

We have reviewed how to rank matrices, that represent the distribution of goods and commodities among people, using a SWF. We noted that this operation generally loses information or strongly restricts the class of evaluation functions. We surveyed some results on multidimensional inequality indices, synthetic measures of the degree of disparity among individuals. Applying a multidimensional inequality index means reducing all variables we want to evaluate to scalars which defeats the aim of our research, namely to analyze inequality when several attributes besides income characterize individuals. Finally, we considered the work of Koshevoy and Mosler, who extended the notion of Lorenz ordering to a multidimensional context, using tools of convex analysis. The outcome is analytically sophisticated, but the results are not so different from those of theory of majorization. Much work remains to be done, including analysis of different possible kinds of transfers between matrices of individuals-characteristics and characterization of order-preserving functions for matrix majorization $\prec$.

Notes

1 Strictly speaking, the Lorenz (dominance) criterion is a preorder because, instead of antisymmetry, only the following weaker condition holds: $x \prec y$ and $y \prec x$ together implies that x is a permutation of the elements of y and then $x = y$.

2 Note that condition (ii) is equivalent to conditions (10.1) and (10.2) in Definition 1.

3 Dasgupta *et al.* (1973) extended this result to the class of S-concave functions.

4 The assumption that at least $(m-r+2)$ of X_i's columns are co-planner means that they belong to a two-dimensional affine space of $\mathbb{R}^m$.
5 Technically, the comparison of bivariate distributions they provide in Atkinson and Bourguiguon (1982), occurs on the basis of differences in their expected utility and of the properties of the social welfare function assessing multivariate inequality.
6 The SWFs are assumed to be addively separable and symmetric with respect to the individuals.
7 The term "named good" is first used by Hahn (1971) in the analysis of equilibrium with transaction costs.
8 For a wide survey of the topic, see Weymark (in this volume).
9 Note that Maasoumi (1982) extends this approach by considering the case in which several attributes are continuously distributed and Maasoumi and Zandvakili (1990) apply this framework to the measurement of mobility.
10 See Marshall and Olkin (1979) for a formal definition of what a cone ordering is.

References

Atkinson, A.B. (1970). "On the measurement of inequality." *Journal of Economic Theory* 2, 244–263.

Atkinson, A.B. and F. Bourguignon (1982). "The comparison of multidimensioned distributions of economic status." *Review of Economic Studies* 39, 183–201.

Bhandari, S.K. (1988). "Multivariate majorization and directional majorization: positive results." *Sankhyā: The Indian Journal of Statistics* 50, 199–204.

Dalton, H. (1920). "The measurement of inequality." *Economic Journal* 20, 348–361.

Dardanoni, V. (1992). "On multidimensional inequality measurement." In: Dagum, C. and Lemmi, A. (eds), *Income Distribution, Social Welfare, Inequality,and Poverty. Vol. 6 of Research on Economic Inequality*. JAI Press, Stamford, CT, pp. 201–207.

Dasgupta, P., A.K. Sen and D. Starret (1973). "Notes on the measurement of inequality". *Journal of Economic Theory* 6, 180–187.

Fishburn, P.C. (1988). *Nonlinear Preferences and Utility Theory*. Baltimore, MD, Johns Hopkins University Press.

Gajdos, T. and J.A. Weymark (2005). "Multidimensional generalized Gini indices." *Economic Theory* 26, 471–496.

Hahn, F.H. (1971). "Equilibrium with transaction costs ." *Econometrica* 39(3), 417–439.

Hardy, G.H., J.E. Littlewood and G. Polya (1934, 1952). *Inequalities*. Cambridge University Press, London.

Joe, H. and J. Verducci (1993). "Multivariate majorization by positive combination." In: *Stochastic Inequalities IMS Lecture Notes:* Monograph Series, vol. 22, pp. 159–181.

Kolm, S.C. (1969). "The optimal production of social justice." In: J. Margolis and H. Guitton (eds), *Public Economics*. Macmillan, London and St. Martin's Press, New York, pp. 145–200.

Kolm, S.C. (1977). "Multidimensional egalitarianism." *Quarterly Journal of Economics* 91, 1–13.

Koshevoy, G. (1995). "Multivariate Lorenz majorization." *Social Choice and Welfare* 12, 93–102.

Koshevoy, G. (1998). "The Lorenz zonotope and multivariate majorizations." *Social Choice and Welfare* 15, 1–14.

Koshevoy, G. and K. Mosler (1996). "The Lorenz zonoid of a multivariate distribution." *Journal of American Statistical Association* 91, 873–882.

Koshevoy, G. and K. Mosler (1999). "Multivariate Gini indices." *Journal of Multivariate Analysis* 53, 112–126.

Lorenz, M.O. (1905). "Methods for measuring concentration of wealth." *Journal of American Statistical Association* 9, 209–219.

Maasoumi, E. (1986). "The measurement and decomposition of multidimensional inequality." *Econometrica* 54, 991–997.

Maasoumi, E. (1989). "Continuously distributed attributes and measures of multivariate inequality." *Journal of Econometrics* 42, 131–144.

Maasoumi, E. and S. Zandvakili (1990). "Generalized entropy measures of mobility for different sexes and income levels." *Journal of Econometrics* 43, 121–134.

Marshall, A.W. and I. Olkin, (1979). *Inequalities: Theory of Majorization and its Applications*. Academic Press, New York.

Mosler, K. (1991). "Multidimensional welfarism." In Eichhorn, W. (ed.), *Models and Measurement of Welfare and Inequality*. Berlin, Springer-Verlag, pp. 808–820.

Muirhead, R.F. (1903). "Some methods applicable to identities and inequalities of symmetric algebraic functions of *n* letters." *Proceedings of Edinburgh Mathematical Society* 21, 144–157.

Ostrowski, A.M. (1952) "Sur quelques applications des functions convexes et concaves au sens de I. Schur." *Journal of Math. Pures App.* 31, 253–292.

Rado, R. (1952). "An inequality." *Journal of London Mathematical Society* 27, 1–6.

Rietveld, P. (1990). "Multidimensional inequality comparisons." *Economics Letters* 32, 187–192.

Rinott, Y. (1973). "Multivariate majorization and rearrangement inequalities with some applications to probability and statistics." *Israel Journal of Mathematics* 15, 60–77.

Schur, I. (1923). "Uber eine Klasse von Mittelbildungen mit Anwendungen die Determinanten." *Theorie Sitzungsber Berlin Matematische Gesellschaft* 22, 9–20 (*Issai Schur Collected Works* (A. Brauer and H. Rohrbach (eds)) vol.II. pp. 416–427, Springer-Verlag, Berlin, 1973).

Sen, A.K. (1997). *On Economic Inequality* (Second eds), extended edition with J. Foster, Oxford, Clarendon Press.

Sen, A.K (1980). "Equality of what?" In: McMurrin, S. (ed.), *Tunner Lectures on Human Values*, vol. 1, Cambridge, Cambridge University Press.

Shorrocks, A.F. (1984). "Inequality decomposition by population subgroups." *Econometrica* 52, 1369–1385.

Tsui, K.Y. (1995). "Multidimensional generalizations of the relative and absolute inequality indices: The Atkinson-Kolm-Sen approach." *Journal of Economic Theory* 67, 251–265.

Tsui, K.Y. (1999). "Multidimensional inequality and multidimensional generalized entropy measures: an axiomatic derivation." *Social Choice and Welfare* 16, 145–157.

Weymark, J.A. "The normative approach to the measurement of multidimensional inequality." This volume.

11 Multidimensional egalitarianism and the dominance approach

A lost paradise?

Alain Trannoy

11.1 Introduction

Although the properties meanings and limits of the Lorenz dominance criterion are now well understood in the univariate case (see, for example, Atkinson, 1970; Kolm, 1969; Sen, 1973) by the theorists and by the practitioners (see for instance, the diverse entries in the *Handbook of Income Distribution* (Atkinson and Bourguignon, 2000)), it is not the case for its various extensions to a multi-attribute context. However, the pressure is growing for such extensions, thanks to the widespread accessibility of data bases where the description of individual units is plural. Besides, a consensus is emerging among many scientists, particularly development economists, about the multidimensional aspect of individual well-being which cannot be reduced to a unique monetary dimension. The economists' awareness of this multiplicity traces back to the ethical analysis of Rawls (1971) and Sen (1985, 1987, 1992). The lack of health attributes in any study on poverty now appears as a major drawback. Education appears as another important dimension which is even more complex to apprehend owing to its impact on income streams in dynamics. It is important to stress that many additional aspects of well-being may not be compared on a true cardinal basis and often a ranking of individuals with respect to these non-pecuniary aspects is the only material to work with. Despite the fact that we are aware of this paucity of information, it is assumed in the following that all attributes are given a cardinal meaning. A solid defense (at least for a review) of such a line comes from the fact that very little is known in a true ordinal setting (see however Allison and Foster (1999)).

As the title suggests, we will focus on dominance criteria of the Lorenz type, since John Weymark provides a complementary review of ethical measures of inequality in a multidimensional context in this volume. The gains ensued by a dominance approach come from the robustness of the obtained rankings. A fairly large range of opinions is compatible with the results. Underterminacy is the price to pay for this benefit. When we are unable to conclude in the comparison between two distributions, it signals a conflict between the points of views captured by the dominance test. The art of dominance analysis is to find classes of opinions which balance the lack of discriminative power with the benefit provided by a larger robustness of the conclusion. A sensible way to proceed in any empirical work starts with dominance criteria before pursuing the analysis with some well-defined indices.

It is important to recall that the dominance approach is associated with four points of view. To a welfare economist, a distribution of attributes appeals to some social welfare function which expresses some value judgements in an explicit manner. To a social scientist, who is not always well-disposed with the apparatus of welfare economics for good and bad reasons, a more direct approach through the transfers to be performed among individuals, in order to be closer to an equal distribution, seems more palatable. It appears to be a natural way to proceed for assessing the deviation between the actual distribution and perfect equality. To a public finance economist, the amount to be given to the poor in order to reach some target in terms of income appears as a way to measure the importance of poverty or inequality from a purely financial point of view. The two first approaches are not implementable since they lead to checking an infinity of conditions. To an applied economist, the more important aspect of dominance approach lies in the user friendly implementation test and in the statistical packages enabling to crash numbers quickly. It is worth stressing that this last aspect is not the least, since it likely commands the success of the dominance tool among the practitioners. The peculiar character of the implementation test relatively to other ones lies in the finite number of steps to be checked. The miracle of the Hardy–Littlewood–Polya theorem make identical all these four approaches in a one dimensional setting. Comparing distributions according to an additive separable social welfare function with concave utilities or to the sequence of Pigou–Dalton's progressive transfers lead exactly to the same conclusion as resorting to Lorenz curves or computing the amount of aggregate poverty gaps.

Ultimately, the game consists in finding again such a neat equivalence in the multidimensional setting. Yet, as it has been understood for some time, and well anticipated by Marshall and Olkin (1979), it is considerably harder to obtain such an equivalence in a multidimensional framework than in one dimension. The equivalence between the transfer approach and the others seems particularly intricate, as exemplified for instance by the investigation of Joe and Verducci (1993) for price dominance.

Without dispute this time, Kolm article (1977) can be regarded as the first one to touch upon these issues of multidimensional dominance criteria. His main idea, to reduce a multidimensional problem into a unidimensional one, was not an importation from the literature on stochastic dominance which, albeit useful, has followed another path (see, for example, Huang *et al.*, 1978; Levhari *et al.*, 1975). It is likely that the attributes considered in the analysis have no true market prices. Anyway, one can sum up the situation of an individual by the value of the required budget to afford his bundle, using some shadow price vector. For given prices, we are back to the comparison of a one-dimension distribution. Since the shadow price vector is unknown, Kolm proposes to say that a distribution of attributes is more unequal than another if the distribution of expenditures is more unequal with the Lorenz criterion for any positive shadow price vector. First, we shall review this line of research which has been deepened by Koshevoy and Mosler in a bunch of papers.

We then divide the remaining literature in two strands. The attributes are given a symmetrical role in the first one, for which the leading article has been done by Atkinson and Bourguignon (1982). The crucial idea introduced here is that of complementarity or substitutability between attributes, which may be expressed as a social taste either for increasing correlation or for decreasing correlation. The two mentioned authors limited themselves to the correspondence between stochastic dominance conditions and the welfare interpretation of the value judgements. The transfers principles underlying these dominance criteria have been introduced by Moyes (1999).

One may oppose this avenue of research to a second one for which an attribute, let us say income, is given a special role owing to its transferability. The intuition behind this line of research comes from the empirical evidence that money is extensively used to compensate for deficiencies in other characteristics in everyday life. Hence, principles of transfers are more easily assessed when they involve transfers of income to compensate health deficiencies than the opposite. We probably agree that the closest to true situations the principles are, the better founded the dominance criterion is. To refer to thought experiment is always an ersatz for a true one. It turns out that an asymmetric point of view deliver specific recommendations which are not captured by the symmetric one. Atkinson and Bourguignon (1987), in a different context, opens the way to this asymmetric view. They are looking for dominance criteria when the statistical units (families) cannot be considered to have the same need. Need has a special status in their analysis, it is just a parameter which distinguishes families. Muller and Trannoy (2003a) plug the asymmetric character of need and income into a truly multidimensional framework.

The chapter consists of four sections. Section 11.2 questions the approach which has been called the price majorization in the statistical area which we here prefer to term *budget* dominance. Section 11.3 presents the results obtained with the symmetric approach. Section 11.4 deals with the asymmetric one, where we borrow from Muller and Trannoy (2003a).

11.2 Budget dominance

We consider the classical model of an exchange economy with n individuals identified by $i = 1, \ldots, n$ and l attributes denoted by $j = 1, \ldots, l$. $N = \{1, \ldots, n\}$ is the set of individuals, and $L = \{1, \ldots, l\}$ the set of attributes. It is assumed that any attribute is experienced as a good thing. An allocation is described by a non-negative matrix $x = (x_{ij}) \in \mathbb{R}^{nl}_{+}$ with n rows and l columns. The row x_i is the endowment of the ith individual, and the column x_j gives the distribution of jth attribute among the n persons.

Comparisons of vectors are denoted as follows: $x_i \geq y_i$ if $x_{ij} \geq x'_{ij}$ for all j, $x_i > x'_i$ if $x_{ij} \geq x'_{ij}$ for all j and $x_i \neq x'_i$, $x_i \gg x'_i$ if $x_{ij} > x'_{ij}$ for all j. For any vector $y \in \mathbb{R}^n_+$, $(y_{(1)}, \ldots, y_{(n)})$ denotes the rearrangement of y such that $y_{(1)} \leq \cdots \leq y_{(n)}$.

Following Sen (1970), we call quasi-ordering a reflexive and transitive binary relation, and ordering a complete quasi-ordering. For the sake of completeness, we recall the definition of the relative Lorenz dominance criterion.

Definition 11.1. *Given $y, y' \in R^n_+$ of means μ_y and $\mu_{y'}$, y dominates y' according to the Relative Lorenz criterion, denoted $y \succcurlyeq_{\mathrm{RL}} y'$, iff*

$$\frac{1}{n}\sum_{i=1}^{k}\frac{y_{(i)}}{\mu_{\mathbf{y}}} \geq \frac{1}{n}\sum_{i=1}^{k}\frac{y'_{(i)}}{\mu_{\mathbf{y}'}}, \quad \textit{for } k = 1, \ldots, n.$$

A good deal of multidimensional dominance analysis concerns 'price majorization' or 'budget majorization'[1] (see Arnold, 1987; Joe and Verducci, 1993; Marshall and Olkin, 1979; Muliere and Scarsini 1989). An allocation is viewed as more unequal than another one if the distribution of the individual budgets for the former is less unequal for the relative Lorenz criterion than the distribution of individual budgets for the latter for all non-negative price vectors.

Definition 11.2. *x is said to budget dominates x' ($x \succeq_B x'$) iff*

$$xp \succcurlyeq_{RL} x'p, \quad \forall p \in \mathbb{R}^l_+.$$

In other terms, the distribution of resources becomes less spread according to the Lorenz test, no matter what values are assigned to resources. Sometimes in the statistical literature (see for example, Bhandari, 1988; Marshall and Olkin, 1979) the qualification of a non-negative price is dropped. Since we have restricted the attributes to be goods, this generalization is unnecessary here. Two questions may be asked for this criterion as for any other one. First, is it possible to check dominance according to this criterion in a finite number of steps? Second, what is the ethical background beneath this criterion, which at first glance looks fine at least for an economist? These two questions are addressed successively.

11.2.1 A generalization of the Lorenz curve

Koshevoy (1995, 1998), and this author with Mosler in two papers (1996, 1999) gave several answers to the first question in generalizing the concept of a Lorenz curve in a multidimensional setting. I will select the answer contained in their latest paper, unfortunately unpublished yet.

The Lorenz curve in the univariate case plots the cumulated proportion of income received by the cumulated proportion of the poorest people. The usual Lorenz curve can also be seen as the graph of the *inverse* Lorenz function: given a proportion of the total income, the inverse Lorenz function indicates the maximum percentage of the population that receives this proportion. In the multivariate case, the analogue is to consider a share of the total endowment in each attribute and to determine the largest proportion of the population which hold these shares.

Let s an element of $[0, 1]^l$ designate a vector of shares and $\bar{x}_{ij} = x_{ij}/\sum_i x_{ij}$ the individual shares. The definition of the inverse Lorenz function reads as follows, where W stands for a set of vectors of individual weights $W = \{w \in [0, 1]^l\}$.

Definition 11.3. *Let x be an allocation. The inverse Lorenz function of x is the function $l_x : [0, 1]^l \longrightarrow [0, 1]$, such that*

$$l_x(s) = \max_{w \in W} \left\{ \frac{1}{n} \sum_{i=1}^{n} w_i \middle| \frac{1}{n} \sum_{i=1}^{n} w_i \bar{x}_{ij} \leq s \right\} \tag{11.1}$$

For any vector of global shares, the inverse Lorenz function gives the maximum percentage of the population holding them. This percentage is computed as an average of individual weights. They are constrained to be identical, whatever the attributes and they enter in a weighted average of individual shares which must be at most equal to the global shares.

Albeit it looks like a bit complicated at first glance, the computation of these weights corresponds to what we do in order to draw the usual piecewise linear Lorenz curve for a discrete distribution. For instance, if the one dimensional allocation is (4, 6, 10), the computation of individual weights solution of the optimization program (1) gives

$$\text{For any } s \in \left[0, \tfrac{1}{5}\right], w = (5s, 0, 0)$$
$$\text{For any } s \in \left[\tfrac{1}{5}, \tfrac{1}{2}\right], w = \left(1, \tfrac{10}{3}\left(s - \tfrac{1}{5}\right), 0\right)$$
$$\text{For any } s \in \left[\tfrac{1}{2}, 1\right], w = \left(1, 1, 2\left(s - \tfrac{1}{2}\right)\right).$$

The above definition allows us to systematize this method to a multidimensional setting. We refer to the quoted paper for further properties of the inverse Lorenz function. Theorem 4.1 in that paper gives the solution to test budget dominance.

Proposition 11.1 (Koshevoy and Mosler, 1999). *Let x and x' two allocations. $x \succeq_B x'$ iff $l_{x'}(s) \geq l_x(s)$ for all $s \in [0, 1]^l$.*

Then an allocation x budget dominates an allocation x' if the graph of the inverse Lorenz function for x stands below that of x' for any vector of attribute shares, that is, the maximum percentage of people who hold a vector less or equal to s is always larger in the dominated distribution than in the dominant one. This theorem constitutes a great achievement in allowing to generalize the Lorenz quasi-ordering to a multidimensional setting in a palatable way. When there are only two dimensions, we keep the advantage of visualizing the disparity inherent in a given distribution.

11.2.2 A flavour of quasi-concavity

Regarding the second question, we are short of a full and satisfying answer, since a complete characterization of this quasi-ordering through either elementary transformations or social welfare functions is still missing (see, however Joe and Verducci (1993) for elementary transformations[2]). I will just point out a property satisfied by budget dominance which casts doubt on its appropriateness to our requirements in a multidimensional setting. More specifically, I would like to argue it requires a property that is not needed.

Consider a matrix x where each row is identical up to a permutation of the attributes, that is for any $i, k \in N$, there exists a permutation π on L such that $x_{ij} = x_{k\pi(j)}$ for any $j \in L$. Now consider an allocation x' which is the same as x, except that a row corresponding to the allocation of some individual i has been averaged: x'_i is a convex combination of the x_{ij}. Then x' budget dominates x. It is easy to show why it is so. To give the intuition, consider an example in a 2 attributes 2 individuals context, with $\begin{pmatrix} a & b \\ b & a \end{pmatrix}$ with $b > a$ and suppose that the allocation of the first individual is averaged. W.l.o.g, we normalize prices in order that they add up to 1. For any price of the first attribute larger than $\frac{1}{2}$, the second individual is the poorest. Here, averaging leaves unchanged his wealth in absolute terms but he remains the poorest. Since the total wealth decreases, it means that the part of total wealth owned by the poorest person increases. A symmetric reasoning applies when the price of the second attribute is smaller than $\frac{1}{2}$. Then, in both cases, the relative Lorenz curves of the budget allocations in x' lies above the relative Lorenz curves of the budget allocations in x and consequently x' budget dominates x. The reasoning may be generalized without difficulty, but for our purpose this simple example is sufficient.

Is there something wrong with this property? Well, admittedly, coming from the one dimensional case where the Pigou–Dalton transfers represent the way to average incomes, there are two possible directions for averaging in a multidimensional setting. We may average in columns, that is performing what have been called by Fleurbaey and Trannoy (2003) Pigou–Dalton transfers of goods, that is, averaging the allocation of a given attribute across individuals. A good deal of multidimensional analysis consists of qualifying when it is desirable to do so, depending on the correlation between the allocations of different goods (see Atkinson and Bourguignon, 1982; Dardanoni, 1995; List, 1999; Tsui, 1999). We may also average in rows, that is averaging the allocation of a given individual across goods. This averaging has a flavour of quasi-concavity and it is open to debate if this kind of prerequisite has to be taken in account.

The discussion may be deployed along two axes. First, quasi-concavity or say the preferences for cocktails may or may be not a property of preferences, depending on the nature of the considered attributes. Second, even if it was so, should we take into account properties of individual preferences in a dominance analysis?

If the attributes are simply oranges and bananas of the first microeconomics course, then there is little doubt that quasi-concavity may be suspected as a generic property of individual preferences. Yet, for tradable goods there is little sense to consider budget dominance, since we only have to use the market price. Multidimensional analysis is generally performed on attributes such as health or education which are often non-tradable goods for many reasons. Beside moral ones, it might be the case that prices would not clear the market (to avoid cancer for instance), because the demand would be discontinuous.

Even if this intuition was proven to be wrong, and quasi-concavity was a robust property, it remains questionable to include it as a requirement in a dominance analysis. The utilitarian shape of the social objective considered in the literature does not imply any commitment to the utilitarian philosophy. The only restriction is additive separability of the social objective, and the utility functions which we refer in the sequel can be viewed as representing either the households' actual utility functions, or the decider's valuation functions embodying ethical principles such as a degree of inequality aversion. Properties of preferences have to be included, only if we favour the first interpretation. Furthermore, if a positive answer is given, the conflict between dominance and Paretianism pointed out by Fleurbaey and Trannoy (2003) arises (see, the echo in Fleurbaey, 2004, Chapter 9 in this volume.)

A last remark to close this discussion. The egalitarian allocation corresponding to the allocation x of the earlier example may be reached by averaging rows or averaging columns. We guess that there is a large support to the proposition that the most natural movement to perform this equalization is through individuals rather than through goods, were only to respect feasibility constraints. To this respect, the two other view points avoid any quasi-concavity assumptions.

11.3 Symmetric treatment of attributes

If the implementation of the dominance criterion remains unchanged when we permute the rows of the allocation matrices, then the dominance criterion is said to be symmetric. This anonymity property with respect to the set of attributes is shared by budget dominance and by the perspective put forth by Atkinson and Bourguignon in their first paper (1982), which is in tune with the models used in the stochastic dominance literature (see, for example, Hadar and Russel, 1974; Huang *et al.*, 1978; Levhari *et al.*, 1975; Levy and Paroush, 1974).

The interest of the Hardy–Littlewood–Polya theorem comes from the fact that it establishes the equivalence not only between transfers of the Pigou–Dalton type and Lorenz dominance, but also between these and welfare dominance. The notion of welfare dominance is based on additively separable social welfare functions which are symmetrical with respect to bundles: An allocation x is said to dominate another allocation x' with respect to the class $\mathcal{U}$ whenever

$$\sum_{i=1}^{n} u(x_i) \geq \sum_{i=1}^{n} u(x_i') \quad \text{for all } u \in \mathcal{U} \tag{11.2}$$

and it will be denoted $x \succeq_{\mathcal{U}} x'$. $\mathcal{U}$ will be defined by imposing a specific sign on the partials of utility functions denoted by subscripts.

This notion of dominance is usually tied to a welfarist point of view, more specifically utilitarianism. Actually, a more neutral interpretation is possible. As already mentioned earlier, the utility function u may not only represent individuals' subjective satisfaction, but may also embody a social aversion to inequality. One may even consider u as the social planner's evaluation of consumption bundles, without any direct relation with individual preferences. In other words, many philosophical approaches can be subsumed under an additively separable social welfare function of the above kind.

Let us consider some of the classes introduced by Atkinson and Bourguignon (1982). Comparatively to the budget dominance which can work with any number of attributes, one obvious limitation of the approach pioneered by these authors comes from the very limited number of attributes that are allowed. Even if theoretically, the restriction is severe, it is not sure that it is detrimental from a practical point of view. In most empirical studies, the number of attributes does not exceed three. The basic message is best understood with two attributes, $j = 1, 2$.

Among their classes of utility functions, we will pick up those which express a kind of substitutability between attributes (for detailed discussion on this issue, see Atkinson and Bourguignon (1982), Tsui (1999), List (1999), Bourguignon and Chakravarty (2003)). This is captured by a negative sign of the cross partial derivative u_{12}. The marginal utility of an attribute decreases with the level of the other. The first class

$$\mathcal{U}_{\mathrm{AB}_1} = \{u_1, u_2 \geq 0, u_{12} \leq 0\}, \tag{11.3}$$

has a flavour of first degree stochastic dominance, since concavity in any dimension is not required. Only increasingness and substitutability are imposed.

The second class is more demanding. A utility function is said to have non-increasing increments if

$$u(x + h) - u(x) \geq u(y + h) - u(y),$$

for all $x, y \in \mathbb{R}^l_+$ such that $x \leq y$, and for all $h \in \mathbb{R}^l_+$. When u is twice continuously differentiable on $\mathbb{R}^l_+$, then u has non-increasing increments if and only if $u''_{jk} \leq 0\ \forall j, k \in L$, a condition known under the label of ALEP substitutability[3] (see Chipman, 1977). When a person gets richer, marginal utility is required to decrease in each dimension. Let us define the intermediate ALEP class by

$$\mathcal{U}_{\mathrm{ALEP}} = \{u_1, u_2 \geq 0, u_{11} \leq 0, u_{22} \leq 0, u_{12} \leq 0\}.$$

The second class given by

$$\begin{aligned}\mathcal{U}_{\mathrm{AB}_2} = \{&u_1, u_2 \geq 0, u_{11} \leq 0, u_{22} \leq 0, u_{12} \leq 0,\\ &u_{121} \geq 0, u_{212} \geq 0, u_{1122} \leq 0\}\end{aligned} \tag{11.4}$$

entails ALEP substitutability and goes far beyond.

We will interpret these conditions on the cross partials at the third and fourth order in relation with what they require in terms of elementary transformations, a translation which has been done by Moyes (1999).

x is obtained from x' by an *increment of attribute* j^*, when some individual i^* has more of good $j^*, x_{i^*j^*} > x'_{i^*j^*}$ given that all other attributes levels remain fixed, $x_{ij} = x_{ij}$ for any i,j different of i^* and j^*. In a compact way, $x > x'$ implies that x is obtained from x' by at least an increment.

All the following discussion can be limited to three types of transformations, the *compensating progressive* transfers (CPT), the *favourable composite* transfers (FCT), and the *favourable composite compensating* permutations (FCCP).[4]

Consider an initial allocation x' where there exists two distinct individuals i^*, k^* such that i^* is strictly poorer in each dimension than k^*. It is not controversial to state that if k^* gives some of his endowment to i^*, in one of the two goods, others things being equal, then equality has been improved. A kind of compensation is taking place. This statement does not seem contentious as long as k^* and i^* exchange their endowment in each attribute. The ensuing definition of a compensating progressive transfer encompasses the usual Pigou–Dalton transfers as well, by allowing as a limit case that the endowments of two individuals are identical in a dimension.

Definition 11.4 (CPT). *An allocation x is obtained from an allocation $x'(x' \neq x)$ by a compensating progressive transfer of good j^* between i^* and k^* if the four following conditions are satisfied*

(1) $x_{ij} = x'_{ij}\ \forall i \neq i^*, k^*\ \forall j = 1,2$

(2) $x_{i^*j^*} + x_{k^*j^*} = x'_{i^*j^*} + x'_{k^*j^*}$

(3) $x'_{i^*j^*} \geq \max(x_{i^*j^*}, x_{k^*j^*}) \geq \min(x_{i^*j^*}, x_{k^*j^*}) \geq x'_{k^*j^*}$

(4) $x'_{i^*j} = x_{i^*j} \geq x_{k^*j} = x'_{k^*j}, \forall j \neq j^*.$

This definition seems at the core of multidimensional analysis, since slightly changes of the definition opens to other interesting concepts. If we change the third requirement of the previous definition such as it becomes,

$$\max(x_{i^*j^*}, x_{k^*j^*}) \geq x'_{i^*j^*} \geq x'_{k^*j^*} \geq \min(x_{i^*j^*}, x_{k^*j^*}),$$

other things being equal, then we get a *deteriorating regressive* transfer.

The view that there are goods and services, such as health care, housing or education, whose availability to different individuals should not depend on their income, is known as specific egalitarianism (Tobin, 1970). If we modify the fourth requirement by substituting an equality sign for an inequality sign, then we obtain the commodity-specific equalizing transfers of the Pigou–Dalton type, that is, the *progressive* transfer can be performed only if the recipient and the donor are equally supplied in other goods than j^*. A regressive transfer is a *deteriorating regressive* transfer under the same proviso.

The earlier definition is somewhat extensive in that it encompasses transpositions. More precisely, a *compensating one-dimension* permutation is a CPT where (3) becomes

$$x'_{i^*j^*} = \max(x_{i^*j^*}, x_{k^*j^*}) \geq \min(x_{i^*j^*}, x_{k^*j^*}) = x'_{k^*j^*}.$$

Whether we change (3) in $\max(x_{i^*j^*}, x_{k^*j^*}) = x'_{i^*j^*} \geq x'_{k^*j^*} = \min(x_{i^*j^*}, x_{k^*j^*})$, we get a *deteriorating one-dimension* permutation.

The following result illuminates the ethical requirement beneath the signs of the partial derivatives of the utility function for the first class of Atkinson–Bourguignon. Clearly, the prerequisites appear as a minimum.

Proposition 11.2 (Moyes, 1999[5]). *If an allocation x is derived from an allocation x' by a compensating one-dimension permutation or an increment, then $x \succeq_{\mathcal{U}_{\mathrm{AB}_1}} x'$.*

Hence, if a distribution stems from another one by a sequence of described earlier elementary transformations, it dominates the other for all utility functions belonging to the first Atkinson–Bourguignon class. The proposition says nothing of the opposite, namely, the fact that a dominant distribution for the AB_1 class may be derived from the dominated distribution through a sequence of increments and compensating one-dimension permutation.

To add concavity among the restrictions imposed on the utility functions is related to the idea of demanding an equalization of consumption in every dimension, among individuals. It is immediate to prove that

Proposition 11.3. *If an allocation x is derived from an allocation x' by a CPT or an increment, then $x \succeq_{\mathcal{U}_{\mathrm{ALEP}}} x'$.*

It remains to present the transformations which entail a gain in welfare for the second Atkinson–Bourguignon's class of utility functions. Obviously they include the previous transformations but it turns out that more complex transformations which involve at least two of the previous ones have to be added. They will be termed favourable in reference to a vocable introduced by Shorrocks and Foster (1987) with their notion of favourable composite transfer. In a one dimensional context, it combines a progressive and a regressive transfers, the former taking place lower down in the distribution than the latter, in such the way that the variance of the original distribution is not affected. Here a *favourable progressive* transfer combines a progressive transfer and a regressive one of the same magnitude. The former involves persons that are lower down that the persons involved in the latter with respect to the distribution of the other attribute. The formal definition of a favourable composite transfer reads as follows.

Definition 11.5 (FCT). *Let x and $x'(x' \neq x)$ be two allocations such that there exists two pairs of individuals $(i^*, k^*), (h^*, m^*)$ for whom the following relation holds for some j*

$$x'_{k^*j} = x'_{i^*j} < x'_{h^*j} = x'_{m^*j}.$$

x is obtained from x′ by a favourable composite transfer if a progressive transfer of the other attribute j^* is performed between i^* and k^*, a regressive transfer of j^* is performed between m^* and h^* and the two following conditions are satisfied as well

(i) $x_{k^*j^*} - x'_{k^*j^*} = x_{h^*j^*} - x'_{h^*j^*}$
(ii) $\min\{x_{k^*j^*}, x_{m^*j^*}\} - \min\{x'_{k^*j^*}, x'_{m^*j^*}\} \geq \max\{x_{h^*j^*}, x_{i^*j^*}\} - \max\{x'_{h^*j^*}, x'_{i^*j^*}\} = 0.$

Two additional conditions have to be respected: The two involved transfers (of the same attribute) are of the same magnitude. The minimum income (respectively the maximum income) among the four actors of the transfer increases (resp. remains the same) in the final distribution with respect to the initial one.

As long as we substitute a strict inequality sign for the inequality sign in (ii), we get a *favourable composite one-dimension* permutation (FCP).

The most complex transformation combined a *compensating one-dimension* permutation between a pair of individuals and a *deteriorating one-dimension* permutation between another pair. The ranking of each pair of individuals according to each dimension initially overlaps, even if the winner of the compensating permutation is in a worse situation than the loser of the deteriorating permutation at the starting point. The precise statement is the following.

Definition 11.6 (FCCP). *Let x and $x'(x' \neq x)$ be two allocations such that there exist two pairs of individuals $(i^*, k^*), (h^*, m^*)$ with $x'_{k^*j} < x'_{m^*j} < x'_{i^*j} < x'_{h^*j}$ for one of the two attributes. x is obtained from x′ by a favourable composite compensating one-dimension permutation if a compensating one dimension of the other attribute j^* is performed between $i^*$and k^*, a deteriorating regressive transfer of j^* is performed between m^* and h^* and the two following conditions are satisfied as well*

(i) $x_{k^*j^*} - x'_{k^*j^*} = x_{h^*j^*} - x'_{h^*j^*}$
(ii) $\min\{x'_{k^*j^*}, x'_{i^*j^*}\} < \min\{x_{m^*j^*}, x_{h^*j^*}\}.$

A more readable interpretation of this property may be grasped through the following example. Four individuals 1, 2, 3, 4 are unambiguously ranked in an increasing way relatively to an attribute, say good 1, and nothing changes in this dimension. 1 and 3 permute their endowments in good 2 and this change can be termed a compensating permutation, because 3 is supposed to be initially wealthier than 1 in good 2. Individuals 2 and 4 permute their endowments in good 2 as well, but the outcome is a deteriorating permutation, since individual 2 is initially better off than individual 4 in this attribute. Condition (i) says that the two transfers are of the same magnitude. Condition (ii) tells us that the loser of the deteriorating permutation (individual 2) is still better off than the loser of the compensating permutation (individual 3) with respect to the transferred good.

Proposition 11.4 (Adapted from Moyes, 1999). *If an allocation x results from an allocation x' by performing any combination of increments, CPT, FCP or FCCP of any attribute, then $x \succeq_{\mathcal{U}_{AB_2}} x'$.*

Le Breton (1986) has questioned the rationale of the second class introduced by Atkinson and Bourguignon on the basis that it is difficult to understand the meaning on the cross forth partial derivative. The findings of Moyes helps to translate the definition of the second class in concrete small changes of the attributes distribution. Admittedly, the latest transformation remains a bit complex and it is still hard to be totally convinced that it must be imposed.

For the sake of completeness, we remind the results obtained by Atkinson and Bourguignon which exhibit the statistical tests equivalent to their criteria of dominance. To any allocation x, we can associate the corresponding joint cumulative distribution function $F_x(x_1, x_2)$, where, by an abuse of notation, x_1, x_2 now denote a couple of values of the random variable $X = (X_1, X_2)$. For the case of discrete random variables considered here, F_x is a step function. ΔF denotes $F_x - F_{x'}$. Introducing,

$$\Delta H(x_1, x_2) = \int_0^{x_1} \int_0^{x_2} \Delta F(s, r)\, ds\, dr. \tag{11.5}$$

one yields:

Proposition 11.5 (Atkinson and Bourguignon, 1982).

(i) $x \succeq_{\mathcal{U}_{AB_1}} x' \Leftrightarrow \Delta F(x_1, x_2) \leq 0, \quad \forall x_1 \in X_1, \forall x_2 \in X_2;$
(ii) $x \succeq_{\mathcal{U}_{AB_2}} x' \Leftrightarrow \Delta H(x_1, x_2) \leq 0, \quad \forall x_1 \in X_1, \forall x_2 \in X_2.$

This result exhibits tests which appear as the natural extensions of the univariate first and second stochastic dominance conditions to a bidimensional framework. Since the earlier criteria are different from the generalization of the Lorenz test presented in Section 11.2, it emerges that the routes of stochastic dominance and inverse stochastic dominances which are converging up to the second order in a one dimensional world are diverging in a multidimensional setting.

11.4 Asymmetric treatment of attributes

Up to now, the two attributes are playing a symmetric role, as in the coefficient of correlation. Let us consider the following two simple examples which illustrate that we may be interested in putting the two attributes in a different footing, as in a simple regression analysis.

For convenience, attribute 1 is income and attribute 2 handicap. There are three income levels, low, middle and high, ranked in increasing order, and two levels of handicap (handicapped and non-handicapped) ordered in that way. The following matrices[6] describe the initial and final distributions of population.

$$A = \begin{pmatrix} 1 & 1 \\ - & - \\ 1 & - \end{pmatrix} \quad B = \begin{pmatrix} - & - \\ 2 & - \\ - & 1 \end{pmatrix}.$$

It is routine to observe that the income distribution in B is better than its counterpart in A according to the Generalized Lorenz criterion. Moreover the marginal distribution of handicap is exactly the same between the two distributions.

Now, it may be observed that the income distribution among the handicapped is completely equalized in B while it is unequal in A. Among the non-disabled, the distribution of income is strictly better in B than in A according to the General Lorenz test. In inspecting columns of the two matrices, we are comparing the conditional distributions of income for a given level of handicap. Another point of view is captured by examining the rows of the matrices. We are looking at the distribution of handicap for a given level of income. Comparing the first rows, the comparison is still in favour of distribution B. The distribution of handicaps among the poors is still better in B. When we compare the distribution of handicaps for the group consisting of poor and middle income people (the cumulated two first rows), there is evidence that the situation has deteriorated.

A symmetric example is provided with the following configuration with two income levels (poor, rich) and three health levels (bad, normal, good).

$$C = \begin{pmatrix} 1 & - & 1 \\ 1 & - & - \end{pmatrix} \quad D = \begin{pmatrix} - & 2 & - \\ - & - & 1 \end{pmatrix}.$$

Here, the distribution of health conditions is better in D than in C for the poor as well as for the rich. Yet, the distribution of income for the group made of the bad and normal health people has deteriorated in D with respect to C.

The asymmetric approach modelizes situations where we favour one of the two points of view: Either, we are primarily interested in the distribution of health or education among the poor (more appropriately, the different cumulated income groups) or, we are interested in the distribution of income among the unhealthy, the uneducated (the different cumulated health or education groups). It is easy to rationalize both points of view, it depends on the context and the perspective we have in mind. For instance, an important literature (see, for example, Wagstaff and van Doorslaer, 2002; Wagstaff *et al.*, 1991) focuses on socio-economic inequalities in health. In this literature, the distribution of health among the poor is emphasized, meaning that health may be used to compensate for a poor income.

To capture these two view points, and having in mind for instance that attribute 1 is income and attribute 2 is health, we consider the following two subsets of

ALEP utility functions. In the first case, income is the compensating attribute, and health the compensated attribute

$$\mathcal{U}_{\mathrm{AS}_1} = \{u_1, u_2 \geq 0,\ u_{11} \leq 0,\ u_{22} \leq 0,\ u_{12} \leq 0,\ u_{112} \geq 0\}, \tag{11.6}$$

while in the second class, it is the opposite

$$\mathcal{U}_{\mathrm{AS}_2} = \{u_1, u_2 \geq 0,\ u_{11} \leq 0,\ u_{22} \leq 0,\ u_{12} \leq 0,\ u_{221} \geq 0\}. \tag{11.7}$$

Our classes are clearly intermediate between the first class of Atkinson and Bourguignon and their second class. Their distinctive features come from the fact that they are no more anonymous with respect to the set of attributes. The first class is designed to capture the view that we are primarily interested in the distribution of income among the unhealthy. To this aim, a specific sign is imposed on the cross third partial derivative u_{112}. It is required to be positive which means that the decrease in marginal utility of income is smaller among the healthy than among the unhealthy. In other words, the differences in marginal utilities of income between healthy persons are smaller than those among unhealthy, which implies that latter group takes priority over the former for public funds.

A symmetric statement prevails for the second class according to which it is the distribution of health among the poor which matters. This time, thanks to the assumption on the sign of u_{221}, the differences in marginal utilities of health between the poor are larger than those among the rich. In other words, poor must have the priority in health care. Anyway, the argument will be made more transparent and more persuasive with the help of permutations and transfers introduced in Section 11.3.

Following the same lines than Moyes, it can be easily established the following implication.

Proposition 11.6. *If an allocation x results from an allocation x′ by performing any combination of increments, CPT of any attribute and FCP of attribute 1 (resp., attribute 2), then* $x \succeq_{\mathcal{U}_{\mathrm{AS}_1}} x'$ *(resp.* $x \succeq_{\mathcal{U}_{\mathrm{AS}_2}} x'$*).*

If we combine a compensation permutation of income among the unhealthy and a deteriorating permutation of income among the healthy, then welfare improves according to the first class, while it changes for the better according to the second class if we combine a compensation permutation of health among the poor and a deteriorating permutation of health among the rich.

Now, by adding a transfer sensitivity condition à la Shorrocks-Foster (1987) on the compensating good to the previous conditions, we define two new classes

$$\mathcal{U}_{\mathrm{ASS}_1} = \{u_1, u_2 \geq 0, u_{11} \leq 0, u_{22} \leq 0, u_{12} \leq 0, u_{112} \geq 0, u_{111} \geq 0\} \tag{11.8}$$

$$\mathcal{U}_{\mathrm{ASS}_2} = \{u_1, u_2 \geq 0, u_{11} \leq 0, u_{22} \leq 0, u_{12} \leq 0, u_{221} \geq 0, u_{222} \geq 0\}. \tag{11.9}$$

These slight changes allow us to consider favourable composite transfers as well, which encompass favourable composite permutations as particular cases.

Proposition 11.7. *If an allocation x results from an allocation x' by performing any combination of increments, CPT of any attribute and FCT of attribute 1 (respectively, attribute 2), then $x \succeq_{\mathcal{U}_{\mathrm{ASS}_1}} x'$ (resp. $x \succeq_{\mathcal{U}_{\mathrm{ASS}_2}} x'$).*

The substance of the argument remains the same. We add more flexibility in operating composite transformations. Since, it is rather odd to allow FCP to improve welfare without permitting FCT to do the same, it seems that the right classes of utility functions which capture an asymmetric argument are the latest.

In order to present the tests to be implemented in order to check dominance for the earlier classes, it is convenient to recall the definition of the Generalized Lorenz test (Shorrocks, 1983). Here is an extension of this notion for the multidimensional framework.

Definition 11.7. *x is said to Generalized Lorenz dominates $x' (x \succeq_{GL} x')$ if:*

$$\forall k \in N, \ \forall j \in L, \qquad \frac{1}{n}\sum_{i=1}^{k} x_{(i)j} \geq \frac{1}{n}\sum_{i=1}^{k} x'_{(i)j}.$$

A natural extension of the *absolute income poverty gap* to a multidimensional setting seems to be the following for a poverty limit of x_1.

$$P_x(x_1 \mid x_2) = \frac{1}{n} \sum_{\{i \mid (x_{i1}, x_{i2}) \leq (x_1, x_2)\}} (x_1 - x_{i1}).$$

We cumulate the absolute poverty gaps for all individuals having an income less than an income limit x_1 and a given health x_2. A similar definition prevails for the *absolute health poverty gap*.

$$P_x(x_2 \mid x_1) = \frac{1}{n} \sum_{\{i \mid (x_{i1}, x_{i2}) \leq (x_1, x_2)\}} (x_2 - x_{i2}).$$

Poverty gap dominance is known to be equivalent to second stochastic dominance in a univariate framework (see Foster and Shorrocks, 1988). Quite naturally, we adopt the following two definitions for multi-attribute distributions.

Definition 11.8. *Let $X = (X_1, X_2)$ a couple of random variables. x is said to income poverty gap dominates x' $(x \succeq_{P1} x')$ if*

$$P_x(x_1 \mid x_2) \leq P_{x'}(x_1 \mid x_2) \quad \forall x_1 \in X_1, \ \forall x_2 \in X_2,$$

x is said to health poverty gap dominates x' $(x \succeq_{P2} x')$ if

$$P_x(x_2 \mid x_1) \leq P_{x'}(x_2 \mid x_1) \quad \forall x_1 \in X_1, \ \forall x_2 \in X_2.$$

The following proposition states sufficient conditions to check dominance according to the asymmetric classes $\mathcal{U}_{\text{ASS}_1}$ and $\mathcal{U}_{\text{ASS}_2}$.

Proposition 11.8. *Muller and Trannoy (2003a).*[7]

$$x \succeq_{GL} x' \quad \text{and} \quad x \succeq_{P1} x' \Rightarrow x \succeq_{\mathcal{U}_{\text{ASS}_1}} x' \tag{11.10}$$

$$x \succeq_{GL} x' \quad \text{and} \quad x \succeq_{P2} x' \Rightarrow x \succeq_{\mathcal{U}_{\text{ASS}_2}} x' \tag{11.11}$$

The two criteria have in common that the marginal distributions of attributes must be more egalitarian in the Generalized Lorenz sense. The poverty gap condition[8] makes the difference between the two, the income poverty gap does not increase for any levels of income and health for the 'distribution of income among the unhealthy' view, while the health poverty gap does not become larger for the 'distribution of health among the poor' view.

The reader can check that in the two examples mentioned earlier B dominates A according to the criterion (11.10), but not according to (11.11) and it is the opposite for D versus C. Our criteria lead to less partial quasi-orderings of bidimensional distributions than Atkinson and Bourguignon's first criterion but to a more partial ordering than their second criterion. The exhibited criteria may be used as well as in poverty analysis by choosing a poverty threshold in income or in health (see Bourguignon and Chakravarty, 2003, for an adaptation of the first criterion of Atkinson and Bourguignon to poverty measurement). For an extension to more than two goods, we refer to the original article and to Muller and Trannoy (2003b).

11.5 Conclusion

The lecture has not been comprehensive, quite the contrary (see for instance, Mosler (1991), Savaglio (2002), and Fleurbaey and Trannoy (2003) to supplement this synopsis). Three simple views of multidimensional dominance have been deployed. Generalization of a main concept used in univariate analysis has been proposed in each section. Budget dominance allows to offer a natural extension of the Lorenz criterion. A symmetric treatment of attributes leads to a generalization of the usual first and second stochastic dominance. The notion of poverty gaps has been fruitfully extended to a multidimensional context, thanks to an asymmetric perspective. In the course of development, principles of transfers have been proposed and discussed. It is quite apparent that these extensions point in different directions and that the beautiful unity of the univariate case seems lost.

We have emphasized the differences between these views, but it is not difficult to find what they have in common. All express the idea that to have more of an attribute compensates for having less of another one, namely, the attributes are substitute rather than complement in individual well-being. This compensation is captured by the negative sign of the cross partial derivative of the utility function when two attributes are considered. This condition has long been studied and interpreted in the risk context (see Richard, 1975), and has been at the heart of a dominance criterion proposed by Bourguignon (1989) when needs differ.

It has been remarked that for each of these views, there is still a lot to be discovered and more specifically, we are far from attaining the analogue of the Hardy–Littlewood–Polya theorem for each of these views. Likely, the most beautiful apples of the research tree are still to come. As long as the burn of egalitarian passions has not been soothed, interest in revisiting the analytical tools used in inequality measurement will not vanish.

Acknowledgements

This article was prepared for the 2003 Summer School on Inequality and Economic Integration organized by the International School of Economic Research at the University of Sienna. I am grateful to Marc Fleurbaey for his comments, to Ernesto Savaglio for a careful reading and to Eugenio Peluso and Louis Eeeckoudt for their help. The usual *caveat* applies.

Notes

1 The terminology is not fixed.We also find directional majorization (Marshall and Olkin, 1979) and positive comparisons majorization (Joe and Verducci, 1993).
2 These authors have a characterization for the case of two individuals.
3 ALEP stands for Auspitz–Lieben–Edgeworth–Pareto.
4 The limit cases of permutations considered by Moyes are allowed by our transfers principles.
5 Indeed, Moyes proved a little bit more. A compensating one-dimension permutation coupled with an increment increase welfare according to (11.2) if and only if u belongs to $\mathcal{U}_{AB_1}$. A similar remark applies for the other classes.
6 These matrices, which convey the joint distribution of the population across the two attributes, differ from the matrices introduced in Section 11.2. For instance, matrix A reads as follows: there is one handicapped individual with a low income level.
7 Conditions in (11.10) (resp.11.11) are also sufficient to check dominance for $\mathcal{U}_{AS_1}$ (resp.11.11) $\mathcal{U}_{AS_2}$.
8 This second condition implies Generalized Lorenz dominance for the compensating variable as well. We state the Lorenz condition independently to make more transparent the common requirements to the two criteria.

References

Allison, R.A. and J.E. Foster, 1999, Measuring health inequality using qualitative data, WP no. 99.10, Harvard Center for Population and Development Studies.

Arnold, B.C., 1987, *Majorization and the Lorenz Order: A Brief Introduction*. Springer, Berlin.

Atkinson, A.B., 1970, On the measurement of inequality, *Theory* 2, 244–263.

Atkinson, A.B. and F. Bourguignon, 1982, The comparison of multi-dimensioned distributions of economic status, *Review of Economic Studies* 49, 181–201.

Atkinson, A.B. and F. Bourguignon, 1987, Income distribution and differences in needs, in G.R. Feiwel (ed.), *Arrow and the Foundation of the Theory of Economic Policy*, Macmillan, London.

Atkinson, A.B. and F. Bourguignon, 2000, Income distribution and economics, in A.B. Atkinson and F. Bourguignon (ed.), *Handbook of Income Distribution*, North-Holland, Amsterdam.

Bhandari, S.K., 1988, Multivariate majorization and directional majorization: positive results, *Sankhyā: The Indian Journal of Statistics* 50, 199–204.

Bourguignon, F., 1989, Family size and social utility. Income distribution dominance criteria, *Journal of Econometrics* 42, 67–80.

Bourguignon, F. and S.R. Chakravarty, 2003, The measurement of multidimensional poverty, *Journal of Economic Inequality* 1, 25–40.

Chipman, J., 1977, An empirical implication of Auspitz–Lieben–Edgeworth–Pareto complementarity, *Journal of Economic Theory* 14, 228–231.

Dardadoni, V., 1995, On multidimensional inequality measurement, in C. Dagum, A. Lemmi. (eds.), *Income Distribution, Social Welfare, Inequality and Poverty. Vol. 6 of Research on Economic Inequality*. JAI Press, Stamford, CT, pp. 201–207.

Fishburn, P.C. and R.G. Vickson, 1978, Theoretical foundations of stochastic dominance, in G.A. Whitmore and M.C. Findlay (eds), *Stochastic Dominance*, Lexington Books, Cambridge, MA.

Fleurbaey, M., 2004, Social welfare, priority to the worst-off and the dimensions of individual well-being, in F. Farina and E. Savaglio (eds), *Inequality and Economic Integration*, Rouledge, London, chapter 9.

Fleurbaey, M. and A. Trannoy, 2003, The impossibility of a Paretian liberal, *Social Choice and Welfare* 21, 243–263.

Foster J.E. and A.F. Shorrocks, 1988, Poverty orderings and welfare dominance, *Social Choice and Welfare* 5, 179–198.

Hadar, J., and Russell, W.R., 1974, Diversification of interdependant prospects, *Journal of Economic Theory* 7, 231–240.

Hardy, G.H., J.E. Littlewood and G. Polya, (1934, 1952), *Inequalities*, Cambridge University Press, London.

Huang, C.C., D. Kira and I. Vertinsky, 1978, Stochastic dominance rules for multi-attribute utility functions, *The Review of Economic Studies* 45(3), 611–615.

Joe, H. and J. Verducci, 1993, Multivariate majorization by positive combination, in *Stochastic Inequalities IMS Lecture Notes:* Monograph Series, vol. 22, pp. 159–181.

Kolm, S.C., 1969, The optimal production of social justice, in H. Guitton and J. Margolis (eds.), *Public Economics*, Macmillan, London, pp. 145–200.

Kolm, S.C., 1977, Multidimensional egalitarianisms, *Quarterly Journal of Economics* 91, 1–13.

Koshevoy, G., 1995, Multivariate Lorenz majorizations, *Social Choice and Welfare* 12, 93–102.

Koshevoy, G., 1998, The Lorenz zonotope and multivariate majorizations, *Social Choice and Welfare* 15, 1–14.

Koshevoy, G. and K. Mosler, 1996, The Lorenz zonoïd of a multivariate distributions, *Journal of the American Statistical Association* 91(434), 873-882.

Koshevoy, G. and K. Mosler, 1999, Price majorization and the inverse Lorenz function, DP in Statistics and Econometrics 03/99, September 1999, Universität zu Koln.

Le breton, M., 1986, Essais sur les Fondements de l'Analyse Economique de l'Inégalité, Thèse pour le Doctorat d'Etat, Université de Rennes I.

Levhari, D., Paroush, J. and B. Peleg, 1975, Efficiency analysis for multivariate distributions, *Review of Economic Studies* 42, 87–91.

Levy, H. and J. Paroush, 1974, Toward multivariate efficiency criteria, *Journal of Economic Theory* 7, 129–142.

List, C., 1999, Multidimensional inequality measurement: a proposal. Working paper in Economics no. 1999-W27, Nuffield College, Oxford.

Marshall, A. and I. Olkin, 1979, *Inequalities: Theory of Majorization and its Applications*, Academic Press, New York.

Mosler, K., 1991, Multidimensional welfarism, in W. Eichhorn (ed.), *Models and Measurement of Welfare Inequality*, Springer-Verlag, Berlin, pp. 808–820.

Moyes, P., 1999, Comparisons of heterogeneous distributions and dominance criteria, *Economie et Prévision* 138–139, 125–146 (in French).

Muliere, P. and M. Scarsini, 1989, Multivariate decisions with unknown price vector, *Economic Letters* 29, 13–19.

Muller, C. and A. Trannoy, 2003a, Multidimensional inequality comparisons: a compensation perspective. Mimeo.

Muller, C. and A. Trannoy, 2003b, A dominance approach to well-being inequality across countries, WP IDEP no. 03–10.

Rawls, J., 1971, *A Theory of Justice*, Harvard University Press, Cambridge, MA, available at http://www.vcharite.univ-mrs.fr/idep/

Richard, C., 1975, Multidivariate risk aversion, utility independence and separable utility functions, *Management Science* 22, 12–21.

Savaglio, E., 2002, Multidimensional inequality: a survey. Working Paper no. 362, Dipartimento di Economia Politica, Universita degli Studi di Siena.

Sen, A.K., 1970, *Social Choice and Welfare*, Holden-Day, San Francisco, CA.

Sen, A.K., 1973, *On Economic Inequality*, Clarendon Press, Oxford.

Sen, A.K., 1985, *Commodities and Capabilities*, North-Holland, Amsterdam.

Sen, A.K., 1987, *The Standard of Living*, Cambridge University Press, Cambridge.

Sen, A.K., 1992, *Inequality Re-examined*, Clarendon Press, Oxford.

Shorrocks, A.F., 1983, Ranking income distributions, *Economica* 50, 1–17.

Shorrocks, A.F. and J.E. Foster, 1987, Transfer sensitive inequality measures, *Review of Economic Studies* 54, 485–497.

Tobin, J. 1970, On limiting the domain of inequality, *Journal of Law and Economics* 13, 263–277.

Tsui, K.Y., 1999, Multidimensional inequality and multidimensional generalized entropy measures: an axiomatic derivation, *Social Choice and Welfare* 16, 145–157.

Wagstaff, A. and E. van Doorslaer, 2002, Overall vs. socioeconomic health inequality: a measurement framework and two empirical illustrations, mimeo.

Wagstaff, A., P. Paci and E. van Doorslaer, 1991, On the measurement of inequalities in health, *Social Science and Medicine* 33, 545–557.

Weymark, J., 2004, The normative approach to the measurement of multidimensional inequality, in F. Farina and E. Savaglio (eds), *Inequality and Economic Integration*, Routledge, London, chapter 12.

12 The normative approach to the measurement of multidimensional inequality

John A. Weymark

12.1 Introduction

Univariate indices of income inequality provide an inadequate basis on which to compare the inequality of well-being within and between populations. Recognition of this fact has lead to an explosion of research recently on multidimensional economic inequality, beginning with the seminal articles by Kolm (1977) and Atkinson and Bourguignon (1982). These articles are primarily concerned with developing dominance criteria for ranking multivariate distributions. When there are multiple attributes of well-being being compared, one distribution may be more equal than a second if the former exhibits less dispersion than the latter or if it reduces the positive dependence between the individual distributions of the attributes. Kolm focused on the first of these ways in which inequality may manifest itself, whereas Atkinson and Bourguignon focused on the second.

Dominance criteria only provide partial orderings of the possible distributions of attributes. In contrast, an inequality index can be used to completely order all distributions. In the normative approach to inequality measurement, a social evaluation (or its representation, a social evaluation function) is used to construct an inequality index. A social evaluation ranks alternative distributions according to their social desirability. The use of a social evaluation makes explicit the value judgements underlying an inequality index. For univariate distributions, the normative approach was pioneered by Atkinson (1970) and Kolm (1969), who introduced general procedures for constructing an inequality index from a social evaluation. Multi-attribute extensions of their methodologies have been proposed by Kolm (1977) and Tsui (1995).[1]

The purpose of this chapter is to provide an introduction to the normative approach to the measurement of multidimensional inequality. While my focus is on indices of inequality, rather than on dominance criteria, it is desirable for an inequality index to be consistent with normatively-based dominance criteria. As a consequence, it necessary to devote some attention to this issue. However, it is beyond the scope of this chapter to provide a systematic survey of the literature on multivariate dominance criteria.[2]

Here, as in much of the literature on the measurement of inequality, it is assumed that the population is homogeneous in the sense that individuals do not differ in welfare-relevant characteristics other than the attributes that are the focus of the analysis. In a heterogeneous society, individuals may differ for a number of reasons – they may belong to households of different size, they may have different preferences, or, even if they have the same preferences, they may have different cardinal utility functions because of differences in their physical characteristics. In the past decade, considerable progress has been made on extending the theory of inequality measurement for homogeneous populations to the heterogeneous case. See, for example, Blackorby *et al.* (1999), Ebert (1995), Shorrocks (2004), and Weymark (1999).

In Section 12.2, some of the notation used in this article is introduced. If a social evaluation is to provide a satisfactory basis on which to construct a normative inequality index, it should satisfy a number of basic properties. These properties are considered in Section 12.3. Among these properties are multi-attribute generalizations of the Pigou–Dalton transfer principle.

The procedure proposed by Atkinson (1970) and Kolm (1969) for constructing relative (i.e. scale invariant) univariate inequality indices and the procedure proposed by Kolm (1969) for constructing absolute (i.e. translation invariant) univariate inequality indices are reviewed in Section 12.4. Multi-attribute generalizations of these procedures are discussed in Section 12.5.

The normative approach has been used by Tsui (1995) to define multi-attribute generalizations of the univariate Atkinson and Kolm–Pollak classes of inequality indices and to axiomatically characterize their underlying social evaluations. These indices are considered in Section 12.6.

The social evaluation functions used to construct Tsui's indices have a two-stage aggregation property. In the first stage, a utility function is used to determine the distribution of utilities and then these utilities are summed. Maasoumi (1986) has suggested constructing inequality indices directly using a two-stage procedure in which a univariate inequality index is applied to the distribution of utilities obtained in the first stage. Maasoumi's proposal is the subject of Section 12.7.

Section 12.8 discusses the multi-attribute generalized Gini indices introduced by Gajdos and Weymark (2005). The social evaluation functions from which these indices are derived also have a two-stage aggregation property, but, in contrast to Tsui (1995) and Maasoumi (1986), the order of aggregation is reversed – first the distributions of each attribute are aggregated using univariate generalized Gini social evaluation functions and then the values of these functions are aggregated into an overall evaluation in a second stage.

Section 12.9 considers a dominance criterion proposed by Tsui (1999) that takes account of the dependence between the individual distributions of the attributes. Some further issues in the measurement of multidimensional inequality are briefly discussed in Section 12.10.

12.2 Preliminaries

There is a fixed set of individuals $N = \{1, \dots, n\}$, with $n \geq 2$. The set of attributes is $Q = \{1, \dots, q\}$. It is assumed that the quantity of each of these attributes can be continuously varied. Examples of such attributes include income, life expectancy, educational attainment, and health status.[3] Attributes need not differ in kind. For example, the attributes could be incomes in different time periods or in different states of the world. In the latter case, we are measuring inequality under uncertainty.

A *distribution* of attributes among the population is an $n \times q$ real-valued matrix. The ijth entry of a distribution matrix X is x_{ij}, individual i's quantity of the jth attribute. The ith row of X is denoted $x_{i\cdot}$ and the jth column is denoted $x_{\cdot j}$. If there is only one attribute, the distribution is written as x rather than as X or $x_{\cdot 1}$. Three sets of distribution matrices are considered for the *domain* $\mathcal{D}$ of admissible distributions. The first, denoted $\mathcal{M}_1$, is the set of all possible distribution matrices. The second, denoted $\mathcal{M}_2$, is the set of all distribution matrices X for which both (a) $x_{ij} \geq 0$ for all $i \in N$ and all $j \in Q$ and (b) $x_{\cdot j} \in \mathbb{R}^{n*}_{+} := \mathbb{R}^n_{+} \setminus \{0_n\}$ for all $j \in Q$.[4] The third, denoted $\mathcal{M}_3$, is the set of all distribution matrices X for which $x_{ij} > 0$ for all $i \in N$ and all $j \in Q$. Note that for distribution matrices in $\mathcal{M}_2$ and $\mathcal{M}_3$, the mean value of any attribute is positive. Except where otherwise specified, $\mathcal{D}$ can be any one of these three domains in the rest of this chapter.

For any $x \in \mathbb{R}^n$, $\mu(x)$ is the mean of x, $\tilde{x}$ is the permutation of x for which $\tilde{x}_1 \geq \tilde{x}_2 \geq \cdots \geq \tilde{x}_n$, and $\hat{x}$ is the permutation of x for which $\hat{x}_1 \leq \hat{x}_2 \leq \cdots \leq \hat{x}_n$. For $u, v \in \mathbb{R}^n$, u *strictly generalized Lorenz dominates* v if $u \neq v$ and for all $k \in N$, $\sum_{i=1}^{k} \hat{u}_i \geq \sum_{i=1}^{k} \hat{v}_i$.[5] If $\sum_{i=1}^{n} \hat{u}_i = \sum_{i=1}^{n} \hat{v}_i$ in this definition, then u *strictly Lorenz dominates* v.

12.3 Basic properties for a social evaluation relation

The inequality indices considered in this chapter are derived from explicit social evaluations of the possible distribution matrices. A *social evaluation* is a binary relation $\succeq$ on the set of distribution matrices $\mathcal{D}$. The relation $\succeq$ is interpreted as meaning "weakly socially preferred to." The symmetric and asymmetric factors of $\succeq$ are $\sim$ and $\succ$, respectively. A function $W : \mathcal{D} \to \mathbb{R}$ that represents $\succeq$ is called a *social evaluation function*.

By defining $\succeq$ directly on $\mathcal{D}$, the analysis is not limited to welfarist social evaluations. *Welfarism* is the principle that the only feature of a distribution that is socially relevant is the vector of utilities associated with this distribution. Welfarist social objectives can be described using a social welfare function. A *social welfare function* is a real-valued function defined on n-tuples of utilities. If the utility functions are known, a social welfare function can be used to construct a social evaluation function – for each distribution, the value of the social evaluation function is the value assigned by the social welfare function to the utilities obtained with this distribution. For example, suppose that the social welfare function is utilitarian and, in keeping with the assumption that the society is homogeneous, that everybody has the same utility function. The corresponding social evaluation function then has the form

$$W(X) = \sum_{i=1}^{n} U(x_{i\cdot}), \quad \forall X \in \mathcal{D}, \tag{12.1}$$

where $U: \mathbb{D} \to \mathbb{R}$ is the common utility function, where $\mathbb{D} = \mathbb{R}^q$ (resp. $\mathbb{R}^q_+$, $\mathbb{R}^q_{++}$) if $\mathcal{D} = \mathcal{M}_1$ (resp. $\mathcal{M}_2$, $\mathcal{M}_3$).[6] Lack of information about individual utility functions limits the applicability of this approach. In contrast, it is possible to use a social evaluation even if nothing is known about the individuals' utility functions other than that they are increasing in their arguments.

There are a number of basic properties that a social evaluation should satisfy if it is to serve as a satisfactory basis from which to construct an inequality index. These properties are formulated as axioms. There are two types of basic axioms: (a) axioms that are not concerned with the distributional sensitivity of the social evaluation and (b) axioms that are multi-attribute generalizations of the Pigou (1912) – Dalton (1920) transfer principle.

12.3.1 Non-distributional axioms

The first axiom requires $\succeq$ to be a complete preorder.

Ordering (ORD). The binary relation $\succeq$ is reflexive, complete, and transitive on $\mathcal{D}$.

The second axiom requires $\succeq$ to be continuous; that is, any strict ranking of two distribution matrices is invariant to small perturbations in these matrices. Continuity ensures that the analysis is not overly sensitive to errors in measurement of the distributions.

Continuity (CONT). The sets $\{Y \in \mathcal{D} \mid Y \succ X\}$ and $\{Y \in \mathcal{D} \mid X \succ Y\}$ are open for all $X \in \mathcal{D}$.[7]

It is assumed that all of the attributes are desirable. Then, regardless of the exact form of individual preferences, the Pareto principle requires that increasing the quantity of any attribute for any individual is socially desirable provided that nobody's allocation of any attribute is decreased. The following monotonicity axiom states this principle formally.

Monotonicity (MON). For all $X, Y \in \mathcal{D}$, if $X \neq Y$ and $x_{ij} \geq y_{ij}$ for all $i \in N$ and all $j \in Q$, then $X \succ Y$.

Equal treatment of individuals is captured by an anonymity axiom. In a homogeneous society, individuals are treated symmetrically if permuting the individual distributions is a matter of social indifference.

Anonymity (ANON). For all $n \times n$ permutation matrices Π and all $X \in \mathcal{D}, X \sim \Pi X$.

12.3.2 Multidimensional transfer principles

Distributional sensitivity of the social evaluation is obtained by requiring $\succeq$ to satisfy some form of the Pigou (1912) – Dalton (1920) transfer principle. The single attribute case is considered first. For concreteness, whenever there is a single attribute, it is supposed that this attribute is income.

A *Pigou–Dalton transfer* is a transfer of income from a richer to a poorer person that results in the initially poorer person ending up with less income than the initially richer person starts with.[8] Formally, if the initial incomes are x_{i_1} and x_{i_2} with $x_{i_1} < x_{i_2}$ and the size of the transfer is $\delta > 0$, then i_1's post-transfer income is $y_{i_1} = x_{i_1} + \delta < x_{i_2}$ (and, hence, i_2's post-transfer income is $y_{i_2} = x_{i_2} - \delta > x_{i_1}$). A Pigou–Dalton transfer can be equivalently expressed in terms of a strict T-transform. A *strict T-transform* is a linear transform defined by an $n \times n$ matrix T of the form

$$T = \lambda I_n + (1 - \lambda)\Pi_{i_1 i_2} \tag{12.2}$$

for some $\lambda \in (0, 1)$ and some $i_1, i_2 \in N$, where I_n is the $n \times n$ identity matrix and $\Pi_{i_1 i_2}$ is the $n \times n$ permutation matrix that interchanges the i_1 and i_2 coordinates. Letting $y = Tx$, it is easy to verify that $y_{i_1} = \lambda x_{i_1} + (1 - \lambda)x_{i_2}$, $y_{i_2} = (1 - \lambda)x_{i_1} + \lambda x_{i_2}$, and $y_k = x_k$ for all $k \notin \{i_1, i_2\}$.

If the distribution y is obtained from the distribution x by a sequence of Pigou–Dalton transfers (possibly involving a number of different pairs of individuals), then *y Pigou–Dalton majorizes x*. As is well-known (see Marshall and Olkin (1979, chapter 1) or Hardy *et al.* (1934)), (a) y Pigou–Dalton majorizes x if and only if (b) y strictly Lorenz dominates x if and only if (c) $y = Bx$ for some $n \times n$ bistochastic matrix B and y is not a permutation of x.[9] The *Pigou–Dalton transfer principle* requires y to be socially preferred to x if y Pigou–Dalton majorizes x. When $q = 1$, a symmetric social evaluation function W satisfies this principle if and only if W is strictly S-concave.[10]

There have been a number of different ways proposed for generalizing the unidimensional Pigou–Dalton transfer principle so that it can be applied when there are multiple attributes. See Kolm (1977), Marshall and Olkin (1979, chapter 15), and Savaglio (2006). Two of these multi-attribute Pigou–Dalton transfer principles are considered here.

In the first of these principles, the definition of Pigou–Dalton majorization is generalized by applying the same sequence of T-transforms to all attributes.

Definition 12.1. *For all $X, Y \in \mathcal{D}$ for which Y is not a permutation of the rows of X, Y uniformly Pigou–Dalton majorizes X, denoted $Y \succ_{PD} X$, if $Y = PX$, where P is the product of a finite number of $n \times n$ strict T-transforms.*

The corresponding multidimensional transfer principle is the *Uniform Pigou–Dalton Majorization Principle.*

Uniform Pigou–Dalton Majorization Principle (UPM). For all $X, Y \in \mathcal{D}$ for which Y is not a permutation of the rows of X, if $Y \succ_{\text{PD}} X$, then $Y \succ X$.

As noted earlier, if there is only one attribute, a sequence of Pigou–Dalton transfers can be equivalently expressed in terms of a bistochastic matrix. This observation suggests using bistochastic matrices to define a multi-attribute version of Pigou–Dalton majorization.

Definition 12.2. *For all $X, Y \in \mathcal{D}$ for which Y is not a permutation of the rows of X, Y uniformly majorizes X, denoted $Y \succ_U X$, if $Y = BX$ for some $n \times n$ bistochastic matrix B.*[11]

Note that the same bistochastic matrix is being used to smooth the distributions of each attibute. The corresponding multidimensional transfer principle is the *Uniform Majorization Principle*.

Uniform Majorization Principle (UM). For all $X, Y \in \mathcal{D}$ for which Y is not a permutation of the rows of X, if $Y \succ_U X$, then $Y \succ X$.

The product of strict T-transform matrices is a non-permutation bistochastic matrix. If either $q = 1$ or $n = 2$, the converse is also true. However, if $n \geq 3$ and $q \geq 2$, there exist non-permutation bistochastic matrices that are not products of strict T-transforms. See Marshall and Olkin (1979, p. 431). As a consequence, except in the special cases noted earlier, UM is a more restrictive assumption than UPM.

Kolm (1977) has shown that if a common increasing and strictly concave utility function U is used to evaluate individuals' allocations of attributes, then for all $X, Y \in \mathcal{D}$, the vector of utilities $(U(y_{1\cdot}), \ldots, U(y_{n\cdot}))$ strictly generalized Lorenz dominates the vector of utilities $(U(x_{1\cdot}), \ldots, U(x_{n\cdot}))$ if $Y \succ_U X$. Hence, the ordering defined by the utilitarian social evaluation function (12.1) satisfies UM if U is increasing and strictly concave.

If $Y \succ_{PD} X$ or if $Y \succ_U X$, then Y exhibits less dispersion than X. Furthermore, the mean value of each attribute is the same in both X and Y. It is for these reasons that UPM and UM have so much appeal as ways of incorporating inequality aversion into a social evaluation. However, in a society in which individuals have different preferences, Fleurbaey and Trannoy (2003) have shown that multi-attribute versions of the Pigou–Dalton transfer principle can conflict with the Pareto principle. Thus, a welfarist would want to limit the domain of applicability of multidimensional transfer principles in heterogeneous societies.

12.4 Normative univariate inequality indices

In the normative approach to inequality measurement, an inequality index is constructed from a social evaluation ordering. This approach has its origins in the articles by Atkinson (1970) and Kolm (1969) on univariate inequality measurement. In this section, I review the procedures that were proposed by Atkinson and Kolm for deriving univariate inequality indices from social evaluation orderings.

12.4.1 The Atkinson–Kolm–Sen inequality index

Suppose that $q = 1$ and that the social evaluation ordering is $\succsim$. The *equally-distributed-equivalent income* $\Xi_{\succsim}(x)$ associated with a given univariate income distribution x is the per capita income that, if distributed equally, is indifferent to the actual income distribution according to $\succeq$. Formally, $\Xi_{\succeq}(x)$ is defined implicitly by

$$(\Xi_{\succeq}(x) \cdot 1_n) \sim x, \quad \forall x \in \mathcal{D}. \tag{12.3}$$

ORD, CONT, and MON ensure that $\Xi_{\succeq}(x)$ is well-defined. The *equally-distributed-equivalent income function* is the mapping $\Xi_{\succeq} \colon \mathcal{D} \to \mathbb{R}$ that assigns the equally-distributed-equivalent income to each income distribution in the domain. $\Xi_{\succeq}$ is a particular representation of $\succeq$.

Now suppose that that $\mathcal{D} \in \{\mathcal{M}_2, \mathcal{M}_3\}$ (so that the mean income is always positive). The *Atkinson–Kolm–Sen inequality index* corresponding to $\succeq$ is the function $I_{\succeq}^{\mathrm{AKS}} \colon \mathcal{D} \to \mathbb{R}$ defined by

$$I_{\succeq}^{\mathrm{AKS}}(x) = 1 - \frac{\Xi_{\succeq}(x)}{\mu(x)}, \quad \forall x \in \mathcal{D}. \tag{12.4}$$

If $\succeq$ satisfies the Pigou–Dalton transfer principle, the value of this index is bounded above by 1 and bounded below by 0 (and the lower bound is only attained if incomes are equally distributed). This procedure for constructing an inequality index was independently proposed by Atkinson (1970) and Kolm (1969), and was later popularized by Sen (1973).[12] This index has a simple interpretation. $I_{\succeq}^{\mathrm{AKS}}(x)$ is the fraction of the total income that could be destroyed if incomes are equalized and the resulting distribution is indifferent to x according to $\succeq$. Thus, the Atkinson–Kolm–Sen inequality index is a measure of the waste due to inequality.

Given any univariate inequality index $I \colon \mathcal{D} \to \mathbb{R}$, (12.4) can be used to determine the underlying social evaluation that generates this index using the Atkinson–Kolm–Sen methodology. This social evaluation is represented by

$$\Xi_{\succeq}(x) = \mu(x)[1 - I(x)], \quad \forall x \in \mathcal{D}. \tag{12.5}$$

A univariate or multivariate inequality index $I \colon \mathcal{D} \to \mathbb{R}$ is *normatively significant* if for all $X, Y \in \mathcal{D}$ for which $\mu(x_{\cdot j}) = \mu(y_{\cdot j})$ for all $j \in Q$, $I(X) \geq I(Y)$ if and only if $Y \succeq X$. By construction, an Atkinson–Kolm–Sen inequality index is normatively significant.

An index is a *relative* index if it is invariant to a proportional scaling of all its variables; that is, if it is homogeneous of degree 0. From (12.4) it follows that $I_{\succeq}^{\mathrm{AKS}}$ is a relative inequality index if and only if $\Xi_{\succeq}$ is homogeneous of degree 1, which is equivalent to requiring $\succeq$ to be homothetic.

12.4.2 *The Kolm inequality index*

As in the preceding subsection, suppose that $q = 1$ and that the social evaluation ordering is $\succeq$. Further suppose that $\mathcal{D}$ is any one of the three domains defined in Section 12.2. Kolm (1969) has proposed an alternative to $I_{\succeq}^{\mathrm{AKS}}$ for the measurement of univariate income inequality. The *Kolm inequality index* corresponding to $\succeq$ is the function $I^{\mathrm{K}}_{\succeq}: \mathcal{D} \rightarrow \mathbb{R}$ defined by

$$I^{\mathrm{K}}_{\succeq}(x) = \mu(x) - \Xi_{\succeq}(x), \quad \forall x \in \mathcal{D}. \tag{12.6}$$

If $\succeq$ satisfies the Pigou–Dalton transfer principle, the value of this index is always nonnegative and it is only equal to 0 if everyone has the same income. $I^{\mathrm{K}}_{\succeq}(x)$ is the per capita income that could be destroyed if incomes are equalized and the resulting distribution is indifferent to x according to $\succeq$. As is the case with $I^{\mathrm{AKS}}_{\succeq}$, $I^{\mathrm{K}}_{\succeq}$ is normatively significant.

An index is an *absolute* index if it is invariant to an increase or decrease of all of its variables by a common amount. Kolm intended for $I^{\mathrm{K}}_{\succeq}$ to be used as a measure of absolute inequality, which implicitly places an invariance restriction on $\succeq$ analogous to the homotheticity requirement for $I^{\mathrm{AKS}}_{\succeq}$ to be a relative index. From (12.6), it can be seen that $I^{\mathrm{K}}_{\succeq}$ is an absolute inequality index if and only if $\Xi_{\succeq}$ is unit-translatable, which is equivalent to requiring $\succeq$ to be translatable.[13]

If one subscribes to Kolm's procedure, the equally-distributed-equivalent income function underlying the univariate inequality index $I: \mathcal{D} \rightarrow \mathbb{R}$ is given by

$$\Xi_{\succeq}(x) = \mu(x) - I(x), \quad \forall x \in \mathcal{D}. \tag{12.7}$$

Comparing (12.5) and (12.7), we see that the social evaluation that provides the normative foundation for an inequality index is indeterminate unless one has adopted a particular procedure for deriving inequality indices from social evaluations.[14] For this reason, Foster (1994), among others, has criticized the various proposals for constructing normative inequality indices.

Both the $I^{\mathrm{AKS}}_{\succeq}$ and $I^{\mathrm{K}}_{\succeq}$ indices are cardinal. Replacing I by an ordinally-equivalent function, say by squaring I, in either (12.5) or (12.7) changes the underlying social evaluation. While there has been some research on ordinal inequality indices for univariate distributions (see Blackorby *et al.*, 1999; Chakravarty, 1990; Dutta, 2002), this is an issue that has not been considered in the multivariate literature.

12.5 Normative multivariate inequality indices

In this section, I describe how the $I^{\mathrm{AKS}}_{\succeq}$ and $I^{\mathrm{K}}_{\succeq}$ indices have been generalized for multivariate distributions by Kolm (1977) and Tsui (1995). Throughout this discussion, it is assumed that $\succeq$ satisfes ORD, CONT, MON, ANON, and UM.

12.5.1 The multi-attribute Kolm inequality index

In this subsection, it is supposed that $\mathcal{D} \in \{\mathcal{M}_2, \mathcal{M}_3\}$. The Kolm (1977) multi-attribute generalization of the Atkinson–Kolm–Sen inequality index measures the inequality of a distribution matrix by the fraction of the aggregate amount of *each* attribute that could be destroyed if every attribute is equalized and the resulting distribution is indifferent to the original distribution according to $\succeq$.[15] To define this index formally, some preliminary definitions are needed.

For all $X \in \mathcal{D}$, let X_μ denote the distribution matrix in which, for all $j \in Q$, the entries in the jth column are all set equal to $\mu(x_{\cdot j})$. Define the function $\Delta_{\succeq} : \mathcal{D} \to \mathbb{R}$ by setting, for all $X \in \mathcal{D}$, $\Delta_{\succeq}(X)$ equal to the scalar that solves

$$\Delta_{\succeq}(X)X_\mu \sim X. \tag{12.8}$$

By ORD, CONT, and MON, this function is well-defined.

The *multi-attribute Kolm inequality index* associated with $\succeq$ is the function $I^{\mathrm{KM}}_{\succeq} : \mathcal{D} \to \mathbb{R}$ defined by setting

$$I^{\mathrm{KM}}_{\succeq}(X) = 1 - \Delta_{\succeq}(X), \quad \forall X \in \mathcal{D}. \tag{12.9}$$

If $q = 1$, $\Delta_{\succeq}(x) = \Xi_{\succeq}(x)/\mu(x)$ for all $x \in \mathcal{D}$. Hence, for univariate distributions, $I^{\mathrm{KM}}_{\succeq} = I^{\mathrm{AKS}}_{\succeq}$.

$\Delta_{\succeq}$ is not a representation of $\succeq$. Nevertheless, for any $X, Y \in \mathcal{D}$ for which $X_\mu = Y_\mu$, MON implies that $\Delta_{\succeq}(X) \geq \Delta_{\succeq}(Y)$ if and only if $X \succeq Y$. It then follows from (12.9) that $I^{\mathrm{KM}}_{\succeq}$ is normatively significant.

Consider an arbitrary inequality index $I : \mathcal{D} \to \mathbb{R}$. While (12.9) can be used to to solve for the $\Delta_{\succeq}$ function that generates I, $\Delta_{\succeq}$ does not provide sufficient information to determine $\succeq$ when $q > 1$. The problem is that the social ranking of X and Y is not known if $X_\mu \neq Y_\mu$ and neither X_μ weakly dominates Y_μ (attribute by attribute) nor Y_μ weakly dominates X_μ.

The value of $I^{\mathrm{KM}}_{\succeq}$ is clearly bounded above by 1. If $X = X_\mu$, then $\Delta_{\succeq}(X) = 1$ and $I^{\mathrm{KM}}_{\succeq}(X) = 0$. Because $X_\mu = BX$ for the bistochastic matrix B in which all entries are equal to $1/n$, UM and MON imply that $I^{\mathrm{KM}}_{\succeq}(X) > 0$ when $X \neq X_\mu$.[16] ANON implies that $I^{\mathrm{KM}}_{\succeq}$ treats individuals symmetrically; that is, $I^{\mathrm{KM}}_{\succeq}(X)$ is invariant to a permutation of the rows of X.

$I^{\mathrm{KM}}_{\succeq}$ is a relative index if and only if $\succeq$ is homothetic. For future reference, this property of $\succeq$ is stated as a formal axiom.

Homotheticity (HOM). For all $X, Y \in \mathcal{D}$ and all $\lambda > 0$, $X \succeq Y$ if and only if $\lambda X \succeq \lambda Y$.

For univariate distributions of income, one justification that has been offered for this axiom is that the social evaluation should be invariant to the units in which income is measured (dollars, euros, yen, etc.). In the multi-attribute case, HOM implies that $\succeq$ is invariant to a common proportional change in the units in which all goods are measured. If the various attributes correspond to different kinds of goods, this line of reasoning suggests that *independent* changes in the units in which different attributes are measured should not affect the social evaluation ordering.

Strong Homotheticity (SHOM). For all $X, Y \in \mathcal{D}$ and all $q \times q$ diagonal matrices Λ for which $\lambda_{jj} > 0$ for all $j \in Q$, $X \succeq Y$ if and only if $X\Lambda \succeq Y\Lambda$.

SHOM was proposed by Tsui (1995). The appeal of this kind of scale invariance assumption has been questioned by Bourguignon (1999, p. 479) when applied to inequality measurement. He has argued that if, say, incomes are doubled, then the contribution of other attributes to overall inequality may well be affected. Even if one accepts SHOM when the atrributes are different kinds of goods, as noted by Gajdos and Weymark (2005), this axiom is not appropriate if some of the attributes are naturally measured in the same units. For example, if the attributes are incomes in different states of the world, their units of measurement cannot be varied independently. For some goods, even stronger invariance properties may be appropriate. This would be the case if an attribute is measured on an ordinal scale.[17]

12.5.2 The multi-attribute Tsui inequality index

In this subsection, it is supposed that $\mathcal{D} \in \{\mathcal{M}_1, \mathcal{M}_2, \mathcal{M}_3\}$. Tsui (1995) has provided a multi-attribute generalization of Kolm's univariate inequality index. Tsui's index measures inequality by the amount of each attribute that must be taken away from every individual in order to obtain an allocation that is indifferent to the original allocation according to $\succeq$ if the distribution of each attribute is equalized.

The formal definition of this index uses the function $\Gamma_{\succeq}\colon \mathcal{D} \to \mathbb{R}$ defined by setting, for all $X \in \mathcal{D}$, $\Gamma_{\succeq}(X)$ equal to the scalar that solves

$$(X_\mu - \Gamma_{\succeq}(X)\mathbf{1}) \sim X, \qquad (12.10)$$

where $\mathbf{1}$ is a distribution matrix whose entries are all equal to 1. By ORD, CONT, and MON, this function is well-defined.

The *multi-attribute Tsui inequality index* associated with $\succeq$ is the function $I^{\mathrm{TM}}_{\succeq}\colon \mathcal{D} \to \mathbb{R}$ defined by setting

$$I^{\mathrm{TM}}_{\succeq}(X) = \Gamma_{\succeq}(X), \quad \forall X \in \mathcal{D}. \qquad (12.11)$$

If $q = 1$, $I^{\mathrm{TM}}_{\succeq} = I^{\mathrm{K}}_{\succeq}$ because $\Gamma_{\succeq}(x) = \mu(x) - \Xi_{\succeq}(x)$ for all $x \in \mathcal{D}$. Using reasoning similar to that used in the discussion of $I^{\mathrm{KM}}_{\succeq}$, it is straightforward to show that $I^{\mathrm{TM}}_{\succeq}$ is normatively significant, $I^{\mathrm{TM}}_{\succeq}(X) = 0$ if $X = X_\mu$, $I^{\mathrm{TM}}_{\succeq}(X) > 0$ if $X \neq X_\mu$, and $I^{\mathrm{TM}}_{\succeq}(X) = I^{\mathrm{TM}}_{\succeq}(\Pi X)$ for any $n \times n$ permutation matrix Π. Furthermore, given an arbitrary inequality index $I\colon \mathcal{D} \to \mathbb{R}$, it is not possible to determine the social evaluation $\succeq$ that generates I using Tsui's procedure.

$I^{\mathrm{TM}}_{\succeq}$ is an absolute index if and only if $\succeq$ is translatable.

Translatability (TRA). For all $X, Y \in \mathcal{D}$ and all $\lambda \in \mathbb{R}$ for which $X + \lambda\mathbf{1} \in \mathcal{D}$ and $Y + \lambda\mathbf{1} \in \mathcal{D}$, $X \succeq Y$ if and only if $X + \lambda\mathbf{1} \succeq Y + \lambda\mathbf{1}$.

If TRA is satisfied, then $\succeq$ is invariant to a common change in the origins from which the quantities of the various attributes are measured. Tsui (1995) has also considered a stronger version of this translatability axiom that requires $\succeq$ to be invariant to independent changes in these origins.

Strong Translatability (STRA). For all $X, Y \in \mathcal{D}$ and all $q \times q$ diagonal matrices Λ for which $X + \mathbf{1}\Lambda \in \mathcal{D}$ and $Y + \mathbf{1}\Lambda \in \mathcal{D}$, $X \succeq Y$ if and only if $X + \mathbf{1}\Lambda \succeq Y + \mathbf{1}\Lambda$.

As with SHOM, STRA would not be appropriate if there are attributes that should be measured in the same units.

12.6 Multidimensional Atkinson and Kolm–Pollak indices

Starting with the work of Atkinson (1970) and Kolm (1969), the procedures described in Section 12.4 have been used to derive new functional forms for univariate inequality indices. Prominent among them are the Atkinson (1970) class of relative inequality indices and the Kolm (1969, 1976) – Pollak (1971) class of absolute inequality indices. In this section, I consider the multi-attribute generalizations of these indices proposed by Tsui (1995).

12.6.1 Multidimensional Atkinson indices

In this subsection, it is supposed that $\mathcal{D} = \mathcal{M}_3$. With minor modifications, the analysis also applies to the domain $\mathcal{M}_2$. Atkinson (1970) considered univariate distributions and assumed that the social evaluation $\succeq$ is represented by a symmetric and additively separable social evaluation function, as in (12.1). Suppose that U is increasing and strictly concave. With these assumptions, $\succeq$ is homothetic if and only if there is a scalar $r < 1$ such that for all $x_i > 0$,

$$U(x_i) = \begin{cases} a + bx_i^r/r, & \text{if } r < 1 \text{ and } r \neq 0; \\ a + b\ln(x_i), & \text{if } r = 0, \end{cases} \tag{12.12}$$

for some $a \in \mathbb{R}$ and some $b > 0$. For the social evaluation function obtained by substituting (12.12) into (12.1), the equally-distributed-equivalent income function is given by

$$\Xi^{\mathrm{A}}_{\succeq}(x) = \begin{cases} \left[\frac{1}{n}\sum_{i=1}^n x_i^r\right]^{1/r}, & \text{if } r < 1 \text{ and } r \neq 0; \\ \prod_{i=1}^n x_i^{1/n}, & \text{if } r = 0, \end{cases} \tag{12.13}$$

for all $x \in \mathcal{D}$. $\Xi^{\mathrm{A}}_{\succeq}$ is a mean of order r function for $r < 1$. The Atkinson–Kolm–Sen relative inequality index corresponding to (12.13) is

$$I^{\mathrm{A}}_{\succeq}(x) = \begin{cases} 1 - \left[\frac{1}{n}\sum_{i=1}^n \left(\frac{x_i}{\mu(x)}\right)^r\right]^{1/r}, & \text{if } r < 1 \text{ and } r \neq 0; \\ 1 - \prod_{i=1}^n \left(\frac{x_i}{\mu(x)}\right)^{1/n}, & \text{if } r = 0, \end{cases} \tag{12.14}$$

for all $x \in \mathcal{D}$. An index of the form given in (12.14) is an *Atkinson index of inequality*.[18]

The multi-attribute generalization of this class of indices proposed by Tsui (1995) was identified axiomatically. This axiomatization requires that $n \geq 3$. Tsui's axioms are multi-attribute analogues of the axioms used by Blackorby *et al.*

(1981) to axiomatize the social evaluation functions for the Atkinson class of indices. They include ORD, CONT, MON, ANON, UM, and SHOM.[19]

Tsui's final axiom is a separability assumption. For all $X \in \mathcal{D}$ and all nonempty $S \subset N$, let X^S denote the submatrix of X containing the distributions of attributes for individuals in S and let X^{S^C} be the submatrix containing the remaining rows of X. The individuals in S are *individual separable* in $\succeq$ from their complement S^C if the conditional ordering of the subdistribution matrices for the individuals in S obtained by fixing the subdistribution matrix of the individuals in S^C does not depend on the choice of the latter submatrix.

Minimal Individual Separability (MIS). There exists a non-singleton set of individuals $S \subset N$ that is individual separable in $\succeq$ from S^C.

ANON implies that if S is individual separable in $\succeq$ from S^C, then any set of individuals with the same cardinality is individual separable from its complement. When $n \geq 3$, combining ANON and MIS with ORD, CONT, MON, and UM implies that there exists an increasing, strictly concave function $U : \mathcal{D} \rightarrow \mathbb{R}$ such that $\succeq$ can be represented by an additive social evaluation function of the form given in (12.1). The function U is a utility function that the social evaluator uses to aggregate any individual's allocation of the q attributes into a summary statistic. The function U need not coincide with any individual's actual utility function. Adding SHOM to the six axioms used to obtain the additive representation of the social evaluation order places considerable structure on the aggregator function U, as the following theorem due to Tsui (1995) demonstrates.

Theorem 12.1. *Suppose that $n \geq 3$. A social evaluation $\succeq$ on $\mathcal{D} = \mathcal{M}_3$ satisfies ORD, CONT, MON, ANON, UM, MIS, and SHOM if and only if there exists an increasing, strictly concave function $U : \mathbb{R}^q_{++} \rightarrow \mathbb{R}$ such that $\succeq$ can be represented by an additive social evaluation function of the form given in (12.1) where, for all $x_{ij} > 0$,*

$$U(x_{i\cdot}) = a + b\prod_{j=1}^{q} x_{ij}^{r_j} \tag{12.15}$$

or

$$U(x_{i\cdot}) = a + \sum_{j=1}^{q} s_j \ln(x_{ij}), \tag{12.16}$$

where $a \in \mathbb{R}$, $s_j > 0$ for all $j \in Q$, and the parameters b and r_j, $j \in Q$, are chosen so that the function U in (12.15) is increasing and strictly concave.[20]

A function $I^{\mathrm{AM}}_{\succeq}: \mathcal{D} \to \mathbb{R}$ is a member of the corresponding class of multi-attribute Kolm relative inequality indices if for all $X \in \mathcal{D}$,

$$I^{\mathrm{AM}}_{\succeq}(X) = 1 - \left[\frac{1}{n}\sum_{i=1}^{n}\prod_{j=1}^{q}\left(\frac{x_{ij}}{\mu(x_{\cdot j})}\right)^{r_j}\right]^{1/\sum_j r_j} \tag{12.17}$$

or

$$I^{\mathrm{AM}}_{\succeq}(X) = 1 - \prod_{i=1}^{n}\left[\prod_{j=1}^{q}\left(\frac{x_{ij}}{\mu(x_{\cdot j})}\right)^{s_j/\sum_j s_j}\right]^{1/n}, \tag{12.18}$$

where the parameters satisfy the restrictions in Theorem 12.1. $I^{\mathrm{AM}}_{\succeq}$ is a *multi-attribute Atkinson inequality index*. If $q = 1$, (12.17) and (12.18) are equivalent to the formulae for the univariate Atkinson index given in (12.14).

12.6.2 Multidimensional Kolm–Pollak indices

In this subsection, it is supposed that $\mathcal{D} = \mathcal{M}_1$. With minor modifications, the analysis also applies to the other two domains.

For the univariate case, assume as in Atkinson (1970) that the social evaluation $\succeq$ is symmetric and additively separable. If the function U in (12.1) is increasing and strictly concave, then $\succeq$ is translatable if and only if there is a scalar $r > 0$ such that for all $x_i \in \mathbb{R}$,

$$U(x_i) = a + b\left(\frac{\exp(-rx_i)}{-r}\right), \tag{12.19}$$

for some $a \in \mathbb{R}$ and some $b > 0$. The equally-distributed-equivalent income function for $\succeq$ is given by

$$\Xi^{\mathrm{KP}}_{\succeq}(x) = -\frac{1}{r}\ln\left[\frac{1}{n}\sum_{i=1}^{n}\exp(-rx_i)\right], \quad r > 0, \tag{12.20}$$

for all $x \in \mathcal{D}$. The Kolm absolute inequality index corresponding to (12.20) can be written as

$$I^{\mathrm{KP}}_{\succeq}(x) = \frac{1}{r}\ln\left[\frac{1}{n}\sum_{i=1}^{n}\exp(r(\mu(x) - x_i))\right], \quad r > 0, \tag{12.21}$$

for all $x \in \mathcal{D}$. An index of the form given in (12.21) is a *Kolm–Pollak index of inequality*. This class of inequality indices was introduced by Kolm (1969) (see also Kolm (1976)). In consumer theory, the functional form in (12.20) was shown by Pollak (1971) to characterize the additive utility functions that have linear Engel curves.

Given an ordering R on the positive orhant of $\mathbb{R}^n$, an ordering R^* on all of $\mathbb{R}^n$ can be defined by setting, for all $u, v \in \mathbb{R}^n$, uR^*v if and only if $(\exp(u_1), \ldots, \exp(u_n))R(\exp(v_1), \ldots, \exp(v_n))$. The ordering R is homothetic if and only if the ordering R^* is translatable. This observation accounts for why the equally-distributed income functions for the Kolm–Pollak indices can be obtained from the equally-distributed income functions for the Atkinson indices by an exponential change of variables.[21]

By substituting STRA for SHOM in the axioms of Theorem 12.1, Tsui (1995) has characterized a class of multi-attribute Kolm–Pollak social evaluation orderings.

Theorem 12.2. *Suppose that $n \geq 3$. A social evaluation $\succeq$ on $\mathcal{D} = \mathcal{M}_1$ satisfies ORD, CONT, MON, ANON, UM, MIS, and STRA if and only if there exists an increasing, strictly concave function $U\colon \mathbb{R}^q \to \mathbb{R}$ such that $\succeq$ can be represented by an additive social evaluation function of the form given in (12.1) where, for all $x_{ij} > 0$,*

$$U(x_{i\cdot}) = a + b\prod_{j=1}^{q} \exp(r_j x_{ij}), \tag{12.22}$$

where $a \in \mathbb{R}$ and the parameters b and r_j, $j \in Q$, are chosen so that the function U in (12.22) is increasing and strictly concave.

The functional form in (12.22) can be obtained from (12.15) by an exponential change of variables. A function $I_{\succeq}^{\mathrm{KPM}}\colon \mathcal{D} \to \mathbb{R}$ is a member of the corresponding class of multi-attribute Tsui absolute inequality indices if for all $X \in \mathcal{D}$,

$$I_{\succeq}^{\mathrm{KPM}}(X) = \frac{1}{\sum_j r_j} \ln\left[\frac{1}{n}\sum_{i=1}^{n} \exp\left(\sum_{j=1}^{q} r_j(\mu(x_{\cdot j}) - x_{ij})\right)\right], \tag{12.23}$$

where the parameters satisfy the restrictions in Theorem 12.2. $I_{\succeq}^{\mathrm{KPM}}$ is a *multi-attribute Kolm–Pollak inequality index*. This class of indices coincides with the univariate Kolm–Pollak class when $q = 1$.

Note that Theorems 12.1 and 12.2 use the stronger forms, SHOM and STRA, of the invariance axioms. The implications of using HOM and TRA instead have not been determined.

12.7 Maasoumi's two-stage aggregation procedure

The multi-attribute social evaluation functions considered in the preceding section are defined using a two-stage aggregation procedure. In the first stage, for each individual, a utility function is used to aggregate the individual's allocation of the q attributes into a summary measure of well-being. This initial aggregation results in a unidimensional distribution of utilities. In the second stage, the individual utilities are summed to provide the overall social evaluation of a distribution matrix.

Maasoumi (1986) (see also Maasoumi, 1999) has suggested that a multi-attribute *inequality index* should be constructed directly using a two-stage procedure. Specifically, he proposed using a utility function in the first stage to aggregate the individual allocations of the attributes into a vector of utilities and then, in the second stage, using a univariate inequality index applied to this distribution to obtain a measure of the inequality in the distribution matrix. He also proposed functional forms for these aggregators. For the second-stage aggregator, he suggested using a member of the class of generalized entropy inequality indices. This class of indices contains the Atkinson class and all of the indices that are ordinally equivalent to some member of the Atkinson class. Using information-theoretic considerations, Maasoumi argued that the utility function should be a weighted mean of order r. The multi-attribute Atkinson and Kolm–Pollak inequality indices are not two-stage aggregators in the sense of Maasoumi, as is apparent from inspection of their functional forms.

Dardanoni (1995) has shown that an inequality index constructed according to Maasoumi's proposal need not satisfy the inequality counterpart of UM. His argument is based on the following example.

Let

$$X = \begin{bmatrix} 10 & 10 & 10 \\ 10 & 90 & 10 \\ 90 & 10 & 10 \end{bmatrix} \quad \text{and} \quad B = \begin{bmatrix} 1 & 0 & 0 \\ 0 & 0.5 & 0.5 \\ 0 & 0.5 & 0.5 \end{bmatrix}.$$

We then have

$$Y = BX = \begin{bmatrix} 10 & 10 & 10 \\ 50 & 50 & 10 \\ 50 & 50 & 10 \end{bmatrix}.$$

Because the distribution matrix Y is obtained by multiplying X by a non-permutation bistochastic matrix, it seems reasonable to say that X exhibits more inequality than Y. Indeed, this is the case for any normatively-significant inequality index if the underlying social evaluation satisfies UM.

Now suppose that the inequality index is constructed using Maasoumi's two-stage procedure. Assume that the univariate inequality index I used in the second stage is a strictly S-convex relative index. Also assume that the utility function U used in the first stage is a symmetric, increasing, concave function of its arguments. We then have $U(x_{1\cdot}) = U(y_{1\cdot}) < U(x_{2\cdot}) = U(x_{3\cdot}) \leq U(y_{2\cdot}) = U(y_{3\cdot})$. If the weak inequality is in fact an equality, there has been no change in the distribution of the utilities, so I registers no change in inequality. If the weak inequality is strict, then the situation of the two individuals with the largest pre-transfer utilities is improved after the transfers and, as can be seen by considering the pre- and post-transfer Lorenz curves for the utility distributions, I regards Y as exhibiting more inequality than X. In either case, the ordering of X and Y differs from the one described in the preceding paragraph.

The conclusion that Dardanoni (1995, p. 202) draws from this example is that uniform majorization is "uninformative for evaluating the amount of inequality in society." This seems unwarranted. A more natural conclusion would be to question the appropriateness of Maasoumi's two-stage aggregation procedure for constructing multidimensional inequality indices.

12.8 Multidimensional generalized Gini indices

The most widely-used univariate index of relative inequality is the Gini index. The Gini social evaluation ordering is a member of the class of generalized Gini social evaluations introduced by Weymark (1981). These social evaluations are both homothetic and translatable. As a consequence, the procedures described in Section 12.4 can be used to define a class of generalized Gini relative inequality indices and a class of generalized Gini absolute inequality indices. In this section, the multi-attribute generalizations of these indices recently introduced by Gajdos and Weymark (2005) are considered.

12.8.1 Multidimensional generalized Gini social evaluations

Before turning to the multidimensional generalized Ginis, it is first necessary to formally define the univariate generalized Ginis. A *generalized Gini social evaluation* is a binary relation $\succeq$ on $\mathcal{D}$ whose equally-distributed-equivalent income function $\Xi^{\mathrm{G}}_{\succeq}: \mathcal{D} \to \mathbb{R}$ has the form

$$\Xi^{\mathrm{G}}_{\succeq}(x) = \sum_{i=1}^{n} a_i \tilde{x}_i, \quad \forall x \in \mathcal{D}, \tag{12.24}$$

where $0 < a_1 < a_2 < \cdots < a_n$ and $\sum_{i=1}^{n} a_i = 1$.[22] The *Gini equally-distributed-equivalent income function* is the special case of (12.24) in which $a_i = (2i-1)/n^2$ for all $i \in N$. As noted earlier, a generalized Gini social evaluation is both homothetic and translatable. The corresponding classes of generalized Gini relative and absolute inequality indices are obtained by substituting (12.24) into (12.4) and (12.6), respectively.

The multi-attribute versions of the generalized Gini social evaluations introduced by Gajdos and Weymark (2005) were obtained by supplementing multidimensional generalizations of the axioms Weymark (1981) used to characterize the univariate generalized Ginis with a assumption that requires the social evaluation to be separable with respect to attributes. Aside from the separability assumption, the only one of these axioms that has not already been introduced is a comonotonic additivity axiom. In order to define this axiom, some additional notation is required.

A distribution matrix X is *nonincreasing comonotonic* if $x_{1j} \geq x_{2j} \geq \cdots \geq x_{nj}$ for all $j \in Q$. In other words, person 1 has at least as much of every attribute as person 2, person 2 has at least as much of every attribute as person 3, etc. Let $\mathcal{D}^{\mathrm{D}}$ denote the set of nonincreasing comonotonic matrices in $\mathcal{D}$.

Weak Comonotonic Additivity (WCA). For all $X, Y \in \mathcal{D}^{\mathrm{D}}$ and all $Z \in \mathcal{M}^{\mathrm{D}}_1$ for which there exists a $j_0 \in Q$ such that (1) $x_{\cdot j} = y_{\cdot j}$ for all $j \neq j_0$, (2) $z_{ij} = 0$ for all

$i \in N$ and all $j \neq j_0$, and (3) $X + Z \in \mathcal{D}^{\mathrm{D}}$ and $Y + Z \in \mathcal{D}^{\mathrm{D}}$, $X \succeq Y$ if and only if $X + Z \succeq Y + Z$.[23]

The distribution matrices X, Y, $X + Z$, and $Y + Z$ in the definition of WCA are all nonincreasing comonotonic and have identical distributions of all the attributes except j_0. Hence, the social ranking of these matrices coincides with the ranking obtained with the conditional ordering of attribute j_0. $X + Z$ and $Y + Z$ are obtained from X and Y by adding a common distribution of attribute j_0 to both $x_{\cdot j_0}$ and $y_{\cdot j_0}$. WCA requires the social ranking of two comonotonic distribution matrices to be invariant to this kind of change. In other words, in any conditional ordering of two distributions of an attribute, the ordering only depends on the amounts by which the distributions differ.[24]

For all $X \in \mathcal{D}$ and all nonempty $M \subset Q$, let X^M denote the submatrix of X containing the distributions of the attributes in M and let $X^{M^{\mathrm{C}}}$ be the submatrix containing the other columns of X. The attributes in M are *attribute separable* in $\succeq$ from their complement M^{C} if the conditional ordering of the subdistribution matrices for the attributes in M obtained by fixing the subdistribution matrix of the attributes in M^{C} is independent of the choice of the latter submatrix. The separability axiom used by Gajdos and Weymark (2005) is given by the following axiom.

Strong Attribute Separability (SAS). For all nonempty $M \subset Q$, M is attribute separable in $\succeq$ from M^{C}.

Gajdos and Weymark (2003) have shown that if a social evaluation $\succeq$ on $\mathcal{D}$ satisfies SAS and ANON, then the two multi-attribute transfer principles, UPM and UM, place equivalent structure on $\succeq$. They have also shown that ORD, CONT, MON, and SAS imply that $\succeq$ has a two-stage aggregation representation, but the order of aggregation differs from that used in the multi-attribute Atkinson and Kolm–Pollak inequality indices. In the first stage, the distributions of each attribute are aggregated, resulting in a q-dimensional vector of scalars. In the second stage, the components of this vector are aggregated to provide an overall evaluation of the distribution matrix. If there are at least three attributes, this second-stage aggregator is additively separable. If it is additionally assumed that $\succeq$ satisfies WCA, then the first-stage aggregators must be generalized Gini equally-distributed-equivalent income functions.

12.8.2 Multidimensional generalized Gini relative inequality indices

Now assume that $\mathcal{D} = \mathcal{M}_2$. The following theorem, due to Gajdos and Weymark (2005), characterizes the set of social evaluations that satisfy HOM in addition to the axioms considered in the preceding paragraph.[25]

Theorem 12.3. *If $q \geq 3$, then the binary relation $\succeq$ on $\mathcal{D} = \mathcal{M}_2$ satisfies ORD, CONT, MON, ANON, UPM, SAS, WCA, and HOM if and only if there exists an*

$n \times q$ matrix A of positive coefficients with $a_{\cdot j}$ increasing in i and $\sum_{i=1}^{n} a_{ij} = 1$ for all $j \in Q$, a positive vector $\gamma \in \mathbb{R}^q$ with $\sum_{j=1}^{q} \gamma_j = 1$, and a scalar r such that $\succeq$ can be represented by a social evaluation function $W_{\succeq}^{\mathrm{GMR}} : \mathcal{M}_2 \to \mathbb{R}$ for which

$$W_{\succeq}^{\mathrm{GMR}}(X) = \left[\sum_{j=1}^{q} \gamma_j \left(\sum_{i=1}^{n} a_{ij} \tilde{x}_{ij} \right)^r \right]^{1/r}, \quad \forall X \in \mathcal{M}_2, \tag{12.25}$$

if $r \neq 0$ and

$$W_{\succeq}^{\mathrm{GMR}}(X) = \prod_{j=1}^{q} \left(\sum_{i=1}^{n} a_{ij} \tilde{x}_{ij} \right)^{\gamma_j}, \quad \forall X \in \mathcal{M}_2, \tag{12.26}$$

if $r = 0$.

Thus, the second-stage aggregator is a mean of order r function, where r is unrestricted, if $\succeq$ is assumed to satisfy the axioms of Theorem 12.3. If HOM is strengthened to SHOM, then only the $r = 0$ case is possible; that is, the second-stage aggregator must be a Cobb–Douglas function.

A function $I_{\succeq}^{\mathrm{GMR}} : \mathcal{D} \to \mathbb{R}$ is a member of the corresponding class of multi-attribute Kolm relative inequality indices if

$$I_{\succeq}^{\mathrm{GMR}}(X) = 1 - \frac{\left[\sum_{j=1}^{q} \gamma_j \left(\sum_{i=1}^{n} a_{ij} \tilde{x}_{ij} \right)^r \right]^{1/r}}{\left[\sum_{j=1}^{q} \gamma_j \mu(x_{\cdot j})^r \right]^{1/r}}, \quad \forall X \in \mathcal{M}_2, \tag{12.27}$$

when $r \neq 0$ and

$$I_{\succeq}^{\mathrm{GMR}}(X) = 1 - \frac{\prod_{j=1}^{q} \left(\sum_{i=1}^{n} a_{ij} \tilde{x}_{ij} \right)^{\gamma_j}}{\prod_{j=1}^{q} \mu(x_{\cdot j})^{\gamma_j}}, \quad \forall X \in \mathcal{M}_2, \tag{12.28}$$

when $r = 0$. $I_{\succeq}^{\mathrm{GMR}}$ is a *multi-attribute generalized Gini relative inequality index.*

12.8.3 Multidimensional generalized Gini absolute inequality indices

Now assume that $\mathcal{D} = \mathcal{M}_1$. Using a simple exponential change of variables, Gajdos and Weymark (2005) have established the counterpart of Theorem 12.3 for translatable social evaluations.

Theorem 12.4. *If $q \geq 3$, then the binary relation $\succeq$ on $\mathcal{D} = \mathcal{M}_1$ satisfies ORD, CONT, MON, ANON, UPM, SAS, WCA, and TRA if and only if there exists an $n \times q$ matrix A of positive coefficients with $a_{\cdot j}$ increasing in i and $\sum_{i=1}^{n} a_{ij} = 1$ for* *all $j \in Q$, a positive vector $\gamma \in \mathbb{R}^q$, and a scalar r such that $\succeq$ can be represented by a social evaluation function $W_{\succeq}^{\mathrm{GMA}}: \mathcal{M}_1 \to \mathbb{R}$ for which*

$$W_{\succeq}^{\mathrm{GMA}}(X) = \frac{1}{r} \ln \left[\sum_{j=1}^{q} \gamma_j \exp \left(r \sum_{i=1}^{n} a_{ij} \tilde{x}_{ij} \right) \right], \quad \forall X \in \mathcal{M}_1, \tag{12.29}$$

if $r \neq 0$ and

$$W_{\succeq}^{\mathrm{GMA}}(X) = \sum_{j=1}^{q} \gamma_j \left(\sum_{i=1}^{n} a_{ij} \tilde{x}_{ij} \right), \quad \forall X \in \mathcal{M}_1, \tag{12.30}$$

if $r = 0$.

The second-stage aggregators in Theorem 12.4 are Kolm–Pollak functions. Note that, in contrast to (12.20), the parameter r can take on any value in $\mathbb{R}$. If TRA is strengthened to STRA, then $r = 0$, in which case the second-stage aggregator is linear.

A function $I_{\succeq}^{\mathrm{GMA}}: \mathcal{D} \to \mathbb{R}$ is a member of the corresponding class of multi-attribute Tsui absolute inequality indices if

$$I_{\succeq}^{\mathrm{GMA}}(X) = \frac{1}{r} \ln \left[\frac{\sum_{j=1}^{q} \gamma_j \exp\left(r \mu(x_{\cdot j}) \right)}{\sum_{j=1}^{q} \gamma_j \exp\left(r \sum_{i=1}^{n} a_{ij} \tilde{x}_{ij} \right)} \right], \quad \forall X \in \mathcal{M}_1, \tag{12.31}$$

when $r \neq 0$ and

$$I_{\succeq}^{\mathrm{GMA}}(X) = \sum_{j=1}^{q} \gamma_j \left[\mu(x_{\cdot j}) - \sum_{i=1}^{n} a_{ij} \tilde{x}_{ij} \right], \quad \forall X \in \mathcal{M}_1, \tag{12.32}$$

when $r = 0$. $I_{\succeq}^{\mathrm{GMA}}$ is a *multi-attribute generalized Gini absolute inequality index.*

12.9 Correlation increasing majorization

The two multi-attribute generalizations of the Pigou–Dalton transfer principle, UPM and UM, ensure that the social evaluation is inequality averse in the sense that uniform mean-preserving decreases in the spreads of the distributions of the attributes are socially desirable. Atkinson and Bourguignon (1982) have argued that a multi-attribute inequality index should also take account of the statistical dependence between the attribute distributions. Tsui (1999) has investigated one way in which an inequality index can be sensitive to the dependence properties of distribution matrices.[26] Tsui's axiom requires the value of a multi-attribute inequality index to increase if two individuals' allocations are rearranged so that one of these individuals receives at least as much of every attribute as the other and strictly more of at least one attribute (and this was not the case before the rearrangement).[27] In this section, the corresponding principle for social evaluations is considered.

For $x, y \in \mathbb{R}^q$, $x \wedge y = (\min\{x_1, y_1\}, \ldots, \min\{x_q, y_q\})$ and $x \vee y = (\max\{x_1, y_1\}, \ldots, \max\{x_q, y_q\})$.

Definition 12.3. *For all $X, Y \in \mathcal{D}$, Y is obtained from X by a correlation-increasing transfer if $X \neq Y$, X is not a permutation of the rows of Y, and there exist $i_1, i_2 \in N$ such that (i) $y_{i_1\cdot} = x_{i_1\cdot} \wedge x_{i_2\cdot}$, (ii) $y_{i_2\cdot} = x_{i_1\cdot} \vee x_{i_2\cdot}$, and (iii) $y_{i\cdot} = x_{i\cdot}$ for all $i \notin \{i_1, i_2\}$.*

Note that a correlation-increasing transfer preserves the mean of each attribute.

Definition 12.4. *For all $X, Y \in \mathcal{D}$, Y is more correlated than X, denoted $Y \succ_C X$, if Y can be obtained from X by a finite sequence of correlation-increasing transfers.*[28]

The social evaluation version of Tsui's dependence-sensitivity axiom requires that if Y is more correlated than X, then X should be socially preferred to Y.

Correlation Increasing Majorization (CIM). For all $X, Y \in \mathcal{D}$, if $Y \succ_C X$, then $X \succ Y$.

Tsui (1999) has shown that CIM and UM (resp. UPM) are independent principles. In other words, any pair of distribution matrices that can be ordered by $\succ_C$ cannot be ordered by $\succ_U$ (resp. $\succ_{PD}$) and vice versa.

A function $f : D \to \mathbb{R}$, where $D \subseteq \mathbb{R}^q$, is *L-superadditive* if for all $x, y \in D$, $f(x \wedge y) + f(x \vee y) \geq f(x) + f(y)$. If the inequality is strict when $x \wedge y \neq x$ and $x \wedge y \neq y$, then f is *strictly L-superadditive*.[29] *L-subadditive* and *strictly L-subadditive* functions are defined analogously by reversing the inequality signs. If f is twice differentiable, then f is L-superadditive (resp. strictly L-superadditive, L-subadditive, strictly L-subadditive) if and only if for all distinct $j_1, j_2 \in Q$ and all $x \in D$, $\partial^2 f(x)/\partial x_{j_1} \partial x_{j_2} \geq 0$ (resp. > 0, ≤ 0, < 0).

It follows from the definition of strict L-subadditivity that the utilitarian social evaluation (12.1) satisfies CIM if U is strictly L-subadditive. Furthermore, a straightforward extension of Proposition 4 in Tsui (1999) shows that, for all $X, Y \in \mathcal{D}$, the vector of utilities $u = (U(x_{1\cdot}), \ldots, U(x_{n\cdot}))$ strictly generalized Lorenz dominates the vector of utilities $v = (U(y_{1\cdot}), \ldots, U(y_{n\cdot}))$ if $Y \succ_C X$ and U is increasing and strictly L-subadditive.[30]

For the two-attribute case, the implications of correlation-increasing transfers for the utilitarian social evaluation function have also been considered by Atkinson and Bourguignon (1982).[31] The two attributes are *substitutes* if the utility function U is strictly L-subadditive and they are *complements* if it is strictly L-superadditive. In contradiction to CIM, the value of a utilitarian social evaluation function increases in response to a correlation-increasing transfer when the two goods are complements. For this reason, Bourguignon and Chakravarty (2003) criticized Tsui's use of CIM, arguing that he has implicitly assumed that all goods are substitutes.

The multi-attribute generalized Gini social evaluations do not satisfy CIM. The reason is quite simple – the separability across attributes implied by SAS is inconsistent with $\succsim$ being sensitive to the statistical dependence of the individual attribute distributions. As Gajdos and Weymark (2005) have shown, the inconsistency with CIM holds even if there is a single attribute that is attribute separable in $\succsim$ from the other attributes if $\succsim$ satisfies ANON.

There are, however, multi-attribute relative inequality indices that satisfy the inequality versions of both UM and CIM. For the domain $\mathcal{M}_3$, Tsui (1999) has axiomatized a class of such indices. They are multi-attribute generalized entropy relative inequality indices. List (1999) has constructed multidimensional generalizations of the Gini and Atkinson indices that also satisfy both of these properties.[32]

List has also proposed a procedure for constructing multidimensional relative inequality indices on $\mathcal{M}_2$ that are consistent with both of these inequality dominance principles. List's construction bears some relationship to the two-stage aggregation procedure proposed by Maasoumi (1986) that is described in Section 12.7. For any $X \in \mathcal{M}_2$, X is first replaced by the distribution matrix $X_C = X\Lambda_C$, where Λ_C is the $q \times q$ diagonal matrix in which $\lambda_{jj} = 1/\mu(x_{\cdot j})$ for all $j \in Q$. The mean value of each attribute in X_C is 1. This step ensures that the resulting index is invariant to independent changes in the units in which attributes are measured. Next, a common utility function is used to aggregate each person's allocation of the attributes in X_C. In order for the resulting index to satisfy both inequality dominance principles, this utility function must satisfy a number of properties, such as strict concavity. Finally, the resulting vector of utilities is aggregated using a generalized-Lorenz-consistent univariant inequality index.

With the exception of List's generalized Atkinson indices, none of the inequality indices proposed by List (1999) and Tsui (1999) are provided with a social-evaluation foundation. List's generalized Atkinson indices are defined using the function $\mu^{\mathrm{e}}_{\succsim} : \mathcal{M}_2 \to \mathbb{R}$, where, for all $X \in \mathcal{M}_2$, $\mu^{\mathrm{e}}_{\succsim}(X)$ is the scalar that solves

$$\mu^{\mathrm{e}}_{\succsim}(X)\mathbf{1} \sim X_C. \tag{12.33}$$

Using this function, a *List multi-attribute relative inequality index* $I^{\mathrm{LM}}_{\succsim} : \mathcal{M}_2 \to \mathbb{R}$ is defined by setting

$$I^{\mathrm{LM}}_{\succsim}(X) = 1 - \mu^{\mathrm{e}}_{\succsim}(X), \quad \forall X \in \mathcal{M}_2. \tag{12.34}$$

List's multidimensional Atkinson indices are defined using a specific functional form for the function $\mu^{\mathrm{e}}_{\succsim}$. $I^{\mathrm{LM}}_{\succsim}$ provides an alternative to Kolm's procedure for constructing multi-attribute relative inequality indices. At present, nothing is known about the properties of $I^{\mathrm{LM}}_{\succsim}$ except when $\mu^{\mathrm{e}}_{\succsim}$ has the particular functional form assumed by List.

12.10 Concluding remarks

It is also natural to investigate the implications of requiring social evaluations to satisfy multivariate versions of univariate transfer sensitivity, decomposability, and population replication invariance axioms. The latter two properties require social evaluations to be defined for different population sizes. Tsui (1999) has employed decomposability and replication invariance axioms in his characterization of a class of multi-attribute generalized entropy inequality indices. However, these indices were axiomatized directly, rather than indirectly using a social evaluation. Moyes (1999) has formulated multivariate transfer sensitivity axioms, but, to the best of my knowledge, multivariate generalizations of univariate transfer sensitivity axioms have yet to be used to help construct normative inequality indices.[33]

A number of functional forms for multivariate inequality indices have been proposed that do not have explicit normative foundations. Examples of such indices are List's multivariate Gini indices (see List, 1999), Tsui's multivariate generalized entropy indices (see Tsui, 1999), and Koshevoy and Mosler's multivariate generalizations of the Gini index (see Koshevoy and Mosler, 1997).

The framework employed here has also been used to analyze inequality under uncertainty. See Ben-Porath *et al.* (1997) and Gajdos and Maurin (2004). In this application, attributes are incomes in different states of the world. By working in this more structured environment, it is possible to formulate axioms that are appropriate for this specific problem that may not be appropriate in other interpretations of the model. Of particular note in this regard is that incomes in different states are measured in the same units, a fact that is exploited in some of the axioms used by Ben-Porath *et al.* (1997) and Gajdos and Maurin (2004).

A related area of research is the measurement of multidimensional poverty. See, for example, Bourguignon and Chakravarty (2003) and Tsui (2002). Multidimensional poverty raises many of the same issues that have been explored in the multidimensional inequality literature. In addition, there are issues that relate specifically to the concern with poverty. For example, there is the basic issue of who should be counted as being poor – someone who is poor in all dimensions or someone who falls below the poverty threshold in any dimension?

Although much has already been learned about multidimensional normative inequality indices, much more remains to be discovered. Compared to the theory of univariate inequality measurement, the analysis of multidimensional inequality is in its infancy.

Acknowledgments

This article was prepared for the 2003 Summer School on Inequality and Economic Integration organized by the International School of Economic Research at the University of Siena. I am grateful to Andrea Brandolini, Satya Chakravarty, Marc Fleurbaey, Thibault Gajdos, Christian List, Ernesto Savaglio, and the participants in the Summer School for their comments. I am especially grateful to Claudio Zoli for the proof that appears in footnote 16.

Notes

1 Inequality is not the only social phenonmenon for which multivariate indices have been developed. For example, the United Nations Human Development Index (see United Nations Development Programme, 1990) aggregates indicators of longevity, education, and command over resources into an overall measure of the standard of living.

2 See Trannoy (2006) for a detailed discussion of multivariate dominance criteria. Some of the issues in the measurement of multidimensional inequality that are not considered here are discussed in the surveys by Maasoumi (1999) and Savaglio (2006).

3 While, in principle, each of these attributes is subject to continuous variation, in practice, they may only take on a finite number of values. For example, qualitative measures of health status employ discrete categories. For an analysis of inequality measurement for categorical data, see Allison and Foster (2004).

4 $\mathbb{R}$, $\mathbb{R}_{+}$, and $\mathbb{R}_{++}$ denote the set of real numbers, nonnegative real numbers, and positive real numbers, respectively. 0_n (resp. 1_n) is an n-vector of zeros (resp. ones).

5 See Shorrocks (1983) for a detailed discussion of generalized Lorenz domination. In the mathematics literature, generalized Lorenz domination is known as weak supermajorization. See Marshall and Olkin (1979, p. 10).

6 This functional form is used by Atkinson (1970) in the unidimensional case and by Atkinson and Bourguignon (1982) in the multidimensional case. However, Atkinson (1983, p. 5) has said that "there is nothing inherently *utilitarian* in the formulation" given in (12.1). If U is not interpreted as a utility function, then (12.1) simply amounts to saying that the social evaluation function is symmetric and additively separable.

7 A matrix in $\mathcal{D}$ can be thought of as a vector in $\mathbb{R}^{nq}$. A subset of $\mathcal{D}$ is open if the corresponding set of vectors is open in $\mathbb{R}^{nq}$.

8 Note that in this formulation of a Pigou–Dalton transfer, the relative positions in the income distributions of the two individuals are permitted to differ pre- and post-transfer. It is sometimes assumed that the transfer does not reverse the rank order. In the presence of Anonymity, this restriction is of no consequence.

9 A nonnegative square matrix is *bistochastic* if all of its row and column sums are equal to 1.

10 A function $f: D \to \mathbb{R}$, where $D \subseteq \mathbb{R}^n$, is *S-concave* if $f(Bx) \geq f(x)$ for all $x \in D$ and all $n \times n$ bistochastic matrices B and it is *strictly S-concave* if the inequality is strict when Bx is not a permutation of x. *S-convexity* and *strict S-convexity* are defined analogously by reversing the inequality signs.

11 The terminology used here is based on Tsui (1999). In the terminology of Marshall and Olkin (1979), $Y \succ_{\text{PD}} X$ is equivalent to saying that X *chain majorizes* Y and $Y \succ_{\text{U}} X$ is equivalent to saying that X *majorizes* Y.

12 Atkinson (1970) assumed that the social evaluation function has the form given in (12.1).

13 A function $f: D \to \mathbb{R}$, where $D \subseteq \mathbb{R}^n$, is *unit-translatable* if $f(x + \lambda 1_n) = f(x) + \lambda$ for all $x \in D$ and all $\lambda \in \mathbb{R}$ for which $x + \lambda 1_n \in D$. A binary relation on a subset of a Euclidean space is *translatable* if it can be represented by a unit-translatable function.

14 While the two procedures described in the text are the most commonly used for constructing normative inequality indices, they do not exhaust the possibilities. For a discussion of some other approaches, see Blackorby *et al.* (1999), Chakravarty (1990), and Dutta (2002).

15 Bourguignon (1999) and List (1999) have proposed alternate multi-attribute generalizations of the $I_{\succsim}^{\text{AKS}}$ index. Bourguignon's index is constructed by first computing the ratio of the utilitarian sum in (12.1) to the utilitarian sum that would have been obtained if everyone had the mean value of each attribute and then subtracting this number from 1. Bourguignon assumes that the utility function used to aggregate the individual allocations is a CES function. List's proposal is considered in Section 12.9.

16 The same conclusion holds if UPM is substituted for UM because, as the following argument demonstrates, when $X \neq X_{\mu}$, X_{μ} can be obtained from X by a finite sequence

of strict T-transforms. If attribute 1 is not equally distributed in X, then by Lemma 2.B.1 in Marshall and Olkin (1979), there exists a finite sequence of strict T-transforms that, when applied to X, results in a distribution matrix Y in which attribute 1 is equally distributed. Note that if a T-transform is applied to Y, the distribution of attribute 1 is unchanged. Hence, reasoning as above, if attribute 2 is not equally distributed in Y, by applying a finite sequence of strict T-transforms to Y, it is possible to equalize the distributions of both attributes 1 and 2. By applying the same argument to each attribute sequentially, it follows that X_μ can be obtained from X by a finite sequence of strict T-transforms.

17 HOM and SHOM (and TRA and STRA defined in Section 12.5.2) are formally equivalent to invariance assumptions used in the literature on social choice with interpersonal utility comparisons. See Bossert and Weymark (2004) and Gajdos and Weymark (2005).

18 The same class of indices was also characterized by Kolm (1969, Theorem 13).

19 Tsui formulated his axioms in terms of a social evaluation function, rather than in terms of the underlying binary relation. Tsui assumed that the social evaluation function is strictly quasiconcave. However, this assumption can be replaced by the weaker assumption UM in his theorems.

20 The parameter restrictions on b and the r_j are quite complicated. See Tsui (1995) for details.

21 In the Kolm–Pollak counterpart to the $r = 0$ case of the Atkinson index, U is concave, but not strictly concave. Furthermore, the equally-distributed-equivalent income function is always equal to average income and inequality as measured by the Kolm index is identically 0.

22 Weymark (1981) merely requires that $a_1 \leq a_2 \leq \cdots \leq a_n$. If any of these weak inequalities hold with equality, $\Xi^{\mathrm{G}}_{\succeq}$ is S-concave, but not strictly S-concave.

23 The definition of WCA given here differs slightly from the one given in Gajdos and Weymark (2005). Theorems 12.3 and 12.4 are valid with either definition of WCA.

24 Gajdos and Weymark (2005) also considered a stronger version of this axiom.

25 Strictly speaking, in this and the following theorem, Gajdos and Weymark used a variant of UM in which the conclusion that $X \succ Y$ is weakened to $X \succeq Y$. With this weaker assumption, the weights $a_{\cdot j}$ only need to be nondecreasing in i, rather than increasing.

26 For an overview of different dependence concepts, see Joe (1997).

27 Dardanoni (1995) has investigated a variant of this principle that requires Y to exhibit at least as much inequality as X if Y is a comonotonic rearrangement of X.

28 Tsui's definition of $\succ_{\mathrm{C}}$ permits the sequence of correlation-increasing transfers to be supplemented with permutations of the individual allocations.

29 See Marshall and Olkin (1979, Chapter 6) for a detailed discussion of L-superadditive functions. Marshall and Olkin define f to be L-superadditive if for all distinct $j_1, j_2 \in Q$ and all $x, y \in D$ for which $x_j = y_j$ for all $j \notin \{j_1, j_2\}$, $f(x \wedge y) + f(x \vee y) \geq f(x) + f(y)$. This definition is equivalent to the one in the text.

30 If, in addition, U is symmetric and additive, then u strictly Lorenz dominates v.

31 Bourguignon (1999) has considered the implications of correlation-increasing transfers for the multi-attribute inequality indices proposed by Maasoumi (1986).

32 These indices are not members of the families of multi-attribute generalized Gini and Atkinson indices discussed in Sections 12.6 and 12.8.

33 For a discussion of transfer sensitivity for univariate distributions, see Shorrocks and Foster (1987).

References

Allison, R.A. and Foster, J.E., 2004. "Measuring health inequality using qualitative data." *Journal of Health Economics*, 23, 505–524.

Atkinson, A.B., 1970. "On the measurement of inequality." *Journal of Economic Theory*, 2, 244–263.

Atkinson, A.B., 1983. *Social Justice and Public Policy*. Cambridge, MA: MIT Press.

Atkinson, A.B. and Bourguignon, F., 1982. "The comparison of multi-dimensioned distributions of economic status." *Review of Economic Studies*, 49, 183–201.

Ben-Porath, E., Gilboa, I., and Schmeidler, D., 1997. "On the measurement of inequality under uncertainty." *Journal of Economic Theory*, 75, 194–204.

Blackorby, C., Donaldson, D., and Auersperg, M., 1981. "A new procedure for the measurement of inequality within and among population subgroups." *Canadian Journal of Economics*, 14, 665–685.

Blackorby, C., Bossert, W., and Donaldson, D., 1999. "Income inequality measurement: The normative approach." In J. Silber (ed.) *Handbook of Income Inequality Measurement*. Boston, MA: Kluwer Academic Publishers, pp. 133–157.

Bossert, W. and Weymark, J.A., 2004. "Utility in social choice." In S. Barberà, P.J. Hammond, and C. Seidl (eds) *Handbook of Utility Theory, 2: Extensions*. Boston, MA: Kluwer Academic Publishers, pp. 1099–1177.

Bourguignon, F., 1999. "Comment on Maasoumi (1999)." In J. Silber (ed.) *Handbook of Income Inequality Measurement*. Boston, MA: Kluwer Academic Publishers, pp. 477–484.

Bourguignon, F. and Chakravarty, S.R., 2003. "The measurement of multidimensional poverty." *Journal of Economic Inequality*, 1, 25–49.

Chakravarty, S.R., 1990. *Ethical Social Index Numbers*. Heidelberg: Springer-Verlag.

Dalton, H., 1920. "The measurement of the inequality of incomes." *Economic Journal*, 30, 348–361.

Dardanoni, V., 1995. "On multidimensional inequality measurement." In C. Dagum and A. Lemmi (eds) *Income Distribution, Social Welfare, Inequality, and Poverty. Vol. 6 of Research on Economic Inequality*. Stamford, CT: JAI Press, pp. 201–207.

Dutta, B., 2002. "Inequality, poverty, and welfare." In K.J. Arrow, A.K. Sen and K. Suzumura (eds) *Handbook of Social Choice and Welfare*. Vol. 1. Amsterdam: North-Holland, pp. 597–633.

Ebert, U., 1995. "Income inequality and differences in household size". *Mathematical Social Sciences*, 30, 37–55.

Fleurbaey, M. and Trannoy, A., 2003. "The impossibility of a Paretian egalitarian." *Social Choice and Welfare*, 21, 243–263.

Foster, J.E., 1994. "Normative measurement: Is theory relevant?" *American Economic Review* (*Papers and Proceedings*), 84, 265–370.

Gajdos, T. and Maurin, E., 2004. "Unequal uncertainties and uncertain inequalities: An axiomatic approach." *Journal of Economic Theory*, 116, 93–118.

Gajdos, T. and Weymark, J.A., 2005. "Multidimensional generalized Gini indices." *Economic Theory*, 26, 471–496.

Hardy, G.H., Littlewood, J.E., and Pólya, G., 1934. *Inequalities*. Cambridge: Cambridge University Press.

Joe, H., 1997. *Multivariate Models and Dependence Concepts*. London: Chapman and Hall.

Kolm, S.-C., 1969. "The optimal production of social justice." In J. Margolis and H. Guitton (eds) *Public Economics*. London: Macmillan, pp. 145–200.

Kolm, S.-C., 1976. "Unequal inequalities. I." *Journal of Economic Theory*, 12, 416–442.

Kolm, S.-C., 1977. "Multidimensional egalitarianisms." *Quarterly Journal of Economics*, 91, 1–13.

Koshevoy, G.A. and Mosler, K., 1997. "Multivariate Gini indices." *Journal of Multivariate Analysis*, 60, 252–276.

List, C., 1999. "Multidimensional inequality measurement: A proposal." Working Paper in Economics No. 1999-W27, Nuffield College, Oxford.

Maasoumi, E., 1986. "The measurement and decomposition of multidimensional inequality." *Econometrica*, 54, 991–997.

Maasoumi, E., 1999. "Multidimensioned approaches to welfare analysis." In J. Silber (ed.) *Handbook of Income Inequality Measurement*. Boston, MA: Kluwer Academic Publishers, pp. 437–477.

Marshall, A.W. and Olkin, I., 1979. *Inequalities: Theories of Majorization and Its Applications*. New York: Academic Press.

Moyes, P., 1999. "Comparisons de distributions hétérogènes et critères de dominance." *Économie et Prévision*, 138–139, 125–146.

Pigou, A.C., 1912. *Wealth and Welfare*. London: Macmillan.

Pollak, R.A., 1971. "Additive utility functions and linear Engel curves." *Review of Economic Studies*, 38, 401–414.

Savaglio, E., 2006. "Three approaches to the analysis of multidimensional inequality." In F. Farina and E. Savaglio (eds) *Inequality and Economic Integration*. London: Routledge, pp. 269–283.

Sen, A.K., 1973. *On Economic Inequality*. Oxford: Clarendon Press.

Shorrocks, A.F., 1983. "Ranking income distributions." *Economica*, 50, 3–17.

Shorrocks, A.F., 2004. "Inequality and welfare evaluation of heterogeneous income distributions." *Journal of Economic Inequality*, 2, 193–218.

Shorrocks, A.F. and Foster, J.E., 1987. "Transfer sensitive inequality measures." *Review of Economic Studies*, 54, 485–497.

Trannoy, A., 2006. "Multidimensional egalitarianism: The dominance approach." In F. Farina and E. Savaglio (eds) *Inequality and Economic Integration*. London: Routledge, pp. 284–302.

Tsui, K.-Y., 1995. "Multidimensional generalizations of the relative and absolute inequality indices: The Atkinson–Kolm–Sen approach." *Journal of Economic Theory*, 67, 251–265.

Tsui, K.-Y., 1999. "Multidimensional inequality and multidimensional generalized entropy measures: An axiomatic derivation." *Social Choice and Welfare*, 16, 145–157.

Tsui, K.-Y., 2002. "Multidimensional poverty indices." *Social Choice and Welfare*, 19, 69–93.

United Nations Development Programme, 1990. *Human Development Report 1990*. New York: Oxford University Press.

Weymark, J.A., 1981. "Generalized Gini inequality indices." *Mathematical Social Sciences*, 1, 409–430.

Weymark, J.A., 1999. "Comment on Blackorby, Bossert, and Donaldson (1999)." In J. Silber (ed.) *Handbook of Income Inequality Measurement*. Boston, MA: Kluwer Academic Publishers, pp. 157–161.

Index